# Revolutionary Marxism in Spain
## 1930–1937

# Historical Materialism Book Series

The Historical Materialism Book Series is a major publishing initiative of the radical left. The capitalist crisis of the twenty-first century has been met by a resurgence of interest in critical Marxist theory. At the same time, the publishing institutions committed to Marxism have contracted markedly since the high point of the 1970s. The Historical Materialism Book Series is dedicated to addressing this situation by making available important works of Marxist theory. The aim of the series is to publish important theoretical contributions as the basis for vigorous intellectual debate and exchange on the left.

The peer-reviewed series publishes original monographs, translated texts, and reprints of classics across the bounds of academic disciplinary agendas and across the divisions of the left. The series is particularly concerned to encourage the internationalization of Marxist debate and aims to translate significant studies from beyond the English-speaking world.

*For a full list of titles in the Historical Materialism Book Series available in paperback from Haymarket Books, visit:*
www.haymarketbooks.org/category/hm-series

# Revolutionary Marxism in Spain, 1930–1937

By
Alan Sennett

Haymarket Books
Chicago, IL

First published in 2014 by Brill Academic Publishers, The Netherlands
© 2014 Koninklijke Brill NV, Leiden, The Netherlands

Published in paperback in 2015 by
Haymarket Books
P.O. Box 180165
Chicago, IL 60618
773-583-7884
www.haymarketbooks.org

ISBN: 978-1-60846-481-4

Trade distribution:
In the US, Consortium Book Sales, www.cbsd.com
In Canada, Publishers Group Canada, www.pgcbooks.ca
In the UK, Turnaround Publisher Services, www.turnaround-uk.com
In all other countries, Publishers Group Worldwide, www.pgw.com

Cover design by Ragina Johnson.

This book was published with the generous support of
Lannan Foundation and the Wallace Global Fund.

Printed in Canada by union labor.

10 9 8 7 6 5 4 3 2 1

Library of Congress Cataloging-in-Publication data is available.

# Contents

# Acknowledgements

This book would not have been possible without the support, encouragement and hard work of a number of people. I am most grateful to Sebastian Budgen and Peter Thomas for suggesting the project of converting my doctoral thesis into a book for the *Historical Materialism* series. This allowed me to revisit the field, update, revise, rethink and extend my original research. As a result, the narrower focus of the thesis has been considerably opened out to allow the book to engage with wider historical debates concerning the politics and activities of revolutionary Marxists in Spain during the 1930s.

For their support, advice and encouragement during the four years of researching and writing the PhD thesis, I would like to thank the following people: my supervisors, Professor Paul Cammack and the late Professor Norman Geras; the staff of the Department of Government of the University of Manchester; the staff of the John Rylands University Library, Manchester; members of the Historical Commission of the Fundación Andreu Nin in Madrid, especially Carmen Grimau and Jaime Pastor; the staffs of the Fundación Pablo Iglesias and the Hemeroteca Municipal in Madrid; and my friend, Martine Waltho, who undertook the daunting task of proof-reading the original thesis manuscript and whose friendship contributed immensely to the completion of the project. Doctoral research was funded through a Research Studentship from the Economic and Social Research Council and a grant from the University of Manchester's Norman Chester Fund.

I would like to thank the editors of the *Historical Materialism* Book Series, especially David Broder and Danny Hayward, for their diligent and painstaking work. Their careful editorship has saved me from numerous stylistic and typographical errors. Thanks also go to Sarah Grey of Grey Editing who did a fantastic job of copy editing the completed manuscript. My appreciation also to Carla Leach for a superb indexing job. Needless to say, any errors that remain are solely those of the author.

Rosanna Woensdregt, Assistant Editor History and Social Sciences at Brill, was of immense help in piloting the whole project through to the production stage. Her advice steered me away from a number of pitfalls. My appreciation also goes to Debbie de Wit for her work as Production Editor at Brill.

Finally, I wish to express my gratitude to my family and friends for their practical and emotional support. I owe particular debts to my parents, Bill and Peggy Sennett (1920–97), to whose memory this book is lovingly dedicated.

# List of Abbreviations

BOC     Bloc Obrer i Camperol – Workers' and Peasants' Bloc (dissident communists)

CEDA     Confederación Española de Derechas Autónomas – Spanish Confederation of Autonomous Right [parties]

CGTU     Confederación General de Trabajo Unitário – General Confederation of United Labour (official Communist trade union)

CNT     Confederación Nacional del Trabajo – National Confederation of Labour (anarcho-syndicalist union)

CPSU     Communist Party of the Soviet Union (official)

CSR     Comités Sindicalistas Revolucionarios – Revolutionary-Syndicalist Committees (Maurín's group in the 1920s)

FAI     Federación Anarquísta Ibérica – Iberian Anarchist Federation

FCCB     Federación Comunista Catalano-Balear – Catalan-Balearic Communist Federation (Maurín's group, expelled from PCE)

FJS     Federación de Juventudes Socialistas de España – Socialist Youth Federation (of Spain)

FNTT     Federación Nacional de Trabajadores de la Tierra – National Federation of Landworkers (Socialist-led trade union)

FOUS     Federación Obrera de Unidad Sindical – Workers' Federation of Syndical Unity (POUM-led trade union)

GPU     State Political Administration, later NKVD (People's Commissariat for Internal Affairs) – (Soviet secret police organisation)

JCI     Juventud Comunista Ibérica – Iberian Communist Youth (POUM youth movement)

JONS     Juntas de Ofensiva Nacional Sindicalista – National Syndicalist Offence Committees (fascist movement)

JSU     Juventudes Socialistas Unificadas – Unified Socialist Youth (merged Socialist and official Communist youth movements)

KPD     German Communist Party

PCC     Partit Comunista Català – Catalan Communist Party (dissident communists)

PCdeC     Partit Comunista de Catalunya – Communist Party of Catalunya (official; fused with three other Catalan organisations to form the PSUC)

PCE     Partido Comunista de España – Spanish Communist Party (official Communists)

PNV     Partido Nacionalista Vasco – Basque Nationalist Party

POUM     Partido Obrero de Unificación Marxista – Workers' Party of Marxist Unification (Nin and Maurín – dissident communists)

PSOE    Partido Socialista Obrero Español – Spanish Socialist Workers' Party (social-
        democratic party)
PSUC    Partit Socialista Unificat de Catalunya – Unified Socialist Party of Cataluña
        (official Communists)
SFIO    French Socialist Party
UGT     Unión General de Trabajadores – General Workers' Union (Socialist)

# Introduction

This study examines the influence of Trotsky's political thought upon those Spanish Marxists who broke with the official Communist movement during the 1930s. The book takes as its central theme the idea which is most evocative of Trotsky's name and lies at the very core of his political thought, the theory of permanent revolution. It argues that Trotsky's theory of revolution and the conception of historical development underpinning it can be shown to have had a major impact upon the Spanish dissident communists' political thought and actions in the period from 1930 to 1937. Trotsky's influence can also be found in the Spanish Marxists' critique of Stalinism and their conceptions of fascism and dictatorship. A large portion of the book focuses upon a primary-source analysis of the writings and political activities of the two most prominent and influential dissident communists, Andreu Nin and Joaquín Maurín. They are generally considered to be the most significant Spanish contributors to twentieth-century Marxist thought, although few of their writings have been translated into English. It is argued here that, although their work deserves to be viewed in its own right, it is underpinned by the influence of Trotsky's Marxism, particularly insofar as Nin's writings are concerned.

It is curious that, given the overwhelming volume of published material concerned in one way or another with the Spanish Revolution and Civil War, comparatively little attention has been directed toward the political ideas and activities of the dissident communists. The same might be said of Trotsky's writings and political interventions in the deliberations of those communists who had become disenchanted with the official line emanating from Moscow. Recent biographies of Trotsky have devoted surprisingly little space to discussing Trotsky's understanding of and connection with Spanish events. Robert Service's biography deals with the Spanish Civil War in under two pages.[1] Geoffrey Swain devotes a couple of paragraphs to the subject.[2] The most extensive and informative coverage is to be found in Ian Thatcher's short political biography.[3] Even there it merits only four pages. Of the monographs that do exist, many are coloured by the fact that they have either been written by ex-members of the organisations concerned or by commentators who have a

---

1  Service 2009.
2  Swain 2006.
3  Thatcher 2003.

particular political axe to grind. Among the notable exceptions to this rule is
the work of the Catalan historian Pelai Pagès. He is the author of the most
authoritative study of Nin's political ideas, *Andreu Nin: su evolución política*;
the principal work on Spanish Trotskyism during the 1930s, *El movimiento
trotskista en España (1930–1935)*; and a full-length biography of Nin, *Andreu Nin:
Una vida al servicio de la clase obrera*.[4] He has also contributed numerous articles on the dissident communists and introductions to collections of Nin's
writings and speeches. Nin's relationship with the Spanish communist movement has been studied in depth by Francesc Bonamusa in his book *Andreu Nin
y el movimiento comunista en España*. Antoni Monreal dealt with Maurín's
political thought of the 1920s and 1930s in his book *El pensamiento político de
Joaquín Maurín*. Other academic studies of particular note are Bonamusa's *El
Bloc Obrer i Camperol 1930–325* and Andrew Durgan's *B.O.C. 1930–1936: El Bloque
Obrero y Campesino*, which is essentially the published version of his Ph.D.
thesis.[6]

Although these studies often deal extremely well with Nin's and Maurín's
political ideas – especially those by Pagès, Monreal and Durgan – they do not
examine the influence of Trotsky's Marxism in depth. Trotsky's involvement in
the dissident communists' affairs is usually addressed either in terms of organisational connections, such as those of the International Left Opposition, or in
relation to Trotsky's personal advice to Nin. The literature cited above, together
with the items mentioned later in chapter footnotes, is concerned rather more
with the history of the dissident communist organisations than with the nature
of the Marxist theory upon which their dissent from the post-Lenin orthodoxy
was based.

The more specific literature devoted to Trotsky's involvement with Spain is
dominated by the various articles and pamphlets of the French Trotskyist historian Pierre Broué. He has defended Trotsky against the criticisms of veteran
dissident communists such as Víctor Alba and Ignacio Iglesias. Although these
debates provide useful discussions of key political issues, they do not adequately address the theoretical issues from a critical perspective. To his detractors, Trotsky simply transposed his model of Russian historical development
and the strategy of the Bolsheviks onto an analysis of Spain, a country with
different conditions and different traditions of mass struggle. But, in responding to such detractors, Broué does not advance a counterargument to explain
how and why Trotsky generalised the conception of historical development

---

4  Pagès 2011.

5  Bonamusa 1974.

6  Durgan 1989.

and theory of revolution he had originally formulated for Russian conditions. Consequently, there is no discussion of whether or not Trotsky's general theory was able to take account of different conditions or whether he successfully adapted it to suit Spain. Indeed, there is little attempt in any of the literature on the subject to place Trotsky's involvement with the Spanish Revolution in the context of his Marxism as a whole.

It is important to stress a few points regarding the scope and content of this book. The present study lays no claim to advance a novel interpretation of Spanish history, nor is it intended as a contribution toward a greater understanding of the genesis of the organisations concerned, other than in the realm of their political thought. However, it does offer some evaluative and critical comments concerning the perspectives and actions of the political groups mentioned. It also sets them in their historical context and considers some issues of a historiographical nature. The main aims of the book are twofold. In the first place, it seeks to outline and assess Trotsky's involvement with the Spanish Revolution and to set this within the overall context of his political theory and historical approach. Secondly, it attempts to measure the influence of Trotsky's political thought upon the Spanish dissident communists through a close examination of the political ideas of Andreu Nin and Joaquín Maurín. It is hoped that the present study will fill a gap in the existing literature on Trotsky's political thought and also contribute toward a greater understanding of a somewhat neglected current of Marxist thought.

Turning to the organisation of the book, Chapter One focuses upon Trotsky's formulation and refinement of his theory of revolution. It begins with a description of the law of uneven and combined development and argues that this law forms the foundation upon which the theory of permanent revolution rests. One of the central concerns, here, is to emphasise the extent to which Trotsky departed from the prevailing Marxist orthodoxy over the question of exactly how proletarian revolutions might develop. Although he was not unique among his contemporaries in using the concept of 'permanent revolution', it will be argued that he formed the most coherent and complete theory of revolution that challenged the prevailing notions of stagism. His dissenting voice, arguably one of the most healthy and creative facets of Trotsky's Marxism, can be heard even in the formative phases of his political evolution. This chapter also considers the controversy over Stalin's doctrine of 'socialism in one country'. In forcefully rejecting this doctrine, Trotsky restated the theory of permanent revolution and expanded it into a theory of world socialist revolution. A lengthy concluding section discusses some of the main theoretical and historical problems with Trotsky's formulation of permanent revolution and attempts to assess its strengths and weaknesses.

The second chapter is devoted to an exposition and analysis of Trotsky's writings on Spain and to his political involvement with the dissident communists. It examines Trotsky's application of the law of uneven and combined development to Spanish historical development in the early modern and modern periods. Chapter Two also considers whether Trotsky was at all justified in applying the prognosis of permanent revolution to Spain. Attention is also given to the relationship between revolutionary theory and political strategy as manifested in Trotsky's advice to the Spanish dissident communists. Since it is impossible to comprehend Trotsky's advice to his followers without appreciating his analysis of the international situation and his warnings of the dangers of fascism and Stalinism, these aspects of his thought are also dealt with in relation to the Spanish context.

The bulk of the book is devoted to the political ideas and actions of the Spanish dissident communists up until 1937. Chapter Three examines the evolution of Nin and Maurín's political thought through to the early 1930s. It outlines their characterisations of Spanish history and their perceptions of the course that Spain's revolutionary process was likely to take. It attempts to clarify the points of convergence and divergence between Trotsky's analysis and their own respective conceptions.

Chapter Four focuses upon Nin's and Maurín's analyses of and participation in the Spanish labour movement during the early 1930s. It compares and contrasts their theoretical understandings of fascism and dictatorship and considers the warnings each gave about the dangers of a new authoritarianism arising in Spain. This chapter also examines the practical efforts of the dissident communists to build a Workers' Alliance against the threat from the far Right. Finally, it discusses the differences in perspective between Nin's organisation and Trotsky's International Left Opposition.

The next chapter looks at the convergence of the two wings of dissident communism in Spain, which culminated in the creation of the Partido Obrero de Unificación Marxista (Workers' Party of Marxist Unification, known as the POUM) in September 1935. Chapter Five thus examines the political basis upon which the POUM was constructed, examining its political programme and orientation toward other political forces on the Left. This chapter also considers its view of and participation in events leading up to the elections of February 1936.

Chapter Six offers a discussion of the POUM's involvement in the Spanish Popular Front. It asks why this new party, an amalgamation of the Spanish Trotskyist organisation led by Nin and Maurín's largely Catalan Bloque Obrero y Campesino (Workers' and Peasants' Bloc, or BOC), involved itself in an electoral alliance that included bourgeois-republican parties. This move led to a massive rift between Trotsky and Nin that was never repaired. It is argued that this crucial phase in the development of the POUM needs to be set within broader historical debates around the nature and significance of the Frente Popular (Popular Front). Hence this chapter situates discussion of the POUM's possible reasons for signing the electoral pact within the wider historiography of this key period in the run-up to the outbreak of civil war in July 1936. Controversy surrounds the question of whether the Spanish Popular Front should be viewed as an official Communist initiative, driven by the Comintern, or whether it is better understood as the product of the domestic political dynamic. Chapter Six goes on to look at the POUM's responses to the war and social revolution sparked off by the military rising of July 1936. Finally, it considers the reasons behind the POUM's participation in the Catalan government in late 1936, in which Nin served a brief spell as minister of justice.

The final chapter looks at the campaign waged against the POUM in the context of the reversal of the social revolution in the first half of 1937. Frequently viewed as a counterrevolution, the motive force behind this development is often associated with the growing influence over the Republican government of Soviet advisors, Comintern agents and the Spanish Communist Party. The situation reached a crisis point in May 1937 as armed conflict exploded in Barcelona. Government suppression of what was seen as an insurrection was followed by the outlawing, persecution and eradication of the POUM as a political force and the murder of Nin. Again, this has generally been explained as the work of Soviet secret service agents and is often tied to Stalin's foreign policy requirements. Yet, in order to fully understand these events, we need to examine the perspectives of the POUM during the early months of 1937 and consider some of the historiographical debates around the causes of the May events. As will be seen, historians disagree considerably over the role played by the official Communists, Soviet advisors and agents, and other political forces in the Republican camp. The chapter ends with an assessment of the role and significance of the POUM's theory and practice during the Spanish Revolution.

An appendix has been provided in order to clarify some of the historical references that cannot usefully be covered through the device of footnotes. It consists of a survey of modern Spanish history up until the end of the Spanish Civil War. The function is to furnish the reader with an overview of the main historical and political problems to which Trotsky and the Spanish dissident communists addressed themselves. The essay is divided into three sections.

The first section deals with the character of Spanish historical development particularly the issues surrounding Spain's transition to capitalism. The second section looks at the emergence of organised labour and the condition of the various workers' organisations in 1930. The final section offers a brief history of the Second Republic, the Revolution and the Civil War.

# CHAPTER 1

# Trotsky's Theory of Revolution

It has long been clear to many scholars that Marx by no means ruled out the notion of a socialist revolution occurring in a relatively backward country like Russia.[1] However, such an idea was far removed from the orthodox understanding of Marx that prevailed among many Second International theorists of the early twentieth century. For them, revolutions in less advanced capitalist countries would not pass beyond what they often referred to as the 'stage of bourgeois democracy'. A truly 'socialist' revolution was only possible in countries that had already experienced a considerable degree of capitalist industrial development. Trotsky's major, if not entirely original, contribution to Marxist political theory thus flew in the face of orthodoxy, insisting that the next round of revolutionary struggle in Russia would not witness a completion of Russia's 'bourgeois revolution', but would combine with and grow into a socialist one. Even a passing acquaintance with Russia's subsequent history is sufficient to confirm the prescience of this analysis. The Bolshevik Revolution, when it arrived in October 1917, was, indeed, not detained at the 'bourgeois-democratic stage' but witnessed the emergence of a new political, social and economic entity that sought to transform Russia into a workers' state. Moreover, Trotsky himself was a key participant in this attempt to reshape society and continued to place this analysis of the dynamics of Russian social development at the core of his subsequent theory and practice. He elaborated and extended this theoretical perspective to other 'backward' countries in which he detected the presence of a revolutionary dynamic, not least Spain. The purpose of this chapter is to present and discuss Trotsky's theory of revolution as it developed within his writings over the space of twenty-five years.

It is important to recognise that Trotsky's Marxism drew far less stimulus from close readings of classic texts than it did from personal involvement in revolutionary events. As he noted, political thought needs to be situated within

---

1   Perhaps the most significant example is Marx's 1881 letter to the Russian revolutionary Vera Zasulich (in McLellan 1977, pp. 577–580). However, there is considerable evidence in the writings of Marx and to some extent Engels that the possibility of socialist revolutions in backward capitalist countries was present in their thought, albeit alongside other ideas that tend to contradict this. See the detailed discussion of Marx's revolutionary thought in Löwy 1981.

the context of the concrete conditions that give rise to it.[2] Hence we would do well to study the evolution and elaboration of what became known as the 'theory of permanent revolution' in relation to the cataclysmic events of the first forty years of the twentieth century. In this respect, Trotsky's development of the theory of permanent revolution cannot be separated from either its historical context or the personal trajectory of its main author. While the term 'permanent revolution' is found in some of Marx's writings,[3] and was discussed as a concept in the context of Russia in the period from 1903 to 1907 by leading Marxists such as Kautsky,[4] it was Trotsky who formulated the complete theory. Moreover, as will be argued below, his formulation rests upon a powerful methodological tool which is missing from other contributions, namely the law of uneven and combined development. That said, the intention here, is less to chart the genesis of the theory and more to present it in its totality as a complete theoretical device which aspires to the status of a universal theory. Many claims have been made as to its theoretical power in revealing the dynamics of revolution in the period of high imperialism and late capitalism. Its validity has been seen not merely to hinge upon its internal coherence as a theory, but also to rest upon the extent to which it may be usefully and profitably applied to the concrete revolutionary situations its author purported to clarify and advance. Trotsky would surely have been the last person to relegate his theory of revolution to the status of an academic exercise. In his terms, and those of his followers, revolutionary theory has but one purpose: to inform revolutionary strategy and tactics in order to assist the struggle of the working class in the conquest of political power and in laying the basis for socialism on a global scale. In this respect, permanent revolution constitutes an integral and indispensable aspect of Trotsky's Marxism and can be said to embody the classic unity of theory and practice often said to have characterised the lives of his peers Lenin and Luxemburg.

This chapter begins by considering the law of uneven and combined development and the sense in which it serves as a foundation for the theory of permanent revolution. It then discusses Trotsky's development of what might be termed the 'permanentist' aspects of Marx's theory of revolution; that is to say, those aspects of Trotsky's theory of revolution that can be traced back to the perspectives adopted by Marx and some Second International Marxists.

---

2  Trotsky 1969, p. 157.
3  For instance: *On the Jewish Question* (Marx 1843); *The Holy Family* (Marx 1845); and *Address to the Central Committee of the Communist League* (Marx 1850).
4  See Day and Gaido (eds.) 2009 for texts by Kautsky, Parvus, Trotsky, Luxemburg, Mehring and Ryazanov in which ideas of the 'revolution in permanence' are elaborated.

We will first look at the way Trotsky elaborated his ideas in relation to the revolutionary experience of 1905, and then explore his extension of the theory to encompass all backward capitalist countries. These formulations were to prove highly influential among the Spanish 'dissident communists' in the 1930s, as will be shown in later chapters. Later sections of the present chapter deal with Trotsky's understanding of the concept of 'revolutionary crisis' and discuss his theory in the light of twentieth-century revolutions. As we will see, this discussion raises a number of problems and questions that will resurface in relation to Spain's historical and political development.

## 1.1      Uneven and Combined Development

Notions of uneven historical development are certainly to be found in the work of Marx and other early Marxists, but Trotsky extended the concept by adding a second aspect, the law of combined development.[5] As he expressed it:

> Unevenness, the most general law of the historic process, reveals itself most sharply and complexly in the destiny of backward countries. Under the whip of external necessity their backward culture is compelled to make leaps. From the universal law of unevenness there derives another law which, for the lack of a better name, we may call the law of combined development – by which we mean a drawing together of the different stages of the journey, a combining of separate steps, an amalgam of archaic with more contemporary forms. Without this law, to be taken of course in its whole material context, it is impossible to understand the history of Russia, and indeed of any country of the second, third or tenth cultural class.[6]

Trotsky thus sees 'uneven development' describing the variable rates of development of a country's productive forces, the spread of which is determined by differing natural conditions and historical conjunctures. It is these variable elements that apportion differential rates of growth to each country, to every branch of the national economy and to institutions and social classes. Therefore, out of unevenness arise particular combinations of characteristics

---

5  Löwy 1981.
6  Trotsky 1980b, pp. 5–6.

from a lower stage of social development with those from a higher stage.[7] These combinations may well be quite different from country to country.

Such a formulation was immensely useful for Marxists when it came to analysing the particular nature of a country's social, economic and political development and its revolutionary potential. Since the Marxist methodology tends to begin with analysis of the economic 'base', it is not surprising that Trotsky took this as his starting point for gauging revolutionary potential. Yet he was well aware of the need to avoid suggesting a mechanistic equation between a country's level of economic development and its degree of preparedness for proletarian revolution. Indeed, he saw this as the essential conceptual power of the notion of uneven development. It suggested that countries whose economies were relatively 'backward' were capable of achieving levels of development in certain economic sectors superior to those of more 'advanced' countries. If this was the case, then it further suggested that these advanced sectors were combined with the traditional, backward sectors. If so, then this raised interesting contradictions in social, economic and political spheres that might open up the prospect of revolutionary crises.

In order to clarify the issue of uneven capitalist development, it is worth reflecting upon Trotsky's explanation for this phenomenon. Two factors essential to the competitiveness of capitalist enterprises are the continual updating of the production process and the organisation of labour so as to increase productivity. Although those countries first to industrialise continued to hold a massive advantage over the later-industrialising states of the mid-to-late nineteenth century, latecomers like Germany and the United States enjoyed the benefits of the most advanced technology and production methods from the outset. They were able to begin their industrialisation with the most up-to-date techniques and processes, thus jumping over the formative stages through which Britain and France had been obliged to pass. The outcome of this was that, in industries where technology had undergone rapid development, the latecomers were not held back by the need to replace outdated machinery, and, in this sense, enjoyed an immediate advantage. They were also able to compete effectively from the outset and move into new branches of industry with relative ease.

---

7    Trotsky's earliest significant elaboration of uneven and combined development came in his 1906 pamphlet, *Results and Prospects*; the formulation also crops up in subsequent writings. Its main application to Russia comes in *The Permanent Revolution* (Trotsky 1969) and *The History of the Russian Revolution* (Trotsky 1980b). This summary draws upon all of these sources. Footnotes in this section are largely restricted to direct quotes.

Trotsky argued that once the world capitalist economy entered its imperialist phase in the late nineteenth century, the majority of relatively backward countries had been unable to experience overall economic growth. Their patterns of development tended to display a *combination'* of modern industrial capitalism, on the one hand, and, on the other, the continuation of an archaic agrarian sector that dominated the national economy and constituted a massive obstacle to dynamic capitalist development. The capitalist industrial sector was often promoted by the state and dominated by foreign capital, whereas agriculture was the preserve of pre-capitalist ruling classes.

### Uneven and Combined Development in Russia

Trotsky applied the law of uneven and combined development in his analysis of the dynamics of the 1905 Revolution in Russia. He notes that, in Russia, the contrasts between modern and archaic productive forces and social relations of production were especially pronounced and seriously hampered the development of capitalism. By the beginning of the twentieth century, Russia's vast precapitalist agriculture contrasted sharply with a developing capitalist industrial sector. Largely foreign and, in part, fostered by the Tsarist state, these capitalist enterprises were highly concentrated, huge in scale and often devoted to heavy industrial production for military purposes.[8] With the exception of a few areas, the dominant agrarian sector remained largely undeveloped and acted as a brake upon the development of a dynamic national economy.[9] Employing the vast majority of the active population at a subsistence level, Russia's backward agriculture prevented the emergence of a strong domestic market. This, in turn, inhibited the growth and diversification of the manufacturing industry. Trotsky notes that any accumulated domestic capital tended to be diverted away from industry and into real estate speculation, usury and hoarding. The bourgeoisie was thus closely related to landed interests and had little stake in the kind of agrarian revolution which would have been necessary to stimulate a dynamic agriculture. Although industrial

---

8   Trotsky 1980b, pp. 5–6; Trotsky 1973b, Chapters One and Two. For modern historical studies of the state and industrial development in Russia see Kemp 1969, Chapter Five; Anderson 1974, Part 2, Chapter Six; Kahan 1967; Milward and Saul 1977; Gerschenkron 1963; and Falkus 1972.

9   According to Lenin, Russian agriculture was developing in the direction of wage labour with large Junker-type estates, but at the time, 1912, 'purely capitalist relations in our country are still overshadowed to a *tremendous* extent by *feudal* relations' (V.I. Lenin, 'The Essence of the "Agrarian Problem" of Russia,' cited in Anderson 1974, p. 350). As Anderson points out, the suggested 'Prussian path' did not materialise in the final years of Tsarism and the slowly spreading capitalist relations were always mixed up with pre-capitalist modes of surplus extraction (Anderson 1974, pp. 351–2).

development established capitalist relations of production in factories which employed very large numbers of people, the overwhelming majority of the population were still involved in feudal and semi-feudal forms of production in the countryside. But even here one could speak of a *combination* of social relations of production, since many factory workers returned to their villages to take part in the harvest.[10]

As mentioned above, the rise of economic imperialism was the major shift in the nature of capitalism that enabled Trotsky to see the development of backward societies as both uneven and combined. Unlike Marx, Trotsky was writing in the age of 'high imperialism', when Second International theorists saw capitalism as incorporating most countries into a global economic system. As he remarked in 1905: 'Binding all countries together with its mode of production and its commerce, capitalism has converted the whole world into a single economic and political organism'.[11] Colonialism and economic imperialism were the means by which capitalism was exploiting 'backward' countries and territories, often employing precapitalist methods. But, in Russia, the state welcomed foreign capital and had been able to transplant onto Russian soil the most advanced technology and the most concentrated organisation of labour. Much of Trotsky's 1906 pamphlet *Results and Prospects* is devoted to an explanation of how Russia developed into what he called a 'semi-colonial country'.

Central to Trotsky's analysis is his argument that the penetration of capital took place with the active encouragement of the Tsarist state. Indeed, in Russia, 'capitalism seemed to be an offspring of the state'.[12] Due to factors such as the country's unfavourable geographical situation, its dispersed population, its slow economic development and the failure of towns to develop as manufacturing centres, Russia found itself lagging far behind its European rivals. Its economy lacked dynamism and its class formation remained primitive. Toward the end of the seventeenth century, Trotsky continued, Russia had found itself faced with competition from other European countries. The state thus attempted to accelerate economic development and, by the late nineteenth century, was actively promoting it.

---

10   Rimlinger (1960) and Von Laue (1961) note this. Even after the emancipation of the serfs in 1861, an act which freed many for work in the new factories, the *mir* system continued to bind the peasant/worker to the soil. He could always be summoned to return to his village. But, by 1917, there were 3.6 million workers, concentrated in particular regions. Most came from the countryside, 'snatched from the plough and hurled into the factory furnace', as Trotsky put it (quoted in Smith 2002, p. 10).

11   From Trotsky's forward to Lassalle's 'Address to the Jury', quoted in Trotsky 1969, p. 107.

12   Trotsky 1969, p. 41.

> In order to be able to survive in the midst of better-armed hostile countries, Russia was compelled to set up factories, organize navigation schools, publish textbooks on fortification, etc.... [But] if the general course of the internal economy of this enormous country had not been moving in this same direction, if the development of economic conditions had not created the demand for general and applied science, all the efforts of the state would have been fruitless.[13]

Economic modernisation was thus state-induced rather than state-created. Government provided and attracted from overseas much of the necessary investment and directed it largely into production for military use. This often conflicted with business interests. However, the lack of a strong tradition of liberal democracy among the indigenous bourgeoisie, which was itself a reflection of its weakness as a class, meant that there was little prospect of it enjoying real political influence. For Trotsky, this revealed a key contradiction of uneven and combined development in Russia: the feudal state form, which maintained its rule only through an enormous coercive apparatus, had come into conflict with the requirements of the very capitalist industrial development it had done so much to foster. Owing to the particular path of capitalist development in Russia and its specific mode of insertion into the imperialist system, the historical agent of democratic revolution – the national bourgeoisie – was incapable of taking the political action necessary to overcome this contradiction. The Russian bourgeoisie thus appeared as a mere shadow of its revolutionary English and French forebears.

Uneven and combined development of social classes also accounted for the relative weakness of the Russian bourgeoisie. As Trotsky notes, the towns had not evolved as economic centres in the way they had in Western Europe. Until the late nineteenth century, the role of Russian towns remained primarily as administrative centres and bases for the military. Industrial development, when it came, was not centred upon an existing urban artisan class, as had been the case in Britain and France. The establishment of large factories tended to concentrate the workforce from the very outset, thus creating a substantial proletariat. Yet, at the same time, the urban petit-bourgeoisie, the traditional social bedrock of Western bourgeois liberalism, remained relatively insignificant. For Trotsky, this accounted for the weakness of this social layer. Trotsky described the big bourgeoisie, the key capitalist class, as 'half foreign'.

---

13    Trotsky 1969, p. 42.

Capitalism in Russia did not develop out of the handicraft system. It conquered Russia with the economic culture of the whole of Europe behind it, and before it, as its immediate competitor, the helpless village craftsman or the wretched town craftsman, and it had the half-beggared peasantry as a reservoir of labour power. Absolutism assisted in various ways in fettering the country with the shackles of capitalism.

...

By economically enslaving this backward country, European capital projected its main branches of production and methods of communication across a whole series of intermediate technical and economic stages through which it had had to pass in its countries of origin. But the fewer obstacles it met with in the path of its *economic* domination, the more insignificant proved to be its political role.[14]

In other words, as long as the economic interests of foreign capitalists were guaranteed by the Tsarist state, there was no need for them to intervene at a political level.

### The Imperialist World System

In *The Permanent Revolution*, written in 1929, Trotsky extended his use of the concept of uneven and combined development to all countries which were experiencing a limited degree of capitalist development and were locked into the imperialist world system. Although he considered that most countries were affected by this global capitalist system and the world division of labour, he realised that each one had a particular location within the overall framework.

The economic peculiarities of different countries are in no way of a subordinate character . . . [N]ational peculiarity is nothing else but the most general product of the unevenness of historical development, its summary result, so to say.[15]

As Marx had stressed, capitalism also created contradictions that had the effect of radically altering the conditions of economic, social and political development. Emerging capitalist societies did not simply repeat the same course of historical development followed by earlier developers. Hence, Trotsky totally rejected Stalin's idea that revolutionary politics should be based

---

14    Trotsky 1969, pp. 49–50.
15    Trotsky 1969, p. 148 (emphasis in original).

upon the 'general features of capitalism' which all countries possessed and not upon the specific characteristics of each country. It was, he argued, a potentially damaging mistake to see the world economy as simply a sum of its constituent national parts.

> In reality, the national peculiarities represent an original combination of the basic features of the world process. This originality can be of decisive significance for revolutionary strategy over a space of many years. Suffice it to say that the proletariat of a backward country can come to power before the proletariat of the advanced countries. This historic lesson alone shows that in spite of Stalin, it is absolutely wrong to base the activity of the communist parties on some 'general features', that is, on an abstract type of national capitalism.[16]

Gauging the specificities of a particular country requires awareness that the effects of uneven and combined development include the development of productive forces at variable rates, the temporal drawing-out or telescoping of 'historical epochs', and the differential speed of evolution of different economic sectors, social classes, institutions and other social phenomena. Each of these variables contributes to the national particularities of a country so that 'the peculiarity of a national social type is the crystallisation of the unevenness of its formation'.[17]

Although Trotsky did not formulate a systematic theory of imperialism, an appreciation of its dynamics was certainly intrinsic to his world view. Revolutionary upheavals were, he maintained, intimately connected to the uneven and combined development of the countries which make up the world system. One of the major contradictions of capitalist development was the inability of its productive forces to develop within the framework of the nation-state. Hence the world system was best viewed as a 'chain' in which most countries formed links because of their enforced relationship with imperialism. The dominant role of the imperial bourgeoisie within the world economy – and the penetration of the economies and political systems of underdeveloped countries by economic imperialism – ensured that the development of backward countries would be distorted and delayed.

World revolution was also a chain that was directly related to the capitalist world system – a chain which might break at its weakest link. This did not necessarily mean the weakest national economy. The notion applied, rather, to a

---

16     Trotsky 1969, pp. 147–8.
17     Trotsky 1969, p. 148.

conjuncture in which a high level of class consciousness and organisation clashed with the least flexible, least 'bourgeois' political system and state form. In this sense, Russia in 1917, Germany in 1919 and Spain in the 1930s were all cases of 'weakest links', irrespective of their very different levels of economic development. According to Trotsky's paradigm, any major upset in the temporary equilibrium in one or more part(s) of the world system would have effects everywhere else in the framework. This would include any radical disturbance to the equilibrium of class forces, the balance between imperialist powers, relations between a core country and its colonies or satellites, imbalances in the market, disruptions between accumulation of capital and a rise in surplus value as a whole, or the equilibrium between mass movements and the bureaucratic apparatuses that normally control them. The resulting shock waves might speed up revolutionary changes in unexpected areas.[18] The cause of such an upheaval could be one or a combination of factors such as capitalist crisis, war, or revolutions in other countries.

Ernest Mandel notes that Trotsky's methodology demanded a highly complex analysis of many features, such as the world economy and its fluctuations; the relationship between each individual country and its integration into the world system; the differential impact of the fluctuations of the world economy on each country; the historically produced relationship between each country's capital and labour, as well as other social classes; the factors involved in any disturbance in that relationship; the specific forms of political struggle at any given point in that country's historical development; and the specific composition and weight of each country's labour movement, its dynamics and relationship to the international class struggle.[19] All of these elements are affected by the law of uneven and combined development as it operates in each country. Obviously, this makes it highly improbable that such a complex of interrelated variables would produce two countries with exactly the same characteristics.

Of course, this did not rule out comparative analysis. There were certain features of both the Russian experience and that of China between 1925 and 1927 that caused Trotsky to suggest these cases held general implications for all backward capitalist colonial and semi-colonial countries. One of the key contradictions of Russian development, which contained massive implications for the character of the Revolution, derived from the fact that as capitalist production grew in size, so, too, did the industrial proletariat. For Trotsky, this ruled out any repeat of previous revolutionary experiences such as those of 1789 or

18    Mandel 1979a, pp. 34–5.
19    Ibid.

1848. The national bourgeoisies in backward countries were simply not strong enough to lead the masses in a struggle for democracy, as in 1789, or to share power with the old ruling classes, as they had tried to do in 1848. In 1905, the Russian proletariat had demonstrated that it was a class sufficiently developed and willing to take the leading role in the Revolution, although it had not been quite strong enough to succeed. Faced with a revolutionary proletariat, Trotsky argued, the national bourgeoisie tended to side with absolutism and thus became a counterrevolutionary force. This led him to the conclusion that in backward countries, the national bourgeoisie was invariably likely to play a reactionary role. This was a key element in Trotsky's analysis of Spain.

It could be argued that Trotsky avoided the crude economism often found in Second International Marxist analyses. For Trotsky, the degree of economic development did not, in itself, determine the presence or absence of revolutionary potential in a particular historical conjuncture. As he noted in 1906:

> It is possible for the workers to come to power in an economically backward country sooner than in an advanced country ... To imagine that the dictatorship of the proletariat is in some way automatically dependent on the technical development and resources of a country is a prejudice of 'economic' materialism simplified to absurdity. This point of view has nothing in common with Marxism.[20]

Hence the prospects for revolution depended less upon the level of productive forces than on the dynamics of the class struggle, the international situation and subjective factors such as the working class's traditions, initiative and readiness to fight.[21]

In this respect, the Russian proletariat enjoyed another advantage of uneven development. It had been able to skip over the long history of development of the labour movement in Britain and France and create strong revolutionary organisations in a very short time. These organisations could achieve what those of more advanced countries had been unable to. They could also adopt the most up-to-date revolutionary theory, Marxism, and learn from struggles in other countries. At a time when the English and German proletariats had represented a similar proportion of the population as the Russian proletariat constituted at the beginning of the twentieth century, he argued, they had played a far less significant political role. Trotsky thus concluded that late-developing

---

20    Trotsky 1969, p. 63.
21    Ibid.

countries with very uneven development tended to have proletariats whose influence and potential far outweighed their relative size and newness.

> There is no doubt that the number, the concentration, the culture and the political importance of the industrial proletariat depend upon the extent to which capitalist industry is developed. But this dependence is not direct. Between the productive forces of a country and the political strength of its classes there cut across at any given moment various social and political factors of a national and international character, and these displace and even sometimes completely alter the political expression of economic relations. In spite of the fact that the productive forces of the United States are ten times as great as those of Russia, nevertheless the political role of the Russian proletariat, its influence on the politics of its own country and the possibility of its influencing the politics of the world in the near future are incomparably greater than in the case of the proletariat of the United States.[22]

Yet Trotsky was aware that no mathematical formula could predict at what point the proletariat would be ready for the conquest of power. This leads us to a consideration of the theory of permanent revolution, which, in Trotsky's Marxism, forms a logical progression from the law of uneven and combined development. We begin by briefly outlining the political and intellectual background to his various statements of the theory.

## 1.2     Permanent Revolution

The key texts in which Trotsky formulated and developed his version of permanent revolution were written from a specific point of involvement in revolutionary events and in response to definite political struggles. They were in no sense academic works and should not be read as such. Nor did Trotsky claim complete originality.[23] This means that it has been necessary to reconstruct the general theory from several texts spanning twenty-five years and which were written with different ends in mind.[24]

---

22    Trotsky 1969, p. 65.

23    For the central role played by Kautsky in the emergence of the term 'permanent revolution', see the introduction to Day and Gaido (eds.), 2009, pp. 1–58.

24    The history of the theory of permanent revolution is outlined in Löwy 1981, pp. 39–46, and Brossat 1974. Brossat argues that Trotsky's initial indications of a permanentist conception can be traced to his pamphlet *Up to the Ninth January* (December/January 1904–5).

However, it is important to note the specific context of the two core works. *Results and Prospects* was written in the aftermath of events in Russia in which Trotsky played a significant role. It was essentially a prediction of how a future revolution might develop in Russia. *The Permanent Revolution*, written 20 years later, was an elaboration of his earlier work and appeared in response to attacks upon his perspective both from the Stalin camp and from his former Left Opposition comrade Radek. The 1928 book drew upon the concrete experience of 1917, the Civil War, the creation of the Third International (Comintern) and the degeneration of the USSR under Stalin's leadership. Here, Trotsky attacked Stalin's notion of 'socialism in one country' and what he saw as the errors of Comintern policy toward China in 1926–7. He also extended the theory of permanent revolution to all backward colonial and semi-colonial capitalist countries. It is clear that he believed that the course of the Russian Revolution had attested to the correctness of permanent revolution as a theory and, moreover, that Lenin had endorsed the theory in practice, adopting it as the basis of his proletarian internationalism. Thus he argued that, when Stalin, Bukharin and Radek appealed to Lenin as their authority, they were actually distorting his true position after February 1917. Trotsky referred, of course, to Lenin's 'Letters from Afar' (March 1917) and the *April Theses*, in which Lenin argued that the socialist revolution had become the order of the day in Russia.[25]

---

Löwy disagrees and cites instead Trotsky's preface to Lassalle's *Address to the Jury* (June 1905) as his first textual statement of the formula 'dictatorship of the proletariat supported by the peasantry', and his July–October articles as the first textual references to a permanentist perspective (Löwy 1981, pp. 44–5). Clearly, the theory of permanent revolution informed all of Trotsky's writings from 1905 onward, but the following texts represent his main statements of it: 'Thirty-Five Years After' (December 1905), reproduced in Trotsky 1970a; the 1906 work *Results and Prospects* (Trotsky 1969); the 1928 book *The Third International After Lenin*; *The Permanent Revolution*, which appeared in 1929 (Trotsky 1970b); and the 1939 article 'Three Concepts of the Russian Revolution' (in Trotsky 1970d). In his 1922 preface to *1905*, which includes an excellent, concise statement of permanent revolution, Trotsky states that he formulated the theory between 9 January and October 1905 (Trotsky 1973b, p. vi).

25   Excerpts from 'Letters from Afar' appear in Mills 1963, pp. 246–56. The *April Theses* can be found in Lenin 1964, pp. 21–4. The total about-face contained in the *April Theses* met with a great deal of opposition among the Bolsheviks. As *Pravda* expressed it: 'As for Lenin's general scheme, it seems to us unacceptable in that it starts from the assumption that the bourgeois revolution is ended, and counts on an immediate transforming of this revolution into a Socialist revolution' (quoted in Shub 1966, p. 223). Against the exaggerated claims that in March and April 1917 Lenin 'went over' to Trotsky's permanentist perspective, it is enough to quote Trotsky on the point: 'Lenin had not come over to my point of view, but had developed his own, and...the course of events, by substituting arithmetic for algebra, had revealed the essential identity of our views' (Trotsky 1975b, p. 345).

### Second International 'Stagism'

Since the controversy surrounding permanent revolution hinges upon Trotsky's break with what he characterised as a stagist conception of revolution, it is worth noting the various positions held by Second International Marxists prior to October 1917. After Engels's death, it was generally considered that the Russian Revolution at least would remain within bourgeois limits in terms of what it would be able to achieve. Within Russian Social Democracy, Plekhanov and the Mensheviks thought that the revolution could only be bourgeois and that the role of the proletariat and its party would be limited to supporting the liberal bourgeoisie against the old régime. Plekhanov believed that a prolonged phase of capitalist industrialisation and modernisation under a liberal democracy was the essential precondition for any future socialist revolution. This view was based upon a rigidly economistic interpretation of Marx's thoughts on the subject. Marx's writings on revolution were taken to mean that historical development would necessarily follow a series of fixed stages through which each country had to pass.[26] However, Plekhanov's interpretation overlooked Marx's emphasis upon the decisive importance of revolutionary political action by the working class.[27]

Up until March and April 1917, Lenin and the Bolsheviks shared the view that the bourgeois-democratic revolution had to be completed before a socialist revolution could become an objective possibility. However, they expressly rejected the idea that the Russian bourgeoisie could play a leading revolutionary role. For Lenin, only the proletariat allied with the peasantry could carry out a successful revolution. The workers and peasants, not the bourgeoisie, would be the ones to take political power and exercise a 'democratic dictatorship'. Yet he also insisted, against Trotsky, that this revolutionary government would oversee the completion of bourgeois-democratic tasks before socialist ones came onto the agenda.[28]

---

26   Plekhanov 1969.

27   Löwy argues that there is ample textual evidence in Marx's writings to identify many of the basic components of a permanentist theory of socialist revolution; so this claim does appear to be well founded. But, as he notes, they were not assembled into anything like a coherent theory and are frequently contradicted by stagist notions (Löwy 1981, pp. 1–29). Indeed, it is difficult to say that Marx and Engels possessed a theory of socialist revolution. Crucial elements such as a theory of imperialism and a complete grasp of the national question were either absent or underdeveloped in their writings. Again, this is not surprising when one considers that the capitalism they were examining had yet to enter its full imperialist phase.

28   Lenin 1970, pp. 121–5. Although, on balance, Lenin's position concerning the bourgeois character of the Russian Revolution did not alter until March/April 1917, he often came to

Another position, which was closer to Trotsky's in terms of methodological approach and informed some aspects of the theory of permanent revolution, was that of Alexander Parvus (Alexander Israel Helphand), who collaborated with Trotsky during the 1905 Revolution.[29] Parvus was already well established as a leading Marxist and provided considerable inspiration to the development of Trotsky's political ideas. He noted the peculiarities of Russian society, its semi-Asiatic character and state form; he also stressed the failure of the towns to develop as economic centres. This backwardness meant that the historic social base of revolutionary democracy, the urban artisan and petit-bourgeois classes, was poorly developed. Such underdevelopment contrasted sharply with the development of a concentrated proletariat in the late nineteenth century. Parvus concluded from this that only the working class could carry a revolution through and, in so doing, would take political power. But even Parvus cannot be said to have broken totally with stagist orthodoxy, since he still held that a workers' government would only be able to introduce gradual social reforms within the confines of a capitalist economic structure.[30]

### Trotsky's Evolving Theory

At the time of his collaboration with Parvus in early 1905, Trotsky had also still to reject a stagist conception of revolution and to realise that in Russia the revolution would go beyond bourgeois-democratic achievements. Commenting upon his own early formulations of permanent revolution, Trotsky later noted that there was never any disagreement that the revolution would be bourgeois, in the sense that its origins lay in the contradictions between developing capitalist productive forces and the anachronistic class and political relations which dominated Russian society. His point was that the bourgeois character of the revolution did not pre-determine which classes would have to solve the democratic tasks or what form the relationship between the revolutionary

---

the brink of adopting a permanentist position. An example of this is his *Farewell Letter to the Swiss Workers*, in which he not only argues that the Russian Revolution would 'initiate a "series of revolutions . . . arising from the imperialist war"', but also that the proletarian revolution 'would create the most favourable conditions for a socialist revolution and in a sense *start that revolution*' (in Mills 1963, pp. 238–40, emphasis in original).

29   See Trotsky's essay (really a series of articles) 'Up to the 9th January', with a preface by Parvus. Reproduced with commentaries in Day and Gaido (eds.) 2009.

30   Parvus's model for such a government was the recently elected Labour government in Australia. See Zeman and Scharlau 1965. Trotsky notes the impact of Parvus's ideas on the theory of permanent revolution in Trotsky 1969, pp. 187–8; Trotsky 1975b, p. 172; and 'Three Concepts of the Russian Revolution' in Trotsky 1970d, pp. 422–33.

classes would take.[31] Trotsky opposed Lenin's formula of 'democratic dictatorship of the proletariat and peasantry' precisely because it suggested an equal role for both classes in the revolution. Yet the peasantry had so far proved incapable of creating its own independent party and of leading a revolution. Thus, Trotsky concluded, the role of the peasants could only ever be to support the leading revolutionary class, which in Russia was the proletariat.

For Trotsky, then, the correct formulation was that of the dictatorship of the proletariat *supported by* the peasantry. Once in power, the proletariat would proceed to implement those democratic tasks outlined by Lenin: solving the agrarian question by radical redistribution of land; overthrowing the monarchy and absolutist state and reconstructing the state along democratic lines; granting the right of self-determination to the oppressed national minorities. Yet Trotsky felt this could not be the end-point of a proletarian dictatorship. As he put it:

> In other words, the dictatorship of the proletariat would become the instrument for solving the tasks of the historically-belated bourgeois revolution. But the matter could not rest there. Having reached power the proletariat would be compelled to encroach even more deeply upon the relationships of private property in general, that is to take the road of socialist measures.[32]

This was the essence of Trotsky's 'break' with existing interpretations of Marx. In a reference to Marx's *1850 Address*, from which the term 'permanent revolution' was appropriated, Trotsky clarifies the essential point of his theory:

> The permanent revolution, in the sense which Marx attached to the concept, means a revolution which makes no compromise with any single form of class rule, which does not stop at the democratic stage, which goes over to socialist measures and to war against reaction from without; that is, a revolution whose every successive stage is rooted in the preceding one and which can end only in the complete liquidation of class society.[33]

---

31    Trotsky 1969, pp. 126–7.

32    Trotsky 1969, p. 129.

33    Trotsky 1969, pp. 130–1. As Löwy points out, the difference between Marx's and Trotsky's
      conceptions of revolution had everything to do with the fact that whereas Marx was writing in the historical epoch of transition between bourgeois and proletarian revolutions,
      Trotsky was writing in the early twentieth century when the proletariat had developed

Here it is worth underlining that Trotsky was not arguing that the Russian Revolution was 'socialist' in content from its outset, still less that it missed out the phase of bourgeois-democratic tasks. As we have seen, a key assumption of Trotsky's theory of permanent revolution was that the objective conditions of the world economy, especially in Europe, were ripe for revolutionary upheavals. Conditions in Russia – its uneven and combined development – suggested that its proletariat could take power sooner than the proletariats of more advanced countries. But, whether or not a socialist society could be constructed in Russia depended upon the 'fate of European and world capitalism'.[34] That is to say, the building of a socialist society rested upon successful revolutions in more developed countries. In this respect, any advances made toward socialism by a proletarian dictatorship in Russia would always be limited by and dependent upon the progress of the international revolution. As he put it:

> The socialist revolution begins on national foundations – but it cannot be completed within these foundations. The maintenance of the proletarian revolution within a national framework can only be a provisional state of affairs, even though, as experience of the Soviet Union shows, one of long duration. In an isolated proletarian dictatorship, the internal and external contradictions grow inevitably along with the successes achieved. If it remains isolated, the proletarian state must finally fall victim to these contradictions. The way out for it lies only in the victory of the proletariat of the advanced countries. Viewed from this standpoint, a national revolution is not a self-contained whole: it is only a link in the international chain. The international revolution constitutes a permanent process, despite temporary declines and ebbs.[35]

Trotsky himself argued that the methodological 'break' with the stagist conception of revolution would not have been possible without rejecting the crude economism of the 'vulgar' Marxists.[36] Here, he again credited Marx with

---

the potential to lead revolutionary movements (Löwy 1981, p. 53). Trotsky was one of the first to realise that the implications of this historical progression ruled out the prospect of new revolutions following the classical bourgeois path. Lenin, Parvus and Luxemburg also recognised this, but Trotsky alone realised that the specific effects of Russia's development ruled out a capitalist stage of development *after* a revolution in which the proletariat had taken political power.

34    Trotsky 1969, p. 129.
35    Trotsky 1969, p. 133.
36    Trotsky 1969, p. 132.

providing an impetus for this in the *Communist Manifesto*, where it is suggested that 1848 could be the 'immediate prologue to the socialist revolution'.[37] He points out that Marx himself did not see the full development of capitalism as a necessary precondition to be fulfilled before the question of socialist revolution could be raised. Had he been aware of Marx and Engels's comments upon Russia's revolutionary prospects, Trotsky would no doubt have quoted the 1882 preface to the Russian edition of the *Manifesto*, in which they note that Russia 'forms the vanguard of revolutionary action in Europe'. They also point out the combined nature of Russian society and mention the question of progression to a 'higher form of communist common ownership' of land. Whether Russia would have to pass along the path trodden by the advancing capitalist countries would depend upon revolutions in the West and in Russia 'complement[ing] each other' and not upon any inexorable law of economic development.[38]

Another important element in Trotsky's political thought was his emphasis upon the need for revolutionaries to be prepared to respond to events. The timing of revolution was not something that could be chosen. Revolutionary upsurges could not be put off, as it were, until the development of capitalism had permitted the proletariat to achieve its optimal point in terms of size, concentration and class consciousness. Capitalism was itself limited by its class contradictions and the revolutionary struggles arising from them. Periodic revolutionary upsurges were thus an inevitable consequence of capitalist development and could arise quite early on in the development of capitalism in any particular country. Trotsky did not doubt that the levels of development, of concentration and proletarianisation, had to reach a certain maturity before class struggles could take on momentous significance. Yet he noted that, in Russia, this stage was achieved within a few decades, owing to the specific results of the country's uneven and combined development.

Trotsky thus rejected economism and endorsed the relative autonomy of politics, just as Marx had done in his political writings on France during the 1850s.[39] It was clear to Trotsky that the revolutionary role of the proletariat was not an index of national economic development. Had it been simply a reflection of economic development, the advanced capitalist countries would have

---

37    Trotsky 1969, p. 85. In *The Permanent Revolution*, Trotsky stresses that the failure of the 1848 revolution does not detract from Marx's methodological correctness: 'The revolution of 1848 did not turn into the socialist revolution. But that is just why it also did not achieve democracy' (Trotsky 1969, p. 131).

38    Preface to the 1882 Russian edition, in Marx 1973a, p. 56.

39    See the collection in Marx 1973b.

experienced far sharper class struggles in the nineteenth century than had in fact been the case. This pointed toward social and political factors as determining factors, conditioned (later theorists might say 'over-determined') by particular combinations of socio-economic relations.

## 1.3    Critical Perspectives on Permanent Revolution

Permanent revolution, as a theory underpinning political action, has been heavily criticised, both at the time (especially during the 1920s and 1930s) and since. Hence the outline of the theory presented above requires a more detailed exploration of some of its key elements. A good place to begin is with Trotsky's view of the relationship between the proletariat and the peasantry. After that the survey moves on to the question of the democratic revolution 'growing over' into the socialist revolution. It then turns first to the question of the need for revolutions in other countries, and second to Trotsky's extension of his theory of revolution to other supposedly backward countries. The purpose here is theoretical clarification and precision rather than any attempt at a 'defence' of Trotsky's theoretical and political perspective. The issues raised here are of considerable importance to understanding Trotsky's approach to the problems faced by the Spanish dissident communists.

### Peasants and Proletarians

A vital question for the theory of permanent revolution, and one of its most often-criticised aspects, concerns Trotsky's view of the peasantry and its relationship to the proletariat during periods of revolution. Peasants, the most numerous and diverse social layer in backward countries, occupy for Trotsky an intermediate position in the revolution owing to their heterogeneous class composition. He believed that the peasantry was incapable of creating an independent party of its own and was therefore compelled to choose between the policy and leadership of the bourgeoisie and that of the proletariat. Yet he did not think this diminished the crucial importance of the peasants during a revolution. As he put it:

> Without the decisive significance of the agrarian question for the life of the whole of society and without the great depth and gigantic sweep of the peasant revolution there could not even be any talk of the proletarian dictatorship in Russia. But the fact that the *agrarian* revolution created the conditions for the dictatorship *of the proletariat* grew out of the inability of the peasantry to solve its own historical problem with its

own forces and under its own leadership. Under present conditions in bourgeois countries, even in backward ones, insofar as they have already entered the epoch of capitalist industry and are bound into a unit by railroads and telegraphs – this applies not only to Russia but to China and India as well – the peasantry is even less capable of a leading or even only an independent political role than in the epoch of the old bourgeois revolutions.[40]

Trotsky agreed with Lenin on the need for a coalition between the peasantry and proletariat, but he insisted that the proletariat had to fulfil a hegemonic function in this alliance. However, it would be true to say that, before 1917, Lenin was rather less convinced that the peasantry would remain politically passive and ignorant during the early phases of a revolution.

Trotsky's 1928 response toward the old Leninist formula of 'the democratic dictatorship of the proletariat and the peasantry', which was so often cited to refute his theory of permanent revolution, did not disguise the original differences in their respective positions. He points out that, from March 1917, Lenin did not try to implement his formula but struggled only for the dictatorship of the proletariat, with peasant support. This had been Trotsky's own perspective, he claims. The reason Lenin held on to the notion of 'democratic dictatorship' until the last minute stemmed from the centrality of the agrarian revolution among the democratic tasks. As Trotsky notes, Lenin even briefly endorsed the idea of the proletariat leading the peasantry in 1909.[41] When it came to the point of forming a government in November 1917, Lenin did not hesitate to demand a majority position for the Bolsheviks.[42]

Trotsky also points out that when Lenin spoke of collaboration between the proletariat and the peasantry, he always stressed that any alliance would be implacably opposed to the bourgeoisie. Lenin's formula could never be an excuse for the kind of collaboration with the bourgeoisie imposed by the Comintern on the Chinese Communists in the late 1920s, he insisted. Any disagreement he had with Lenin was not over the need for joint action with the peasants, but stemmed from debates on the programme, party form and political methods such an alliance should adopt.[43]

Thus it would seem clear that both Lenin and Trotsky came to share the view that the proletariat, once in power, was the class which would

---

40     Trotsky 1969, p. 194.
41     Trotsky 1969, pp. 195–6 and p. 198.
42     Trotsky 1969, p. 203. See also Dukes 1979, pp. 92–3.
43     Trotsky 1969, p. 190.

emancipate the peasantry. To do so, it would have to convince the peasants of the benefits of supporting a workers' government. In order to do this it would be necessary to widen the social base of the revolution. However, this did not extend to permitting an equal share in government for the peasants. Indeed, they both agreed that the proletariat had first to win state power before the agrarian question could be tackled adequately.[44] Only then might peasants be mobilised properly.

Neither Lenin nor Trotsky doubted that the mobilisation and radicalisation of the peasants was itself a prerequisite for the continuation of the proletariat in power. In *Results and Prospects*, Trotsky states that one of the earliest and most pressing tasks of the new proletarian régime would be the expropriation of land and the collectivisation and modernisation of agricultural production. Only by carrying this through could the peasantry obtain a real stake in the continued existence of a workers' government. This would also cement the links between the peasantry and the proletariat.[45] This question of agrarian collectivisation was to be posed in a new and remarkable way during the summer revolution in Spain in 1936.

Behind Trotsky's thoughts on the peasant-proletarian relationship was the concern that, as the workers' government developed, it would be threatened by the disintegration of the revolutionary coalition with the peasantry.[46] Since this government would progressively become the class rule of the proletariat, there was a danger that some elements among the peasantry would not accept the government's policies of collectivism and internationalism because they might believe such measures held nothing for them. Thus the government would need to canvass support in the countryside and build a bloc against the richer peasants and the agrarian bourgeoisie. This was indeed to be a problem facing the new Soviet state; Lenin devoted much time in the final years of his life to the issue of links between workers and peasants.[47]

In his unpublished critique of the theory of permanent revolution, Radek argued that the democratic dictatorship was actually realised in Russia in 1917. Trotsky replied that even Lenin had only identified the existence of such a regime between April and October. However, the real point was that the democratic dictatorship, which in any case was not one of the proletariat and peasantry, failed to solve the democratic tasks. These only received proper attention

---

44    Trotsky 1969, pp. 184–5.
45    Trotsky 1969, pp. 70–2.
46    Trotsky 1969, p. 76.
47    See the collection of Lenin's texts of 1922 and 1923 on the worker-peasant alliance in Lenin
        1980.

from the workers' government, formed as a result of October 1917.[48] Hence, we can see that for both Lenin and Trotsky the peasant revolution would not be realised as a bourgeois one. Only as the revolution began to take up socialist measures under a proletarian government could the peasantry satisfy its own demands.

### The 'Growing Over' Controversy

This brings us to the issue of the 'growing over' of the democratic revolution into the socialist revolution. In *Results and Prospects*, Trotsky explicitly formulated the relationship between the initial bourgeois character of the revolution and its uninterrupted transition toward socialist measures in the following manner:

> It is possible to limit the scope of all the questions of the revolution by asserting that our revolution is *bourgeois* in its objective aims and therefore in its inevitable results, closing our eyes to the fact that the chief actor in this bourgeois revolution is the proletariat, which is being impelled towards power by the entire course of the revolution.
>
> We may reassure ourselves that in the framework of a bourgeois revolution the political domination of the proletariat will only be a passing episode, forgetting that once the proletariat has taken power into its hands it will not give it up without a desperate resistance, until it is torn from its hands by armed force.
>
> We may reassure ourselves that the social conditions of Russia are still not ripe for a socialist economy, without considering that the proletariat, on taking power, must, by the very logic of its position, inevitably be urged toward the introduction of state management of industry. The general sociological term *bourgeois revolution* by no means solves the politico-tactical problems, contradictions and difficulties which the mechanics of a *given* bourgeois revolution throw up.[49]

This seems a clear explanation of the idea of 'growing over', but it raised some questions at the time. What did Trotsky mean by suggesting that bourgeois-democratic tasks would fuse with socialist ones? Did this mean he thought the revolution would simply skip the bourgeois stage altogether?

---

48   As Lenin realised after March 1917 when he spoke of the need to abandon the antiquated slogans of the past. See 'Letters on Tactics' in Mills 1963, pp. 228–38.

49   Trotsky 1969, pp. 66–7.

Responding to Radek's criticism that he had confused two quite separate 'stages', that of bourgeois democracy and that of socialism, Trotsky argued that, in practice, the tasks of each would combine into a single, uninterrupted process. The proletarian offensive would certainly address bourgeois tasks such as the agrarian question, but their solution would not take the form of a separate bourgeois stage. This was not because such a stage was theoretically inconceivable, but rather because Russia's peculiar development suggested that only the proletariat had the capacity to conquer state power. In Russia, 'history combined the main content of the bourgeois revolution with the first stage of the proletarian revolution – did not mix them up but combined them organically.'[50]

> [T]he *skipping of stages* (or remaining too long at one stage) *is just what uneven development consists of* ... [T]he prediction that historically backward Russia could arrive at the proletarian revolution sooner than advanced Britain rests entirely upon the law of uneven development.
>
> One stage or another of the historical process can prove to be inevitable under certain conditions, although theoretically not inevitable. And conversely, theoretically 'inevitable' stages can be compressed to zero by the dynamics of development, especially during revolutions, which have not for nothing been called the locomotives of history.[51]

Even Kautsky, in 1906, had argued that the Russian Revolution could not be bourgeois because the national bourgeoisie was not one of its driving forces.[52]

Trotsky went further, asserting that, once in power, the proletariat would seek to resolve the 'tasks' of the bourgeois-democratic revolution. However, the workers would be forced far beyond the limits of bourgeois class demands because these would simply not satisfy the requirements of the class whose representatives were now in control: 'It would be the greatest utopianism to think that the proletariat, having been raised to political domination by the internal mechanism of a bourgeois revolution, can, even if it so desires, limit

---

50    Trotsky 1969, p. 239.

51    Trotsky 1969, p. 241.

52    Karl Kautsky, 'The Driving Forces and Prospects of the Russian Revolution'. Cited in Löwy 1981, pp. 36–7. Also reproduced with commentaries in Day and Gaido (ed.) 2009, p. 567. Dick Geary notes that when Kautsky uses the term 'the revolution in permanence' it is not in the same sense as Marx or Trotsky. Geary 1987, p. 79.

its mission to the creation of republican-democratic conditions for the social domination of the bourgeoisie'.[53]

Once the proletariat took power, the revolution would assume a continuous character as the dictatorship of the proletariat grew out of the bourgeois-democratic revolution. This was really what Trotsky meant when he used the terms 'permanent' or 'uninterrupted' to describe the revolutionary process. In Trotsky's revolutionary calendar, the dictatorship of the proletariat did not come after the completion of democratic tasks, but rather preceded this process and was the precondition for the solution of these tasks as well as the

---

53   Trotsky 1969, pp. 101–2. Nicolas Krassó accuses Trotsky of 'sociologism', by which he means an overemphasis upon social structures at the expense of underestimating the efficacy and autonomy of political institutions, especially those of the proletarian party. According to Krassó, in Trotsky's writings both before and after 1917, 'mass forces are presented as constantly dominant in society, without any political organisations or institutions intervening as necessary and permanent levels of the social formation'. For Krassó (1967, p. 72), this was the source of Trotsky's theoretical errors as well as his differences with Lenin over the party.

But Krassó overlooks the fact, or refuses to believe, that in 1917 Trotsky changed his view on the nature of the party and adopted that of Lenin. Even a cursory glance at Trotsky's post-1917 writings reveals the centrality of the proletarian party in his thought. His voluminous pamphlets, articles and letters on the Third International demonstrate a veritable obsession with this particular institution. Indeed, he was to see the building of revolutionary parties upon Leninist principles as a key task of the International Left Opposition and, later, the Fourth International. Mandel, in reply to Krassó, notes that Marx posed the question not of autonomy of political institutions, but of their *relative* autonomy. Moreover, it was Marx who insisted that class struggles were the motive forces of history. Political institutions only have efficacy in relation to the social forces they serve or represent. Once this relationship breaks down, they cease to be functional.

Mandel argues that although it is the vehicle for the working class to win power, the revolutionary party is not only a product of the class it represents. Moreover, without favourable objective conditions, the class will not be won over *en masse* to such a party. Even under favourable conditions, there was no guarantee that the programme and leadership of the party would ensure its success (Mandel 1968, pp. 34–6). Even if there are errors in Krassó's argument, he is surely justified in questioning the mechanical identification between the proletariat and the revolutionary party. Was the post-1917 dictatorship in the Soviet Union that of the proletariat or really of the Bolshevik Party? Trotsky himself realised that proletarian parties could sometimes constitute obstacles to revolutionary activity, yet his fetishisation of the party and its programme led him, in the 1930s, to devote an enormous amount of time and effort to correcting the line of dissenting sections of the Left Opposition and to intervening in petty squabbles. This was time which, given the relative insignificance of the Left Opposition and the gravity of the world situation, could perhaps have been spent more profitably.

starting point for socialist measures. He argued that the dictatorship of the proletariat in Russia would not have been possible if the agrarian question had already been solved.[54] Thus he thought that the proletariat could come to power on the basis of the unresolved bourgeois-democratic tasks precisely because it was the only social force able to solve them.

If it provides the starting point, the bourgeois revolution is never actually completed. For Trotsky's theory, the minimum programme for revolution – which includes 'tasks' such as unemployment relief, the eight-hour day and improved working conditions – will, on the assumption of power by the proletariat, combine with the maximum programme, which is the business of the socialist revolution. In order to understand Trotsky's thinking on this point, it is necessary to recall that he did not believe that the bourgeoisies of backward countries were capable of sustaining radical democratic reforms. Everything boils down, ultimately, to class interests. Any attempt to implement an eight-hour day, for example, would meet implacable opposition from capitalists if it came during a period of revolutionary upheaval. Even a progressive bourgeois government would abandon such a demand when faced with lock-outs and factory closures. However, a workers' government would be forced to expropriate factories and socialise production because of immense pressure from its own social base, upon which such a government would ultimately depend to remain in power. What began as a minimum demand would, through force of circumstance, require a maximum programme to bring it into being. Because of the weight of the peasantry, the agrarian question would be a priority for the new government. It would be forced to implement some form of collectivisation, either in the form of communes or state collectives.[55] Trotsky thought that a workers' government would need to adopt two tactics to preserve its power: agitation and organisation in the countryside, and collectivism. Only these would ensure the survival of the proletarian régime.

It was clear to Trotsky that there could be no question of a proletarian party entering a revolutionary government by, on the one hand, assuring the workers that it would implement a minimum programme and, on the other, promising the bourgeoisie that it would respect bourgeois legality. The proletarian party would simply be unable to realise this undertaking because it constituted the leading force in the government. In practice, Trotsky concluded, there could be no intermediate régime, no 'democratic dictatorship'.[56] This issue was to

---

54    Trotsky 1969, p. 182.

55    Trotsky 1969, p. 80 and pp. 102–4.

56    There has been a debate within the Trotskyist movement over the significance of the theory of permanent revolution. Unfortunately, the motivation behind this has little to do

surface with particular power in Trotsky's responses to the Popular Fronts in France and Spain in the mid-1930s.

Recognising the possibility of failure was an important aspect of Trotsky's perspective. A proletarian revolution would not inevitably succeed; even if it did, as it would in Russia, it would not necessarily go on to build a socialist society. He outlined several possible scenarios. First, the revolution could fail entirely, as it had in 1905. Second, a successful proletarian insurrection might be defeated if the bourgeoisie succeeded in winning mass peasant support. In this case, the revolution would achieve very little, since the bourgeoisie would probably reach a compromise with the old ruling classes. But should the proletariat hold on to power and begin to set in motion the means whereby the revolution might break out of the national framework, a third path became possible. In this third scenario, the Russian Revolution might 'become the prologue to the world socialist cataclysm'.[57]

### World Revolution

The revolution in Russia did succeed in transferring political power into the hands of the revolutionary party that, in Trotsky's view, represented the class interests of the proletariat. But this was not followed by successful revolutions in more advanced countries. Indeed, it was the hotly disputed issues of how the USSR, a 'workers' state' in Trotsky's mind, might survive and whether a socialist society could be built independently of the global revolutionary

---

with any desire to achieve analytical clarity or to calmly assess the theory in the light of historical events since Trotsky's death. The overtly sectarian nature of the controversy has tended to obscure any contributions it might have to make to a scholarly analysis of the theory. An indication of the level of the debate can be grasped from the contribution of Jack Barnes, a leader of the Socialist Workers, Party of the United States. He argues that Lenin thought in permanentist terms *prior* to 1917. Barnes cites approvingly the programme of the Cuban CP at its first congress in 1975, in which the concept of uninterrupted transition from democratic to socialist revolution is attributed to Lenin. He cites Radek's and Stalin's distortion of Trotsky's view to the effect that Trotsky is seen to reject an alliance between the proletariat and the peasantry. Barnes sees this, and not Lenin's stagism, as the main difference between Lenin and Trotsky prior to 1917. This historical and textual mistake unfortunately detracts from the more tenable argument Barnes advances concerning Trotsky's tendency to underestimate the revolutionary potential of the peasantry (Barnes 1983, pp. 11–12, 13, 14 and 42–3). The Australian Socialist Workers' Party has also taken the 'Third Worldist' approach to revolution, which appears to be a reversion to a stagist perspective. For a trenchant critique of this and a powerful restatement of Trotsky's theory, see Mandel 1986.

57    Trotsky 1969, p. 183. Here Trotsky is quoting his own 1908 view.

process that preoccupied Trotsky in his 1928 book *The Permanent Revolution*. He had never viewed the Soviet Union in any terms other than its relation to the rest of the world. For him, other revolutions and struggles were never subservient to or of less importance than the survival of the Soviet Union. As will be shown, it was axiomatic to his thought that these struggles were all interdependent. This is not to say, of course, that he underestimated the tremendous boost and inspiration afforded to other revolutionary movements by October 1917.

Even in *Results and Prospects*, Trotsky had referred to the 'real historical prospects' for socialist revolution across Europe. Yet it was not possible to assign a time scale to the process.[58] He was convinced even then that, if a successful workers' government came to power in Russia, it would require the assistance of revolutionary movements in other countries:

> *Without the direct state support of the European proletariat the working class of Russia cannot remain in power and convert its temporary domination into a lasting socialist dictatorship.*[59]

> Should the Russian proletariat find itself in power, if only as a result of a temporary conjuncture of circumstances in our bourgeois revolution, it will encounter the organized hostility of world reaction, and on the other hand will find a readiness on the part of the world proletariat to give organized support ... Left to its own resources, the working class of Russia will inevitably be crushed by the counter-revolution the moment the peasantry turns its back on it. It will have no alternative but to link the fate of its political rule, and, hence, the fate of the whole Russian Revolution, with the fate of the socialist revolution in Europe.[60]

Hence a revolution in Russia would spark off revolutionary movements in more developed countries, he thought. According to Trotsky's pre-1914 views in *Results and Prospects*, such a revolution would have been unlikely to survive without successful proletarian seizures of power elsewhere. In the event, Russia did lead the way but was left isolated after the failure of revolutions in other European countries in the post-war years (1918 to 1923). Yet the new 'workers' state' in Russia was not 'crushed' as he had predicted, despite attempts by the forces of 'world reaction' to do so. Indeed, by 1928, Trotsky believed that

---

58    Trotsky 1969, p. 81.
59    Trotsky 1969, p. 105 (emphasis in original).
60    Trotsky 1969, p. 115.

the greatest danger to the revolution came from within, from what he saw as the disastrous policies of Stalin and the Comintern.

From the mid-1920s, Trotsky devoted a great deal of attention to combating the theory of 'socialism in one country' and what he considered the subordination of the Comintern and world revolution to this rigid perspective. He accused Stalin of separating Russia's national revolution from the international revolution. Stalin, he thought, presented the conquest of power within the 'national' confines of Russia as the final act of the revolution. Consequently, Soviet ideologues now saw the idea of world revolution as a means of defending the Russian Revolution as redundant. Yet Trotsky, as ever, maintained that October 1917 had been merely the initial act in a global socialist revolution which would extend over decades. For him, the defence of the USSR was now more than ever bound up with the success of revolutions in other countries.[61]

Trotsky's argument was essentially that the seizure of state power by the proletariat did not somehow allow Russia to exit the world economy. The workers' state could not exist as an independent and self-sufficient socialist economy. As he saw it:

> The passing of power from the hands of Tsarism and the bourgeoisie into the hands of the proletariat abolishes neither the processes nor the laws of world economy ... The international division of labour and the supranational character of modern productive forces not only retain but will increase twofold and tenfold their significance for the Soviet Union in proportion to the degree of Soviet economic ascent.[62]

At best, the fledgling workers' state might lay the national foundations for a future socialist society. But the ultimate realisation of socialism in Russia depended entirely upon the final victory of the world revolution.

Trotsky added that the contradictions between the existence of a workers' state and the requirements of an imperialist world order meant that one of them had to perish. During the 1920s, capitalism had gained time to stabilise and to prepare a new military action against the USSR. The resistance of the world proletariat to imperialism would no doubt increase, but the existence of this pressure could itself provoke the bourgeoisie into striking at the Soviet heartland of proletarian internationalism. He concluded that the increasingly authoritarian character of some European régimes strongly indicated that the

61      Trotsky 1969, p. 154.
62      Trotsky 1969, p. 152.

continued existence of the USSR was even more dependent upon the success of revolutions in Europe.

With hindsight, we can see that Trotsky greatly underestimated the USSR's capacity for survival under Stalin. He certainly failed to anticipate the degeneration of the proletarian régime into a bureaucratic dictatorship. Indeed, he wrote surprisingly little on the USSR itself in the early 1930s, compared to his output on other world affairs.[63] Only after Hitler's rise to power in Germany did Trotsky conclude that the Soviet Communist Party and the Comintern could not be salvaged and that a further political revolution would be necessary for the workers to reclaim what he believed to be their usurped power. While his 1936 book *The Revolution Betrayed* proved an important and timely expression of his critique of Stalinism, it also portrayed the Soviet Union as a 'degenerated workers' state' that should nevertheless be defended.

Trotsky's theory of revolution has often been caricatured as a call for 'a continuous conflagration at all times and all places – a metaphysical carnival of insurrection'.[64] In fact, both Lenin and Trotsky had been quick to oppose any adventurist actions by workers in advanced countries in support of the USSR. According to them, the best defence of the Soviet Union was to prepare and consolidate the new Communist Parties in readiness for real revolutionary situations. It was senseless to risk total destruction through premature insurrections. Perhaps Trotsky can best defend himself on this score:

> Naturally, I never shared the Bukharinist version of the theory of the 'permanent' revolution, according to which no interruptions, periods of stagnation, retreats, transitional demands, or the like, are at all conceivable in the revolutionary process ... The consciousness that real dangers actually threatened the Soviet power did not prevent me from waging an irreconcilable struggle shoulder to shoulder with Lenin at the Third Congress against this putschistic parody of a Marxian conception of the permanent revolution ... [W]e declared tens of times to the impatient Leftists: 'Don't be in too great a hurry to save us. In that way you will destroy yourselves and, therefore, also bring about our destruction.'[65]

Krassó also accuses Trotsky of conflating the question of the class nature of the revolution – that is to say, the growing over of democratic into socialist demands – with the different issue of the ability of the revolution to sustain

---

63    Thatcher 2003, p. 190.
64    Krassó 1967, p. 68.
65    Trotsky 1970b, pp. 88–9.

itself on an international plane.[66] Yet it would appear Krassó begins from the twin assumptions that, first, socialism could be and was constructed in a single country, and second, the success or failure of this venture did not depend upon a global revolutionary process and was not constrained by the relationship of the USSR to the world capitalist economy. It seems, from events since 1989, that history has tended to vindicate Trotsky's original contention and has demonstrated the emptiness of claims that the USSR was a socialist society. It seems reasonable to argue that Trotsky was correct to predict that, should the world revolution fail to produce victories in advanced countries, the USSR would remain a transitional society and would not progress toward socialism.

Having said this, there is little doubt that Trotsky, who was no economist, did underestimate the Soviet economy's capacity to sustain itself in a hostile environment. He also overestimated the revolutionary enthusiasm of the working class in advanced countries. But it would seem rash to accept Krassó's dismissal of the significance of revolutionary crises in Western Europe during the 1920s and 1930s, such as Germany from 1918 to 1923, France in 1936, and Spain in 1934 and in 1936 and 1937.[67] Nor is it tenable to argue that all of these conflicts were decided upon a national rather than international level. The civil war in Spain was a clear example of social, political and military conflict on an international as well as a national scale. The spread of fascism and dictatorship in Europe during the 1930s suggests that the original intentions of Lenin and Trotsky for the Third International – to provide a means of building

---

66    Krassó 1967, p. 68.

67    In his rejoinder to Mandel's 'anti-critique', Krassó rejects this list of revolutionary crises. Commenting on events in Spain in 1936 and 1937, Krassó argues that the Spanish Communist Party was initially a very weak force and that the Republic had little chance of winning the war. He also says that the conflict, like all the others on Mandel's list, was resolved nationally, not internationally (Krassó 1968). This ignores two crucial historical facts. First, a revolution did occur as a consequence of the nationalist military rising in July 1936. Whether it was a 'permanent revolution' or not is another matter. Secondly, the Spanish Civil War is often characterised as involving the participation of international forces on both sides. It is popularly seen as the first international attempt to halt the spread of fascism in Europe. On the 'Nationalist' side, Franco enjoyed considerable Italian and German help. The supposed 'neutrality' of the democracies needs to be examined in terms of whether a state was truly impartial or in reality assisted the Nationalist side. Also, for many on the international Left, Spain's was a revolutionary war fought to defend socialist achievements and to stem the advance of fascism. It could also be argued that the official Spanish Communists played a counterrevolutionary role, assisting in the destruction of the truly revolutionary forces.

an international revolutionary leadership which would both promote world revolution and defend the USSR – were far from utopian. Indeed, this continued to be, in theory at least, the stated purpose of the Comintern throughout the 1930s. The powerful attraction of working-class internationalism at a time of relentless onslaught by authoritarian forces in Europe goes a long way toward explaining the success of the pro-Moscow Communist Parties during those years. That Stalin might be said to have utilised the Comintern as an instrument for promoting his own foreign policy, and in so doing suppressed genuine revolutionary movements, are charges with which many national Communist Parties had great difficulty coming to terms.

### Permanent Revolution as a General Theory

It will already be clear that just as with the law of uneven and combined development, Trotsky came to regard the theory of permanent revolution as a general theory, applicable to all backward capitalist countries. As he noted:

> With regard to countries with a belated bourgeois development, especially the colonial and semi-colonial countries, the theory of the permanent revolution signifies that the complete and genuine solution of their tasks of achieving *democracy and national emancipation* is conceivable only through the dictatorship of the proletariat as the leader of the subjugated nation, above all of its peasant masses.[68]

In such countries, the 'dictatorship of the proletariat' would appear quite varied in terms of its social base, political forms, immediate tasks and tempo of development. The specific consequences of uneven and combined development in each country would shape the precise nature of the struggle for power.

> The peculiarities of a country which has not accomplished or completed its democratic revolution are of such great significance that they must be taken as the basis for the programme of the proletarian vanguard. Only upon the basis of such a *national* programme can a Communist Party develop its real and successful struggle for the majority of the working class and the toilers in general against the bourgeoisie and its democratic agents.[69]

---

68    Trotsky 1969, p. 276.
69    Trotsky 1969, p. 254.

Hence the extent of a revolutionary party's success would be determined by the role of the proletariat in the economy and therefore by the level of development of capitalism.

No less important were the crucial issues of the 'agrarian revolution' and the 'national question'. Addressing these questions, Trotsky argued, a young and relatively small proletariat could come to power on the basis of a *'national democratic* revolution sooner than the proletariat of an advanced country on a purely *socialist* basis'.[70] Yet he was careful to add that this did not mean that all countries were ripe for revolution. While the world economy might be ripe for socialism, no isolated country could build a socialist society. In fact, he added, a country might well be ready for the dictatorship of the proletariat before becoming open to changes of a socialist order.[71]

Nor was every backward country ripe for the dictatorship of the proletariat or every colonial country ready for national liberation. Under imperialism, the national democratic revolution could only be won when social and political relations in a given country were able to place the proletariat in power and permit it to lead the masses. In any other situation, the national liberation struggle would achieve only partial results which were not in the interests of the working class or peasantry. But no one could say when and under what conditions 'ripeness' would occur in colonial countries. The most that could be said was that the revolutionary process in colonial and semi-colonial countries could pass through several phases. One phase might see the national bourgeoisie veering to the left and later turning on the masses, as in China.[72]

---

70    Ibid.

71    Trotsky 1969, pp. 254–5.

72    Trotsky notes that he had returned to the issues first outlined in 1906 and restated the theory of permanent revolution only when the Stalinist campaign and policy of the Comintern threatened to sabotage the Chinese revolution. Stalin and Bukharin said in 1924 that China was in the throes of a revolution of national liberation in which the Chinese bourgeoisie was a leading element. They advised the Chinese Communists to join the Kuomintang and accept its discipline, to halt the agrarian movement and not to form soviets. To do otherwise, Stalin insisted, would alienate the 'reasonable ally' Chiang Kai-shek. Stalin said this in April 1927, only days before the Kuomintang turned on its Communist 'allies' and massacred thousands of them. Following this disaster, the Comintern compounded its error by seeing the left wing of the Kuomintang as a potential ally. Again this 'ally' turned upon the Chinese Communists.

Trotsky argued that the Comintern's Chinese policy promoted what he considered to be ridiculous alliances and hopeless adventurism simply to suit Moscow's foreign policy, even arranging a rising in Canton to coincide with the CPSU congress. (According to C.P. Fitzgerald (1977, pp. 35–6), the orders for this rising came from Moscow.) The Sixth

As already noted, Trotsky thought that the development of capitalism on a truly global scale had prepared the world economy for a transformation to socialism. Furthermore, he considered it probable that many backward countries would be able to realise the dictatorship of the proletariat sooner than advanced countries. However, in the context of the process of world revolution, he thought that the advanced capitalist countries would still arrive at socialism soonest.[73] This appears to constitute something of a paradox in Trotsky's thought: that less developed countries would be the first to see socialist revolutions, whereas their complete socialist transformations would have to wait not simply for later revolutions in advanced countries, but also for socialist transitions to take place in those countries. In other words, this was a promise of revolutionary struggle today but socialist desserts at some unspecified and contingent point in the future. This paradox may partly account for the many confusions and misunderstandings surrounding interpretations of the meaning of 'permanent revolution' by both supporters and detractors of

---

Congress of the Comintern approved the slogan 'democratic dictatorship of the proletariat and peasantry' for China, but gave no advice to the Chinese Communists on how to distinguish between this and the dictatorship of the Kuomintang. However, Stalin also deprived them of democratic slogans, since he ruled out the tasks of a constituent assembly, universal suffrage, etc. Trotsky notes that the Bolsheviks had organised around such slogans in 1917; only when soviet power conflicted with them were they abandoned in favour of the dictatorship of the proletariat. He argued that it was crucial for the Comintern to destroy the theory of permanent revolution in order to pursue its anti-Bolshevik Chinese tactic. Trotsky saw China as a semi-colonial country in which the question of democratic tasks also involved liberation from colonialism and national unification. Although the Kuomintang was in power, it could not solve the democratic tasks and no independent agrarian revolution was possible. Thus the 'national revolution' against imperialism advocated by Stalin and Bukharin could neither be bourgeois-democratic nor could it result in a democratic dictatorship. It would be socialist in character or it would be no revolution at all (Trotsky 1969, pp. 133–4, 138–42, 190, 205, 254–60, 271–5; Trotsky 1970b, pp. 167–230; see also the collection of writings on China, Trotsky 2009).

The example of China is certainly instructive when examining the Comintern's relationships with national Communist Parties and in understanding the way its directives were often accepted without question. In the report of his interview with Mao Zedong on the 1927 events, Edgar Snow says that Mao blamed Ch'en Duxiu, then leader of the Party, and the Soviet adviser Borodin. The latter had been ready to placate the Kuomintang even at the expense of disarming the Communists. For his part, Ch'en merely followed Moscow's directives and, initially, accepted the argument that the 'defence of the USSR' took priority over all other political considerations (Snow 1968, pp. 162–5, and notes pp. 432–4).

73    Trotsky 1969, p. 279.

Trotsky's Marxism. However, taken in hindsight, the notion that socialist revolutions would not necessarily deliver socialism seems a reasonable summary of many of the revolutionary events and processes unfolding across the span of the 'short' twentieth century, not least in 'backward' capitalist, colonial and semi-colonial countries.

## 1.4    Theorising Revolutionary Crises

While he thought of capitalism, revolution and socialism as global processes, Trotsky nevertheless realised that the nation-state would continue to be the immediate arena for inter-capitalist struggles and revolutionary conflicts. Therefore another important aspect of Trotsky's revolutionary thought, one which has a direct bearing upon his analysis of Spain, is his conception of 'revolutionary crisis'. As we have seen, Trotsky thought that the world revolution would develop through a succession of crises, perhaps in several states at once. The result was the revolutionary chain effect noted above. But how did he conceptualise the dynamics of revolutionary crises in individual nation-states?

### Structural Preconditions
In an article devoted to precisely this issue, Trotsky stressed the need to distinguish between the objective economic and social preconditions for a revolutionary crisis and the subjective political prerequisites.[74] Economic and social factors in backward capitalist countries have already been mentioned in earlier sections. As far as advanced countries are concerned, Trotsky saw the objective preconditions for revolutionary crises arising from a number of sources, such as a country's declining productive power and loss of relative importance in the world market. Other causes might include the decrease in incomes and perpetual unemployment resulting from declining economic fortunes. All of these causes may themselves originate from or be exacerbated by global economic crisis, inter-imperialist rivalries or war.

### Political Preconditions
Turning to the subjective political factors without which a revolutionary crisis could not develop at all, Trotsky stressed the need for a radical change in the political consciousness of all classes. Only when the proletariat begins to seek a revolutionary solution to the crisis of society – a solution which is opposed to the interests of the existing social and economic order – would the revolution-

---

74    'What Is a Revolutionary Situation?', 17 November 1931, in Trotsky 1973c., pp. 352–5.

ary crisis mature, he thought. In order to achieve the critical mass of revolutionary consciousness, the proletariat would need to lose confidence in the parties of the Right, Centre and reformist Left and to be won over to a revolutionary programme. Hence the key task of the proletarian party in the pre-revolutionary phase was to struggle for such a transformation of proletarian consciousness.

Trotsky argued that a revolutionary crisis opens up the possibility for the proletariat to become the ruling power in society. Yet the nature of the crisis and the tactics of the proletarian leadership would be influenced a great deal by the political attitude and actions of the petty-bourgeoisie and the peasantry. Of crucial importance in this respect would be the extent to which these oppressed classes lose confidence in the big bourgeoisie, the landed oligarchy and their traditional political parties. Other key factors included the will of the oppressed classes for radical social change and the degree to which they looked to the forces of the revolutionary proletariat for political leadership. Trotsky knew only too well that the petty-bourgeoisie and peasantry could play either a progressive role on the side of the revolution or a profoundly reactionary one which would support authoritarian solutions to the crisis.[75]

A key factor governing the development of a revolutionary crisis concerned the attitude of the ruling class itself. For such a crisis to emerge, the ruling class (or classes) must both lose confidence in their ability to control the situation and also feel marginalised in relation to proletarian forces. The proletariat, petty-bourgeoisie and peasantry would respond positively to the disintegration of the old ruling classes and the revolution would derive momentum from this. As Lenin had formulated it: 'When the "lower classes" no longer want to be ruled in the old way, and when the "upper classes" cannot carry on ruling in the old way'.[76] In order for this scenario to come about and for a revolutionary crisis to materialise, the repressive apparatus of the state must already have reached an advanced level of decomposition. This constitutes the loss of authority and initiative on the part of the ruling classes. Just as with the attitudes and political actions of the petit-bourgeoisie, this crisis of power held dangers as well as opportunities for the proletarian movement.

Clearly, the actions of the working class would be of decisive importance in the development of a revolutionary situation. A general strike of great magnitude and force might totally unsettle the repressive forces of the state. But it would also be vital to develop dual-power organs of workers' representatives to such a point that a substantial section of the masses identifies with these alter-

---

75    This emerges strongly in his analysis of fascism. See Chapter Two.
76    Lenin, cited in Mandel 1979b, p. 6.

native organs rather than with those of the ruling classes. Only then would it be possible to speak of a situation of 'dual power' as existed in Petrograd in 1917.

Following on from the last point, Trotsky stressed that he was talking about a profound crisis of legitimacy for the existing state institutions in the eyes of the masses. Dual-power organs (workers' councils) must be seen to enjoy greater legitimacy. If this was not the case, the revolutionary crisis would probably not reach full maturity. Hence in order to be able to speak of a dual-power situation, it was not enough that the masses merely rejected the old institutions. Workers and peasants needed to identify with the new legitimacy represented by organs of workers' power; otherwise the revolutionary situation would not develop and the crisis would simply be another crisis of the old regime. Trotsky was well aware that only experience in struggle could lead the masses beyond a simple rejection of the old régime and toward embracing a revolutionary alternative.

It was thus impossible to predict the exact point during these changes at which the revolutionary situation would become fully mature. Only during the struggle to win over the workers, peasants and petty-bourgeoisie against the resistance of the ruling classes would the revolutionary party discover the correct moment to move. All that could be said was that the deeper the original crisis, the faster these changes would take place. However, Trotsky did not believe that all of the political preconditions would necessarily ripen at the same time. For instance, the revolutionary party might mature less rapidly than either the changes in consciousness of the workers, peasants and petty-bourgeoisie or than the political disintegration of the ruling classes. So a revolutionary situation might develop in the absence of an adequate revolutionary party, as was indeed the case in Spain. During the 1930s, Trotsky advanced, as the Left Opposition's main objective, the construction of revolutionary communist parties capable of tackling the tasks posed by the revolutionary crises he felt certain would develop. This preoccupation informed all of his interventions in the debates within the independent communist Left, not least in Spain.

### Assessment

Trotsky's notion of revolutionary crisis may be judged to have broken with an orthodox Marxist position, since it does not simply connect the prospects for proletarian revolution with a capitalist crisis of overproduction via a causal relationship. Class struggles are attributed a degree of relative autonomy which, in his analyses of specific cases, shows that he was able to break with an economistic and reductionist Marxism. He advances a 'primacy of politics' argument when determining the outcome of revolutionary situations, although this is over-determined by structural socio-economic factors. It could be argued that this is an affirmation of Marx's dictum that people, rather than abstract forces, make history but not in circumstances of their own choosing. Although Trotsky frequently outlines the objective conditions which make social revolution a possibility, he is no less aware of the subjective factors involved in 'making' a revolution.

As has been noted many times already, Trotsky's placement of the revolutionary party at the core of proletarian revolutionary strategy has become one of the best-known aspects of his political thought and that of his followers. He assigned to the party a key role in the preparation of the proletariat for decisive revolutionary action. However, this did not in itself ensure that the party was in possession of a ready-made revolutionary solution which would guarantee the proletariat success in a power struggle. The party aspired to the status of revolutionary leadership of the proletariat, but it could only actually achieve this by participating in working-class struggles and drawing lessons from these struggles. Only in this way could the revolutionary party win the respect of those it sought to lead and achieve a full understanding of the specific problems the revolution would have to overcome.

It would seem, then, that the view of revolutionary crisis outlined above is incompatible with the notion often attributed to Trotsky that revolution is possible at all times and in all capitalist states. In reality, he thought that, for a revolutionary opportunity to present itself, there needed to be a conjunction of a crisis of bourgeois society (including a crisis of the state) with the intense radicalisation of a mature working class. By definition, such crises appear only periodically and are certainly not present at all times.[77] It is also clear from Trotsky's later writings that he did not think the success of the proletariat was ever guaranteed. He recognised that it was quite possible that a revolutionary crisis would result in the stabilisation of capitalist society. None of this makes sense unless it is situated within Trotsky's worldview of the international capitalist system in which everything is connected and interdependent. Hence, the outcome of a revolutionary crisis in a single country might have decisive implications for the course of the world revolution as a whole. A victory of the order of October 1917 could give a tremendous boost to global revolutionary struggles for decades to come. However, a defeat such as the one in Germany in the period between 1918 and 1923 might greatly assist capitalist stabilisation in other countries.

---

77    Mandel 1979a, p. 39.

## 1.5     Permanent Revolution since Trotsky

If the theoretical tools of uneven and combined development and permanent revolution are to be considered useful contributions to Marxist political and historical sociology, it is necessary to examine the strengths and weaknesses of these concepts in the light of seventy years of revolutionary upheavals. Although an examination of the individual cases of twentieth-century revolutions lies beyond the scope of this study, it is possible to outline the general argument that, when taken together, these revolutions constitute a continuation of the process of world revolution which began in 1917. Such an exercise inevitably leads to criticism and qualification of some of Trotsky's initial assertions and provides the opportunity to pose a series of questions that need to be addressed in a case study of Trotsky's involvement with the Spanish Revolution.

Many Marxists who place themselves squarely within the tradition of Trotskyism have argued that the 'successful' socialist revolutions of the twentieth century can indeed be said to have followed a permanentist path. They also maintain that the history of the countries in which such revolutions have occurred can usefully be understood in terms of uneven and combined development.[78] It is often stated that in the cases of the Russian, Yugoslav, Chinese, Vietnamese, Cuban and Nicaraguan revolutions, a revolutionary party inspired by Marxist-Leninist principles led a proletarian and peasant movement which took state power and proceeded to exercise it for a significant length of time.[79] It is argued that these were all peripheral capitalist countries, affected in various ways and to different degrees by imperialism. Their revolutions cannot be said to have witnessed an initial bourgeois phase in which a proletarian-peasant dictatorship presided over the resolution of the democratic tasks necessary to liberate the creative forces of national capitalism. Nor did these revolutions jump over the unresolved bourgeois-democratic problems and move directly to implementing purely socialist measures. It would be more accurate to say that they combined democratic and socialist tasks within a

---

78    See, for example, the works by Mandel already cited and the various essays by George Novack, the American Trotskyist, in Novack 1972.

79    In Nicaragua, the Frente Sandinista de Liberación Nacional (Sandinista National Liberation Front, or FSLN) was a revolutionary party influenced by Marxism and inspired by the example of the Cuban revolution. On taking power, the Sandinistas replaced Somoza's armed forces with a popular militia. However, the case of Nicaragua stands out from all of the previous socialist revolutions in terms of its approach to the question of political democracy. The Sandinistas were able to establish a democratic political framework, the results of which they were prepared to accept. After their electoral defeat in February 1990, the FSLN duly handed power over to the victorious opposition coalition.

single, uninterrupted process.[80] Confirming the validity of this argument would obviously require a detailed analysis of each individual revolution. While such a task cannot be attempted here, there are a number of issues arising from the concrete experiences of post-1917 revolutions that reveal problems in Trotsky's general theory. These will be addressed below. But before doing so, it is worth briefly considering the role played by what Trotsky himself considered the first workers' state in the process of world revolution.

### The Soviet Union and World Revolution

When Trotsky argued that the revolutionary proletarian party's arrival in power did not signal the end of the revolution but only its initial act, he effectively identified the central problem of the Russian Revolution, a problem that could never be solved in his view other than as a consequence of the development of the world revolution. The confusion of two quite distinct problems – namely, the survival of the proletarian régime on the one hand and the construction of a socialist society on the other – does appear to have hampered Soviet thinking from Stalin onwards. The conflation of these distinct questions into the single problematic of 'socialism in one country' signalled the end of the brief hegemony of the 'permanentist' theoretical perspective in Russia between 1917 and 1923. Thereafter, the conception of proletarian internationalism, which was fundamental to the revolutionary thought of both Lenin and Trotsky, appears to have been subordinated to the perceived requirements of the USSR's own survival. From Trotsky's critical viewpoint, the ideological camouflage for this was Stalin's notion that socialism could be achieved within the boundaries and out of the resources of the Soviet Union alone.

In reality the new Soviet state followed a path no one had foreseen. The October Revolution proved strong enough to resist a counterrevolution backed by the advanced capitalist states, themselves severely weakened by the effects of the world war and the ensuing economic crisis. But, by the same token, the defeat of revolutionary bids in other countries left the USSR in an

---

80   This is the argument advanced in Löwy 1981, pp. 103–59. The notion that revolution will begin at the periphery of the world capitalist system and spread to its core has proved attractive to those who follow a 'third worldist' approach. While it is undoubtedly true that revolutionary successes in peripheral areas of the capitalist world system have influenced revolutionary crises in advanced countries, there has been no case in which a proletarian revolutionary movement has taken state power. In recent years, moreover, the objective and subjective conditions for such crises have been noticeably absent in advanced states. Whether or not this is a temporary hiatus in the process of world revolution, we are forced to conclude that the thesis that socialist revolution can spread from less developed to developed countries has yet to be confirmed.

isolated position. The outcome was neither a restoration of capitalism nor the construction of a socialist society. In hindsight, it seems reasonable to endorse Trotsky's characterisation of the USSR as a 'contradictory society halfway between capitalism and socialism'.[81] By this Trotsky meant that it was a society that possessed the potential to progress toward socialism, yet could still slide backward toward capitalism. Whether the USSR would remain 'stuck' in this halfway situation or move forward to socialism rested, he thought, upon the success of socialist revolutions in advanced capitalist countries. It was with great reluctance that Trotsky concluded that the USSR under Stalin had become a major obstacle both to the advance of world revolution and to its own transition to socialism.

It is a matter of considerable debate to what extent the foreign policies of the Soviet leadership, arguably expressed through the Comintern until its dissolution in 1943, contributed to the failure of revolutionary movements in advanced capitalist countries and of revolutions in not a few peripheral ones.[82] As will be seen in the case of Spain, it is certainly arguable that Stalin evolved a deliberate counterrevolutionary strategy. On the other hand, there is much historical debate over the degree of autonomy exercised by national Communist Parties in initiatives such as the Popular Front strategy, the level of criticism and dissent from the Moscow 'line' within official parties, and the extent of *de facto* control Moscow exercised over local agents and political activists on the ground. There is also room for debate over the degree to which the requirements of Soviet foreign policy actually determined the tactics of the Comintern in the way Trotsky and others maintained they did.

In global terms, it might be argued that the doctrine of 'socialism in one country' has in practice led to the exact opposite of its stated aim. No country has built a socialist society which in any meaningful sense approaches or has ever looked like approaching a classical Marxist definition of a society politically, economically, socially and culturally superior to the most advanced capitalist societies. Those countries that did witness attempts to create socialism within national boundaries usually resorted to methods so morally repugnant as to discredit the socialist project itself in the eyes of their populations and many outside observers. Thus in a very real sense, although perhaps for many reasons unforeseen by Trotsky, his rejection of the possibility of socialism developing in a single state would appear to be a prescient one.

---

81    Trotsky 1972a, p. 255. Mandel later developed Trotsky's thesis in the light of developments in the USSR during the 1980s. See Mandel 1989.

82    See the extensive discussion of the Comintern in Rees and Thorpe 1998.

If Trotsky was correct to say that no country can solve its socialist tasks in isolation, one is prompted to ask: 'To what extent can key democratic tasks be resolved within the socialist revolution?' Trotsky's suggestion that the USSR could at best lay down the national foundations for a future socialist society indicates that democratic tasks, emptied of their bourgeois class content, could be adequately addressed by a workers' government. But in all countries that experienced 'successful' socialist revolutions (proletarian seizures of power), the national, agrarian and democratic questions invariably still awaited 'full and complete' resolution. Indeed, these unresolved problems re-emerged in the post-1989 upheavals in Eastern Europe. It would appear that in their 'socialist' phases, the most these bureaucratic régimes were able to achieve was to suppress and paper over some fundamental developmental problems. One searches in vain for any meaningful democracy. Whatever Stalin's evident crimes and distortions, it can be cogently argued that Lenin and Trotsky were largely responsible for stifling early manifestations of workers' democratic demands.

Trotsky's old prophesy that Lenin's conception of the party would lead to the party substituting itself for the class it represented would come true in practice after 1917. It could be said that by colluding in this act of substitution, Trotsky contributed to the creation of the very structures Stalin was to utilise as he fulfilled to the letter Trotsky's 1904 prediction that a 'dictator' would substitute himself for the central committee of the party.[83] Having achieved so much, it seems that the Bolsheviks were not willing to place their revolution in jeopardy by allowing the people in whose name they had acted to pass judgement on their government by means of free elections or even via free workers' organisations. This fundamental absence of democracy at a critical moment – and its justification by the blunt assertion that soviet democracy would be a higher, more progressive form than pluralist parliamentary democracy – is perhaps the weakest aspect of Trotsky's political thought. Even in later writings, it is clear that he envisaged a workers' government implementing a programme which, although taking account of peasant aspirations, could not, by its very nature, admit democratic accountability in the short term. A workers' state was, by definition, a minority régime in a predominantly agrarian country like Russia. Therefore Trotsky felt the only way in which the working class might preserve its power was by actually transforming the demands of a significant proportion of the peasantry into socialist ones.

It is true that in some respects Trotsky did move back toward a more pluralistic view of socialist democracy during the 1930s. In a response to the official

---

83    Deutscher 1954, p. 487.

Communist-inspired campaign to restrict the right-wing press in Mexico, Trotsky reminded the Mexican Communist Party that since Mexico was a bourgeois state, such measures would only rebound upon the workers' movement. He also made a plea for democratic freedoms. In a workers' state, he argued, the means of communication must be placed at the disposal of society as a whole.

> Once this fundamental socialist step has been taken, all currents of public opinion that have not taken up arms against the dictatorship of the proletariat must be given the opportunity to express themselves freely. It is the duty of the workers' state to make available to them, in proportion to their numbers, all the technical means they may require, such as presses, paper and transport.[84]

Hence he certainly recognised the immense importance of democratic freedoms for workers' parties operating within bourgeois democracy and also came to see that they would be a vital safeguard against bureaucratic degeneration in a workers' state. Yet Trotsky remained convinced that, however democratic a bourgeois parliamentary régime might appear, in the final analysis it remained a class dictatorship of the bourgeoisie. Nothing less than the dictatorship of the proletariat could lay the basis for a socialist democracy. Yet, given his own record when in power in the years after October 1917 and his often intolerant attitude toward those whose political perspective differed only slightly from his own, it is hard to believe that Trotsky ever fully embraced the concept of democratic pluralism.

There is, then, a strong case that the theory of permanent revolution offers a plausible explanation for the tendency for revolutions that have taken on a socialist character to occur in backward rather than advanced capitalist countries. However, there are certain problems with the theory that cannot be ignored and that, as we will see, have relevance for the Spanish case.

### General Theory or Revolutionary Strategy?

The first problem concerns the extent to which a theory initially intended to explain the specificities of Russian historical development can be said to have the universal validity of a general theory. One of the most frequent criticisms of Trotsky's theory of revolution is that it imposes the model of October 1917 upon countries whose paths of development have been very different to that

---

84    21 August 1938. From the Mexican Trotskyist journal *Clave*, October 1938, written 21 August 1938, in Trotsky 1972b, p. 418.

of Russia.[85] However, there is often some confusion over whether this charge refers to permanent revolution as a mode of analysis or as a political strategy. For Trotsky, the theory of permanent revolution was intended to be both. Yet it did not offer a blueprint for revolution. It was still necessary to elaborate specific programmes and strategies that corresponded to the particular situation in each country. In this respect, permanent revolution could only ever be a general framework within which the particular conditions and problems of an individual case could be made sense of and through which the accumulated experience of previous revolutionary struggles could be assimilated. We might also add that the theory was based upon a conception of historical development which seems very flexible. The following chapter will consider the extent to which Trotsky drew upon the law of uneven and combined development in his writings on Spain, but it is worth noting here that it was precisely this historical and sociological tool that suggested the parallel between the general courses of Russian and Spanish history. It is curious, then, that the law of uneven and combined development is barely mentioned by those who criticise Trotsky's analysis of Spain.

We can say, then, that, despite its reputation, the theory of permanent revolution as Trotsky articulates it makes no claim to represent a total strategy for revolution or to serve as a 'model'. It seeks only to identify general trends within the dynamics of revolution in peripheral capitalist countries. It might be boiled down to the assertion that should the representatives of the working class conquer state power, they will not be able, even if they so desire, to remain within the limits of bourgeois legality. If this can be proved false, the entire theory collapses. It is also true to say that aspects other than permanent revolution entered into Trotsky's revolutionary strategy: soviets, the party, revolutionary crises and so on. Permanency, in terms of the 'growing-over' question, was only one aspect of what was essentially a Leninist revolutionary strategy.

### Revolutionary Leadership

One of the main problems with the theory of permanent revolution as Trotsky formulated it concerns the assertion that *only* the proletariat can lead the democratic revolution in peripheral capitalist countries. It will be recalled that the class nature of this leadership determined that there would not be a period of bourgeois democracy and national capitalist development akin to those the

---

85    As we have seen, the essential aspects of permanent revolution had been formulated at least eleven years before 1917. But the charge of schematisation based upon the model of 1917 is frequently levelled against Trotsky, not least by those who wish to argue that his theory has no relevance to Spain.

advanced countries experienced after their bourgeois revolutions. As has already been noted, the statement that there could be no bourgeois-democratic revolutions in backward capitalist countries, only socialist ones, has of course been contradicted by history. Since 1945 a succession of revolutions in colonial and semi-colonial countries have been led by the national bourgeoisie and/or petty-bourgeoisie. These revolutions have gone some way toward addressing the basic democratic tasks of political democracy, agrarian reform and the national question. Examples of such bourgeois revolutions include Mexico, Algeria, India and Egypt.[86] Ongoing events would appear to suggest that many of these revolutions were partial and incomplete. It would seem that the era of bourgeois revolutions is very far from played out.

In defending Trotsky's theory of revolution against the criticism that it rejects formulations other than working-class leadership, Ernest Mandel argued that it is not a question of denying that any bourgeois-democratic task can be achieved without the proletariat in charge or that a revolutionary process cannot begin without proletarian hegemony over the peasantry. He stressed that Trotsky's contention was simply that there would be no 'full and genuine' completion of *every* bourgeois-democratic task.[87] But this leads us to ask: 'What constitutes full and genuine completion?' Does, for instance, the transition to capitalist relations of production in agriculture constitute the solution of the agrarian question? As we will see in the Spanish context, such a transition neither guarantees the dynamic development of capitalist agriculture nor resolves rural social conflicts. We might even wish to question whether any advanced country has totally resolved its own democratic issues. An answer to this point might be that such tasks are fulfilled to a sufficient degree once the central problems – the agrarian revolution, the national question and basic democratic rights – are resolved in the eyes of the overwhelming majority of the population. Yet it seems clear that these are not necessarily adequate or once and for all 'solutions'. For instance, in the United Kingdom, as in several

---

86    Löwy calls these 'unfinished bourgeois revolutions'. He identifies two distinct varieties: 'interrupted popular revolutions' and 'semi-revolutions from above'. He argues that both forms have been incomplete and have failed to combine all of the key democratic tasks (Löwy 1981, pp. 160–88). In Europe, the late-developing peripheral capitalist countries Ireland, Portugal, Spain and Greece have all experienced revolutionary crises of greater or lesser intensity. Yet these countries differ from non-European peripheral ones in the sense that, apart from Ireland, their connections with imperialism have been weaker. Spain and Portugal have even been imperialist powers in their own right. As we will see in Chapter Two, Trotsky saw Spain as a semi-colonial country and in this sense similar to Russia.

87    Mandel 1979b, p. 70.

other Western European states, there is a huge question mark over the issue of national and regional devolution up to and including complete independence. It is hard to believe that the current configuration of nation-states will remain unchanged in the future.

### The Democratic Tasks

It is worth clarifying what is meant by 'democratic tasks' and emphasising that they are seen to vary according to the character of the country in question. In those countries said to have experienced classic bourgeois revolutions, these 'tasks' were primarily abolishing autocratic political rule; ending feudal or precapitalist residues among the relations of production; establishing a parliamentary democracy based upon universal (male) suffrage; and national unification or liberation.[88] The modern period clearly presents rather different issues from those arising from the backwardness of France at the time of its revolution.[89] Here, the democratic tasks were complicated by profound backwardness and the weight of imperialism. In these cases, the tasks might usefully be reformulated in the following way. The *agrarian revolution* constitutes the most difficult task facing peripheral capitalist countries. It demands abolishing precapitalist relations of production and other residues, expropriating all large landowners and redistributing land to the peasants. *National liberation* involves both national unification and emancipation from imperialist domination. It also demands the creation of a national market protected from cheap foreign goods and the control of key resources which have been taken out of the hands of multinational capitalist enterprises. The establishment of *democracy* is also a broader task than in the classical cases. Beyond the establishment of democratic freedoms based upon a republic, accomplishing democratic tasks might entail ending military rule and creating the social and cultural conditions for popular participation in politics: literacy, an eight-hour day, or other similar social reforms and innovations.

Such concerns have considerable relevance to the Spanish case discussed in the following chapters. Spain's revolution (1931–1937) may appear closer to the semi-colonial/colonial model than first impressions would suggest. Yet its

---

88    Those states which were able to establish the basis of their advanced industrial capitalist economies by means of semi-revolutions from above – Germany, Italy and Japan – were either not subjected to or proved able to resist the constraints of imperialist domination. For an insightful discussion of England, France and Prussia from a Marxist perspective, see Mooers 1991.

89    Mandel 1979b, p. 73.

classification as such is complicated by its relatively high degree of industrial development and stronger national bourgeoisie relative to those of other peripheral capitalist countries. Given a comparatively strong proletariat, Spain appears closer to the Russian case than to any other country that has experienced what might be described as a socialist revolution. Its peculiar combination of advanced and backward features makes it an interesting and challenging case to examine.

According to Mandel, the acid test for judging whether any backward country has solved its bourgeois-democratic tasks is simply that the tasks now facing its proletariat must approximate those facing the proletariats of advanced capitalist countries.[90] That is to say, its proletariat must think in terms of purely socialist tasks. However, the reality would seem to be that after 1945 the more industrialised countries on the periphery of global capitalism became *more*, not less, dependent upon imperialism for their technology, markets, capital and technical expertise. Their national bourgeoisies became ever more intimately tied to the multinational corporations and international credit agencies and, as a consequence, their economies showed greater vulnerability to the economic fluctuations of the advanced economies.[91] Yet it cannot be denied that it has been possible for national bourgeoisies to carry out reforms and establish stable regimes with a relatively high degree of political and economic independence. The national bourgeoisie has often been able to gain long-term hegemony over the masses by implementing popular democratic reforms. In Latin America and Asia, especially, this has produced relatively stable and pluralistic capitalist democracies, often with considerable dynamism.

---

90    Mandel 1979b, p. 89.

91    Mandel argues that, under 'late capitalism', a term which denotes a shift within the structure of core imperialist countries, the incomplete industrialisation of certain peripheral countries becomes a feature of the altered world capitalist economy. The logic of this is that the producers of industrial machinery and technology in core countries need to expand their export outlets into underdeveloped countries. Imperialism therefore promotes the industrial development of some countries and, in so doing, alters the relationships between imperialist and national bourgeoisies. This, in turn, has the effect of altering the composition of the power bloc in the peripheral countries. The old bloc of landowners, comprador bourgeoisie, and imperialist capital based around raw materials and primary products is replaced by one made up of the indigenous industrial bourgeoisie, state and military technocrats, and those multinationals interested in exporting machinery (Mandel 1979b, pp. 71–2; see also Mandel 1978b).

So where does this leave the theory of permanent revolution on the question of 'democratic tasks' in today's globalised capitalism? It would seem that Trotsky's pessimistic prognosis regarding the ability of the petty-bourgeoisie and bourgeoisie of underdeveloped and developing countries needs serious revision. Mandel is no doubt correct to caution that it is easy to overestimate the depth and durability of democratic achievements, since history tends to suggest that, even in countries enjoying periods of considerable democratic freedoms, political democracy can be very fragile. He is also surely justified in questioning whether such 'intermediate' cases such as Mexico, Brazil, Algeria, Egypt and India have witnessed a 'complete and genuine solution' to their problems of democracy. But it is difficult to sustain his argument that imperialism still exerts a limiting and blocking effect upon the ability and willingness of bourgeois and petty-bourgeois forces to address questions of democracy in meaningful ways. Of course, this need not mean that in an economic and political crisis as profound as the post-2008 depression and the ongoing Arab revolutions, Trotsky's argument about the national bourgeoisie's 'reversion to type' might still not apply. The point is to what extent it can revert to authoritarian solutions in the face of profound advances in democratic culture and democratisation of the means of communication. Perhaps these are things Trotsky can be forgiven for failing to anticipate.

### Dependency

An important aspect of Trotsky's global perspective was the argument that colonial and semi-colonial countries are tied into an imperialist world system. Hence they are dependent countries with dependent bourgeoisies. Although not necessarily directly manipulated by the imperialist powers, they are still subject to the economic power of imperialist capital which ensures an indirect political control over them.[92] In the post-1945 controversy between dependency theorists and those who argue that capitalism actually develops peripheral countries, the law of uneven and combined development seems to contain much that is still of analytical interest. It could be argued that imperialism, by spreading capitalist exploitation on the one hand and by promoting transitions to capitalist production (however partial) on the other, *both* under-develops and develops these economies. It *both* ties them into an unequal relationship of mutual dependency with advanced countries *and* creates the conditions for relatively independent (if limited) capitalist industrial

---

92    Mandel 1979b, pp. 77–80.

development.[93] Once again, this argument may hold some validity for the period with which this study is mainly concerned, Europe in the 1930s, but it has difficulty accounting for the dynamics of globalised capitalism over the last thirty years.

Indeed, it is hard to argue that globalisation fails to facilitate economic development along a path similar to that followed by the older, more advanced capitalist states. One only has to look at the emergence of the BRIC countries to see that globalisation provides considerable opportunities for national bourgeoisies. The claim of dependency theory that peripheral countries rely upon advanced ones for their economic survival and are thus underdeveloped by capitalism may have a certain descriptive allure, yet fails to convince today. As Trotsky noted in 1930, dependency was never a one-way process:

> Every backward country integrated with capitalism has passed through various stages of decreasing or increasing dependence upon the other capitalist countries, but in general the tendency of capitalist develop-ment is toward a colossal growth of world ties, which is expressed in the growing volume of foreign trade, including, of course, capital export. Britain's dependence upon India naturally bears a qualitatively different character from India's dependence upon Britain. But this difference is determined, at bottom, by the difference in the respective levels of

---

93    In his attack upon 'dependency theory', Bill Warren argued in favour of a view which rec-ognises the dynamic and modernising role played by imperialism in promoting capitalist development in ex-colonial countries. Warren maintained that the establishment of capi-talist democracy was a vital prerequisite for the socialist education of the working class. He saw imperialism as a force that encouraged rather than hindered the development of productive forces in peripheral countries. He argued that this led to a qualitative improve-ment in social conditions for colonial and semi-colonial countries (Warren 1980). Although this is reasonable as a general statement and builds upon Marx's own writings on India, it ignores the contradictory nature of capitalism. In particular, Warren's thesis overlooks the tendency of capitalism to combine progressive and regressive features, modern technology and modern social relations with barbaric oppression and a rein-forcement of precapitalist social relations of production (such as slavery). As Löwy has noted, if socialism can be arrived at through capitalist development, Warren is forced to oppose anti-capitalist revolutionary movements in peripheral countries. He would also have to explain why a long history of advanced bourgeois democracy has not produced a working class with a socialist consciousness in a country like Britain. Another problem lies in the fact that there is no reason to suggest a causal connection between capitalist economic development and the emergence of democracy. For a development of these objections to Warren, see Löwy 1981, pp. 223–7 and the critique in Lipietz 1992, pp. 48–58.

development of their productive forces, and not at all by the degree of their economic self-sufficiency. India is a colony; Britain, a metropolis. But if Britain were subjected today to an economic blockade, it would perish sooner than would India under a similar blockade. This, by the way, is one of the convincing illustrations of the reality of world economy.[94]

Hence it would seem that, for Trotsky, imperial relationships were in a very real sense reciprocal when set within the framework of the world capitalist system, even if political power flowed outwards from the metropole.

In the post colonial world, the power of global capital is harder to locate in particular metropolitan centres since it is far more widely diffused. Now it seems more accurate to speak of a transnational bourgeoisie. Yet revolutions still take place within 'national' contexts; it would seem that national bourgeois forces, perhaps assisted by those of other states, can gain long-term hegemony over the popular masses through national-democratic reforms. It is almost certain that, in such cases, Trotsky would have reiterated his warning that a revolutionary party must in no way assist the bourgeoisie in power to fulfil its tasks. The party ought rather to take advantage of any weakness or indecision on the part of bourgeois forces and struggle to secure hegemony over the proletarian and peasant masses. Only then can it pull the revolution in a socialist direction. The combination of democratic and socialist tasks under proletarian leadership would not, therefore, depend upon the prior completion of the bourgeois-democratic revolution. Such a revolutionary combination rested in the first place upon the failure or the inability of the bourgeoisie to accomplish its own tasks and, in the second place, upon the capacity of the proletarian party to win leadership of the revolution. Later chapters will deal with this particular problem in the context of the Spanish Revolution and Trotsky's specific advice to the dissident communists.

### Class
Any Marxist analysis is, first and foremost, a class analysis. This is certainly the key concept at the heart of everything Trotsky had to say about the nature of revolution. However, this does not mean that Trotsky's characterisation of the role of classes in revolutions was unproblematic or unchanging. The following

---

94    From Trotsky's 1930 preface to the German edition of *The Permanent Revolution* (Trotsky 1969, pp. 152–3). This analysis seems rather prophetic when one considers Britain's position during the Second World War, after the fall of France.

comments are limited to those points that have direct bearing upon the Spanish case.

In *The Permanent Revolution*, the petty-bourgeoisie is portrayed as incapable of playing a leading revolutionary role and as predestined to follow either the bourgeoisie or the proletariat. However, the most advanced national-democratic revolutions have been led by the petty-bourgeoisie rather than by the more conservative national bourgeoisie. Indeed, national bourgeoisies have displayed a propensity to repress popular democratic movements and side with the old ruling classes. As we will see, the Catalan industrial bourgeoisie represents a prime example of this tendency. By 1938, Trotsky's views on this point had altered to the extent that he now accepted that the petty-bourgeoisie could break with the bourgeoisie and participate in a workers' and farmers' government.[95] In fact the petty-bourgeoisie (especially the military) has shown a tendency to substitute itself for weak national bourgeoisies and lead the democratic revolution or semi-revolution. It often introduces reforms of a more radical nature than the bourgeoisie actually wants. The petty-bourgeoisie also tends to produce the intellectuals vital to revolutionary movements. This is certainly the case in countries where the national bourgeoisie's fear of the masses is one reason why it sides with the landowners and imperialism, as in Spain. In such a climate, liberalism finds little or no articulation among a national bourgeoisie that is traditionally conservative and anti-democratic. Petty-bourgeois intellectuals are in a sense forced to rely upon the proletariat and/or the peasantry as the only available revolutionary agency. Consequently, the left petty-bourgeois position, which can even extend to a socialist ideology, is explicitly anti-imperialist and anti-bourgeois because of the close relationship between national bourgeoisies and imperialist interests. While this may speak to the Spanish case to some extent, one of the weaknesses of Trotsky's approach was to underestimate the significance of liberal bourgeois and petty-bourgeois political forces.

In October 1917, the Russian industrial working class was unquestionably the decisive social force enabling the Bolsheviks to take power. Moreover, the party was undeniably proletarian in its ideology, programme and social

---

95    It should be said that the characterisation 'workers' and farmers' government' had nothing to do with the Comintern's use of the same slogan. For Trotsky, the term had been used in 1917 merely as another name for the dictatorship of the proletariat and was not counterposed to such a dictatorship. A workers' and farmers' government would be totally independent of the bourgeoisie. Even in the unlikely event of this regime materialising, it would be but a brief prelude to the full dictatorship of the proletariat (Trotsky 1980a, pp. 37–40).

composition. But this formula has yet to be repeated by any socialist revolution in which state power has been taken. Despite varying degrees of proletarian involvement, the shock troops of successful post-1917 revolutions have been drawn from the peasantry. This is less surprising when one considers the agrarian nature of the societies in question and their low levels of industrial development compared to Tsarist Russia. Yet the fact remains that the language, programmes, ideology and politics of these mainly peasant movements were still essentially proletarian. This attests to the massive impact of the Bolshevik Revolution, the vibrations of which can be detected in many of the major political events of the short twentieth century.

With the exception of the Yugoslav case, all of the post-1917 socialist revolutions which were at all successful saw large sections of the peasantry supporting the collectivisation of agriculture. This was a major feature of the Spanish Revolution of 1936 and 1937 and sets it apart not only from the Russian Revolution but also from other Western European revolutionary crises, like those of Germany in 1919 and France in 1936. As we will see, it is possible to explain the importance of socialist and anarchist ideas to rural revolt in Spain by using the framework of the law of uneven and combined development.[96] However, Trotsky's contention that the peasants were unable to organise and mobilise themselves – that they would always require the leadership of a proletarian party which imported a revolutionary socialist consciousness – has not proved to be the case.

Anyone wishing to make sense of the historical position of the peasantry will inevitably be forced to break down this heterogeneous social mass into its component parts. As a general rule, we find that the better-off peasants (peasant proprietors) have been hostile to revolutionary movements. Curiously enough it is the middling peasant, the small-holder, who is generally the first to become politically mobilised. The poorest peasants, sharecroppers, tenants

---

96    Löwy contends that although the 'huge historical fact' of its revolutionary role contradicts Trotsky's view of the peasantry, it is the theory of permanent revolution which enables us to understand the reasons for the revolutionary actions of peasants in colonial and semi-colonial countries. He argues that the uneven and combined development of capitalism has caused a deep uprooting of rural populations and decomposition of village life. The political, military and economic penetration of imperialist capital has been a key factor in provoking revolutionary crises. Uprooted peasants have been the prime movers in organising the political action which has been decisive in successful socialist revolutions. The other key aspect has been the failure of the national bourgeoisie to offer radical democratic solutions to the agrarian and national questions. The peasantry has had no choice but to look toward communist movements for leadership (Löwy 1981, pp. 210–11). This specific analysis cannot be applied in full to Spain, but elements of it might be useful.

and others, tend to join the revolutionary movement only when it has achieved its first successes. Löwy has argued that this is because the poor peasant lacks the sense of political independence afforded to the middling peasant by the possession of land. Since they are totally controlled by large landowners, the poor peasant and rural wage labourer do not join in until the revolutionary movement appears strong enough to challenge this immediate authority.[97] It remains to be seen whether this holds true for Spain or whether the country's peculiar development, with its many regional variations, makes it a special case.

## 1.6   Conclusion

One of the contentions of this presentation and discussion of Trotsky's Marxism has been that his political thought differs from that of Second International Marxists over the key issue of how socialist revolutions develop. This is not to say that in formulating his version of the theory of permanent revolution Trotsky can be said to have come closer to Marx's 'true intentions' than other theorists. Marx provided the raw material for *both* permanentist and stagist theories of revolution. While Trotsky certainly drew upon and developed certain themes present in Marx's work, he worked out his major theoretical formulations in relation to personal political involvement in and observation of the revolutionary struggles in Russia and other countries. This was equally true when it came to the elaboration, extension and application of his theoretical perspective to other cases of 'backward' development. It could also be argued that Trotsky was closer than most of his contemporaries to the spirit of Marx's thought in the sense that they both recognised alternative paths of development in human history and rejected any predetermined or guaranteed socialist future. Trotsky reaffirms Marx's contention that people make their own history, adding the crucial rider that failure to grasp the opportunities history throws up can have tragic consequences for humanity as a whole. This concern motivated his active interest in all of the major world issues of the 1930s, ranging from the struggle against fascism to the Revolution and Civil War in Spain. It is to this aspect of Trotsky's political engagement and influence that we now turn.

---

97    Löwy suggests that this applies generally to revolutions in Mexico, Russia, China, Vietnam, Cuba and Algeria (Löwy 1981, p. 212).

# Trotsky on Spain

For Trotsky, the 1930s were years of personal tragedy, constant danger, hurried departures and bitter struggle against his *bête noire*, Stalin. Yet they were also highly productive. Following his expulsion from the Soviet Union in 1929, he devoted most of his energy to overseeing the work of the International Left Opposition and, later on, to founding the Fourth International. His writings from this period include *The History of the Russian Revolution*, *The Stalinist School of Falsification*, and *The Revolution Betrayed*, as well as numerous pamphlets, articles and letters (many of which are now collected in the 14-volume *Writings of Leon Trotsky*). To the list of published works we must add his writings on Germany, France and Spain, as well as unfinished biographies of Lenin and Stalin. Given his many and varied literary and political activities, it is a testament to the significance of events in Spain that Trotsky devoted so much valuable time to analysing them.[1]

---

1 In September 1937 Trotsky communicated to his literary agent his eagerness to write a book on Spain which would include 'not only a general analysis of the Spanish Revolution and its development, but also a merciless condemnation of the Stalinist leadership of the revolution and of the attitude of the so-called European "democracies"'. However, the book did not materialise other than as a much shorter article under the title 'The Lessons of Spain: The Last Warning'. See the extracts from Trotsky's letters to Charles Mumford Walker of 17, 28 and 30 September and 6 October 1937 in Blanco Rodríguez 1982, pp. 115–17. Trotsky's writings on Spain between 1930 and 1940 are collected in Trotsky 1973a. Various articles referring to Spanish events are also to be found in the fourteen-volume collection (Trotsky 1970–9).

   Trotsky's involvement with Spain has received its most sympathetic treatment from the French historian Pierre Broué (1966; 1967; 1975; 1982; 1988). Other contributions from a Trotskyist perspective are the introductions: L. Evans 1973, Orozco 1977. Also from a Trotskyist perspective, see Hassel 1982. Critics of Trotsky's writings on Spain are headed by the POUM veteran Ignacio Iglesias. He produced two books or, rather, the same book twice: Iglesias 1976 and 1977. Other articles of interest are Rovida 1980 and Thornberry 1982; an interesting reference to Trotsky's analysis of the Primo dictatorship is Pastor 1978. Of lesser interest are Velarde Fuentes 1968 and Thornberry 1978. The standard works on Trotsky devote little space to his involvement with Spain. For example: Deutscher 1963; Howe 1978, pp. 128–31; Hallas 1979, pp. 71–5. I am indebted to the Fundación Andreu Nin in Madrid for putting at my disposal the unpublished transcript of a *Mesa redonda* (roundtable) discussion on Trotsky and Spain. Participants include Javier Maestro (historian), Juan Pablo Fussi (director of the

Trotsky's writings on Spain, which span the 1930s, fall into distinct phases in both their volume and political intensity. This fact reflects the way in which events in other countries often took precedence over those in Spain as well as Trotsky's growing dissatisfaction with the actions of his Spanish followers. During the first phase, 1930 to 1932, Trotsky outlined the situation in Spain, which he believed would produce a momentous revolutionary opportunity. He argued that this would have massive implications for the world proletarian revolution and the struggle against fascism and dictatorship in Europe. His writings of this period occupy nearly half of the volume of collected works devoted to Spain. Most of these pieces were intended to assist dissident Spanish communists such as Andreu Nin, who looked to Trotsky for political guidance.[2] However, between 1933 and 1935, he wrote little about Spain. This lapse is probably explained by his preoccupation with the European situation following Hitler's rise to power and his own change of political direction, which took him away from attempts to rescue the Third International and toward building a new international organisation. It was also a particularly unsettled period in Trotsky's life. In July 1933, he moved to France from Turkey, where he had been in exile from the Soviet Union since February 1929; then from France to Norway in June 1935; and, finally, to Mexico in January 1937. During this time he was engaged in writing his major critique of Stalinism, *The Revolution Betrayed*, and was subject to increasingly violent attacks by Stalin's agents. When, in 1936, he returned to the issues of the Spanish Revolution, he was faced with a situation that had altered dramatically in the space of less than two years. In addition to the problems of a country in revolutionary turmoil, there were the questions of the Popular Front, the POUM and the Civil War.[3]

---

Biblioteca Nacional), Wilebaldo Solano (an ex-POUM leader), and the French historian Pierre Broué (Fundación Andreu Nin, n.d.).

2   Between May 1930 and December 1932, Trotsky wrote more than 60 letters, articles, pamphlets and Left Opposition bulletins which dealt wholly or partly with Spanish matters. These include 36 letters to Nin, which Trotsky later published along with some of Nin's letters. Since the Trotsky-Nin correspondence was stolen by GPU agents in November 1936, and given comments by Trotsky to this effect, there was certainly much more than what has survived. See Reed and Jakobson 1987, pp. 363–75.

3   Biographical information on Trotsky relies heavily upon the following works: Deutscher 1954, 1959 and 1963; Segal 1983; Thatcher 2003; Swain 2006; and Service 2009. However, it seems that little written by or about Trotsky is uncontroversial. The three latest biographies are heavily critical of Deutscher. Yet they themselves have been criticised from within the Trotskyist movement; significant parts of Service's biography have been seriously challenged for factual accuracy by some (non-Trotskyist) Eastern European specialists. A key critic from

These writings, like Trotsky's entire political thought during the 1930s, need to be viewed within the dual context of what many on the dissenting communist Left saw as the struggle against Stalin's abandonment of the principles of Bolshevik internationalism.[4] We must also set Trotsky's perspective on Spain alongside his acute awareness of the threat posed by fascism in Europe. From the late 1920s up until 1933, his political energies were devoted to the building of a Left Opposition *within* the Comintern and national Communist Parties. He also advocated the construction of united fronts made up of workers' organisations as the key to confronting the spread of fascism. After Hitler's triumph, he abandoned all hope of salvaging the Comintern and began to think in terms of a new forum for revolutionary Marxists, a Fourth International. These factors played a critical role in Trotsky's relationship with the Left Opposition in Spain and deeply influenced his understanding of events there.

The purpose of this chapter is to present and discuss Trotsky's characterisation of Spain's historical development and his commentaries upon the revolutionary process in Spain. It examines the way the theories outlined in the previous chapter informed Trotsky's approach to revolution in a backward capitalist country. In what ways does his analysis draw upon the theoretical apparatus he employs to such impressive effect when assessing the likely course of the Russian Revolution? Do his theoretical tools – permanent revolution and uneven and combined development – display the flexibility required to explain the particular conditions present in Spain? And can we detect in Trotsky's approach a refinement or extension of these earlier concepts?

Since our principal concern is to chart the trajectory of Trotsky's thoughts on Spain, much which relates to the micro-politics and organisation of both the International and Spanish Left Opposition has been omitted.[5] Yet we must always remain conscious that, for Trotsky, theory was never separate from practice. While, in hindsight, it may appear unfortunate that he devoted so much time and energy to seemingly trivial factional disputes within the organisation he headed, to Trotsky, these practical issues were inseparable from his analytical writings. Just as the advice he offered to the Spanish Left Opposition is incomprehensible without the optic of the theory of permanent revolution,

---

within the Trotskyist camp is North 2010. For a review of both Service and North see Patenaude 2011, pp. 900–2.

4   In March 1936, Stalin remarked to an American interviewer that the idea that the USSR stood for world revolution had been a 'tragi-comic misunderstanding' (Deutscher 1966, p. 414).

5   See subsequent chapters for more on this. On the international Trotskyist movement, see Frank 1979. For the Spanish Trotskyist movement, see the admirable study Pagès 1977a. See also Maestro 1978 and the unpublished Ph.D. dissertation Fatherree 1978.

so the vehemence of Trotsky's criticisms of Nin and the POUM can only be understood from an appreciation of his absolute belief in their capacity to influence events. Underpinning the whole of Trotsky's involvement with the Spanish Revolution – and arguably his whole worldview after 1917 – is the conviction that, however minuscule the initial nucleus of revolutionaries may be, with the correct theory, leadership and programme, this tiny grouping could be transformed into a revolutionary party with mass support in a time of revolutionary crisis.

## 2.1    Spain's Uneven and Combined Development

Trotsky's connection with Spain dates back to the First World War. Expelled from France, he spent November and December 1916 as an unwilling tourist and guest of the Spanish police.[6] During his brief stay in Madrid, Cadiz and Barcelona, Trotsky gained an impression of the country's massive regional differences. He describes Madrid as a city which, although possessing many of the facets of a modern metropolis, seemed reluctant to leave the nineteenth century. Its modernity, suggested by the impressive Prado museum, magnificent banks and busy cafes, stood in stark contrast to the great churches, an apparent absence of industry and the city's manifest poverty. 'In spite of its electricity and banks', he wrote, 'Madrid is a provincial city'.[7] While the architecture bore witness to great material and cultural wealth, the signs of economic dynamism were lacking. 'Spain, to the point I have been able to see it (and I have hardly seen it), appears like Romania, or to put it better, Romania is a Spain without a past'.[8] The old port city of Cadiz 'belonged more completely to the past than did the whole of Spain'.[9] Barcelona, by contrast, was a veritable hive of industry and commerce. It was the capital of Cataluña, 'today the most enterprising region of Spain'. The historic claims of the Catalan people to separation were not mere expressions of a conservative mentality. On the contrary,

---

6   In 1924, Andreu Nin persuaded Trotsky to publish extracts from his diary relating to his sojourn in Spain. The Spanish translation, by Nin, was published in 1929 under the title *Mis peripecias en España*. The version which will be referred to here is Trotsky 1975a. A much shorter account of his experiences is to be found in his autobiography, Trotsky 1975b, pp. 266–78. Concerning Trotsky's brief stay in Spain, see Márquez Reviriego 1975, pp. 116–20.

7   Trotsky 1975a, p. 24.

8   Trotsky 1975a, p. 25.

9   Trotsky 1975a, p. 99.

Trotsky perceived that the content of their nationalist aspirations was constantly being renewed.[10]

Passing encounters, such as one with a young student from Cadiz, afforded Trotsky some revealing insights into Spaniards' perceptions of their own country. According to the student, Spain was hopelessly backward, a 'third-order' nation which lacked industry and adequate investment in education and infrastructure. Wages were low, illiteracy levels were high and the moneyed classes displayed little inclination to improve the national economic situation. Political life was corrupt and geared solely to perpetuating the system.[11] In Cadiz, Trotsky spent much of his time in the city library studying the history of his host country. He remarked in his journal upon the slowness of Spanish development, noting the decline from imperial splendour into what he was later to call the status of a 'nation thrown backward'.[12] European rivalries had brought about the eclipse of Spanish power well before the onset of industrial capitalism. Britain had been the chief instigator and beneficiary of Spain's defeat, robbing it of many key markets and colonies as well as taking control of Gibraltar.

Given the preoccupations of Europe in 1916, it is perhaps not surprising that Trotsky noted the presence of foreign business interests, including Germans in Madrid and French in Barcelona. The war and Spain's neutrality allowed both groups to cultivate considerable influence. Yet it seemed to Trotsky that local entrepreneurs had been rather slow to take advantage of the commercial opportunities afforded by wartime demand from both sides. Indeed, Spain seemed strangely unaffected by the conflagration taking place on the other side of the Pyrenees. However, it was also clear that there was a major distinction to be made between the much more industrialised and dynamic region of Cataluña and Spain's rather backward capital. His French socialist contact, Després, informed him that the rather conservative Spanish Socialist Party, based in Madrid, held very similar social-patriotic views to those of his own party, the French Section of the Workers' International (SFIO). However, in Barcelona, the syndicalists presented an altogether more combative and subversive political culture.[13] Such indications of regional and structural diversity

---

10    Trotsky 1975a, pp. 131–2.

11    Trotsky 1975a, p. 88.

12    Trotsky 1973a, p. 72.

13    Després tried to assist Trotsky when the police caught up with him. They held him temporarily in the Model Prison in Madrid. A press campaign for his release was mounted but it met with a counter-campaign from the conservative papers. The latter referred to Trotsky as a 'pseudo-anarchist', much to his displeasure.

feeding into political cultures were not lost on Trotsky, as he was to demonstrate when events in Spain led him to attempt a much closer analysis of its historical development more than a decade later. Indeed, Trotsky's early exposure to aspects of Spanish history, culture and politics were to serve as a useful introduction to some of the key issues that presented themselves in the course of the 1930s. Perhaps his first-hand experiences helped him place Spain within an international historical context rather than, as was common at the time, seeing it as an exotic anachronism closed off from the rest of Europe.[14] Yet, as we have already seen, a contextualising approach had long been an integral part of Trotsky's methodology.

Between 1917 and 1930 it seems Trotsky made few references to Spanish affairs. However, Joaquín Maurín records an interview with Trotsky in 1921 in which he suggests that a Spanish revolution was unlikely to precede other revolutionary explosions in Western Europe. Affirming support for both Moroccan independence and the Catalan struggle for self-determination, Trotsky thought that Spain's national question would be resolved in a similar manner to that of Russia: an Iberian federation of socialist soviet republics. When it came, he concluded, Spain's revolution would undoubtedly have a great impact upon revolutions in Latin America.[15]

### Spain's Revolutionary Prospects

Trotsky's renewed interest in Spain was occasioned by the growing domestic political crisis in the late 1920s that led to the downfall of the dictatorship of General Miguel Primo de Rivera in January 1930. This exposed King Alfonso XIII, who had backed the dictator, to a rising tide of criticism and the revival of a broad Republican coalition. Trotsky picked up on the predictions of political observers that a change of régime was imminent. In letters to the Spanish Left Opposition, busy forming itself in Belgium, and in a key article completed in January 1931, Trotsky analysed the developing crisis by applying his law of uneven and combined development to Spain's historical development.[16]

In 'The Revolution in Spain', Trotsky compared Spain's development to that of Russia. Spain at the beginning of the 1930s appeared to be one of the

---

14   Javier Maestro in Fundació Andreu Nin, n.d.
15   Cited in Maurín 1966, p. 264. The CNT was the anarcho-syndicalist trade union.
16   Letter to the editors of *Contra la corriente*, 25 May 1930, in Trotsky 1973a, pp. 57–63. See also 'The Revolution in Spain', 24 January 1931, in Trotsky 1973a, pp. 67–88. The letter was translated and published as a pamphlet by the Communist League of America in March 1931.

dinosaurs of Europe. Unlike Russia, whose backwardness stemmed from its slow economic development, primitive social forms and low level of culture, Spain had been a hegemonic and enormously wealthy European power. Yet its subsequent decline and failure to develop its economy apace with other great powers was rooted in its former imperial affluence, for little of the great wealth flowing into Spain from the mines of the Americas was used to develop agriculture, manufacture or commerce.[17]

Critics of Trotsky's interpretation of Spanish history and politics invariably claim that he simply applied the schema of Russian development to Spain. Ignacio Iglesias accuses him of 'theoretical intoxication' and argues that he ought to have viewed Spain 'without preconceived theories'.[18] This seems a curious statement – not merely because theories are by their very nature preconceived, but also considering that it comes from someone writing within the Marxist tradition and frequently citing Marx as an authority. One might point out that it was Marx himself who established the pattern of historical referencing which those influenced by him have followed ever since. Perhaps the real question is not whether it is acceptable to use historical parallels, but whether in so doing the generally acknowledged historical data is respected. Trotsky commits no glaring errors of historical fact and while it is certainly true that many of his political recommendations draw upon the Bolshevik experience, he is well aware that Spain's historical development was very distinct from that of Russia. As he puts it:

> Spain is unmistakably among the most backward countries of Europe. But its backwardness has a singular character, invested by the great historic past of the country. While Russia of the Tsars always lagged far behind its western neighbours and advanced slowly under their pressure, Spain knew periods of great boom, of superiority over the rest of Europe and of domination over South America.[19]

In stating that the Spanish monarchy, like that of Russia, had more in common with Asiatic despotism than European absolutism, Trotsky was merely echoing remarks Marx made in 1854. Trotsky's comparison was again with Russia:

---

17    24 January 1931, in Trotsky 1973a, pp. 67–9.
18    Iglesias 1976, p. 7.
19    Trotsky 1973a, p. 67.

The difference is only that Tsarism was formed on the *extremely slow* development of the nobility and of primitive urban centres, whereas the Spanish monarchy took shape under conditions of the *decline* of the country and the decay of the ruling classes. If European absolutism generally could rise only thanks to a struggle by the strengthened cities against the old privileged estates, then the Spanish monarchy, like Russian Tsarism, drew its strength from the impotence of the old estates and the cities. This accounts for its obvious resemblance to Asiatic despotism.[20]

In other words, while Russia was a genuine case of a country entering the modern age from a very low level of socio-economic development and thus beginning at a disadvantage, Spain saw its development curtailed after a privileged beginning. Hence its backwardness stemmed from an arrested development, a phenomenon Marx described as 'inglorious and protracted putrefaction'.[21]

How could the evident slowness and unevenness of capitalist development in Spain be explained? According to Trotsky, there were several contributing factors. First, there had been imperial failings. Spain proved unable to exploit its early advantages. From the sixteenth century, Dutch and English competition for American markets had gradually eroded Spanish power. The loss of its colonies in the nineteenth century was a further blow to Spain's economic development. Second, there was a structural weakness within the Spanish state. Unlike England or France, the historical ties between Spain's cities and between provinces had tended to weaken in the modern era. This prevented the formation of a truly unified nation-state and retarded the development of a bourgeois social stratum. Hence Spain's weak early bourgeois development deprived the state of the centripetal pressures usually exerted by capitalist development. A third barrier Trotsky identified to the emergence of modern bourgeois society was the political system of the Restoration monarchy that emerged in the late nineteenth century. As Trotsky put it, 'Madrid held the elections but the king held the power'. He argued that the ruling classes depended upon the monarchy because they were too divided to rule in their own name. It was, he contended, a political system which could be described as 'degenerated absolutism, limited by periodic military coups'.[22]

It is important to stress at this point that, however backward Spain may have been, Trotsky still insisted that it was a capitalist society. Indeed, he had no doubt that Spain had already passed well beyond the point at which it required

---

20    Trotsky 1973a, pp. 68–9. For Marx's comments, see Marx and Engels 1975, p. 26.
21    Marx and Engels 1975, p. 23.
22    Trotsky 1973a, pp. 67–9.

a political revolution to overthrow feudalism and set down the legal foundations for capitalist production. This was to be a key difference in the analyses
offered by various socialist and communist commentators. As in the Russian
case, the interpretation of historical development adopted would have critical
implications for political strategy. So how did Trotsky assess Spain's 'bourgeois
revolution'?

To begin with, he was adamant that 'Spain has left the stage of bourgeois
revolution far behind'.[23] Yet to affirm this did not mean to claim that the 'bourgeois-democratic tasks' of this revolution had been successfully completed.
The agrarian problem, the national question, issues of political democracy and
the question of church and state were all still unresolved. Although it was
clearly in the interests of the bourgeoisie to address these outstanding issues,
they had shown neither the desire nor ability to do so. Trotsky perceived their
dilemma in terms of the law of uneven and combined development:

> Now even less than in the nineteenth century can the Spanish bourgeoi-
> sie lay claim to that historic role which the British and French bourgeoi-
> sies once played. Appearing too late, dependent upon foreign capital, the
> big industrial bourgeoisie of Spain, which has dug itself like a leech into
> the body of the people, is incapable of coming forward as the leader of
> the 'nation' against the old estates, even for a brief period. The magnates
> of Spanish industry face the people hostilely, forming a most reactionary
> bloc of bankers, industrialists, large landowners, the monarchy and its
> generals and officials, all devouring each other in internal antagonisms.
> It is sufficient to state that the most important supporters of the dictator-
> ship of Primo de Rivera were the Catalan manufacturers.[24]

He noted that the nineteenth century had witnessed a succession of 'revolutions' during which the army tended to adopt the role of arbiter in political
affairs. Yet these liberal *pronunciamientos* did not constitute serious attempts
to address the bourgeois-democratic tasks. Trotsky continues, 'All these
Spanish revolutions were movements of a minority against another minority:

---

23   Letter to *Contra la corriente*, Trotsky 1973a, p. 60. 'With all its backwardness', Trotsky wrote,
     'Spain has passed far beyond France of the eighteenth century. Big industrial enterprises,
     10,000 miles of railway, 30,000 miles of telegraph, represent a more important factor for
     the revolution than historical reminiscences'. Trotsky 1973a, p. 76. For further historical
     details and a discussion of Spain's industrial development, see the 'Historical Overview' in
     the appendix to this volume.

24   Trotsky 1973a, p. 74.

the ruling and semi-ruling classes impatiently snatching the state pie out of each other's hands'. They were manifestations of the country's particular backwardness.

> If by the term 'permanent revolution' we are to understand a succession of social revolutions, transferring power into the hands of the more reso-lute class, which afterwards applies this power for the abolition of all classes, and subsequently the very possibility of new revolutions, we would then have to state that, in spite of the 'uninterruptedness' of the Spanish revolutions, there is nothing in them that resembles the *perma-nent revolution*. They are rather the chronic convulsions expressing the intractable disease of a nation thrown backward.[25]

Yet, as he was well aware, this backward development was combined with a degree of capitalist industrialisation. It was this combination which suggested the presence of contradictions not dissimilar to those he had identified in the Russian case. Spain's economy and social structure had, he argues, altered as a consequence of the mini-boom afforded by neutrality during the world war. The growth of industry and its diversification established 'a new relationship of forces and opened up new perspectives'.[26] But when post-war normalisation of international trade deprived Spain of its new-found markets, it imposed high tariffs to protect domestic industry from foreign competition. This caused inflation which, together with the poverty of the general populace, held back the emerging modern industrial sector.

Economic modernisation was also retarded by the fears of the bourgeoisie itself. In another parallel with Russia, Trotsky argued that the reliance of the bourgeoisie upon the old political oligarchy increasingly came to contradict the needs of developing capitalism. The native bourgeoisie owed a great deal of its economic success to the strength of foreign capital. It had proved either unwilling or unable to cast off the restrictions of a society and political system dominated by landed interests that lacked dynamism. Under these conditions the national bourgeoisie had come to fear the very class upon whose existence and enlargement its own prosperity rested. So rather than welcome a potential ally, the bourgeoisie came to fear the proletariat more than it hated the oligarchy.[27]

---

25    Trotsky 1973a, p. 72.

26    Trotsky 1973a, p. 73.

27    Trotsky 1973a, pp. 72–5.

It is not surprising that Trotsky vested huge significance in recent structural changes in the relative weight of industrial and agricultural workers in Spanish society. The working class now comprised a very significant proportion of the population and would undoubtedly play a decisive part in political life. Indeed, he noted that the workers had already entered the arena during Spain's nineteenth-century revolutions, but this had been in a subordinate role to the bourgeoisie. The events of the 'tragic week' in 1909 and subsequent strike movements indicated growing proletarian independence. But the workers' movement had really come of age during the 'red years', 1917 to 1920. Here, the increased pace of industrial growth occasioned by war demand established the workers' movement as a potentially revolutionary force. Primo's dictatorship was in essence a reaction to this perceived threat. Catalan industrialists' support for the dictatorship acknowledged both the power of the working class and the bourgeoisie's own preference for authoritarian solutions.[28]

Trotsky's conclusion to 'The Revolution in Spain' was that now, in 1931, Spain occupied the position in the process of world revolution that Russia had held in 1917. It constituted the 'weakest link' in the imperialist chain.[29] Spain was thus poised on the brink of a revolutionary crisis which could not be resolved by a separate bourgeois revolution because the only class with revolutionary potential was the working class. Should a crisis develop, there could be only two possible outcomes: either a proletarian revolution would ensue or the opportunity would be lost. In Trotsky's mind, an analysis of Spain's modern historical development ruled out a further bourgeois revolution, since this had already taken place in the nineteenth century.

### Trotsky's 1931 Perspective: An Appraisal

It is perhaps worth pausing to reflect upon Trotsky's characterisation of Spain in the light of what has been said so far concerning Trotsky's methodology and approach. In the first place, his purpose in offering an interpretation of Spanish history was polemical rather than academic. Trotsky never claimed more than a superficial knowledge of the country and was entirely reliant upon information conveyed to him by his correspondents and through the foreign press. Javier Maestro argues that this did not prevent Trotsky from bringing his powerful analysis to bear upon the problems of the Spanish Revolution. Maestro argues that he applied a historical method which, while recognising national peculiarities, nevertheless insisted upon viewing individual countries as parts of a world economy. The dynamics of this relationship were such that

---

28    Trotsky 1973a, p. 75.
29    Trotsky 1973a, p. 67.

no individual country constituted a 'special case' somehow immune from the
effects of imperialism and class struggles in other countries.[30]

There seems little doubt that, viewed from within a Marxist paradigm at
least, Trotsky was justified in insisting upon the essentially capitalist nature of
Spanish society and on not being distracted by the precapitalist residues that
led many observers to label the country 'semi-feudal'. However, it must be said
that Trotsky himself applied the phrase 'semi-feudal exploitation' when
describing agrarian conditions. Although this terminology might appear contradictory, for him it denoted the *form* in which capitalism operated in backward conditions. That is to say, capitalist landowners employed feudal or
semi-feudal methods in exploiting the peasantry. Therefore, he argued, 'to aim
the weapon of the revolution against the remnants of the Spanish Middle Ages
means to aim it against the very roots of bourgeois rule'.[31] His analysis of the
peculiar effects of uneven and combined development upon class relations
convinced him that the bourgeoisie was not a revolutionary class in waiting.
Nor did the bourgeoisie rely upon the working class to carry out the bourgeois-
democratic revolution, as the Socialists believed. In the light of modern historical research, we may wish to question Trotsky's belief that a significant part
of the bourgeoisie had become integrated into the landowning oligarchy. Yet,
in recognising that the interests of both groups had converged and that they
felt equally threatened by the organised working class, he certainly anticipated
some of the conclusions of future historians.[32]

As far as the comparison with Russia's capitalist development is concerned,
Iglesias is no doubt correct to observe that conditions in Spain in 1930 were
very different from those in Russia in 1917.[33] But, in stressing the uniqueness of
Spanish development, he appears to miss the point that Trotsky based his analysis on a conception of underlying historical processes which were not particular to a single country. As Trotsky explained to Spanish Left Opposition
comrades:

---

30    Fundació Andreu Nin, n.d. Pelai Pagès confirms Maestro's general point when he com-
      ments on the fact that Trotsky was never able to study Spanish society in depth and relied
      upon a 'standardised' Marxist class analysis. 'On the other hand', Pagès adds, 'his enor-
      mous theoretical baggage enabled him to characterise the political positions of social
      classes whose specific peculiarities and behaviour he had no direct knowledge of' (Pagès
      1977a, p. 113).
31    Trotsky 1973a, p. 77.
32    See the appendix to this volume for further discussion of modern historical
      perspectives.
33    Iglesias 1977, pp. 11–12.

Not to know these [national] peculiarities would of course be the great-est idiocy. But underneath them we must know how to discover the moti-vating forces of international developments and grasp the dependence of national peculiarities upon the world combination of forces. The tremen-dous advantage of Marxism and consequently of the Left Opposition consists precisely in this international manner of solving national prob-lems and national peculiarities.[34]

Hence, conjunctural factors were vital in determining the outcome of a politi-cal crisis, but it was necessary to examine the contradictions and tensions which gave rise to it in the first place. By identifying certain common threads in the development of both countries, Trotsky concluded that Spain in 1930 and 1931 faced a situation analogous to Russia's in 1917. However, from the per-spective of uneven and combined development, it was immediately apparent that Spanish society combined the archaic with the modern in a rather differ-ent way to that of Tsarist Russia. In Spain, industrial development had taken place over a much longer time scale, was very partial and restricted to certain regions, and lacked the stimulus of state inducements so crucial in the Russian case. Spanish industrial enterprises clearly did not approach the scale of those of Russia. In contrast to Russia's heavy industrial base, Spanish industry ranged from light industry (textiles) to services and mineral extraction. The low demand in the domestic consumer market meant that there was little incen-tive to mass-produce manufactured goods. Reliance upon foreign capital had resulted in an export sector heavily based upon minerals, wine, fruit and tex-tiles, which afforded the economy its 'semi-colonial' appearance. Although relations of production in agriculture on the large estates were capitalist, Spanish rural society shared the crippling poverty and lack of dynamism of its Russian counterpart. The dominant agrarian sector was indeed bound up in a traditional matrix which had little to do with modern capitalist farming and which retarded the country's overall economic modernisation.[35]

### The Coming of the Second Republic
We now turn to Trotsky's analysis of the political situation in 1930 and early 1931. Following the fall of the Primo de Rivera dictatorship in January 1930

---

34  'Message to the Conference of the Spanish Left Opposition', 7 March 1932, in Trotsky 1973a, p. 173.

35  Elements of this perspective are discussed in relation to modern historical approaches to Spain's development in the appendix to this volume.

without the need for a revolution, Trotsky offered the opinion that this turn of events was far from accidental.

> On the one hand, the dictatorial régime, in the eyes of the bourgeois classes, was no longer justified by the urgent need to smash the revolutionary masses; at the same time, this régime came into conflict with the economic, financial, political and cultural needs of the bourgeoisie. But up to the last moment, the bourgeoisie avoided a showdown struggle with all its might. It allowed the dictatorship to rot and fall like a wormy fruit.[36]

Trotsky saw the fact that the king was still able to cling onto power as an indication of the bourgeoisie's continued support for the monarchy. If many bourgeois now declared themselves Republicans, then they would do so with the intention of deceiving the Republican petty-bourgeoisie and thus retaining its confidence. As subsequent events demonstrated, this was a serious underestimation of the importance of Republican sentiments among significant sections of Spain's middle classes. It also points to a major weakness in Trotsky's analysis, namely the tendency to put forward a functionalist explanation that runs the risk of missing significant differences between political and economic interest groups.

It is thus tempting to accept Iglesias's criticism that subsequent events failed to bear out Trotsky's prediction that the development of the Revolution would drive not only the traditional ruling classes but also the Republican bourgeoisie over to the side of the monarchy.[37] However, this functionalist prognosis was in fact only one of several possible outcomes to the crisis which are outlined in 'The Revolution in Spain'. When quoting Trotsky, Iglesias omits the following sentence: 'A combination of circumstances is possible, to be sure, in which the possessing classes are compelled to sacrifice the monarchy in order to save themselves (for example: Germany!)'.[38]

---

36  Letter to *Contra la corriente*, in Trotsky 1973a, p. 57.

37  Iglesias 1976, p. 13. He refers to the pamphlet *The Revolution in Spain*. Full text in Trotsky 1973a, p. 76.

38  Trotsky 1973a, p. 76. Trotsky had noted the Republican aspirations of the left wing of the bourgeoisie, especially the intellectuals. He also pointed out that this Republicanism was conservative and took the French Republic as its model. Trotsky 1973a, p. 72.

One could argue that this is exactly what was to happen, although it is clear that Trotsky thought the acceptance of the Republic and parliamentary democracy by the bourgeoisie would only be transitory. Iglesias may be correct in suggesting that Trotsky underestimated the popular attractions of a republic and that his analysis of the many political actors in the centre ground of Spanish political life lacked nuance, but this was perhaps inevitable given Trotsky's focus upon what he saw as the main business: the interests and perspectives of the bourgeoisie *as a class*. He simply refused to believe that their class interests led them to prefer a democratic government to an authoritarian one. His thinking on this matter is revealed in a critical passage from May 1930 which is worth quoting at length:

> The same bourgeois parties that because of their conservatism had refused to conduct a serious struggle, no matter how small, against the military dictatorship [of Primo], now have put all the blame for that dictatorship on the monarchy and declared themselves republicans. As though the dictatorship had been hanging by a thread from the balcony of the royal palace the whole time, and as though it had not been kept up at all by the support, sometimes passive, sometimes active, of the most substantial layers of the bourgeoisie who, with all their strength, paralysed the activity of the petty bourgeoisie and trampled underfoot the workers of the city and countryside.
>
> And what is the result? While not only the workers, the peasants, the urban petty bourgeoisie, and the young intellectuals, but also almost all of the big bourgeoisie either are or call themselves republicans, the monarchy continues to exist and to function. If Primo did only hang by a thread from the monarchy, then by what thread did the monarchy hang in such a 'republican' country? At first glance it appears to be an insoluble riddle. But the answer is not so complicated. The same bourgeoisie that was 'tolerating' Primo de Rivera was actually supporting him, as today it supports the monarchy by the only means available, that is, by calling itself republican and thus adapting itself to the psychology of the petit-bourgeoisie, the better to deceive and paralyse it.[39]

Here Trotsky's understanding of the Marxist concept of bourgeois revolution seems to anticipate the modern contributions of Blackbourn and Eley to the

---

39    Letter to *Contra la corriente*, in Trotsky 1973a, pp. 57–8.

study of German historical development.[40] Trotsky saw no necessary causal connection between the development of capitalism and the emergence of liberal bourgeois democracy. Although he recognised that resolving the outstanding democratic tasks would create more stable conditions in which capitalism could mature, the permanent internal contradictions of capitalist society ensured that representative democracy and its political freedoms would always be conditional. Hence, for Trotsky, a political crisis might easily result in dictatorship even in the most supposedly 'democratic' of countries. It seemed that, in backward capitalist states, this tendency toward dictatorship was still more pronounced because the bourgeoisie, aware of its own relative weakness, had good reason to fear the freedom of movement a liberal political system afforded to workers' organisations.

It could be argued that Trotsky's prediction that the bourgeoisie would ultimately prove to be a counterrevolutionary force was borne out by events in Spain. Once it had become sufficiently well organised to win power constitutionally, between 1933 and 1935, the big bourgeoisie reversed the modest achievements of the early Republican administration. Abandoning legalist methods in July 1936, the bourgeoisie placed itself in the Nationalist camp alongside the old oligarchy, monarchists and fascists.[41] Whether or not one accepts this interpretation of the 'historical role' of the bourgeoisie, such a conception was undoubtedly central to Trotsky's worldview and helps explain the depth of his opposition to the Comintern's popular-front tactic. However, this perspective is open to the criticism that it ignores real political divisions within the bourgeoisie.

Trotsky's scepticism of the democratic and republican credentials of the Spanish bourgeoisie did not, however, blur his vision when analysing the twists and turns of the political situation in 1930 and 1931. Contrary to the impression Iglesias gives, Trotsky quite clearly anticipates a parliamentary phase in the political crisis.

---

40    Blackbourn and Eley 1984. In this book the authors attack the *Sonderweg* view of German history that sees it as different from the development of other Western European countries due to German society's supposed 'peculiarities'. Like Trotsky, they reject the notion of a 'missing bourgeois revolution' and the notion that there is a predetermined historical path through which countries must pass to achieve 'modernisation'. As Eley concludes in his part of their joint book, 'the bourgeoisie may come to social predominance by other than liberal routes'. (Blackbourn and Eley 1984, p. 155).

41    This sequence of events is outlined and discussed in the appendix.

Can the Spanish revolution be expected to skip the parliamentary stage? Theoretically, this is not excluded. It is conceivable that the revolutionary movement will, in a comparatively short time, attain such strength that it will leave the ruling classes neither the time not the place for parliamentarism. Nevertheless, such a perspective is rather improbable. The Spanish proletariat, in spite of its combativeness, still recognises no revolutionary party as its own, and has no experience with soviet organisation. And besides this, there is no unity among the sparse communist ranks. There is no clear programme of action that everyone accepts. Nevertheless, the question of the Cortes is already on the order of the day. Under these conditions, it must be assumed that the revolution will have to pass through a parliamentary stage.[42]

This was written in January 1931, while the king was still in place. The coming of the Republic three months later confirmed that the political consciousness of the majority of advanced workers was dominated by the promise of democratic freedoms and reforms. Trotsky felt that only bitter experience could demonstrate the illusory nature of 'bourgeois democracy'. Hence, in the short term, a key task of the communists was to build a united front to link workers and peasants. The basis of this had to be a political programme organised around the most radical democratic demands.

### The Role of the Communists

It was clear to Trotsky that there was total confusion in the minds of many Spanish communists over the nature of the revolution taking place. The tiny Partido Comunista de España (the official Communist Part of Spain, PCE) appeared to accept uncritically the Comintern view that there would be an intermediate 'workers' and peasants' revolution' between the Republican takeover and the proletarian revolution.[43] The party was instructed to play the 'leading role' in creating soviets, which were supposed to be the 'motive force' in both completing the democratic revolution and ensuring that it 'grew over'

42    'The Revolution in Spain', in Trotsky 1973a, pp. 78–9.
43    *Pravda*, cited by Trotsky in 'The Spanish Revolution and the Dangers Threatening It', 28 May 1931, in Trotsky 1973a, p. 120.

into a socialist one.[44] Yet the Spanish party was under strict instructions not to enter into alliances or pacts with other political forces.[45]

In 'The Spanish Revolution and the Dangers Threatening It', Trotsky warned that Comintern policy on Spain was as mistaken as it had been for China. He questioned how the 'intermediate revolution' proposed by Moscow differed from a proletarian revolution. What was its class base and how would the two distinct revolutions differ in method and programme? In reality, he argued, the Comintern was advocating an evolutionary conception of the transition from capitalism to socialism. It was a stagist position whereby 'the decisive moment in this process in which one class wrests the power from another is unnoticeably dissolved'.[46] Once again, Trotsky continued, Stalin was misrepresenting Lenin's notion of the 'growing over' of the bourgeois-democratic revolution into a socialist one. In China, Stalin had announced that the Kuomintang dictatorship would initially 'grow over' into a 'workers' and peasants' dictatorship' and then again into a proletarian dictatorship. He had predicted that the forces of the Right would split away and that those of the Left would increase in strength. This was the logic behind Stalin's 'bloc of four classes' slogan. But Trotsky pointed out that this ran contrary to Marx's class analysis, according to which the character of régimes and revolutions is ultimately determined by the class holding power. Power can therefore only change hands from one class to another through a revolutionary overthrow, not by any process of 'growing over'.[47]

Once again, Trotsky returned to Lenin's 1917 conception of revolution and sought to explain how it corresponded to the theory of permanent revolution.

---

44    Open letter to the PCE from the Executive of the Comintern, 21 May 1931, cited in Claudín 1972, p. 4.

45    See the discussion of the Comintern's 'ultra-Left' policy at this time and Trotsky's critique of it in this Chapter and in Chapters Three and Four.

46    'The Spanish Revolution and the Dangers Threatening It', Trotsky 1973a, p. 121. In his correspondence with the newly created Italian Left Opposition, Trotsky had underlined the central importance of democratic slogans in the fight against fascism. Spanish events suggested that the Italian revolution would also experience a democratic phase of a fairly lengthy duration. Hence it was crucial to reject the myth of the 'popular revolution' which the Comintern had promoted in China and Spain. This position suggested a revolution of a neutral, non-class nature which was alien to Marxism. Trotsky's criticism was directed against the Bordigists of the Prometeo group, who rejected the united front tactic and the use of democratic slogans on principle. See Trotsky's Preface to the Italian version of 'The Spanish Revolution and the Dangers Threatening It', 9 June 1931, in Trotsky 1973c, p. 262, and 10 June 1931 in Trotsky 1979b, pp. 84–5.

47    Trotsky 1973a, pp. 120–2.

The workers took power, Lenin had argued, in specific national conditions and in order to solve specific 'tasks' which, in backward countries, were democratic in nature. These tasks included national liberation or self-determination, the agrarian revolution, and so on. Indeed, Trotsky reminded readers, Lenin went so far as to state that in October 1917 the proletariat had seized power as the agent of the bourgeois-democratic revolution. Only once it began to tackle the democratic tasks did the logic of its class rule oblige it to move on to tasks of an explicitly socialist character. Trotsky stressed that it was to this process, the inevitable movement by the proletariat toward socialist tasks *after it had taken political power*, that Lenin applied the phrase 'growing over'. This is why Lenin maintained that the transition from capitalism to socialism could only take place under the régime of a proletarian dictatorship. It also explained why he did not consider the accomplishment of the socialist revolution to be synonymous with the establishment of the dictatorship of the proletariat.[48]

According to Trotsky's understanding of Lenin on revolution, the period of bourgeois parliamentary rule which had opened in April 1931 with the proclamation of the Second Republic could not represent the first of two or three separate revolutions, as the Socialists and Comintern 'experts' believed. Rather, it amounted to the first phase in a continuous revolutionary process which, Trotsky predicted, would culminate in the struggle for political power by the proletariat, backed up by the peasants. Although no timescale could be specified for a revolution, past experience suggested that certain factors would help determine the tempo of events. The French Revolution had taken three years to arrive at the Jacobin dictatorship; the Bolshevik dictatorship had been realised in eight months. The key difference between the two revolutions was that the Jacobins did not exist as a party on the eve of revolution, whereas the Bolsheviks did. In addition, the Russian Revolution had the great benefit of a 1905 'dress rehearsal' containing all the elements of the February and October Revolutions. This factor hastened the speed of developments. But the key factor present in 1917 was the war, a solution to which could not be delayed. Without the war, Trotsky emphasised, the Revolution would probably have lasted far longer than it did.[49]

It was clear to him that the situation in Spain was very different. The lack of recent revolutionary experience, the weakness of the Communist Party and the absence of a foreign war meant that the Revolution was likely to take far longer to reach full maturity. In this respect, as well as on the question of the

---

48  Trotsky 1973a, p. 123.

49  Trotsky 1973a, pp. 129–30. See also Trotsky's letter to Nin of 20 April 1931 in Trotsky 1973a, pp. 106–7.

parliamentary phase, Trotsky thought the classic French revolutionary example more instructive than the Russian. An extended process would allow time for the revolutionary party to prepare to seize power. However, there were negative factors to be considered, such as the anarcho-syndicalists' predisposition toward spontaneous action and the dangers of adventurism on the part of the official Communists. In view of this, Trotsky thought it quite possible that the Revolution would miscarry.[50]

He noted that unlike in the Russian case, where the Constituent Assembly had been convened *after* the decisive revolutionary battle and was quickly liquidated without much trouble, in Spain the Cortes had arrived *before* the real battles had begun. The Communists could at best hope to win a handful of parliamentary seats. But this did not justify a putschist attempt to overthrow the Cortes. Such an act would fail to solve the question of power, since there could be no substitute for a genuine revolutionary insurrection by the organised proletariat. The absence of a revolutionary party and the confused political orientation of the key workers' organisations suggested that the parliamentary period would be lengthy. Summing up the general situation at the end of 1931, Trotsky commented:

> Needless to say, the Spanish revolution has not yet ended. It has not solved its most elementary tasks (the agrarian, church and national questions) and is still far from having exhausted the revolutionary resources of the popular masses. More than it has already given, the bourgeois revolution will not be able to give. With regard to the proletarian revolution, the present internal situation in Spain may be characterised as pre-revolutionary, but scarcely more than that. It is quite probable that the offensive development of the Spanish revolution will take on a more or less protracted character. In this manner, the historical process opens up, as it were, a new credit account for Spanish communism.[51]

But what did he think Spanish revolutionary Marxists should actually do in concrete political terms?

### Trotsky's Political Advice

At this time Trotsky was still addressing his political advice to all communists in Spain, those who adopted the official Moscow 'line' as well as those who

---

50    Trotsky 1973a, p. 131.
51    'Germany, the Key to the International Situation', 26 November 1931, in Trotsky 1971, p. 115, and Trotsky 1973a, p. 170.

dissented from it. This would only change in 1933 after Hitler came to power in Germany. The political programme Trotsky outlined in response to events in Spain was a good deal more sophisticated than we might gather from Iglesias's summaries.[52] Far from simply advocating the creation of soviet-style organisations, Trotsky was aware that '[f]or a certain time all the questions of the Spanish Revolution will in one way or another be refracted through the prism of parliamentarism'.[53] He advised the communists to make use of the Cortes as a link with the masses, competing in elections where possible. Out of this engagement, political actions would emerge that would go beyond the limits of bourgeois legality. The immediate task of the communists was therefore not to struggle for power in the mode of October 1917, as the Comintern argued, but to win the masses over from Republican illusions and from their faith in the Socialists.[54] Only experiencing the limitations of the new political democracy would dispel in workers' minds the illusions surrounding it. In order to channel this popular experience toward progressive ends, the communists had to participate in everyday political life. But they should not adopt either the 'parliamentary cretinism' of the Socialists or the 'anti-parliamentary cretinism' of the anarcho-syndicalists.[55] Rather, a combination of democratic demands and transitional socialist ones was the logical strategy for taking advantage of the uneven and combined nature of Spanish society:

> Such a combined programme, reflecting the contradictory construction of historic society, flows inevitably from the diversity of the problems inherited from the past. To reduce all the contradictions and all the tasks to one lowest common denominator – *the dictatorship of the proletariat* – is a necessary, but altogether insufficient, operation.[56]

In concrete terms, Trotsky argued, this project required a campaign for basic democratic demands such as unemployment relief, the seven-hour day, agrarian reform and regional autonomy. For instance, the basic democratic question of universal suffrage from the age of 18 occupied a transitional position between the parliamentary phase and the struggle for power. A young worker of 18 was considered old enough to be exploited by capitalism yet was deprived

---

52   Iglesias 1976, pp. 14–16, and Iglesias 1977, pp. 36–9.
53   Trotsky 1973a, p. 118.
54   Trotsky 1973a, p. 128.
55   Trotsky 1973a, p. 115.
56   Trotsky 1973a, p. 80.

of the right to vote.[57] This injustice formed part of the workers' radicalisation toward a revolutionary consciousness. Lowering the voting age would also bring into the political arena hundreds of thousands of young workers and peasants. Trotsky argued that such demands could help turn the youth against the Socialists, whose base was among older workers, and would help drive a wedge between the working masses and the Partido Socialista Obrero Español (Spanish Socialist Workers' Party, PSOE).[58] In short, the task was to advance democratic demands in conjunction with class demands.[59]

So how precisely did Trotsky formulate these demands in the Spanish case? He viewed the right to national self-determination for the Catalan and Basque peoples, even up to the point of separation from Spain, as a fundamental democratic demand. Yet acknowledging this did not oblige the communists to advocate separatism. Separation from the rest of Spain would, Trotsky argued, greatly weaken the workers' movement as a whole, especially since the Catalan workers were in many respects its vanguard.[60] Retaining the economic unity of the country was desirable, but with '*extensive autonomy of national districts*'.[61] Clearly the prospects for separation were only likely to become real in the event of a successful national revolution. Yet Trotsky warned that separatism had also been incorporated into the reactionary project of the Catalan bourgeoisie. Referring to the undemocratic nature of the May 1931 Catalan elections, he suggested that the petty-bourgeois nationalists – always subordinate to big capital, in his view – were effectively deciding the destiny of Cataluña. For Trotsky, then, the slogan of national self-determination meant nothing unless accompanied by demands for the widest possible political democracy.

As we have seen, Trotsky's appreciation of the contradictions of uneven and combined development permitted him to cut through the surface appearance of Spain's agrarian society and avoid the conclusion that the rural economy had to experience a capitalist transition first before a socialist agrarian revolution would become possible. Precapitalist practices and culture had survived in many regions in more or less modified forms, and the absence of a strong and dynamic class of capitalist farmers was conspicuous. But he saw no dual economy in Spain. However strong the residue of feudalism may have been, it

---

57    Voting rights were granted from the age of twenty-three. Trotsky might have added that in 1931 women had yet to be enfranchised, a demand that the dissident communists were to take up.
58    Trotsky 1973a, p. 117.
59    Letter to *Contra la corriente*, in Trotsky 1973a, p. 60.
60    Ibid.
61    Trotsky 1973a, p. 78. Emphasis in original.

had been articulated to a capitalist economy. As such, rural backwardness held back dynamic economic growth, yet the bourgeoisie could not overcome it. Such was the fundamental contradiction of uneven and combined development in Spain. But in spite of their great weight in society, Trotsky did not believe the peasants and rural workers could play an independent or leading revolutionary role, though they were clearly of crucial importance to the success of the Revolution. It would be a mistake, Trotsky warned, to expect the peasants to embrace the slogan 'dictatorship of the proletariat', since it offered them nothing. The issue of radical land redistribution had therefore to be advanced in conjunction with slogans of political democracy.[62] The agrarian issue, he argued, would be fought out in the Cortes, with the peasants paying close attention. They would see that a parliament was unable to solve the land question. Ultimately, this question could only be resolved by the militant actions of the peasants themselves, under the leadership and programme of the revolutionary party and in conjunction with the urban proletarian struggle. To prepare for this, it was important that the communists gain access to the Cortes and put forward their own agrarian programme.[63] Hence electoral politics mattered in the current political climate.

On the question of the Church, Trotsky recognised that the clergy constituted a traditional conservative force. They were financially dependent upon the state and provided the 'firmest axis of reaction'. Certainly the Church's domination over social life presented the Revolution with the democratic task of separating church and state, and transferring the wealth of the Church into public hands. If this wealth could demonstrably be shown to go into assisting agrarian schemes, this demand might win peasant support.[64]

Trotsky noted that the army had been essential to the old régime as a key centralising force in a country notorious for its 'particularism and separatism', and served as both the monarchy's power base and a vehicle for the discontent of the ruling classes. Like the clergy, the officer corps also looked to the state for its livelihood. As the key weapon of the ruling classes, it had become accustomed to playing a political role during the frequent political crises of the old régime. When unable to find stable support among the dominant classes, the monarchy had relied upon the military to keep it in power. Although interclique rivalries often displaced the monarchy, as in the 1873–4 Republic, this was only temporary, owing to the lack of any class prepared to lead a

---

62    Trotsky 1973a, p. 60.

63    Trotsky 1973a, p. 118.

64    Trotsky 1973a, p. 69 and p. 77.

thoroughgoing democratic revolution.[65] Yet, as Trotsky noted, many officers had displayed liberal tendencies in the 'Jaca coup' attempt of December 1930. Here, Republicans and Socialists had arranged a bid for power in which a military rising would be supported by a general strike. Premature action by two army officers at Jaca was followed by the arrest of most of the provisional government and the failure of the Madrid strike. For Trotsky, this rebellion indicated a transition from one phase of struggle to another. It showed unity in action between left Republicans and workers' organisations. However, the workers had not been armed and the workers' organisations had been wrong to think that a military plot could complement a revolutionary general strike. The army had stayed sufficiently loyal to put down the strike; the workers lacked independent aims and leadership, tied as they were to the left Republican project of a bourgeois republic. This did not mean Trotsky rejected the revolutionary role of the army rank and file. But it only made sense when they were organised in soldiers' councils as part of the proletarian movement: that is to say, when they stood in opposition to the classes whose interests the army had traditionally served.[66] It was clear, as it had always been to Trotsky, that ultimately the revolutionary struggle was bound to be faced at some stage with the question of arming the workers.

### The Menace of Fascism

Mention of the military leads us to a key element in Trotsky's political thought of the time – his theorisation of the nature, function and danger of fascism. If we are to fully understand Trotsky's response to developments in Spain and his perception of their significance in relation to events in other countries, it is vital to appreciate the priority he gave to the threat of fascism. In his mission to arm the European workers' movement against a force which he believed would liquidate all of its historical achievements, Trotsky produced some of his most insightful and prophetic political analysis. Few if any other Marxist commentators signalled the dangers posed by the rise of German fascism as early or as comprehensively. In formulating and promoting a political strategy to defeat Nazism before it could take power, he had to counter the Comintern's hostility toward any dissent from its 'general line'. Moscow ideologues labelled even Social Democrats as 'social fascists', making collaboration in the workers' movement impossible. As Trotsky argued, this was a disastrous approach. His alternative was a policy envisaging a 'united front' to be formed against fascism

---

65    Trotsky 1973a, pp. 70–1.
66    Trotsky 1973a, pp. 87–8.

by all genuine workers' organisations. Only such a common front could mobilise sufficient forces to confront the fascist menace successfully.[67]

Trotsky viewed fascism in a functionalist way, as the bourgeoisie's last-ditch 'solution' to the severe structural crisis of capitalism. Far deeper than normal periodic slumps, the world crisis of the late 1920s and early 1930s was a crisis of the very conditions of production and realisation of surplus value. The prevailing character of international competition – the levels of real wages, labour productivity and access to raw materials and markets – constituted an obstacle to capital accumulation posing capitalism with what was potentially an existential crisis. In the case of Germany, which experienced a profound economic depression between 1929 and 1933, a powerful workers' movement enjoying the relative freedoms of the Weimar Republic had been able to win social and economic gains and defend its class interests. The National Socialists rose to power by means of a war against the labour movement in which they demonstrated their utility to the bourgeoisie and gained its material support. As a movement, fascism appeared radical, winning mass support from the petty-bourgeoisie. But once the labour movement had been severely defeated, fascism established itself as a régime and purged its mass base of radical elements. In power, fascism reverted to what Trotsky termed 'Bonapartism of fascist origin'. Once established as a central executive authority, a state, fascism turned its attentions to colonial and semi-colonial conquest by means of military adventure.[68]

If the ongoing world economic crisis posed an existential threat to capitalism, for Trotsky, fascism posed the same order of menace to the workers' movement and, indeed, all democratic and liberal achievements of modern societies. Hence he portrayed the conflict as one of barbarism versus human civilisation.[69] Yet, for the bourgeoisie, this was a risky business, made necessary by the economic crisis underpinning the crisis of parliamentary democracy. The capitalists underwrote the fascist side in what amounted initially to a war waged to crush workers' organisations and thereafter to a régime in which the paymasters would have no direct control. Should the workers repulse the aggressive onslaught, they would not be content merely to reconstruct a bourgeois-democratic political system. Indeed, Trotsky maintained, only if

---

67    Trotsky's key writings on fascism are collected in Trotsky 1971.

68    For a useful overview of Trotsky's theorisation of fascism, see Ernest Mandel's introduction to Trotsky's writings on Germany: Mandel 1971, pp. 9–46; Mandel 1995, pp. 106–26; Beetham 1983, pp. 33–8. On fascism and Bonapartism, see Kitchen 1976, pp. 71–82.

69    See, for instance, Trotsky's essay of 10 June 1933, 'What Is National Socialism?', in Trotsky 1971, pp. 399–407.

they went on to establish a proletarian dictatorship could fascism be decisively eliminated. It followed that, however preferable bourgeois democracy might be when compared with fascism, it simply could not be defended by parliamentary means.

It is important to mention here that Trotsky differentiated between fascism and other forms of authoritarian rule in a way the Comintern's 'theoreticians' did not. As he observed, with reference to the Spanish dictatorship of Primo:

> What is Fascism? The name originated in Italy. Were all counterrevolutionary dictatorships Fascist? We refer to the antecedents of Italian Fascism. The last Spanish dictatorship of Primo de Rivera (1923–30) is called Fascist by the Comintern. Is this correct? We believe it is not. In Italy the Fascist movement was a spontaneous movement of the broad masses, with new leaders emanating from its base. In its origins it is a plebeian movement directed and financed by big capitalism. It arose from the petit-bourgeoisie, from the lowest proletarian layers and, up to a point, from the proletarian masses. Mussolini, an ex-socialist, is the man who formed it and he himself comes from this movement. Primo de Rivera was an aristocrat. He held high military office, occupied an important administrative position, and was governor of Cataluña. He built his movement with the help of state and military forces. The Spanish and Italian dictatorships are two completely different dictatorial forms. Mussolini had difficulty reconciling many old military institutions with the Fascist militia. The problem did not exist for Primo de Rivera.[70]

Manuel Pastor has argued that Trotsky's brief references to Primo, if taken together with his conception of Bonapartism, form the basis for a characterisation of the dictatorship as 'preventative Bonapartism'. Pastor notes that such régimes tend to surface in capitalist countries where the survival of feudal or semi-feudal residues prevents the state structure from adopting a fully 'bourgeois' character. Typically occurring in periods of unstable class equilibrium and following fairly deep economic crises, such régimes offer a temporary solution to a crisis which neither the bourgeoisie nor the working class is yet strong enough to resolve. 'Preventative' Bonapartism differs from fascism in the crucial sense that its mission is *not* to liquidate the workers' movement. Indeed, the PSOE-UGT (Unión General de Trabajadores, or General Workers' Union) had collaborated with Primo. Nor does Bonapartism possess a clear ideology or

---

70    Letter to Max Shachtman, 30 November 1931, in Trotsky 1979b, pp. 99–100.

base itself upon a party with mass petty-bourgeois support. Instead, it rules largely through military and bureaucratic methods.[71]

While we may take issue with Pastor's argument or some of its details, it is sufficient for present purposes to note that Trotsky's references to Spain have inspired an interpretation of the Primo period which departs significantly from others.[72] The fact that Trotsky did not consider the Primo régime to have been fascist does not mean that he thought the danger of fascism in Spain to be slight. In a letter to the Politburo of the CPSU, Trotsky warned that unless the communist forces in Spain united under a common programme and organisation, the Revolution would inevitably fail. The consequences of this would, he wrote, 'lead almost automatically to the establishment of *genuine* fascism in Spain in the style of Mussolini'.[73] This would have dire implications for the USSR and Europe. Many might argue that Trotsky's prediction was to be fulfilled eight years later. In the first place, the dictatorship of General Franco could be labelled 'fascist' on the grounds that it systematically annihilated both the personnel and organisations of the Left. Second, the victory of extreme reaction in Spain gave valuable military experience to Italy and Germany and gained them a potential ally in a strategically vital location.

## 2.2      The Problems of Revolutionary Agency

Clearly, the Spanish situation was not yet at the core of Trotsky's political concerns in the period covered so far, 1930 and 1931. His main attention was drawn, as ever, to what he saw as Stalin's distortion of the Soviet workers' state and the increasingly worrying prospect of fascism in Germany. In assessing the significance of Spanish events we must therefore always bear in mind the wider picture. However, he did register his awareness of the danger of a fascist movement emerging and coming to power in a country whose pattern of capitalist development was uneven and combined in the way Spain's was, and this added urgency to his advice to Spanish communists. Moreover, his prediction that

---

71    Pastor 1978, pp. 137–43.

72    See also Pastor 1975.

73    Letter to the Politburo of the Communist Party of the Soviet Union, 24 April 1931. In Trotsky 1973a, p. 108. See also Trotsky's letter to Nin, 21 November 1930, in which he suggests Spain might pass through the same cycle as Italy (1918–22) with, initial strikes and factory occupations but that, lacking revolutionary leadership, these would be followed by the decline of worker militancy, the rise of a fascist movement and a counterrevolutionary dictatorship. Trotsky 1973a, pp. 63–4.

the outstanding 'democratic tasks' would not be adequately addressed by a bourgeois parliament appeared to be borne out by the experience of the first two and a half years of the Second Republic. The electoral victory of a right-wing coalition in 1933 which proceeded to reverse the modest reforms of the early Republican period only confirmed his scepticism. Spain's Revolution had become 'stuck' in the parliamentary phase, in which there was a stand-off between the workers' movement and the forces of the radical Right. This stale-mate situation allowed time for the extreme Right to build its forces, inspired and abetted by Italy and Germany. Such a situation meant that the Spanish Revolution took on increasing significance in the struggle against fascism in Europe. For Trotsky, it was no longer just a question of a rare 'historic opportu-nity' to continue the world revolution. The future of the European workers' movement and the continued existence of the Soviet Union had now come to hinge upon events in Spain. It is with this in mind that we turn to Trotsky's impression of and involvement with the Spanish labour movement.

Although he suggested different tactics for achieving this end as circum-stances changed, the cornerstone of Trotsky's revolutionary strategy remained the construction of a Bolshevik-type revolutionary party able to lead a prole-tarian insurrection, backed up by the peasantry. From the outset, he argued for creating just such a party in Spain, initially advising the Spanish Left Opposition to work as a faction of the official PCE in the hope that it could be won over to a revolutionary perspective. However, with Hitler's rise to power, Trotsky reluc-tantly, although not immediately, abandoned all efforts to rescue the Comintern and its national parties. He turned instead to the left wing of the social-democratic parties as a source for recruitment to the revolutionary party. This was coupled with his final political project: the construction of the Fourth International.

A fundamental problem facing Trotsky's initial strategy was that Spain sim-ply did not possess a communist movement of any great size or influence. The workers' movement was dominated by the twin pillars of social democracy and anarcho-syndicalism. Unlike in Russia, where the mass proletarian move-ment developed in the midst of revolution, the Spanish workers and peasants had long been organised. This meant that there was little space for a 'third force', since it would face the monumental task of drawing the more advanced workers away from these well-established organisations. However, Trotsky did not consider this to be an insoluble problem. One of the recurrent themes of his political advice to the Spanish communists was that, given correct and audacious leadership, a coherent programme and favourable conditions, a small nucleus of revolutionary Marxists could quickly attract the advanced workers and build a mass party. This question of revolutionary leadership was to dominate Trotsky's relationship with the Spanish dissident communists. His inflexible position has received much criticism.[74]

Trotsky identified converting anarcho-syndicalist workers to revolutionary Marxism as one of the key challenges facing the communists:

> The National Confederation of Labour (CNT) indisputably embraces the most militant elements of the proletariat ... To strengthen this confederation, to transform it into a genuine organisation of the masses, is the obligation of every advanced worker and, above all, of the communists ... As far as the Anarcho-syndicalists are concerned, they could head the revolution only by abandoning their anarchist prejudices. It is our duty to help them do this. In reality, it may be assumed that a part of the syndicalist leaders will go over to the Socialists or will be cast aside by the revolution; the real revolutionists will be with us. The masses will join the communists, and so will a majority of the Socialist workers.[75]

Here it would seem that Trotsky really did lack a sufficient appreciation of the strong attraction anarchist and syndicalist ideas held for many peasants and workers in Spain. Iglesias argues that the CNT's appeals to violent direct action, together with its rejection of the state and conventional 'politics', connected more readily with Spanish traditions of popular revolt than any notions derived from Marxism.[76] While this explanation of anarcho-syndicalism's popularity requires further elaboration, it would appear far more realistic than Trotsky's wishful thinking that the presence of a revolutionary party organised upon Leninist principles would attract large numbers of workers currently supporting the CNT.[77]

If his prediction that, in the throes of revolutionary crisis 'the real revolutionists will be with us' was to be shown utterly mistaken as far as anarcho-syndicalist militants were concerned, it nevertheless retained certain validity with respect to the left wing of the Socialist Party. Trotsky viewed the PSOE as a typical reformist party that had allied itself with the left Republican bourgeoisie for short-term political gains. Its leadership would not accept sole

---

74    It is often claimed, with much justification, that Trotsky's position was just another reflection of his supposed tendency to apply the Bolshevik strategy to Spain regardless of the unique character and history of the Spanish workers' movement. For example see Iglesias 1977, p. 22; also Alba and Schwartz 1988, p. 223.

75    Trotsky 1973a, p. 84.

76    Iglesias 1977, p. 48.

77    See the Appendix for further discussion of anarcho-syndicalism in Spain.

responsibility for political power because it feared the advance this would signify for the Revolution.[78] However low Trotsky's opinion of the PSOE leadership may have been, he nevertheless totally rejected the Comintern's characterisation of them as 'social fascists'. To dismiss the PSOE this way merely in order to reject any collaboration with them was to ignore the progressive potential to be gained from their periodic vacillations to the Left. It also alienated the Socialist workers from the Communists who sought to win them over. He argued, instead, that the Communists had to force, by mass pressure, the Socialists into taking power themselves. Once in power, the inability and unwillingness of the leaders to deliver the promised reforms would then be evident to their own supporters. From the platform of the Cortes, the Communists could expose the conservatism of the Socialist project compared with their own radical democratic demands. This strategy, Trotsky maintained, would encourage the mass base of the Socialist Party to make the kind of progressive demands the leadership would be unwilling to support and thus reveal its tendency to tail-end its Republican partners. The Communists' aim should thus be to drive a wedge between the Socialists and the Republicans and between the PSOE leaders and their mass base.[79]

In response to this it might be argued that the Communists simply lacked the influence among the working class to implement Trotsky's proposals. However, events both in Spain and beyond were to have a huge impact upon the left wing of the PSOE, especially the youth movement. Responses to the 'two black years' (*bienio negro*) of reactionary government, from 1933 to 35, would open up fresh opportunities. During these years, the emergence of a fascist movement and the repressive measures of the government caused many Socialists to reject the reformism of their party and seek a revolutionary alternative. This corresponded to a major shift in Trotsky's thought, the origins and nature of which require some explanation.

### Germany as Turning Point
As we have seen, Trotsky's attention had long been drawn toward events in Germany, which he described in November 1931 as 'the key to the international situation'. 'On the direction in which the solution of the German crisis develops', he wrote, 'will depend not only the fate of Germany herself (and that is already a great deal), but also the fate of Europe, the destiny of the entire

---

78    'Letter to the International Secretariat'. 1 July 1931, in Trotsky 1973a, pp. 147–51.
79    'Down with Zamora-Maura', 24 June 1931, in Trotsky 1973a, pp. 144–5; and 'The Spanish Kornilovs and the Spanish Stalinists', 20 September 1932, in Trotsky 1973a, pp. 183–4.

world, for many years to come'.[80] The defence of the USSR itself hinged upon a correct policy, since 'a victory for Fascism in Germany would signify an inevitable war against the USSR'.[81] He believed that a fascist Germany would lead the forces of the world bourgeoisie against their common *bête noire*. Thus, with Hitler's chancellorship in January 1933, Trotsky's worst fears were realised. In response to this event, Trotsky and the International Left Opposition began to move away from what they now saw as the unworkable strategy of 'straightening out' the Comintern and national Communist parties and toward constructing a new international communist movement in opposition to the Stalinists. This stemmed from the final realisation that the Comintern would not learn the 'lessons of history'. Hitler's victory had not caused it to reject the disastrous policy of the 'Third Period'. Indeed, in April 1933, the Comintern stated that its policy had been correct up to and during the rise of Hitler, and that the proletarian revolution would follow in the wake of fascism. This came at a time when the German Communist Party was being liquidated. Reacting to this enormous defeat, Trotsky wrote of the need to construct a new party in Germany, completely separate from the KPD (German Communist Party).[82] However, it still required further evidence of the Comintern's total incomprehension of the altered situation, manifested in the complete lack of criticism of its former line by the Communist Parties, to drive Trotsky to completely abandon the International he had helped to build.[83]

Nazism's successful rise to power, and the part played by the official Communist movement, forced Trotsky to systematise his interpretation of Stalinism and what he saw as the 'degeneration' of the Soviet Union. While he acknowledged that, within the USSR, the bureaucracy defended itself both against its own working class and the hostility of international capitalism, he believed that the Comintern no longer played an anti-capitalist role in the outside world. Since Russia had now ceased to be the 'key to the international situation', changes in Western Europe would force a political realignment in Russia.[84] He was later to add that the Soviet bureaucracy and Comintern would play a counterrevolutionary role in the world revolution, actively seeking to prevent the victory of socialist revolutions because their example would

---

80    'Germany, the Key to the International Situation', Trotsky 1971, pp. 121–2.

81    Trotsky 1971, p. 126.

82    'The Tragedy of the German Proletariat: The German Workers Will Rise Again – Stalinism, Never!' 14 March 1933, Trotsky 1971, pp. 375–84.

83    'It Is Necessary to Build Communist Parties and an International Anew', 15 July 1933, in Trotsky 1971, pp. 419–26.

84    'The Class Character of the Soviet State', 1 October 1933. Cited in Deutscher 1963, p. 202.

undermine Stalinist power in the USSR itself. Trotsky now believed that only a political revolution within the USSR could overthrow Stalinist hegemony. Despite this, the USSR was still a 'workers' state' and had to be defended externally against the world bourgeoisie.[85]

Only a disaster on the order of Hitler's victory could have forced such changes in Trotsky's orientation. He believed that the Comintern leadership, along with the Social-Democratic parties, had allowed the Nazis to come to power and, in so doing, destroyed the powerful German workers' movement without a struggle. This was, he argued, a criminal action which opened up the distinct possibility of another world war and the general defeat of the European working-class movement. Hence the Third International was doomed, just as the Second had been in 1914. Yet he recognised that, as with the crisis of the world war and its aftermath, a new International would not be created overnight. For most Communist workers, the Third International still embodied the ideals of the October Revolution. Thus, the immediate aim could be no more than to prepare the ground for the Fourth International by winning enough support to make it a feasible proposition. Indeed, four years passed before the new International held its founding conference.

Trotsky's radically altered stance regarding the Soviet Union and the Comintern coincided with his July 1933 move to France, where he was to spend an unhappy couple of years.[86] During this period, and in the context of a rapidly deteriorating political situation in France and Spain, he embarked upon what was to become known within the somewhat limited ranks of the International Left Opposition as the 'French turn'. This consisted of advice to the hundred or so French oppositionists to join the Socialist Party (SFIO) and constitute its revolutionary wing. Its huge membership, or 'advanced' elements of it, could be won over to revolutionary Marxist ideas. He was to extend this tactic, often referred to as 'entryism', to most Left Opposition groups, including those in Spain.[87] Trotsky thought it offered a final chance to construct a united front against fascism. However, the majority of his Spanish co-thinkers – led by Nin, with whom he already had strained relations – concluded that the path to working-class unity did not pass through the PSOE Left. The tiny faction that did take this detour was soon, like its French counterpart, expelled from the

---

85    Anderson 1983, pp. 51–2.

86    Facilitated by the revocation, subject to certain conditions, of his 1916 expulsion order on the part of the French authorities. On his French sojourn, see Deutscher 1963, pp. 260–90.

87    'Two Letters to the International Secretariat', 1 November and 16 December 1934, excerpted in Trotsky 1973a, p. 202 and p. 206.

Socialist Party. The great majority of the Spanish Trotskyists (or Left Communists, as they were now called) chose to ignore the advice of their mentor and instead joined forces with other dissident communists grouped around the Workers' and Peasants' Bloc (BOC) to create a Party of Marxist Unification, the POUM.[88]

In the third volume of his influential biography of Trotsky, Isaac Deutscher argued that the tactic of entering the Socialist parties was Trotsky's desperate attempt to salvage his final political project, the Fourth International.[89] It soon became obvious that, within the French Socialist Party, the Trotskyists, with their total hostility to the leadership's reformism, could only appeal to a small minority, mainly the youth. The 'turn' to the socialist parties also left the Trotskyists open to the Stalinist accusation that they were no longer revolutionaries. Within the ranks of the Trotskyist movement, the new policy proved hugely divisive. The effect on the Spanish Left Communists was to exacerbate the personal and political differences between the national leadership and the International Secretariat as well as between Nin and Trotsky.[90]

Rejecting both the tactic of 'entering' the Socialist Party and the project of a new international signalled the point of rupture between the Left Communists and Trotsky. This would become apparent in the September 1934 issue of the theoretical journal *Comunismo*, where Nin's group announced a break with the Paris-based international Trotskyist movement. Iglesias, a participant in and defender of the POUM, has maintained that the Left Communists' subsequent fusion with Maurín's BOC to form the POUM was a means of breaking out of political isolation. He argues that, had they taken Trotsky's advice and submerged themselves in the PSOE, they would have sacrificed their political identity and would in any case have faced expulsion. By joining forces with those who were politically close to them, the Spanish Trotskyists gained far more than the few who actually followed Trotsky's advice.[91] Had it not been for Trotsky, Iglesias argues, this fusion would probably have taken place long before September 1935.[92]

---

88  See the next section and Chapter Three for a fuller discussion of the political differences between Trotsky and the Spanish Left Communists.

89  Deutscher 1963, p. 272.

90  The International Secretariat was the central body of the International Left Opposition. Frank 1979, p. 38.

91  Iglesias 1977, p. 75.

92  Letter of 2 September 1988, reproduced in Fundació Andreu Nin 1989b. Other ex-POUM militants who blame Trotsky for what they consider to have been two or three lost years prior to the creation of the POUM are: Francisco de Cabo, Letter to Ignacio Iglesias of 28 February 1973, in Fundació Andreu Nin 1989b. Also, Wilebaldo Solano's contribution to

In Trotsky's defence, it has been argued that in proposing the tactic of entryism for Spain he was most concerned with influencing the Socialist Youth, who were highly radicalised yet lacked a proper revolutionary orientation.[93] With hindsight, it could be argued that Trotsky's concerns were borne out in April 1936, when the Communist youth movement absorbed its Socialist equivalent. However, it is hard to think that even Trotsky could have predicted such an occurrence in 1934. More concretely, it has been suggested that had Nin and Maurín responded positively to overtures made by Socialist Youth leader Santiago Carrillo in 1934 and 1935, the PCE might not have enjoyed such a sweeping success.[94] This issue is pursued further in Chapter Four. It seems fair to say that Nin and Maurín made the mistake of being deceived by the small size and relative weakness of the PCE. It may be that they underestimated the authority afforded by the official party's links to the Comintern and, by virtue of this fact, its association with the Russian Revolution. Yet these arguments only gain force with the knowledge of events in 1936 and the particular national and international circumstances of Spain's Civil War.

The Trotskyist historian Pierre Broué has reconstructed Trotsky's reasons for advocating entry into the PSOE. After the Asturian Revolution of 1934, Spain appeared to be on the brink of a profound revolutionary crisis. But there was not now sufficient time for the revolutionary elements to build a mass base before events came to a head, because the advanced workers' allegiance still lay with the PSOE and CNT. Therefore, the best way of influencing politics was to build upon the wave of revolutionary enthusiasm currently sweeping the left wing of the PSOE by entering the party. Once inside, they could link up with the youth with a view to leading them. For Broué, an invitation (if such it was) from the Socialist Youth movement to the Trotskyists to join forces indicates that such a policy was practical. In any case, he argues, entryism was a more realistic and potentially profitable project than the construction of a new party.[95] However, the Spanish Left Communists seemed intent upon building a new party by joining forces with other dissident communists. Movement in this direction had already led to strained relations between Nin and Trotsky.

---

      Fundació Andreu Nin (n.d.). The nature of the differences between the Trotskyists and the BOC prior to 1935, which were not insubstantial and did not disappear with the founding of the POUM, is discussed in subsequent chapters.

93     Pierre Broué in Fundació Andreu Nin (n.d.).

94     Heywood 1990, p. 169.

95     Broué 1966, p. 28. He cites the issues of the Socialist Youth paper *Renovación* in which these overtures were made as No. 127 (27 January 1934) and No. 132 (3 March 1934). See also Broué 1983.

### Trotsky and the POUM

As noted above, it seems doubtful that Trotsky gave much thought to the Spanish situation in the period between mid-1933 and November 1934.[96] This was a particularly unsettled time in his life. He was forced to move house constantly due to threats from French fascists and Stalinists and the hostility of his host government. His political energies were devoted primarily to preparing the ground for the Fourth International. The situation in Europe following Hitler's victory had, he believed, altered substantially. Insurrections in Austria and Spain (February and October 1934) had shown the willingness of workers to enter into armed conflict with the forces of reaction. Trotsky thought that the key short-term tactic had to be the radicalisation of Socialist parties in France, Spain, Belgium and Switzerland to the extent that they would become more receptive to revolutionary ideas. Hence, the main innovation of the Spanish dissident communists in this period, the creation of the POUM in September 1935, did not comply with this tactic.

Given the depth of difference of opinion between Trotsky and his Spanish followers over the best way to influence the workers' movement in a revolutionary direction, it is worth briefly tracing the origins of these disagreements. Trotsky had long been aware of the close ties between the Spanish Left Opposition and Maurín's BOC.[97] The Central Committee of the Spanish Left Opposition (which since March 1932 had called itself the Spanish Left Communists, or Izquierda Comunista de España) had moved from Madrid to Barcelona.[98] Deeply suspicious of the BOC, which he considered petty-bourgeois and provincial, Trotsky was nevertheless forced to recognise the political reality of Cataluña as the key stronghold in the struggle against reaction in Spain.[99] But if this region was to be the incubator of revolutionary militancy, the Catalan proletariat would first have to assume leadership of the struggle for regional autonomy. This could not come about as long as the proletariat's representatives – Maurín's BOC – proposed simply to support a struggle initiated by petty-bourgeois nationalists. Trotsky believed that

---

96    There appears to be a break in his writings on Spain of almost one year between his letter to *Adelante* of 3 October 1933 and his letter to the International Secretariat of the summer of 1934. The former appears in Trotsky 1977, p. 223, but it does not appear in the English version of his writings on Spain, Trotsky 1973a. The second letter is reproduced in Trotsky 1979c, pp. 496–9.

97    For a history of the BOC, see Bonamusa 1974. The BOC is discussed further in Chapter Three.

98    The most comprehensive discussion of the relationship between Trotsky and the Spanish Trotskyists, and between the latter and the International Secretariat, is Pagès 1977a.

99    Letter to the International Secretariat, Summer 1934, in Trotsky 1979c, pp. 496–9.

the BOC, which led the only approximation to a united front, the Alianza Obrera (Workers' Alliance), merely tail-ended the petty-bourgeois politics of the nationalist Esquerra party.[100] To succeed, he felt that the Catalan workers' movement would have to show the way forward for the whole of Spain, and not confine its objectives within the boundaries of Cataluña. Hence, the task of revolutionary Marxists was to win over the mass forces on which the Esquerra was based. To gain this hegemony, the dissident communists would need to put forward radical democratic demands as well as the class demands of the proletariat and specific demands of the peasantry and petty-bourgeoisie. Trotsky concluded that all of this presupposed the existence of a Bolshevik-type party.[101] The POUM was not what he had in mind at all.[102]

It would be incorrect, however, to conclude from this that Trotsky immediately adopted a hostile attitude toward the POUM or considered the Spanish Trotskyists lost to revolutionary Marxism. Despite the POUM's rejection of both the Fourth International project and the entryist tactic, Trotsky wrote of the importance of insisting 'in a friendly way on the need for theoretical and political precision in the interests of the future of the new Spanish party'.[103]

Curiously, perhaps, it is not clear whether the POUM considered itself to be a revolutionary 'party' at all. Ex-POUM activists appear to disagree over the organisation's status and function. Iglesias is adamant that it was not designed as a Bolshevik-style party, since the Revolution did not require one.[104] He argues that the POUM was created in advance of the future revolutionary party.[105] Such a party would only be constituted by *all* the revolutionary Marxist groups working together. The POUM's task was to establish the conditions and framework for this unity.[106] However, another ex-POUM leader, Wilebaldo Solano, has stated that the fusion of dissident communist elements within the POUM embodied the aim of constructing a revolutionary party opposed to the PCE.[107] Whether the POUM constituted a revolutionary party or

---

100   On the Workers' Alliance, see Alba 1977. The Esquerra was a petty-bourgeois nationalist party with broad support in Cataluña. Its leader was Lluís Companys.

101   See Trotsky's articles and letters of 16 December 1932 to 16 December 1934, in Trotsky 1973a, pp. 187–206.

102   For the circumstances of the creation of the POUM in September 1935, see Chapter Three.

103   Letter to the Dutch Revolutionary Socialist Workers Party (RSAP), 18 October 1935, in Trotsky 1973a, p. 207.

104   Iglesias's reply to Pierre Broué, part of a symposium held in Barcelona in September 1985 to commemorate the fiftieth anniversary of the founding of the POUM (Fundació Andreu Nin 1989b).

105   Iglesias 1977, p. 78.

106   Ibid. Iglesias cites *La Batalla* (the POUM newspaper), 18 October 1935.

107   Wilebaldo Solano in Fundació Andreu Nin, n.d.

an instrument of Marxist unity, it seems curious that its supporters should consider this to be more appropriate to the 'realities' of the Spanish labour movement than Trotsky's notions. Both approaches faced the difficult question of why working-class militants in the massed ranks of the PSOE-UGT and CNT should have been influenced by a small group of dissident communists whose organisation barely existed outside of Cataluña. This is a central issue in the history of the POUM to which we will return time and again. Indeed, it is arguably a central factor in the decision of the new organisation's leaders to support the electoral pact in the run-up to the February 1936 elections.

### The Spanish Popular Front

While the Spanish Left Communists earned Trotsky's stern criticism by rejecting his advice to work inside the Socialist organisations and joining forces with Maurín's BOC, this was nothing compared with his condemnation over their participation in the Popular Front electoral alliance. Trotsky now disowned the actions of his Spanish followers Nin and Juan Andrade, labelling them 'treachery'.[108] For Trotsky, the notion of a formal coalition between genuine workers' organisations and bourgeois forces was anathema. He had been arguing for some time that such a cross-class alliance had nothing to do with the Leninist conception of a united front, precisely because it included bourgeois forces. To him there was no difference between the Spanish Popular Front electoral pact and the earlier French version he had attacked so strongly.[109] The Front's programme was actually less radical than that of the 1931–3 Republican

---

108   'The Treachery of the POUM', 23 January 1936, in Trotsky 1973a, pp. 207–11.

109   Trotsky's critique of the French Popular Front is to be found in Trotsky 1976; Trotsky 1958; and Trotsky 1979a. Trotsky's Spanish writings are often seen to be dominated by the question of the Popular Front; see, for instance, Löwy 1981, p. 86, note 52. It is certainly true that he considered it to be 'the question of questions' and 'the main question of proletarian class strategy for this epoch' and devoted a great deal of time to criticising what he believed was a fundamentally Menshevik strategy. But his critique of the popular fronts was clearly based upon the law of uneven and combined development and the theory of permanent revolution. In the case of Spain, he argued, this coalition did not fit the pattern of Spain's development or correspond to the dynamics of its revolution. It was in reality an attempt to impose a schema first elaborated during the Russian Revolution, with the difference that it fitted the current conjuncture even less than it had that of 1917. As he put it at the end of a vitriolic attack on Nin and Maurín: 'All the Popular Fronts in Europe are only a pale copy and often a caricature of the Russian Popular Front of 1917, which could, after all, lay claim to a much greater justification for its existence, for it was still a question of the struggle against Tsarism and the remnants of feudalism'. 'Letter to the Central Committee of the RSAP', 16 July 1936, in Trotsky 1973a, pp. 218–21. Full text is in Trotsky 1976.

government. Trotsky noted that the Socialists' proposals for nationalising the banks and for workers' control of industry had been rejected; the Republicans would not even agree to guarantee the right to strike. However, his most bitter rebuke was reserved for the POUM.

By signing the pact, Trotsky wrote, the POUM shared responsibility for enabling a left bourgeois government to be elected to power with popular support. This was nothing less than a 'betrayal of the proletariat for the sake of an alliance with the bourgeoisie'.[110] Having so recently rejected his advice and the overtures of Carrillo on the grounds that to enter the PSOE would be opportunist, it seemed hypocritical for the POUM now to campaign on a joint electoral platform with them. To Trotsky, it appeared that the POUM was adopting in practice the Stalinist policy of the Comintern's Seventh Congress. It was typical of what he termed the POUM's 'centrism' – by which Trotsky meant a wavering between reformism and revolution. As soon as the Popular Front government took office, the POUM's leadership began to distance itself from the government and behaved as if its victory had been none of their doing.[111]

Trotsky's harsh condemnation of Nin, Andrade and the POUM has understandably drawn much comment from those who were involved in signing the Popular Front pact. It has been claimed that the agreement was no more than a short-term electoral pact that should not even be seen as a Popular Front.[112] Iglesias even argues on this basis that the POUM never actually joined the Popular Front, since it was not part of the government.[113] If it is true that the electoral programme signed by Juan Andrade did not contain the words 'popular front' and in fact owed nothing to the influence of the Comintern, one cannot escape the fact that the pact did constitute a common political programme upon which a government was elected. That the PSOE's left wing and the POUM subsequently refused to co-operate with the Republicans does not alter the fact that they campaigned on behalf of this programme. Nor can they honestly absolve themselves of all responsibility for putting in place the Manuel Azaña administration, which they knew would be composed of bourgeois and petty-bourgeois representatives.

Andrade himself advances rather stronger arguments in defence of signing the pact. He mentions the fear that, if the Right had won another election, the

110 'The Treachery of the POUM', Trotsky 1973a, p. 209.
111 Trotsky 1973a, p. 208. Also see the letter to Central Committee of the RSAP, Trotsky 1973a, p. 220.
112 Contribution by Wilebaldo Solano in Fundació Andreu Nin, n.d.
113 Iglesias 1976, p. 41.

result might have been akin to an elected dictatorship.[114] A desire to release the thirty thousand prisoners taken in October 1934 was a massive incentive and probably explains why the CNT's supporters voted for Front candidates. It is also clear that the POUM believed it politically dangerous to isolate itself from such an overwhelmingly popular movement.[115] Some argue that the national platform afforded by Front rallies enabled the POUM to put its politics across to a much wider audience than would otherwise have been possible.[116] Another justification is that the electoral system favoured coalitions and the POUM would not have won Maurín's seat in the Cortes had it not been part of the Front; a voice in the Cortes gave the POUM greater political legitimacy.[117]

Some of these justifications could be said to endorse Trotsky's allegation of 'opportunism'. Aware of this implication, the POUM leaders declared that the pact had been a political manoeuvre and that the interests of the proletariat were opposed to those of the Popular Front government.[118] Both Andrade and Enrique Rodríguez note that neither Largo Caballero nor the POUM leadership placed any significance upon the contents of the pact. Moreover, the POUM had warned against supporting any government that might result from the pact; only a united front which excluded the bourgeoisie was acceptable.[119] The apparent contradiction upon which Trotsky focused – why sign an electoral agreement when you know beforehand that the government it will elect will be opposed to you? – can only be appreciated if the weakness of the workers' movement and the prospects of a fascist-type régime are taken into account. These two factors led the POUM to conclude that a left Republican government would at least permit the workers' organisations to rebuild themselves and prepare for the next round of class struggles.

Whatever the arguments over signing the electoral agreement, Trotsky's observation shortly after the elections was that the altered domestic and international situations meant that a return to the 1931–3 political compromise in Spain was impossible and that the country was entering an *'acute revolutionary period'*.[120] Spanish workers and poor peasants would not be satisfied with mere

114 Andrade 1986. Solano makes the same point in his contribution to the roundtable discussion. Fundació Andreu Nin, n.d.
115 Nin, cited in Broué 1977, p. 90; Andrade 1986, p. 29; Iglesias 1976, p. 44; Solano, Fundació Andreu Nin, n.d.
116 Iglesias 1976, p. 4; Andrade 1986, p. 29.
117 Andrade 1986, p. 29.
118 Nin, 'Después de las elecciones del 16 de febrero', in Nueva Era 1976, pp. 183–8. See also Maurín, 'Statement in the Cortes', 15 April 1936, cited in Iglesias 1976, p. 48.
119 Andrade 1986, p. 33; Enrique Rodríguez in Fundació Andreu Nin 1989b.
120 Letter to a Spanish comrade, 12 April 1936, in Trotsky 1973a, p. 212. Emphasis in original.

promises again; this time, they would seek revolutionary solutions. He thought the Popular Front would simply prove to be a brake upon this process. It is clear, then, that Trotsky now believed the Revolution had passed the 'parliamentary phase' and stood on the threshold of the struggle for power. As he noted in a reference to the POUM's use of the term 'democratic-socialist revolution':

> Marx wrote in 1876 on the falseness of the term 'Social Democrat': socialism cannot be subordinated to democracy. Socialism (or communism) is enough for us. 'Democracy' has nothing to do with it. Since then, the October Revolution has vigorously demonstrated that the socialist revolution cannot be carried out within the framework of democracy. The 'democratic' revolution and the socialist revolution are on opposite sides of the barricades. The Third International theoretically confirmed this experience. The 'democratic' revolution in Spain has already been carried out. The Popular Front is renewing it. The personification of the 'democratic' revolution in Spain is Azaña, with or without [Largo] Caballero. The socialist revolution is yet to be made in uncompromising struggle against the 'democratic' revolution and its Popular Front. What does this 'synthesis', 'democratic socialist revolution' mean? Nothing at all. It is only an eclectic hodgepodge.[121]

If one places the word 'bourgeois' before 'democratic', Trotsky's meaning immediately becomes clear and is wholly consistent with the theory of permanent revolution. The term 'democratic-socialist revolution' had been advanced by the POUM in opposition to the PCE's characterisation of the Revolution as bourgeois-democratic.[122] In the next chapter, we will discuss whether the differences between Trotsky and the POUM on this point were purely semantic or contained fundamental differences of analysis and theory.

## 2.3    War and Revolution

When Trotsky stated that the parliamentary phase of the Revolution had long since ended, he clearly did not mean that he thought the 'democratic tasks' had been resolved. The point he was making was rather that now that the

---

121    Trotsky 1973a, p. 213.
122    See the article by Maurín, '¿Revolución democráticoburguesa o revolución democrático-socialista?', in Nueva Era 1976, pp. 261–71.

promises of reformist socialism had been shown to be empty, the workers and peasants would seek a more direct means of satisfying their class interests. It was also evident from the experience of five years of a bourgeois republic that 'democracy' (meaning bourgeois democracy) was an inadequate defence against movements of a fascist nature. In other words, the Popular Front government did not correspond to the current phase of the Revolution, which was now a question of attacking the bourgeoisie head-on. Since the Popular Front included representatives of bourgeois interests, Spain's government could hardly be expected to support a revolution against itself. Hence the very existence of a Popular Front in such an unstable climate caused key sections of the bourgeoisie to turn to fascist-style solutions as the best guarantee against a proletarian revolution. Trotsky noted, in response to the July military rising against the Second Republic:

> Incapable of solving a single one of the tasks posed by the revolution, since all these tasks boil down to one, namely, the crushing of the bourgeoisie, the Popular Front renders the existence of the bourgeois régime impossible and thereby provokes the Fascist coup d'état. By lulling the workers and peasants with parliamentary illusions, by paralysing their will to struggle, the Popular Front creates the favourable conditions for the victory of Fascism. The policy of coalition with the bourgeoisie must be paid for by the proletariat with years of new torments and sacrifice, if not by decades of Fascist terror.[123]

It might be argued that Trotsky rather overstated the case when he claimed that the left bourgeoisie feared the workers more than they did the fascists.[124] Most historians would retort that, in reality, their representatives had very good reason to fear the extreme Right more than the labour movement.[125] Yet, viewed from Trotsky's perspective, the question was one of class interest rather than the personal allegiances of a few more liberal-minded capitalists. A Popular Front government was, by definition, incapable of dealing with the situation. It had been unable and unwilling to radically reform the army precisely because it required the military to defend private property. This would always trump any temporary political alliance with sections of the workers' movement.[126]

---

123  Postscript to 'The New Revolutionary Upsurge and the Tasks of the Fourth International', July 1936, in Trotsky 1973a, p. 229.

124  Ibid.

125  See, for instance, Casanova 2010 and Preston 2012.

126  Letter to the International Secretariat, 27 July 1936, in Trotsky 1973a, p. 231.

Hence such a government was powerless to prevent military conspiracies against itself, such as the one which began the Civil War.

According to Trotsky, the Revolution had now reached the stage at which the task of the proletariat was nothing less than the overthrow of the bourgeois state apparatus and its replacement by councils of workers, soldiers and peasants.[127] Only by carrying the Revolution forward toward measures of a socialist nature could the threat of fascism be successfully dealt with, he argued. Thus from the very opening of the Civil War, he considered the Revolution and the War to be inseparable. His reference point was, as often in the past, the Bolsheviks in 1917. The political weapon of the Revolution could offset any military advantage enjoyed by the Nationalists (the military). Revolution might even win the army rank and file away from the officer corps. The fact that, in the summer of 1936, workers' militias had taken effective power in many parts of Republican Spain indicated a first step toward creating the kind of alliance of workers, peasants and soldiers that was required. Trotsky now urged consolidating the initial revolutionary gains as a means of establishing the ground to be defended. Tangible social changes would begin to erode the social base upon which the Nationalists counted.[128]

Much later, in December 1937, Trotsky was to reflect upon the Spanish situation in terms of the theory of permanent revolution, employing parallels with Russia 20 years before. The Socialists and Stalinists, he recalled, believed the Revolution could solve only bourgeois-democratic problems. They considered a socialist revolution 'premature' and declared the immediate priority to be the fight against Francisco Franco. But, Trotsky argued, Franco represented not feudal but bourgeois reaction; only a proletarian revolution could defeat him. If the proletariat came to power, it would certainly address unfinished democratic tasks but, in doing so, would have no option but to take socialist measures as well. This, he argued, had happened on the ground after July 1936.[129] Only by transforming agrarian relations could the peasantry be won over to the struggle against fascism. Due to the intimate links between landowners and the industrial, commercial and financial bourgeoisie, 'the agrarian revolution could have been accomplished only *against* the bourgeoisie'.[130] The Spanish workers' level of combativeness and maturity left Trotsky in no doubt that 'in its specific gravity and in the country's economic life, in its political and

---

127    Postscript to 'The New Revolutionary Upsurge and the Tasks of the Fourth International', in Trotsky 1973a, p. 230.

128    'The Lesson of Spain', 30 July 1936, in Trotsky 1973a, p. 235.

129    'The Lessons of Spain: The Last Warning', 17 December 1937, in Trotsky 1973a, p. 307.

130    Ibid.

cultural level, the Spanish proletariat stood on the first day of the Revolution not below but above the Russian proletariat at the beginning of 1917'.[131] However, as long as the Revolution lacked adequate leadership, it could never reach its October. The construction of a party to play the Bolshevik role would, in Trotsky's opinion, have to contend with the 'Menshevik' policies of the Stalinists and Socialists. Yet, as Trotsky warned, it would be wrong to think that Stalin's policy toward the Spanish Revolution was based upon a theoretical error. Indeed it was not guided by theory at all, but rather by the requirements of the Soviet bureaucracy.[132] By the time he wrote this, however, the prospects of a successful outcome to the war, let alone the Revolution, were fast diminishing.

### July 1936 to April 1937

During the early stages of the war in Spain, Trotsky's stateless existence again prevented his full and unhindered engagement with key world events. He had moved in June 1935 from France to Norway, where he had been granted temporary asylum by the newly elected Labour government. But, as Ronald Segal comments, 'apparently disturbed at the implication of their own generosity', the government soon obliged him to refrain from publicly commenting upon Norwegian affairs as a condition of his continued residence.[133] Indeed, the Soviet government exerted pressure upon the Norwegians to expel him, especially in the context of the first Moscow show trial, in which Trotsky was the main defendant. Trotsky refused a further demand from the Norwegian authorities that he refrain from writing or giving interviews about international affairs and was promptly placed under house arrest.[134] These circumstances help account for the break in his written commentary on Spain between September 1936 and January 1937.[135]

Under increasing attack from both the Stalinist and fascist press in Norway and effectively gagged, Trotsky was happy to accept a somewhat unexpected offer of help from the POUM in obtaining a visa to enter Cataluña. Jean Rous, a French Left oppositionist, liaised with Nin in Barcelona in August and

131    Trotsky 1973a, p. 322.
132    Trotsky 1973a, p. 308.
133    Segal 1983, p. 353, and Thatcher 2003, p. 189.
134    Trotsky's internment lasted from 26 August until the end of December 1936. For details, see Deutscher 1963, pp. 336–45; and Segal 1983, pp. 362–6. See also the text of Deutscher's amusing conversation with Trygve Lie, the Minister of Justice responsible for interning and then expelling Trotsky from Norway. Deutscher 1984, pp. 169–77.
135    For a useful account of Trotsky's final exile in Mexico, see Patenaude 2009.

September 1936 over this matter. According to Ignacio Iglesias, the POUM executive accepted Nin's suggestion to approach the Generalitat (the Catalan regional government) to request asylum for Trotsky.[136] Trotsky seems to have been enthusiastic about this prospect, writing about his willingness to overcome differences with Nin and Andrade at such a critical time.[137] However, there was very little prospect of the Generalitat agreeing to offer Trotsky a visa, which would have been likely to jeopardise the promise of Soviet aid to the Republic.[138] This episode is significant because it suggests that the relationship between Trotsky and Nin may not yet have been beyond repair. Since April 1936, Trotsky had been corresponding with the writer Victor Serge, recently released from Soviet detention and expelled from Russia. Serge had been a fellow Left Oppositionist and friend of both Nin and Trotsky in Russia during the 1920s. He was now in France and in touch with the Trotskyists but remained unconvinced of the need for a Fourth International. Serge also demurred over Trotsky's unequivocal condemnation of the Spanish Popular Front. In the absence of the full correspondence between the two, and of that between Serge and Nin, it is difficult to be certain who was taking the initiative, but it is clear from the surviving letters that Trotsky was willing to welcome Nin back to the ranks of revolutionary Marxism. He urged Serge to sound Nin out over this. But to bring about a rapprochement, Nin would have to 'openly unfurl the banner of the Fourth International in Spain'.[139] He would need to break his alliance

136   Alba and Schwartz 1988, p. 166 and p. 170, note 31.
137   Letter from Trotsky to Jean Rous, 16 August 1936, in Trotsky 1973a, pp. 239–41. This letter, written in response to a telegram from Rous, was intercepted by Italian agents in Barcelona and only discovered in the Italian police archives in 1970 by Paolo Spriano. Trotsky displays not only his readiness to travel to Barcelona, but also his desire to settle the old dispute with Nin and Andrade. The situation in Spain was too momentous to be guided by past disagreements: 'It would be shameful pettiness to turn towards the past if the present and the future open the way for common struggle'. He suggests that Nin *et al.* could be shown the letter if Rous thought it expedient. As to his situation in Norway, he felt 'bound hand and foot'.
138   Víctor Alba, a POUM veteran, argues forcefully that Nin made a 'major tactical error' in proposing the POUM petition the Generalitat for a visa for Trotsky. This assisted the Stalinists in portraying the POUM as Trotskyist (Alba and Schwartz 1988, p. 166). Yet it is difficult to believe that the proposal made any difference to the actual course of events in Spain. The PCE had long claimed the POUM were Trotskyists; while the former Left Oppositionists had broken with Trotsky organisationally and on important political grounds, they did not disclaim all theoretical and historical links with him. Moreover, the POUM fiercely condemned the Moscow 'show trials' and expressed solidarity with Trotsky, as Alba himself notes with apparent approval (Alba and Schwartz 1988, p. 132).
139   Letter from Trotsky to Serge, 5 June 1936, in Trotsky 1973a, p. 217.

with 'the sworn enemies of the Fourth International', by which Trotsky meant the 'petty-bourgeois' POUM.[140] This was prior to Trotsky's house arrest, although it was very evident that his continued residence in Norway was problematic. From Trotsky's letters of 3 and 5 June, we also learn that in previous (now lost) communications Serge had criticised the Trotskyists' treatment of Nin as 'sectarian'.[141] Hence it may be the case that Serge was unwilling to act as go-between in a dispute about political strategy in which he increasingly came to prefer Nin's and the POUM's stance to that of the Trotskyists.[142]

Unwelcome and under attack in Norway, seemingly with nowhere to go, Trotsky finally found refuge in Mexico. This was due in considerable part to the offices of the artist Diego Rivera, who asked his country's reformist president, Lázaro Cárdenas, to offer Trotsky asylum.[143] The move to Mexico, where Trotsky arrived with his wife Natalia Sedova on 9 January 1937, allowed him to resume commentary on and analysis of the Spanish Revolution. As he said to the Dewey Commission in April 1937, it was clear that Stalin was attempting to sabotage the Spanish Revolution as a means of strengthening Soviet foreign policy. In order not to jeopardise his treaty with France, Stalin would endeavour to crush the Revolution and adopt the role of 'the guard of private property in Spain'.[144] As Trotsky had pointed out in earlier press interviews, by only giving enough aid to the Spanish government to save its face in the eyes of the international workers' movement, the USSR was merely prolonging the defeat of the Republic. The implications of this policy for the rest of Europe and the USSR were clear:

> If Fascism wins in Spain, France will find itself caught in a vice from which it will not be able to withdraw. *Franco's dictatorship would mean the unavoidable acceleration of European war*, in the most difficult conditions for France ... On the other hand, the victory of the Spanish workers and peasants would undoubtedly shake the régimes of Hitler and Mussolini.[145]

---

140   Ibid.

141   See the surviving correspondence in Cotterill (ed.) 1994, pp. 62–4 and p. 67.

142   See Serge's letter to Nin of 7 August 1936 and various letters and articles relating to Spain collected in Cotterill (ed.) 1994, pp. 125–47.

143   Segal 1983, p. 365.

144   Excerpt from *The Case of Leon Trotsky*, in Trotsky 1973a, p. 252. The 'Dewey Commission', as it became known, was more formally the 'Preliminary Commission of Inquiry into the Charges Made against Trotsky in the Moscow Trials' and heard evidence from 10–17 April 1937 at Trotsky's new residence in Coyoacán, Mexico City.

145   'Interview with Havas'. 19 February 1937, in Trotsky 1973a, p. 244. Emphasis in original.

Trotsky had repeatedly warned that, if fascism gained more ground in Europe, the fascist states would eventually turn on the Soviet Union. The resulting war would be fought on far less favourable terms than were available at the moment.[146]

In response to the argument often advanced by the Republican, Socialist and Stalinist press that in Spain the key question was the 'defence of democracy', Trotsky agreed that democracy was indeed preferable to fascism:

> However, we always added: We can and must defend bourgeois democracy not by bourgeois democratic means but by the methods of class struggle, which in turn pave the way for the replacement of bourgeois democracy by the dictatorship of the proletariat. This means in particular that in the process of defending bourgeois democracy, even with arms in hand, the party of the proletariat takes no responsibility for bourgeois democracy, does not enter its government, but maintains full freedom of criticism and of action in relation to all parties of the Popular Front, thus preparing the overthrow of bourgeois democracy at the next stage.[147]

If this view was reasonable and consistent with the theory of permanent revolution, Trotsky's argument that 'without the proletarian revolution the victory of "democracy" would only mean a roundabout path to the very same Fascism' has been criticised for failing to anticipate different possible outcomes.[148] Trotsky's point was that, even if Franco were defeated by what he called 'the republican army of capital', the requirements of capitalism were such that he would still look for authoritarian solutions in the current international situation. Thus if the Republicans won in military terms, there would still be an intensification of attacks on workers' organisations so as to pre-empt any attempted socialist revolution. He anticipated that the commanding circles of the Republican Army would then move toward a 'Bonapartist' solution, which would differ little from a Franco dictatorship.[149] His perception of the Republican side was thus rooted in what he saw as its essentially bourgeois class character.

---

146   Interview with *News Chronicle*, 24 or 26 August 1936, in Trotsky 1978, pp. 415–16.

147   'Is Victory Possible in Spain?', 23 April 1937, in Trotsky 1973a, p. 257.

148   Trotsky 1978, p. 258. Emphasis in original. The criticism is raised by the historian J.P. Fusi in Fundació Andreu Nin, n.d.

149   Trotsky 1973a, pp. 259–60.

Given the growing influence of Soviet political and military advisors upon the Republican state apparatus, it is really quite unclear what the outcome of a Republican victory would have meant for Europe. Yet it certainly seems that a perception on the part of some British and French observers that a Republican victory might in fact be a victory for Stalin played a part in diplomatic calculations.[150] However, for mainstream liberal and Socialist opinion, the defeat of authoritarianism in Spain would surely pose a major setback for Hitler and Mussolini. While one may wish, even without invoking hindsight, to reject Trotsky's prediction of dictatorship in Spain regardless of a Republican victory, it is important for our purposes to understand that his view stemmed from a genuine belief in the incompatibility of democracy and capitalism in a period of world crisis. Given the political climate of the 1930s, it is perhaps not so difficult to understand Trotsky's worldview: that humanity was presented with a stark choice between fascist barbarism and socialism. The flaw in this argument is precisely the point Trotsky insisted upon most, namely the possibility that bourgeois-capitalist interests were prepared to support bourgeois-democratic political structures.

Trotsky's attitude toward Nin and the POUM changed profoundly during the course of 1936 and 1937 in response to the twists and turns of events in Spain. As we have already seen, in July 1936 he voiced openness to 'lasting rapprochement' with Nin and Andrade, although this letter never reached its intended recipient.[151] Here it is important to be clear that Trotsky made a critical distinction between his former Left Oppositionist comrades and Maurín's Catalan communist organisation, whose militants formed the majority of the POUM. Maurín himself had been caught in the Nationalist zone at the start of the military rising, and now Nin was generally seen as the party's most prominent figure. It would seem that the earlier separation between Nin and the POUM in Trotsky's mind no longer held. Nin's gravest mistake, in Trotsky's mind, had been committed during Trotsky's enforced Norwegian silence, but now he was free to attack Nin in the strongest terms while expressing admiration for the heroic actions of the POUM militias at the front.[152]

For Trotsky, the POUM's entry into the Generalitat in September 1936 signalled an even greater political betrayal than its signing of the Popular Front pact. As he later expressed it, by actually entering a bourgeois government which then participated in reversing the gains of the Revolution, Nin had

---

150   See Moradiellos 1999, pp. 111–14.
151   Letter to Jean Rous, 16 August 1936, in Trotsky 1973a, p. 240.
152   'Interview with Havas', in Trotsky 1973a, p. 242.

'transformed the Leninist formula into its opposite'.[153] In a comment upon the POUM's 'thirteen points for victory', published in *La Batalla* on 4 April 1937, Trotsky suggested that it was pointless to seek to 'advise' such a government. Why should it accept the POUM's call for it to give way to a congress of workers', peasants' and soldiers' deputies? Having disbanded the militias, why would a bourgeois government relinquish military command to an army controlled by workers?[154] Trotsky, alluding to an earlier assertion by Nin that the workers could seize power by peaceful means, argued that this totally ignored the fact that political and military power lay in the hands of the bourgeois Republicans and Stalinists. While it was certainly correct to argue that the workers should not surrender their arms to the authorities, in doing so one had to acknowledge that this would inevitably mean civil war within the Republican camp.[155]

As ever, Trotsky insisted that the solution to the Spanish situation lay in creating a revolutionary party. Apart from a small group of former Left Oppositionists who had already parted company with Nin and Andrade, the POUM was the only contender for this. Yet still nothing in its actions suggested that the party leaders realised the 'criminality' of their collaboration with the bourgeoisie. Nin was behaving like the Menshevik Martov, one of those Trotsky had famously consigned to the 'dustbin of history' after the Bolsheviks seized power in 1917.[156] By entering the Generalitat as 'minister of bourgeois "justice"', as Trotsky put it, Nin made a mockery of the whole concept of proletarian revolution.[157] Trotsky was convinced that 'if this policy continues, the Catalan proletariat will be the victim of a terrible catastrophe comparable to that of the Paris Commune of 1871'.[158]

### May 1937

In a sense, the events of May 1937 in Barcelona appeared to fulfil this gloomy prediction.[159] In 'preliminary remarks' just after the insurrection, Trotsky suggested that what had occurred was a spontaneous action by the advanced Catalan workers which could have led to their seizing power in Barcelona.

---

153    'Ultralefts in General and Incurable Ultralefts in Particular', 28 September 1937, in Trotsky 1973a, p. 294.

154    For the historical background to this, see the Appendix.

155    'Is Victory Possible in Spain?', in Trotsky 1973a, pp. 260–1.

156    Letter to Harold Isaacs, 25 February 1937, in Trotsky 1973a, p. 245.

157    Letter to the editorial board of *La Lutte Ouvrière*, 23 March 1937, in Trotsky 1978, p. 249.

158    Trotsky 1973a, p. 250. A few days before the May insurrection, Trotsky warned that the POUM was frequently caught unawares by events. He predicted that 'the worst experiences still lie ahead!' (Trotsky 1973a, p. 262).

159    See the Appendix for an outline of the May Days in Barcelona.

It demonstrated the falsity of Nin's belief that the workers could assume power without recourse to armed struggle.[160] Later on, he added that the POUM and CNT had failed to grasp this opportunity and had thus handed the initiative to the counterrevolution. Had they led a successful offensive, the insurrection might have spread to other regions, even to those occupied by the Nationalists. Although it might ultimately have failed, such an attempt to take power would have left the proletariat in a far more advantageous position than was in fact the case after May. Moreover, the revolutionary leadership would have proved itself to the workers and hence guaranteed its own future.[161] Instead, Trotsky noted, the Catalan proletariat was now 'ten times weaker than before the May events'.[162]

Although there was in the May events a clear analogy with the July Days in Petrograd, Trotsky considered the differences to be more significant than the obvious similarities.[163] In Russia, the insurrection took place after only four months of revolution and before the Bolsheviks were ready to launch an attack on power. They called a halt in order to prevent a hopeless situation turning into a decisive defeat. In Spain, the insurrection came after six years of revolutionary struggle; the situation in Barcelona was far from hopeless.[164] Trotsky asked why the POUM and CNT had failed to take the initiative. He cited the anarcho-syndicalist paper *Solidaridad Obrera*, which had later claimed that the workers could have taken power in Barcelona.[165] They had not attempted to do so, the paper said, because the CNT rejected any concept of a proletarian dictatorship. In Trotsky's eyes, this merely confirmed his view that the anarcho-syndicalists did not want power. For its part, the POUM had trailed passively behind the anarcho-syndicalists.[166] In a revolution, Trotsky argued, the dictatorship of the revolutionary party was an unavoidable step if the counterrevolutionary forces were to be defeated. No such dictatorship was even suggested in May and the Stalinist-led counterrevolution was able to step in and fill the vacuum.[167]

---

160    'The Insurrection in Barcelona (Some Preliminary Remarks)', 12 May 1937, in Trotsky 1973a, p. 264.

161    'A Test of Ideas and Individuals through the Spanish Experience', 24 August 1937, in Trotsky 1973a, p. 279.

162    'Answer to Questions on the Spanish Situation', 14 September 1937, in Trotsky 1973a, p. 289.

163    Trotsky 1973a, p. 266. Also, Letter to Jean Rous, 22 October 1937, in Trotsky 1973a, p. 301.

164    Trotsky 1973a, p. 278.

165    Letter to Jean Rous, 22 October 1937, in Trotsky 1973a, p. 303. Also, Letter to Margaret de Silver, 23 October 1937, in Trotsky 1978, p. 513.

166    Letter to Jean Rous, 22 October 1937, in Trotsky 1973a, p. 303.

167    Letter to Margaret de Silver, 23 October 1937, in Trotsky 1978, p. 514.

Thus, in Trotsky's analysis, the defeat of the revolutionary Catalan workers in May 1937 was yet another result of the POUM's inability to create a Bolshevik-style party.[168] Consequently, the POUM had been effectively decapitated. Together with the CNT-FAI (the Federación Anarquista Ibérica, or Iberian Anarchist Federation) they had led the Spanish proletariat to the brink of defeat. However sincere its intentions may have been, the POUM had posed the 'chief obstacle on the road to the creation of a revolutionary party'.[169] As we will see, it is arguable that this condemnation was possibly the harshest and least justified of the many Trotsky levelled against the POUM. It failed to appreciate, on the one hand, the hegemony of the Socialists and anarcho-syndicalists over the Spanish labour movement, and, on the other, the rapid expansion in membership and power of the PCE and PSUC (Unified Socialist Party of Catalonia, the PCE's Catalan counterpart) after July 1936. There was little room for a new political force. It is remarkable that the POUM, which was largely confined to Cataluña, achieved as many adherents and wielded as much influence as it did. It must also be said in criticism of Trotsky's position that there is in his writings on the Civil War something of an absence of comment upon the war itself. No political force opposed to Franco's Nationalists and their allies could offer the Spanish workers what the Bolsheviks had been able to in 1917: peace.

That said, it would be equally wrong to misinterpret the nature and purpose of Trotsky's criticism of the POUM and its leaders. He believed that the POUM had the potential to play a Bolshevik role in the Spanish Revolution and sought to correct what he considered to be its mistakes. This did not mean that he doubted their integrity as revolutionaries. Upon learning of Nin's torture and murder at the hands of the GPU, he acknowledged his revolutionary credentials: 'Nin is an old and incorruptible revolutionary. He defended the interests of the Spanish and Catalan peoples against the agents of the Soviet bureaucracy'.[170] Trotsky also recognised that, unlike the CNT-FAI leaders, the POUM leadership had supported its own militants during the May insurrection and should be considered 'the most honest political organisation in Spain'.[171]

---

168   Interview with *New York Herald-Tribune*, 23 August 1937, in Trotsky 1978, p. 411. Also, see
       Trotsky's criticisms of the POUM in his Letter to the Third Congress of the French JSR and
       in 'Answer to the Associated Press', both 22 May 1937, in Trotsky 1978, p. 300 and pp.
       304–305.
169   Trotsky 1973a, p. 318.
170   'The Murder of Andreu Nin by Agents of the GPU', 8 August 1937, in Trotsky 1973a, p. 267.
171   Trotsky 1973a, p. 326.

### The Negrín Government

After the 'May Days', Largo Caballero was replaced by Juan Negrín as head of the Republican government. Trotsky characterised the new administration as one of 'decaying bourgeois democracy'.[172] He thought it represented the protection of capitalist interests every bit as much as Franco and would quickly discard its democratic pretence. Even if the Republic won the war, Trotsky again insisted, the post-war régime would differ little from a Francoist government. Here, we encounter a curious contradiction in Trotsky's thinking regarding Spain which stems from his general pessimism concerning even the most advanced forms of capitalist democracy. Although he believed it was necessary for the Spanish workers to prepare for Negrín's overthrow,[173] he argued,

> The Stalin-Negrín government is a quasi-democratic obstacle on the road to socialism; but it is an obstacle, not a very reliable or durable one, but an obstacle nonetheless, on the road to Fascism. Tomorrow or the day after tomorrow, the Spanish proletariat may perhaps be able to break through this obstacle and seize power. But if it aided, even passively, in tearing it down today, it would only serve Fascism. The task consists not merely of theoretically evaluating the two camps at their true worth, but moreover of utilising their struggle in practice in order to make a leap forward.[174]

One is prompted to ask why Trotsky thought Negrín's government would become a dictatorship. How could a government described by Trotsky himself as a bourgeois-democratic obstacle to fascism be essentially no different to a régime led by Franco?

A partial answer lies in the fact that, by the middle of 1937, it was apparent that the Revolution had gone seriously off track. Trotsky described it as a 'despoiled and disfigured halfway revolution'.[175] Any gains for the working class had now been reversed. No revolutionary party had emerged; the question of

---

172    Trotsky 1973a, p. 282; Trotsky 1978, pp. 407–13.

173    Letter to James P. Cannon, 21 September 1937, in Trotsky 1973a, p. 291. Trotsky insisted that 'without social revolution, the victory of Fascism or of a semi-Fascist militarism in Spain is completely unavoidable, regardless of the outcome of the military operations'. He believed the generals on both sides would agree upon a joint military dictatorship. See also 'Answers to the *New York Herald Tribune*', 24 August 1937, in Trotsky 1978, pp. 407–8.

174    Trotsky 1973a, p. 296.

175    Trotsky 1973a, p. 295.

state power had never been seriously addressed. Since the Negrín government at least opposed fascism, it was necessary to fight alongside Negrín, just as in 1917 the Bolsheviks had fought with Kerensky against Kornilov. But this step had been taken without assuming responsibility for the government's policies. Once Franco was beaten, the struggle would be between the Communists and Negrín. But, here, Trotsky's historical analogy is stretched to breaking point. First, the revolutionary forces in Spain had, by September 1937, already been crushed or neutralised by the Republican government.[176] Secondly, Franco could not be beaten as easily as Kornilov. In Russia, the question of state power had been resolved in favour of the Bolsheviks *before* the Civil War really got going. In the Spanish case, the Revolution had only 'solved' the question of power locally and, as we have seen, for only a short period. The workers' organisations had immediately been confronted with the problem of fighting a war without a unified command or army. Hence, the two civil wars cannot be compared from this angle precisely because one was fought under a Communist (Bolshevik) government and the other under a government of the Republican bourgeoisie and its allies. In Spain, the situation was further complicated by the involvement of the USSR, the intervention of the fascist powers and wider European issues.

As we have seen, Trotsky viewed Stalin's Spanish policy as an extension of Soviet diplomacy. Stalin feared that Paris and London might be drawn into an anti-Soviet coalition with Berlin. This was precisely why, according to Trotsky, Stalin had intervened to prevent the Largo Caballero government permitting attacks upon foreign capitalist interests.[177] Trotsky had no doubt that the suppression of the POUM and CNT – and the murders of Nin and others – were calculated to further Stalin's diplomatic goals.[178]

> The so-called Communist International has become an indispensable transmitting mechanism to the diplomats of London and Paris. In the struggle to win the confidence of the French and British bourgeoisie, Stalin's chief concern throughout has been to prevent the Spanish workers from taking the path of the socialist revolution.[179]

---

176    There is a major historical debate about the extent of the official Communists' role in crushing the social revolution, which is referred to in later chapters and in the Appendix.

177    Trotsky referred to this letter in his discussion with C.L.R. James in April 1939 (Trotsky 1973a, p. 349) and in 'The Kremlin in World Politics', 1 July 1939 (excerpted in Trotsky 1973a, p. 350).

178    Trotsky 1978, p. 410.

179    'The Beginning of the End', 12 June 1937, in Trotsky 1978, pp. 326–7.

Yet the rather obvious argument that Stalin had traded arms for influence over the Republican government was not sufficient to explain why the Republic accepted these conditions. It was evident to Trotsky that the Republicans actively welcomed a reversal of the Revolution and that this suited Socialist and anarcho-syndicalist leaders, who feared losing their control over the labour movement. Hence, Stalin provided these otherwise divergent forces with a convenient solution by supplying the military hardware and freeing them from responsibility for the counterrevolution.[180]

One might ask, however, whether Largo Caballero calling Stalin's bluff and refusing to halt the Revolution would have simply left the Republicans defenceless against Franco. Trotsky did not think so: had Stalin then refused to continue supplying arms to a genuine workers' government, he would have exposed himself and his bureaucracy for the frauds they were. Moreover, Stalin feared fascism more than he did the proletarian revolution; he would have been forced to send arms, perhaps at lower prices. Trotsky went further, arguing that, even without Russian arms, the revolutionary workers would have been able to fight the fascists as long as they were united around a 'bold social programme' based upon common interests which would be seen as worth defending far more than the bourgeois republic.[181]

Hence it is worth stressing that Trotsky associated the crushing of the Spanish Revolution less with Stalin's blackmail or the presence of his secret police than with the collaboration by the leaders of all of the workers' organisations with the bourgeoisie for their own sectarian interests. After July 1936, he remarked, the Popular Front did not even include the bourgeoisie itself, but rather its 'shadow'.[182] Most of the bourgeoisie had gone over to Franco's side, leaving the professional politicians such as Azaña and Companys as its 'political attorneys'. Thus it maintained a presence in both camps. But this was possible only because the workers' leaders allowed bourgeois representatives to remain in the government. Why, Trotsky asked, maintain bourgeois property and bourgeois legality when the bourgeoisie itself had largely deserted to the fascist camp? Why did those who believed themselves to be revolutionaries not distance themselves from the Republican government?[183]

In other words, Trotsky ascribed the main blame for the defeat of the Revolution to a failure of political leadership on the part of those organisations with genuine revolutionary potential: the CNT-FAI and the POUM. For their

180   Trotsky 1973a, pp. 312–13.
181   Trotsky 1973a, pp. 319–20.
182   Trotsky 1973a, p. 309.
183   'Once Again on the Causes of the Defeat in Spain', 4 March 1939, in Trotsky 1973a, p. 339.

part, the anarcho-syndicalist leaders played no independent role, in spite of the revolutionary actions of their rank and file. Failing to acknowledge the question of political power as the key problem, they joined the Popular Front government and became prisoners of the state.[184] In May 1937, their militants had been prepared to take part in an insurrection, but, at the crucial moment, their leaders renounced the seizure of power. Later, the CNT-FAI would complain that the world proletariat had failed to come to their aid. They forgot, Trotsky noted, that revolutions only attract international support relative to the social programmes they seek to carry out.[185] Given the extent of the anarcho-syndicalist–inspired collectivisation and socialisation of the means of production – in Cataluña especially – this would seem, in hindsight, to be a rather harsh judgement, to say the least.

As for the POUM, Trotsky thought it had failed to establish itself as a revolutionary party during the parliamentary phase of the Revolution, prior to 1936. When the Revolution moved into the period of open class war, between February and July 1936, Nin, Maurín and Andrade had failed to detect the crucial change. As a result, the transition from the democratic phase to the struggle for state power was marked not by the POUM openly discrediting the other left parties, but by it seeking a share in government alongside them.[186] Although it did not intentionally follow the Stalinist line, by supporting the Popular Front, the POUM effectively subordinated the workers and peasants to the bourgeoisie. This made it all the easier for the counterrevolution to turn and crush them. Trotsky accepted that the POUM had based itself upon the theory of permanent revolution', but theoretical correctness was not enough. Political analysis could not be divorced from a Leninist strategy. Rather than mobilise the masses against their reformist leaders, the POUM had tried to win these leaders over to a revolutionary position by argument.[187] It abstained from factional activities within the CNT so as to avoid conflict with its leadership. Nor did the POUM work inside the Republican army, instead creating its own unions and militias to guard its own organisations, occupying its own part of the front. By isolating the revolutionary vanguard from the working class in this way, they rendered it impotent and effectively left the working class

---

184   Trotsky 1973a, p. 315. See also the unfinished article on Spain in 1938–9, Trotsky 1979c, p. 871.

185   'Traitors in the Role of Accusers', 22 October 1938, in Trotsky 1973a, p. 329.

186   Trotsky 1973a, p. 318; see also 'The Class, the Party and the Leadership: Why Was the Spanish Proletariat Defeated? (Questions of Marxist Theory)', 20 August 1940, in Trotsky 1973a, pp. 363–4.

187   Trotsky 1973a, p. 317.

leaderless.[188] An evaluation of Trotsky's critique needs to be set within the context of the POUM's own understanding of the situation. This will be one of the main tasks of subsequent chapters.

### The End of the War

The Civil War dragged on until April 1939. Trotsky's prediction that, among other things, it was a dress rehearsal for a global conflagration has become a common assertion among historians.[189] But he did not believe the Spanish conflict could ever be properly understood in terms of a struggle between democracy and fascism. The great 'democracies' – Britain, France and the United States – had all resolutely refused to assist a fellow parliamentary régime. They did so, he stressed, precisely because their governments saw the situation in Republican Spain as revolutionary. To them, Franco, not the Republic, appeared the guarantee against a successful proletarian revolution. Hence Britain's and France's somewhat premature recognition of Franco's régime appeared to Trotsky simply as a continuation of their existing policy. When it had been unclear that Franco would win, 'non-intervention' had been a convenient way of supporting him without appearing to take sides. Once the situation in Spain had been stabilised to their satisfaction, Britain and France could warn Germany and Italy to withdraw their forces. In this way, Chamberlain and Daladier clearly aimed to restore the balance of power in the Mediterranean, a vital route to their colonies.[190]

Trotsky certainly reserved particular condemnation for Stalin's and the Comintern's role in the defeat of the Spanish Revolution. As he put it in February 1939, as the war was reaching its bitter end with the Nationalist offensive in Cataluña, Franco had been assisted 'from the opposite side of the battlefront':

> His chief assistant was and still is Stalin ... [T]he honourable republicans did everything in their power to trample, to besmirch, or simply to drown in blood the cherished hopes of the oppressed masses ... Under the label of the Popular Front they set up a joint stock company. Under the leadership of Stalin they have assured the most terrible defeat when all the

---

188 Trotsky 1973a, p. 318.
189 For instance, Moradiellos 1999. Trotsky noted, in a characteristically perceptive comment, that Spain's war would be seen by historians as an 'episode' on the path leading to another European war. 'Mysteries of Imperialism', 4 March 1939, in Trotsky 1973a, p. 336.
190 Trotsky 1973a, pp. 333–4. This analysis has certainly found resonance in more recent academic studies. See for instance: Little 1985.

conditions for victory were at hand ... The revolution was brought to ruin
by petty, despicable and utterly corrupted 'leaders'. The downfall of
Barcelona signifies above all the downfall of the Second and Third
Internationals, as well as anarchism, rotten to its core.[191]

As we have seen, Trotsky viewed the Comintern as simply an instrument
of Stalin's foreign policy and the Popular Front as a means of projecting a moderate and non-revolutionary Soviet face – one that would allow the USSR
to pursue a policy of collective security with the democratic powers in the
face of Nazi Germany. It seems clear, though, that Trotsky greatly overestimated the degree of Moscow's influence over national Communist parties,
over Comintern agents, and over political allies within the Popular Fronts.[192]
In the case of Spain, recent research has questioned both the degree of Soviet
influence over wartime Republican governments and even the extent to which
Soviet political agents and advisors intended to control domestic politics.[193]
It is also important to realise that Trotsky's view of the Popular Fronts, especially the French and Spanish, was heavily one-sided: it rather ignored proper
consideration of the motivations and relative balance of other political forces
in the Popular Fronts.[194]

   At the end of the war, Trotsky's reflections upon the defeat in Spain consisted, in considerable measure, of recriminations, placing much blame upon
the POUM and Nin for failures of leadership.[195] He refers to the 'treachery
of the POUM' and to Nin as a 'left Menshevik', accusing them of indulging in
centrism and class collaboration:

> The politics of the POUM were determined by capitulation before the
> bourgeoisie at all critical times, and not by this or that quotation from an
> article by Nin. *There can be no greater crime than coalition with the bour-*
> *geoisie in a period of socialist revolution.*[196]

191   'The Tragedy of Spain', February 1939, in Trotsky 1973a, pp. 330–2.

192   Thatcher 2003, pp. 204–5.

193   Durgan 2007, p. 96.

194   See Graham and Preston 1987.

195   See 'Once Again on the Causes of the Defeat in Spain', *Socialist Appeal*, 21 March 1939
       (written 4 March 1939); Trotsky to Daniel Guérin, 10 March 1939; and 'The Class, the Party
       and the Leadership', unfinished manuscript 20, August 1940. All in Trotsky 1973a, pp. 337–
       46 and pp. 353–66.

196   '"Trotskyism" and the PSOP', 15 July 1939, in Trotsky 1979a, p. 237 (emphasis in original).

115

The Spanish proletariat, which had shown itself to be highly combative and more revolutionary than its leadership, had, he concluded, become 'victim to a coalition composed of imperialists, Spanish republicans, Socialists, Anarchists, Stalinists, and on the left flank, the POUM. They all paralysed the socialist revolution, which the Spanish proletariat had begun to realise'.[197] While the POUM's leaders did not set out to cripple the Revolution, of course, their failure to break fully with centrism meant that they 'fell victim to the contradictions of their own policy'.[198] This was indeed a harsh condemnation of Nin and his comrades. We will test its justness or otherwise in subsequent chapters.

One final point to note in relation to Trotsky's perspective on the Spanish Revolution is his attempt to set events in the context of the international situation – the coming 'imperialist war', as he characterised it. Had Spain's Revolution succeeded, he noted, it would have given a powerful impetus to revolutionary movements in the rest of Europe which might have prevented another world war. In the event, defeat in Spain 'postponed a revolutionary perspective for the imperialist war'.[199] Right up until his murder in August 1940, Trotsky maintained that the new world war was no more the business of the workers' movement than the First World War had been. Indeed, he tended to view the slide into war in 1939 at something of a repeat of 1914. He believed the war attested to the historical decay of capitalism and spelled the end of its most developed political form, bourgeois democracy. This prompted Trotsky to remark that 'the victory of the imperialists of Great Britain and France would be not less frightful for the ultimate fate of mankind than that of Hitler and Mussolini'.[200] This was clearly a major misjudgement on his part. Yet Trotsky did not equate bourgeois democracy with fascism; rather, he saw the world capitalist system in terminal crisis. This crisis presented humanity with the historic alternative: socialist revolution or bureaucratic totalitarian dictatorship.[201] Hence, his final scenario did not admit the possibility that, in

---

197    Trotsky 1973a, p. 365.
198    Ibid.
199    Interview with Sybil Vincent for the *Daily Herald*, 18 March 1939, in Trotsky 1973a, pp. 346–7. Also an interview on 23 July 1939 published in *Intercontinental Press*, 8 September 1939. Reprinted in Trotsky 1978, pp. 24–5.
200    'Manifesto of the Fourth International on the Imperialist War and the Proletarian World Revolution', May 1940, in Trotsky 1978, p. 221.
201    'The USSR in War', 25 September 1939, in Trotsky 1973d, pp. 8–9 and p. 13. In the 'Manifesto of the Fourth International on the Imperialist War and the Proletarian World Revolution', Trotsky wrote: 'Naturally there exists a difference between the political régimes in bourgeois society just as there is a difference in comfort between various cars in a railway train. But when the whole train is plunging into the abyss, the distinction between

the aftermath of the war capitalism might regenerate itself, let alone that this might occur under conditions of parliamentary democracy.

## 2.4     Conclusion

This survey of Trotsky's writings on Spain in revolution makes an effort to demonstrate the ways in which his analysis rests upon the theory of permanent revolution. This theory itself relies heavily upon an appreciation of the uneven and combined manner in which Spanish capitalism developed. It seems reasonable to conclude from the evidence presented here that a consistent methodology underpins and connects Trotsky's writings on fascism, on Stalinism and on the Popular Front. Thus, from a solid theoretical base, refined and elaborated during the struggle against Stalin in the mid-1920s, Trotsky was able to sketch an outline of the course of Spain's development without a detailed knowledge of its history. It allowed him to predict with some accuracy that in the event of a political crisis such as the one Spain entered in 1930 and 1931, the upheaval might turn into a revolutionary opportunity. Drawing explicit parallels with Russia, he realised that the dynamics of Spain's uneven and combined development suggested the possibility not of a bourgeois-democratic revolution but of a socialist one. Any notion of 'bourgeois-democratic revolution' was, he thought, false precisely because Spain had already passed through that transformative process, albeit in an incomplete way compared with Britain or France. Yet there was no guarantee of success for the revolutionary class, the working class. Success rested upon correct leadership and strategy, and it was precisely this that he believed to be lacking in Spain.

Spain's Revolution took on far greater importance than it might have in the past, owing to the particular historical conjuncture of the mid-to-late 1930s. A successful socialist revolution added to Russia's would surely have imparted a huge impetus to the process of world revolution and offered a turning point in the struggles against both fascism and Stalinism. Hence Trotsky's disappointment at the outcome stemmed from what he believed to be the implications for humanity as a whole: the prospect of fascist barbarism, as the bourgeoisie sought ever more extreme ways out of the terminal crisis of capitalism.

The analytical and methodological propositions of Trotsky's characterisation of Spanish historical development are still of some relevance to modern

---

decaying democracy and murderous Fascism disappears in the face of the collapse of the entire capitalist system' (Trotsky 1978, p. 221).

historical debates. Unlike approaches that insist upon Spain's exceptionalism and draw their impressions of its nineteenth- and early-twentieth-century history largely from surface phenomena, Trotsky's approach reveals some of Spanish society's underlying forces and contradictions. While it outwardly appeared to be a predominantly rural and semi-feudal society, the fact that capitalism had evolved and penetrated to a significant degree indicates that Spain was tied into the world capitalist system. While historians may be justified in pointing to Trotsky's overestimation of the extent of feudal and semi-feudal residues, they would be unlikely to question his contention that capitalism was the dynamic force in the economy by the period in question.[202]

Trotsky's insistence that the 'bourgeois revolution' had long since ended also seems to tie into some recent thinking on the subject. It would appear that his conception of bourgeois revolution did not require that a country undergo the transformation of its political régime to one of parliamentary democracy. This may have been one of the 'democratic tasks', but it did not in any sense define the bourgeois revolution. Such an idea is part and parcel of a species of modernisation theory which equates capitalist development with necessarily enhanced political freedoms. Trotsky rejected this assumption, especially with respect to countries whose capitalist development was backward. He stressed, instead, the contradictions of uneven and combined development that produced, on the one hand, a growing industrial proletariat and, on the other, a relatively weak industrial bourgeoisie. This meant that even those fractions of the bourgeoisie one would normally think of as progressive would in practice tend to prefer authoritarian rule to what they might perceive to be the perils of parliamentary democracy. Yet, if this held for a relatively backward capitalist country, the implication was that advanced bourgeois states might enjoy liberal democracy. This seems to contradict Trotsky's growing conviction in the late 1930s that liberal democracy was no longer sustainable and that the choice was socialism or barbarism.

Clearly, the picture Trotsky presents of Spanish society and its historical development is neither complete nor unproblematic. There is, for example, little analysis of the petty-bourgeoisie and the fundamental part it played in the Republican and Nationalist movements. Trotsky tends to subsume this class into the bourgeoisie or the peasantry without allowing it an independent political role. Yet the Republican politicians who made up much of the 1931–3 government and the Popular Front government of 1936 were predominantly petty-bourgeois. Trotsky even states that explicitly in some of his late writings

---

202    See the Appendix for references to ongoing historical issues.

on Spain. Yet instead of analysing their role as modernisers and reformers whose political project genuinely encompassed representative democracy and who utterly rejected authoritarianism, he dismisses them as the 'shadow' of the bourgeoisie.[203]

Another important omission in Trotsky's account is a thorough appreciation of the rural labour force. As we saw in Chapter One, Trotsky was well aware of the vital revolutionary role of the peasants under proletarian leadership. But his insistence that key revolutionary movements were always focused around industrial centres had already been proved incorrect by the Chinese experience. In some areas of the Spanish countryside, the socialisation of production was carried out with great force. In spite of this omission, an understanding of uneven and combined development may provide us with the theoretical means to comprehend this aspect of the Revolution. This peculiar combination of archaic practices with capitalist relations of production suggests a peasantry structurally distinct from the one identified by classical Marxism. We will return to this issue later.

Other aspects of the revolutionary period that do not receive systematic or adequate treatment in Trotsky's writings include the anarcho-syndicalists, the Alianza Obrera and the Asturian Revolution of October 1934. Although he makes numerous references to the CNT-FAI and often praises the courage and revolutionary commitment of its militants, Trotsky's advice to the communists was simply that they should expose the theoretical and political bankruptcy of the leadership and present its rank and file with the 'correct' revolutionary programme. This failed to engage with the reality that anarcho-syndicalism had deeper roots and enjoyed far greater currency than revolutionary Marxism among large numbers of workers, rural and urban. Trotsky offers neither an explanation of its appeal nor an analysis of its social base. The Alianza Obrera is barely mentioned, and Trotsky says nothing concrete or constructive about it.[204] The Asturian Revolution likewise receives scant coverage.[205] As we will see, the dissident communists in Spain extensively covered all these issues in their analyses.

Trotsky returned time and again to what proved to be an intractable problem of the Spanish Revolution: the absence of a revolutionary party capable of achieving hegemony over the politically advanced workers and peasants.

---

203   See, for instance, Trotsky 1973a, p. 309.

204   The most extended reference to it appears in Trotsky's letter to the International Secretariat, summer 1934, in Trotsky 1979c, pp. 496–8.

205   The most significant discussion of to the Asturian Revolution appears in 'Whither France?', excerpted in Trotsky 1973a, pp. 204–5.

His initial response to this was to advise his co-thinkers everywhere to attempt to win over the official Communist parties. In Spain, as elsewhere, this proved a hopeless task because of the influence of the Comintern. The Spanish party's small size and political insignificance also rendered this an inappropriate policy. However, the 'French turn' toward the Socialist parties did have much to commend it as a tactic in the Spanish case. A strong argument could be made for this as the only realistic means by which revolutionary Marxism might have gained a foothold within the PSOE. Even so, only its adoption at a national level would have had a significant impact upon the course of the revolution. Evidently this 'turn' was rejected by Nin and most of his comrades in the Spanish Left Communists, who took an alternative route leading to the formation of the POUM. Whether or not the key ingredient lacking in the Spanish Revolution really was a Bolshevik party, it remains an inescapable fact that Spain's Revolution lacked a focal point, a central revolutionary body willing and able to fill the power vacuum created by the events of July 1936. In this respect, it seems appropriate to enquire whether the POUM's answer to this question really was better suited to Spanish conditions than the one furnished by Trotsky. This will be addressed in subsequent chapters.

It could be argued that some of the weaknesses of Trotsky's position stem from a combination of his personal predicament and the dramatic shift in his political thought provoked by the Nazis' rise to power. What he saw as the utter bankruptcy of the Comintern's response to Hitler led him to conclude, 'There is now no one except me to carry out the mission of arming a new generation with the revolutionary method over the heads of the leaders of the Second and Third Internationals'.[206] It may have been less his own arrogance that made him assert his own indispensability than his genuine fear that an absence of proletarian leadership would render the European working class defenceless in the face of fascism and a new world war. His condemnation of Nin, Andrade and the POUM may be due less to a fit of pique at their rejection of his advice[207] and more to a sense of the extreme urgency and gravity of the situation. His answer, which can hardly be said to have been widely supported either then or since, was to seek to construct a new Marxist international which would 'restore to the proletariat . . . its historical leadership'.[208] Yet it is hard to avoid the conclusion that, by labelling Nin, Andrade and the POUM 'traitors', Trotsky merely alienated many of those who might otherwise have rallied to his wake-up call in some shape or form.

---

206    Trotsky's diary entry for 25 March 1933, cited in Hansen 1975, p. ix.
207    Iglesias 1976, p. 58.
208    'Luxemburg and the Fourth International', 24 June 1935, in Trotsky 1970c, p. 454.

Lastly, it is worth underlining Trotsky's opinion of the Comintern's role in the Spanish Revolution and Civil War. In 1928, he had warned that Stalin sought to subordinate the world class struggle to his project of building 'socialism in one country': 'The task of the parties in the Comintern assumes . . . an auxiliary character; their mission is to protect the USSR from intervention and not to fight for the conquest of power'.[209] Stalin, he argued, needed to sustain the centrality of the USSR to world revolution in order to maintain the prestige and consolidate the position of his own bureaucracy. Hence Stalin's argument that the achievements of October 1917 had to be protected as an example to the world was used to justify the subordination of struggles in other countries to the requirements of Soviet foreign policy. This expediency, Trotsky observed, had caused Stalin to 'turn the Bolshevik strategy on its head' and force the Spanish Revolution at gunpoint back into the bourgeois stage it ought never to have left.[210] Just as in China, so the Comintern's actions in Spain rested upon the theoretical quicksand of stagism. Trotsky argued that the Spanish Revolution 'refutes once again and once and for all the old Menshevik theory, adopted by the Comintern, in accordance with which the democratic and socialist revolutions are transformed into two independent historic chapters, separated from each other in point of time. The work of the Moscow executioners confirms in its own way the correctness of the theory of permanent revolution'.[211] While this is a good example of the consistency of Trotsky's application of his version of a Marxist theory of revolution, it is far from an adequate assessment of the role of the Soviet Union in Spain's Revolution and Civil War. It is useful in helping us understand the theoretical contortions of Soviet Marxism in the 1930s, but rather less so in revealing Stalin's motivations and intentions and the degree to which he was actually able to shape events – the latter being something Trotsky often overestimated.

---

209   Trotsky 1970b, p. 61.
210   Trotsky 1973a, p. 323.
211   Trotsky 1973a, p. 314. Trotsky's view finds support from E.H. Carr, who writes: 'The issue of the subordination of the Comintern to the interests of Soviet foreign policy was ever present in Spain' (Carr 1984, p. 85).

# CHAPTER 3

# Revolutionary Marxists in Spain, 1930–1934

In his survey of Western Marxism, Perry Anderson observes that, despite having the most revolutionary proletariat in 1930s Europe, Spain did not produce 'any significant Marxist theory as such in this period'.[1] The following chapters of this study represent an attempt to revise this general statement. While Anderson may be correct to note that Spain did not produce a Labriola or a Gramsci, it is wrong to think that the Spanish labour movement was totally devoid of talented theorists with considerable influence. However, one would indeed struggle to find very much in the way of theoretical sophistication among the ranks of Spain's Socialist or official Communist parties. The Socialists (PSOE) subscribed to a brand of Marxism which was, in the words of a major study, 'rigid, schematic and derivative, bearing little obvious relation to the socio-economic or political situation in Spain'.[2] As for the Communists in the PCE, their adherence to the Moscow line progressively alienated most of the intellectuals who had been drawn to communist ideas through the Bolshevik example. Yet, among those intellectuals and militants who dissented from official Communist orthodoxy, we do find a handful of individuals whose political thought in the 1920s and 1930s does constitute a vibrant and sophisticated school of revolutionary Marxism. While not all considered themselves followers of Trotsky, they were nevertheless united by a common conviction that the Spanish Revolution would be a socialist revolution and would not be prefaced by a separate bourgeois stage. The following chapters advance the thesis that their analysis, based upon solid theoretical and historical foundations, set them apart from all other currents of Spanish Marxism and shaped their political actions during the Spanish Revolution.

The two individuals who came to lead and influence Spanish dissident communism were Joaquín Maurín and Andreu Nin. Since we are primarily concerned with an understanding of their political thought, what follows is not a study of the political organisations in which they were involved. However, some reference to the groups that fused in September 1935 to create the POUM is vital, as well as to their relations with international organisations. It should be said that the communist groupings with which Nin and Maurín were originally involved arose in response to distinct political situations and

---

1  Anderson 1979, p. 28.
2  Heywood 1990, p. 1.

were subject to different political influences. But it is hard to disentangle the political thought of their key figures; indeed, fusion occurred within the context of a dialogue between the two leaderships. With this in mind, the material has been divided in the following manner. The present chapter looks at the evolution of Maurín's and Nin's political thought up until 1935. It focuses upon their characterisations of Spanish historical development and the nature of the revolution they believed to be imminent. Chapter Four examines their analyses of the Spanish workers' movement, the dangers of fascism in Spain, attempts to build a united front and the question of 'entryism' which confronted both Nin and Maurín. Chapter Five considers their joint attempts to solve the problem of revolutionary organisation and 'Marxist unity' through the creation of the POUM. Chapter Six situates the POUM within debates around the Popular Front up to and including the early phases of the civil war. Finally, in Chapter Seven, we examine the POUM's political response to the revolutionary events of 1936 and 1937.

To begin with, it is important to look at the particular conceptions of revolutionary Marxism Nin and Maurín held. It is worth considering how far their interpretations of Spanish development and the revolutionary process drew upon, coincided with, diverged from, extended or corrected Trotsky's perspective. Why did Nin and Maurín reach rather different political conclusions to Trotsky's?

## 3.1      From Socialism and Syndicalism to Revolutionary Marxism

In order to understand the particular forms of Marxism Nin and Maurín had adopted by the early 1930s, it is important to sketch out their early political biographies briefly. Both came from Catalan-speaking areas: Nin from El Vendrell in Cataluña and Maurín from Bonansa in the province of Huesca (Aragón). Virtual contemporaries in age, they both became teachers and journalists by profession and were both involved in different ways in the intense militancy of the period from 1917 to 1923. During these years, Barcelona especially experienced violent social, political and industrial conflicts that had profound effects upon both men's political formation.

Nin had been politically active since 1910 as a member of the Catalan Republican movement, the Unió Federal Nacionalista Republicana, and in the PSOE's Federación Socialista Catalana. Between 1911 and 1919 he wrote for the Catalan-language periodicals *El Poble Català* and *La Publicitat* and taught in workers' schools in Barcelona. His belief in the inextricable links between the struggle for national emancipation and the struggle for socialism, together with his experience of the August 1917 general strike, led him toward the syndicalists. He officially broke ties with the PSOE in 1919 and, in the same year, participated in the CNT congress, at which he defended the Russian Revolution and advocated for the CNT's affiliation to the Third International. Nin became CNT Secretary General early in 1921 and represented the National Committee as part of the CNT delegation to the founding congress of the International Red Union (Profintern) in Moscow in July 1921. He remained in the USSR for the rest of the decade, marrying a Russian, joining the Soviet Communist Party (CPSU) and working for the Profintern. Nin's trade union activities required him to travel to Germany, France and Italy, which helped him develop a sophisticated and detailed understanding of the European political landscape at a critical moment. Now a committed Communist, Nin felt bound to take sides in the power struggle following Lenin's death. While his sympathies were initially with Bukharin, after 1926 he aligned himself with the platform of the Left Opposition. After being excluded from his trade union work and increasingly isolated and treated with suspicion by the Soviet authorities, Nin was finally expelled in 1930. Despite their political closeness, there is no evidence to suggest, as some more general works on the Spanish Civil War often do, that Nin was ever Trotsky's secretary. Indeed, Nin was not highly active in the Left Opposition at this time; he was making ends meet by translating Dostoyevsky, Lenin and Trotsky into Spanish and Catalan. His relationship with Trotsky might be described as one of political co-operation and personal friendship.[3]

Maurín's politics also evolved from an early mixture of Catalan nationalism, socialist pragmatism and what he described as the 'combative revolutionary spirit' of anarcho-syndicalism.[4] As a student and teacher in Lérida, Maurín became involved with the pro-republican Catalan-language paper *El Ideal*. He was attracted to revolutionary syndicalism and became active in the local Syndicalist Federation, wrote articles for its weekly paper *Lucha Social*, and directed the Lérida workers' school. He participated in the 1919 CNT congress and, like Nin, represented Cataluña as part of the 1921 delegation to the founding of the Profintern. Maurín later remembered being very impressed by Lenin as a strategist and Trotsky as an orator.[5] However, he never completely

---

3  The statement that Nin had once been Trotsky's secretary crops up time and again in English-language histories. Recent examples include Graham 2005, p. 65, and Casanova 2010, p. 267. For a definitive summary of Nin's period in the USSR, his political and literary activities and his relationship with the Left Opposition, see Pagès 2011, pp. 155–79.

4  Maurín, cited in Alba and Schwartz 1988, p. 6.

5  Joaquín Maurín, 'Sobre el comunismo en España'. Appendix to Maurín 1966, p. 255 and pp. 258–9.

abandoned his somewhat eclectic approach to politics in favour of an orthodox Leninist position.

Upon his return to Barcelona, Maurín became secretary of the CNT National
Committee, but he was arrested in February 1922. His removal from the scene
allowed the more purely anarchist-minded elements to gain control of the
Committee. They demonstrated their hostility toward the Russian Revolution
by securing an end to the CNT's provisional affiliation to the Profintern. Maurín
objected to the irregular manner in which this decision had been taken and
insisted that only a full national congress could reverse the original affiliation.
He participated in an oppositional grouping, the Comités Sindicalistas
Revolucionarios (Revolutionary Trade Union Committees, CSR), which stood
against the influence of anarchist tendencies in the CNT and promoted a fusion
of Bolshevism and libertarian communism.[6] Forced underground by the Primo
dictatorship's ban on union meetings, Maurín and other CSR militants decided
to join the Catalan Federation of the Communist Party (PCE), the Federación
Comunista Catalano-Balear (FCCB).[7] It is significant that, while Maurín
became a member of the PCE Executive Committee, neither he nor the other
FCCB members wholly accepted the political line emanating from Moscow,
particularly that of the 'third period'.[8] They did not, however, wish to split the
weak Spanish communist movement at a time (the late 1920s) when the Left
was under constant attack. By 1930, though, the FCCB had effectively ceased to
function within the PCE and was seeking links with communist groupings out-

---

6   The CSR paper, *La Batalla*, first appeared in December 1922 and was edited by Maurín. The
    new CNT leadership withdrew provisional affiliation to the Profintern, which meant Nin now
    only represented the CSR in Moscow, not the CNT.

7   According to Alba and Schwartz, the FCCB had about thirty members (Alba and Schwartz
    1988, p. 11). In fact, the CSR probably had more members than the PCE as a whole.

8   Maurín was arrested again early in 1925. On his release from prison in late 1927, he went to
    France, where he worked as a correspondent for the Soviet news agency Tass. The PCE leader-
    ship, which was also in exile in Paris, had taken Stalin's side in the power struggle within the
    USSR. Maurín, increasingly unhappy with the leadership and politics of the PCE and
    Comintern, concluded after the announcement of the 'social fascist' line that, in its current
    form, the party could play no part in the Spanish Revolution. He opposed the new PCE lead-
    ership's submission to Moscow's dictates, a situation he called 'revolutionary colonialism'.
    Although some of his comrades in the FCCB left to join the Partit Comunista Català (PCC) in
    1928, Maurín still believed the PCE could be reformed. According to Alba, Maurín relin-
    quished this hope after the 1929 PCE congress adopted the slogan 'democratic dictatorship of
    workers and peasants'. He argued that the mission in Spain should not be to replace one
    dictatorship with another but to struggle first for democratic freedoms. He also criticised the
    PCE for ignoring the Catalan question, which he felt was of fundamental importance for the
    revolution (Alba 1975, pp. 111–12).

side of the official party. Given their close friendship and previous political collaborations, it is not surprising that one of these groups was the one to which Nin belonged, the newly formed Spanish Left Opposition.[9]

### Dissident Communist Organisations

The Spanish national section of the International Left Opposition emerged during 1930 and 1931.[10] Upon his arrival in Cataluña in September 1930, Nin began to collaborate with Maurín in the interest of political unity. Maurín's FCCB was in the process of uniting with the larger Partit Comunista Català (PCC).[11] Nin now cooperated with the resulting new organisation, the Bloc Obrer i Camperol (BOC), writing for its publications *La Batalla* and *L'Hora*. His letters to Trotsky during this period reveal that, up until June 1931, Nin

---

9    See the detailed analysis of Nin and Maurín's correspondence between 1928 and 1930 in Pagès 2011, pp. 166–75.

10    The key individuals were Juan Andrade, Loredo Aparicio and García Palacios. They were initially able to gain considerable support among certain regional PCE Federations such as Bilbao and Valencia. The persecution of Trotsky and his co-thinkers was by no means universally understood and supported among Communists who remained loyal to the Moscow line. As for those who faltered in their acceptance of Moscow's orders, it seems that, in the end, the attraction of the October Revolution and the Communist International was strong enough to pull them back into line. The PCE took a long time to realise the significance of the power struggle in Russia. Its organ, *La Antorcha*, continued to publish Trotsky's articles; only in December 1927 did it adopt the official Stalinist critique of the Left Opposition (Pagès 1977a, pp. 36–7).

    The Spanish Left Opposition was first organised in Paris by those involved with *La Vérité*, such as 'Lacroix' (Francisco García Lavid), and in Spain Andrade and 'Gorkín' (Julián Gómez). Its first paper, which appeared in 1929, was *Contra la corriente*; its first congress was held in Belgium in February 1930. However, it was April 1931 before a properly organised Left Opposition section got going in Madrid. In Cataluña, it had no support until Nin's return. Even then, it was not organised until well after the Republic had been proclaimed in April 1931. Elsewhere, it is hard to say at what moment the Opposition became a definite organisation. It tended to emerge as individuals were expelled from the PCE. The break with the PCE was a slow and painful experience for many, especially those who had been among its founding members (Pagès 1977a, p. 48).

11    The PCC was, with 250 members, the largest independent communist party. It was set up in Lérida in 1928 by dissident communists such as Víctor Colomer, Joan Farré and Jordi Arquer who saw no potential for reforming the PCE from within. Its journal *Treball* (Labour), published in Barcelona, was retained by pro-PCE elements that rejoined the PCE in 1931 and later became very pro-Moscow.

    The BOC collaborated with other independent communists to produce one of the few serious theoretical journals available on the Spanish Left. *La Nueva Era* was founded in Paris in 1930 by the *La Batalla* group and moved to Barcelona after the fall of Primo.

combined building the Spanish Left Opposition with attempts to 'enter' the
FCCB-BOC, as it was initially called, though without success.[12] Nin was unconvinced that Trotsky's strategy of reforming the Communist Parties was appropriate for Spain because of the PCE's weakness and lack of influence in the
workers' movement. He predicted that the revolutionary party would be
formed outside of the official party.[13] His strategy, at least with regard to

---

12 Letters of 17 January, 7 March, 4 April, 12 April, 25 June and 29 June 1931, in Trotsky 1973a,
pp. 371, 373, 374, 375 and 376. Initially, Nin believed Maurín could be won over to the Left
Opposition. (See his letter to Trotsky, 12 November 1930, in Trotsky 1973a, p. 371.) In spite
of being expelled by the PCE leadership and, in July 1931, by the Comintern for 'Trotskyism',
Maurín in fact never actively supported Trotsky against Stalin; he merely refused to condemn Trotsky. As he pointed out in his letter to the Comintern Secretariat, the Trotskyist
organ *La Vérité* had been highly critical of him (letter of 8 July 1930, published in
*International Correspondence*, No. 65, 22 July 1931, p. 812, cited in Broué 1977, p. 157).
Lacroix's accusations, published in *La Vérité*, of 'political tight-rope walking', 'bureaucra-
tism' and being a potential recruit to Stalinism may well have influenced Trotsky and
contributed to his very poor opinion of Maurín. See Trotsky's letters to Nin, collected in
Trotsky 1973a. On Lacroix, see Pagès 1977a, pp. 45–6.

   Throughout March and April, Nin continued to assure Trotsky that he would soon be
admitted to the FCCB and warned against attacking it. In March, Nin wrote of the proba-
bility of his candidacy for the BOC in the April municipal elections (Letter to Trotsky,
13 March 1931, in Trotsky 1973a). Nin was not accepted as a candidate due to Maurín's
fears that it would wreck relations with the Comintern. In his letter of 4 April, Nin noted
that his Left Oppositionist propaganda had provoked a rupture with the leadership,
although not with the rank and file (Trotsky 1973a, p. 374). Eleven days later, he said that
the FCCB had invited him to join its Central Committee (Letter of 15 April 1931, in Trotsky
1973a, p. 375).

   As noted in Chapter Two, most of the Trotsky-Nin correspondence was stolen in Paris
by Soviet agents, along with some of Trotsky's other archives, on 6 November 1936. The
reasons for the theft remain unclear, since the stolen documents were not used against
Trotsky, Nin or the POUM (see Reed and Jakobson 1987, pp. 363–75). According to Trotsky,
the correspondence was substantial. In a letter to Victor Serge, he remarked: 'I think that
my letters to Nin over a period of two or three years would make up a volume of several
hundred pages: that should indicate how important I regarded Nin and friendly relations
with him' (3 June 1936, Trotsky 1973a, p. 215). Trotsky published an edited and highly selec-
tive version of the Nin letters in 1933 in an attempt to help the Spanish Left Opposition
clear up what he saw as major obstacles to its development. This means that the only
known surviving letters are those Trotsky selected and edited himself. We should therefore be alert to the fact that Trotsky had a political reason for making them public that
had to do with internal disputes within the International Left Opposition and his growing
dissatisfaction with Nin. Care should thus be exercised when attempting to judge Nin's
actual views from such fragmentary evidence.

13 Letters to Trotsky, 3 December 1930 and 17 January 1931, in Trotsky 1973a, pp. 371–2.

Cataluña, was to work as closely as possible with Maurín and to disseminate the ideas of the Left Opposition among those who would be most receptive to them. Unfortunately, relations with the FCCB-BOC frequently broke down and by June 1931 Nin had become highly critical of its political stance.[14] After this rupture, Nin turned his attention toward building the Spanish Left Opposition and shaping its political programme.

While Trotsky initially supported Nin's joint work with the FCCB-BOC, he increasingly felt that the priority should be to build the Left Opposition in Spain. Nin's contention that the Spanish workers lacked even a rudimentary knowledge of communism should not, Trotsky argued, prevent him from putting the Left Opposition's platform forward.[15] By posing the political problems of the Revolution, the opposition could rapidly gain a leading position in the revolutionary movement.[16] The FCCB appeared to Trotsky as a provincial grouping which could be credible only as part of a broader national revolutionary movement. He felt that the PCE's historical connections to the Russian Revolution and, through the Comintern, to struggles in other countries made it the party to work in, regardless of its current weak leadership and lack of influence.[17] Hence the task in Spain, Trotsky insisted, was to promote the unity of the communist movement around an agreed-upon programme and to seek a united front with the advanced CNT and PSOE militants. 'Nobody outside of the Left Opposition', he wrote to Nin, 'is capable of giving a correct orientation nor of laying down a proper policy in the revolutionary conditions in Spain'.[18] Yet, as Trotsky himself lamented, the Left Opposition had yet to get off the ground in Spain.

This brief summary of the position of the various groups of dissident communists at the close of the Restoration monarchy and the beginning of the Republican period in Spain (1930–1) is intended to provide a context within which to view the political thought of Nin and Maurín. As the most influential contributors to the strategy and tactics of their respective organisations, their thinking underwent important changes during the course of the Revolution. Hence it is useful to begin by outlining the historical and theoretical foundations of their approaches to the problems of the Revolution. Given that both Nin and Maurín were profoundly influenced by the Bolsheviks' achievements, it is interesting to consider what comparisons and lessons they drew out of the

---

14      Letters to Trotsky of 25 June, 29 June and 13 July 1931, in Trotsky 1973a, p. 376.

15      Trotsky to Nin, 29 November 1930, in Trotsky 1973a, p. 383.

16      Trotsky to Nin, 12 December 1930, in Trotsky 1973a, p. 383.

17      Trotsky to Nin, 31 January 1931, in Trotsky 1973a, p. 384.

18      Trotsky to Nin, 29 March 1931, in Trotsky 1973a, p. 387.

Russian experience and applied to Spain. To what extent did their analyses approximate or conflict with those of Trotsky? We start with Nin's perception of Spanish development and the nature of the coming Revolution.

## 3.2    Nin and the Problems of the Spanish Revolution

During his nine years in the Soviet Union, Nin assimilated the method and theory of a Marxism that relied heavily upon Lenin's political and intellectual legacy. In his important study of Nin's political thought, Pelai Pagès stresses that Nin's contribution to Marxism stemmed from developing certain key issues in the thought of Marx, Lenin and Trotsky rather than any theoretical originality of his own.[19] Stalin's official adoption of the theory of 'socialism in one country' certainly provoked Nin to align with the Left Opposition in 1926 and tends to suggest that he implicitly accepted the theory of permanent revolution.[20] However, the unsystematic and diverse nature of Nin's writings leads us to examine the broad perspective of his thought if we wish to detect the influence of notions of uneven and combined development and permanent revolution. Later chapters deal with other aspects of his Marxism, but, here, we will focus upon his view of Spain's backwardness and the immediate political situation he faced upon his return in 1930 and up to the early phase of the Republican period.

Nin's understanding of Spain's economic and political backwardness certainly appears to be informed by a mode of analysis similar to the one Trotsky employed in his characterisation of Russian development.[21] Nin had no doubt that Spain was capitalist. However, his references to the overwhelming weight of Spain's very backward agriculture, compared with its small-scale, dispersed and unevenly developed industry, suggest that he considered Spain somewhat less developed than Trotsky did.

---

19    Pagès 1975, p. 276.

20    According to Pagès, Nin's shift to the Left Opposition may well have occurred in May 1926 as a reaction to the Anglo-Russian Committee abandoning the British General Strike in favour of 'defending the USSR'. Given Nin's close connection with syndical matters, this would seem a reasonable supposition (Pagès 1975, p. 125).

21    In 1931 Nin translated Trotsky's *History of the Russian Revolution* and *Permanent Revolution* into Spanish. See the list of Nin's translations in Pagès 1975, p. 334.

Spain is a largely agrarian country. Seventy per cent of the working population work on the land. In the Spanish economy, the specific gravity of
agrarian production is greater than that of industry. Technology is
extremely primitive . . . A notable feature of our agrarian economy is the
dominance, especially in the south, of large semi-feudal property. This is
characterised by vast estates, either poorly cultivated or absolutely uncul-
tivated, and a miserable and cruelly exploited mass of peasants. All of
this stamps the agriculture of our country with the mark of evident backwardness; a backwardness which determines the impoverishment of the
countryside and the diminution of the purchasing power of the great
majority of peasants and rural workers. This lessens, in turn, the chances
of industrial development.[22]

Agrarian property and social relations, he argued, tended to be semi-feudal not
only on the *latifundios* dominating southern Spain, but also in areas of small-
and medium-scale land ownership.[23]

But much of Nin's characterisation of Spain's backwardness agrees with and
is influenced by Trotsky's formulations.[24] Rural poverty and the technical
backwardness of farming had severely limited the prospects for industrial
development. What industry there was, Nin remarked, had scarcely emerged
from the Industrial Revolution and rarely came close to the industries found in
advanced capitalist countries. With important exceptions, such as iron and
steel in the Basque Country, key industries (such as textiles) were characterised by small unit sizes and low levels of technology. Although the textile
industry employed more than a hundred thousand workers, they were still
using hand looms.[25] New industries such as artificial silk had recently sprung
up, but these were mainly foreign-owned and had not significantly modified

---

22   'El proletariado español ante la revolución', late 1931, in Nin 1971, pp. 45–6.

23   Nin 1971, p. 46. Nin referred to the persistence of many feudal practices such as *aparecías*,
     in which the landowner provided part or all of the capital and land in return for some of
     the product of the harvest; *rabassa morta*, under which the vine growers in Cataluña
     (*rabassaires*) rented their land for the lifetime of the vine; *foros*, a hereditary lease with a
     fixed ground rent; and *arriendos*, leasing to tenant farmers.

24   Nin had translated Trotsky's little book *Mis peripecias en España* about his 1916 'stay' in
     Spain (Trotsky 1975a). Trotsky had also been corresponding with the Spanish Left
     Opposition and writing articles on the situation in Spain since the middle of 1930. Hence
     Nin had ample opportunity to absorb Trotsky's general approach.

25   Nin 1971, p. 46. See also: Nin, '¿Por qué nuestro movimiento obrero ha sido anarquista?',
     *L'Opinió*, 11 August 1928, in Nin 1978a, p. 25.

the basic picture of backwardness. Since Spanish capitalists preferred speculation to consolidation and diversification, the opportunities offered by neutrality during the first world war had been wasted. Any foreign markets acquired
were subsequently lost; even the domestic market contracted.[26]

Nin believed that the main obstacle to capitalist development had been
posed by the political regimes cloaked by the Restoration monarchy and its
supporters. As he put it:

> The country's economic structure found its political expression in the
> monarchy which was supported by the *caciquismo* of the large landown-
> ers, in the Church which possessed – and still does – a powerful economic
> base, in an enormous military, bureaucratic and police apparatus and in
> a despotic and regressive centralism which stifles all the vital forces of
> the country. This political and economic régime constituted an insuper-
> able obstacle to the development of the country's productive forces.[27]

As in Russia, a unified and centralised state was imposed from above before
capitalism had a chance to develop. In other words, the formation of the
national state had not been a consequence of capitalist development.
The Spanish absolutist state was thus characterised by the nationalist aspirations of those regions whose more dynamic economic potential was stifled by
the backwardness of a politically dominant centre (Madrid).[28] Under these
conditions, a weak national bourgeoisie had been unable to resolve the basic
problems of the bourgeois revolution. Power therefore remained in the hands
of a large landowning oligarchy that was intimately connected to the industrial
bourgeoisie through banking capital.[29]

Nin was sharply critical of the official Communist perspective, which held
that the *latifundios* and all the feudal vestiges they contained rested squarely
upon the institution of the monarchy. They thought that, if they supported the
bourgeois Republicans in destroying the monarchy, all obstacles to capitalist
development would be swept away. Yet, in reality, Nin argued, it was the king
who rested upon the large landowners, not vice versa. He considered the *latifundios* to be woven into the fabric of Spanish capitalism because they represented the practical form in which capitalism had been able to exploit the land

---

26    'El proletariado español ante la revolución', in Nin 1971, pp. 46–7.

27    Nin 1971, p. 47.

28    Nin 1971, p. 64.

29    'A propósito de la declaración política del C.E. del PCE', *La Batalla*, 5 March 1931, in Nin
       1978a, p. 69.

in such a backward country.[30] This evidently draws heavily upon Trotsky's 25 May 1930 letter to *Contra la corriente*.[31] Nin reiterates Trotsky's analysis of the way in which precapitalist forms of property and social relations had been harnessed to the capitalist mode of production. This analysis suggests that not only was Spanish development uneven, with both archaic and modern forms of property and social relations, but that these forms had combined with each other. The result was that the bourgeoisie could not simply throw off the precapitalist vestiges that held back dynamic capitalist development, because to do so would entail rejecting the hybrid form of capitalism in which many of them were involved.

Primo's dictatorship, Nin continued, represented an attempt on the part of the bourgeoisie and the most powerful feudal forces to confront the contradictions of Spain's combined and uneven development. Yet it had offered no solution to what Nin called Spain's 'permanent economic crisis'. This was down to the fact that the régime was itself a mass of contradictions. Hence the dictatorship attempted to satisfy the demands of both agrarian and industrial interests. It initially relaxed tariff barriers to encourage the import of foreign industrial goods. This satisfied agrarian interests. However, Primo later pursued a highly protectionist policy in order to win favour with the industrial bourgeoisie. He also followed a policy supportive of those interests closely linked to international finance capital. It was therefore not surprising that Primo managed to antagonise most sections of the ruling classes, especially the industrial bourgeoisie. He even alienated his most solid supporters, the army. In wider society, unemployment and rising prices fuelled the resentment of the workers, peasants and urban petit-bourgeoisie. As Nin later reflected, the dictatorship finally collapsed under the weight of its own contradictions.[32]

Much earlier, Nin had noted that the political situation immediately after Primo's departure in January 1930 was such that neither the industrial bourgeoisie nor the working class had been able to assume power. Hence, two outcomes to the ongoing crisis were possible. The first, and least likely, was that a new Constituent Cortes would be convened. This presupposed a mass mobilisation of workers and peasants to overthrow the monarchy. Yet, even the more progressive bourgeois elements feared losing control during a full-scale revolution. The second scenario, and in his estimation of early 1930 the most probable one, was a pseudo-constitutional agreement between elements of the old

---

30    Nin 1978a, p. 70.
31    In Trotsky 1973a, pp. 57–63.
32    Nin 1971, pp. 45–6.

régime, the oligarchy and the big bourgeoisie. Nin thought the PSOE might even play a part in this arrangement. Such an outcome could work to the advantage of the revolutionary movement, since it would permit a degree of political freedom within which the working class could organise itself. The depth of the economic and political crisis suggested that the question of power would soon resurface and that the Communists had to prepare for this.[33] Nin's forecast was to some extent confirmed by the events of 1930 and 1931. General Berenguer and Admiral Aznar indeed formed temporary semi-constitutional governments, but these failed to resolve the political and economic crisis. However, Nin's anticipation that this crisis would turn into a revolutionary situation in which the working class could take power proved to hit wide of the mark.

Commenting in hindsight upon the actual events of 1931, Nin maintained that the objective conditions for proletarian revolution had indeed existed since the end of the dictatorship. He thought that the reason why a revolutionary situation had not materialised was the disorganisation and ideological disorientation of the working class and the absence of a strong Communist party. In other words, the subjective conditions were not sufficiently mature to make a revolutionary bid possible.[34] The monarchy fell, he argued, because it had outlived its usefulness to the more far-sighted bourgeoisie and big landowners, not because of any revolutionary action on the part of the working class. April 1931, when the Republic was proclaimed, did not constitute a 'democratic revolution' because the new régime actually served to strengthen existing property relations. Indeed, many of the semi-feudal elements were represented in the newly formed provisional government.[35] This was indeed quite literally the case. The prime minister, Niceto Alcalá-Zamora, and his interior minister, Miguel Maura, were both Catholic-traditionalist politicians who had 'converted' to Republicanism overnight in order to save those interests the monarchy could no longer defend and to avert the prospect of proletarian revolution. Thus, Nin argued, it was totally false to see the change to a republic as a revolution in any meaningful sense of the word.

---

33    'La crise de la dictadure militaire en Espagne', *La Lutte de Classes*, January 1930, reproduced as 'La crisis de la dictadura militar', in Nin 1978b, p. 26. See also Nin's letter to Maurín, 4 January 1930, in Pagès 1982b, p. 38.
34    Nin 1971, p. 49.
35    Nin 1971, p. 54.

> The events of 14 April have not at all altered the economic base of the
> régime, so it follows that there has been no revolution. As if to dispel any
> doubt about it, the Provisional Government, in its first semi-official dec-
> laration, published two days after the fall of the Monarchy, solemnly pro-
> claimed the inviolability of property rights.[36]

The real significance of the coming of the Republic, Nin insisted, lay in the
destruction of a key feudal vestige, the monarchy, whose restoration in 1874
had brought the nineteenth-century bourgeois revolution to an abrupt halt.

Nin thought it was a shame that the workers' movement's disorganisation,
confusion and disunity had prevented it from offering revolutionary leadership to the workers at the moment of the monarchy's collapse. Yet the Spanish
proletariat had become obsessed by the notion that the monarchy was responsible for all its ills. Exploiting popular illusions about the advantages of a democratic republic, the Socialists had openly collaborated with the bourgeois
Republicans. For their part, the anarcho-syndicalists had also been deceived by
democratic delusions and had abandoned their political independence and
radical edge in order to support the Republican movement.[37]

Commenting upon the nature of the Second Republic, Nin explained
that during the Restoration monarchy, only a section of the dominant classes
had really held political power, though, after 14 April, the entire bourgeoisie
had claimed to rule in the name of the people. It was clear that any attacks
upon the privileges of the bourgeoisie and large landowners would be presented as an attack upon the Republic – and therefore upon the entire nation.
Nin predicted that the bourgeoisie was now preparing itself for an assault
against the revolutionary elements among the proletariat. He suggested that,
in order to discredit the revolutionary communists in the eyes of the masses,
the bourgeoisie would accuse them of combining with the extreme Right
in the same way that the Russian provisional government had accused the
Bolsheviks of being German agents.[38] Hence, Nin anticipated not only a political struggle to win leadership of the advanced working class in Spain, but that
this struggle would be made more urgent by the likelihood of a fresh assault
upon the workers' movement. This perspective was informed by his already

---

36    Ibid.

37    Nin 1971, p. 55.

38    Nin 1971, p. 56. This was precisely the allegation levelled at Nin and the POUM in early 1937
      by the official Communists, Soviet agents and some Republican elements: namely, that
      they were agents of Germany.

fairly sophisticated analysis of European fascism, an aspect of his Marxism considered in the following chapter.

The first six months of the Republic confirmed Nin's belief that the key issues of the democratic revolution would not be seriously confronted by a government whose principal aims were, first, to protect the very same economic interests that had supported the monarchy and, second, to avoid a popular uprising by the masses whose expectations had been aroused. Such a government would never attack the rights of the large landowners, he argued. Nor would it permit the Catalan people to exercise their right of self-determination. Nin even doubted the extent to which it would reduce the power of the Church. Here it might be noted that Nin, like Trotsky, rather underestimated the political importance of petty-bourgeois politicians in the 1931–3 government and the genuine commitment of figures such as Manuel Azaña to radical reforms. However, Nin drew attention to the petty-bourgeois character of the Catalan Generalitat. For him, this simply meant that the Catalan regional government would express the characteristic vacillations of this class, reflecting its lack of political independence and its tendency to follow the leadership either of the bourgeoisie or the proletariat. In practice, the first three years of the Republic witnessed a partial attempt to resolve certain democratic tasks (the land, church and national questions), but the resistance to its reforms demonstrated the intransigence and conservatism of those holding real economic and political power. Nin was, however, proved correct in predicting that the Republicans would leave intact the bureaucratic and repressive apparatus of the old régime and use it to suppress worker and peasant protest.[39]

At this point (mid- to late 1931), Nin emphasised the similarities between the Spanish situation and that of Russia in 1917 with greater force even than Trotsky. Both countries, he noted, possessed burning national questions that would not be addressed by their despotic and absolutist states. Neither country had witnessed the completion of a bourgeois revolution along the lines of those experienced by the advanced capitalist countries. Their bourgeoisies were weak, conservative and incapable of resolving the basic obstacles to full modernity. Upon the fall of the Tsar in February 1917, the Russian bourgeoisie had taken fright at the prospect of a deeper social revolution and had assumed power itself in order to prevent this from happening. The same had occurred in Spain in April 1931. Nin nonetheless recognised key differences in the two situations. Apart from the fact that Spain was not at war, he identified two crucial factors that favoured the Russian proletariat and that were not present in the Spanish

---

39      Nin 1971, p. 58.

case. First, the Russian proletariat had been able to count upon the soviets as organs of dual power. Second, in Russia there existed a revolutionary party, the Bolsheviks, with a clear view of the dynamics of the Revolution and the actions that needed to be taken. Only the Bolsheviks realised that there could be no solving the tasks of the bourgeois-democratic revolution under the hegemony of the bourgeois provisional government. Lenin had pointed out that the middle road the petty-bourgeois Mensheviks and Social Revolutionaries advocated was a dangerous illusion. This path would lead to the forces of counterrevolution crushing the Revolution. Nin recalled the situation in China between 1925 and 1927, in which the Communists had followed the Comintern's advice and collaborated with the bourgeois nationalists. The latter had taken advantage of this alliance to turn and massacre the revolutionary workers and peasants.[40]

In the light of historical experience, Nin concluded, it was vital for the Spanish proletariat to break with the fiction of bourgeois democracy and 'struggle for the true democratic revolution, which implies the struggle against the bourgeoisie'.[41] He noted that the failure of the Republican government to address popular demands had begun to erode many of the illusions the workers and petty-bourgeoisie had initially entertained about the new democracy. The impact of the world economic crisis deepened this domestic discontent. The absence of an indispensable ingredient for revolution, a strong revolutionary party, did not diminish Nin's belief that Spain would witness a permanent revolution:

> In Spain, history has furnished the working class with a magnificent chance to attack the bourgeois régime, perform the democratic revolution which the bourgeoisie is unable to carry through and begin the period of socialist achievements.[42]

However, he was well aware that the bourgeoisie was highly unlikely to permit the peaceful development of the workers' organisations. As he noted:

---

40    Nin 1971, pp. 64–8.

41    Nin 1971, p. 68.

42    Nin, 'El deber del momento', *El Soviet*, 15 October 1931, in Nin 1978a, p. 124. Nin had already affirmed that 'the democratic revolution can only be the work of the working class which, at the head of all the exploited and oppressed masses of the countryside and the city – peasants, petty-bourgeois – will destroy all the feudal remnants and embark upon the path towards socialist objectives'. 'La revolución democrática y el bolchevismo', *L'Hora*, 21 January 1931, in Nin 1978a, p. 55.

The coming period is not, then, a period of peace but of fierce struggle. And in this struggle the fundamental interests and whole future of the working class will be at stake. The working class will be defeated if it cannot call upon the necessary weapons at the critical moment. It will win if it can count on these weapons, if it breaks all contact with bourgeois democracy, practises true class politics and knows how to take advantage of the opportune moment for making its bid for power.[43]

### 3.3    Maurín and the Problems of the Spanish Revolution

#### *Maurín on the Bourgeoisie*

In Maurín's explanation of the development and nature of Spanish capitalism we find a far more complete and detailed historical account than any furnished by Nin. Whereas Nin's extended writings of the 1930s, *Las dictaduras de nuestro tiempo* and *Los movimientos de emancipación nacional*, deal with key problems in Marxist theory, such as fascism, dictatorship and the national question, Maurín's three major works, *Los hombres de la dictadura*, *La revolución española* and *Hacia la segunda revolución*, focus specifically upon modern Spanish history and the problems facing the workers' movement in the early 1930s.

At the core of Maurín's historical account lies the familiar Marxist theme of the inability of the indigenous bourgeoisie to accomplish its 'historic mission'. This failure came in spite of the fact that at the end of the fifteenth and beginning of the sixteenth centuries, Spain had become a unified absolutist state of great economic and military power. Yet victory over the Moors had been achieved with the aid of that key bastion of feudalism, the Catholic Church, and the resulting bond between church and state ensured that the latter was a prisoner of the former and was not able to act as the transmission mechanism between feudal and bourgeois society. For Maurín, this was one of the prime causes of the weakness of the Spanish bourgeoisie and the persistence of feudalism.[44]

According to Maurín's analysis, the struggle of Spanish feudalism against the emerging bourgeoisie took on three forms: expulsion, emigration and extermination. The Arabs' expulsion from Spain in 1492 deprived the country of a potential agrarian bourgeoisie. The long 'crusade' against the Arabs all but wiped out the beginnings of a productive agrarian system, replacing it with large estates (*latifundios*) which proved spectacularly undynamic. By expelling

---

43   Nin 1971, p. 70.
44   Maurín 1977b, pp. 5–6.

the Jews, in the same year, Spain also lost much of its commercial bourgeoisie. As if to clear away any remaining bourgeois elements by means of terror, the Church and state set up the Inquisition. The War of the Communities (1520–2) offered the Church the opportunity to attack the urban bourgeoisie. Maurín argues that this conflict represented an unsuccessful attempt at a bourgeois revolution more than a century before the English Revolution. It failed, he says, because the Catalan bourgeoisie did not support their revolutionary cousins in Castilla. The victory of the monarchy, nobility and Church was followed by a period of repression which forced the most adventurous and enterprising bourgeois to seek their fortunes in the New World.[45]

However, the Spanish colonial conquest of the Americas proved yet another contributory factor to the bourgeoisie's failure to become hegemonic. It did not invest the enormous wealth secured in domestic modernisation but used it simply as a fund to provide Spanish feudalism with the material means to prolong its domination. Its natural development blocked at home by expulsion and persecution, the bourgeoisie was forced to carry out its 'historic role' by emigrating to the New World. As Maurín saw things:

> Without the Americas, the bourgeoisie would necessarily have developed within national frontiers and the inevitable clashes with feudalism would, by historical imperative, have given it victory as in the rest of Europe. From the outset, America was the escape valve.[46]

Under the influence of the American War of Independence and the French Revolution, and owing to the weakness of Spain itself, the expatriate bourgeoisie could later sever their colonial ties with metropolitan Spain and convert their adopted homelands into independent republics. Those who remained on the Iberian peninsula tended to concentrate in those areas which offered the best commercial prospects: the Atlantic seaboard of Portugal and the Mediterranean coast, especially Cataluña. This exacerbated the impetus for regional nationalism, Maurín argued.

Separatism, he noted, had also been the route taken by areas of Europe that had fallen under Spanish control: the Low Countries, Naples, Sicily and Portugal. Even Cataluña had attempted to break away in 1640. Maurín argued that Spain's European empire disintegrated because the feudal state constituted a brake on economic development.

---

45    Maurín 1977b, pp. 13–19.
46    Maurín 1977b, p. 12.

The decadence of the Hispanic feudal empire can be expressed by the history of separatism of those peoples it subjugated. Upon breaking the chains placed upon it by the empire, that portion of Europe which had been subjected to its domination brought about its own bourgeois revolution. In this struggle for secession, the bourgeoisie and the feudal state found themselves face to face. The battle between them was fierce, as is unavoidable when the class struggle reaches the peak of its intensity ... Separatism expressed the rebellion of the enslaved bourgeoisie which felt forced to distance itself from a state that no longer corresponded to its class conditions.[47]

The decisive point in the collapse of the feudal state came at the beginning of the nineteenth century, with the separation of Spain's American colonies. According to Maurín, this constituted the triumph of the émigré bourgeoisie in its revolution against the feudal metropolis. But in spite of the damage this did to the Spanish state, what remained of the national bourgeoisie was in very poor condition to challenge for political power. The Napoleonic invasion had signalled the beginning of the bourgeoisie's recognition of its historic mission to rid Spain of its feudal past and build a modern economy and society. The loss of the American colonies contributed to the decay of the autocracy; the period between 1808 and the late 1830s saw the national bourgeoisie strive, with the support of the working class, to overthrow the oligarchy of clerics, nobles and large landowners. Yet it lacked sufficient economic strength to prevail; in the following period, from 1840 to 1874, the military entered the political arena through a series of *pronunciamientos*. Although briefly victorious in the years between 1868 and 1874, the bourgeoisie subsequently abandoned its revolutionary aspirations in favour of collaboration with the oligarchy. Maurín saw this as a pragmatic response to the working class's newly discovered political independence.[48]

We can see, then, that, for Maurín, the old régime had come to rest upon a contradictory equilibrium of agrarian, financial and industrial interests. The large landowners of Castilla and Andalucía dominated this arrangement, with Galician interests acting as a cohesive factor within this ruling bloc. He believed that the remnants of Spanish feudalism had adapted to the political formula of the Restoration and could proclaim, like their Junker counterparts had in Prussia, that 'the monarchy can be constitutional as long as we can do

---

47    Maurín 1977b, pp. 23–4.
48    Maurín 1977b, pp. 30–4 and p. 67.

as we please'.[49] The political economy of the Restoration period was thus wholly geared toward maintaining the 'dictatorship' of large landed property. This was reinforced by the mechanism of *caciquismo*. Rather than invest their accumulated capital in industry and agricultural modernisation, the large landowners preferred to practise usury. Although Spain exported agricultural products, the lack of investment, low level of technology and strength of foreign competition held back industrial development. Yet the main obstacle to economic prosperity was the bourgeoisie's post-1874 collaboration with the ruling oligarchy.[50]

Maurín thus viewed what he saw as the contradiction between agrarian and industrial interests as the underlying structural determinant of current political events in Spain. The feudal oligarchy had obstructed the development of the productive forces because they realised this would reduce their own political, economic and social power. Yet the Spanish economy was already part of the world capitalist system; it required a government which would defend and promote its interests in the face of competition from the advanced industrial nations. While Spain exported wine, fruit and oil, it imported manufactured goods that competed with those produced domestically. If, on the other hand, protectionist barriers to industrial imports were raised, they would adversely affect exports of agrarian produce.

> This basic duality, this divergence between industrial capitalism and the agrarian interests is at the root of all the political events that have taken place in Spain for a long time. The coup of Primo de Rivera was the first violent outburst of that contradiction.[51]

He believed that unfettered industrialisation would have spelled the end of this situation. Yet it was not only the immediate interests of the large landowners that stood behind the monarchy: 'The monarchy was not only the government of the agrarians and of Spain's industrial backwardness, but also the true representative of foreign capitalism. The latter required a backward Spain with a rudimentary economy'. Mining and certain other industries were owned by foreign capital to such an extent that Spain constituted a 'semi-colony of the great imperialist powers'.[52] In other words, foreign capital had been exploiting

---

49    Maurín 1977b, p. 42; and Maurín 1977a, p. 78 and p. 80.
50    For a fuller explanation of this terminology and an account of the twists and turns of
      nineteenth-century Spain, see the historical essay in the Appendix.
51    Maurín 1977b, p. 58.
52    Maurín 1977b, p. 59.

Spain's natural resources and its market while, at the same time, sustaining the country's industrial backwardness. This analysis would seem to accord quite closely with that of Trotsky discussed in the previous chapter and may well have been influenced directly or indirectly by Trotsky's thoughts on Spanish development. Yet Maurín seems to have formulated his own analysis of the Catalan bourgeoisie.

Maurín notes that the wartime boom afforded to industry between 1914 and 1918 spurred the Catalan industrial bourgeoisie, represented by the Lliga Regionalista, into political action against the monarchy. But the Lliga's political vision was limited to Cataluña – and it was frightened by the revolutionary actions of the working class. Almost immediately, the bourgeoisie retreated to the safety of the old coalition with the agrarian interests. Yet the alliance broke down in 1921 and 1922 as the post-war economic crisis deepened and the crisis of the Restoration political system was intensified by military defeat in Morocco. It was at that point that Catalan industrial interests sought a solution over and above mere collaboration with agrarian interests. They welcomed the dictatorial régime of Primo de Rivera.[53] Primo offered the bourgeoisie a guarantee against the threat from organised labour, ensuring an alteration in the balance of forces between agrarian and industrial interests. Drawing upon Marx, Maurín described the dictatorship as a Bonapartist solution in which the state ruled on behalf of the dominant economic classes after they had proved unable to do so themselves. It confirmed the weakness of the national bourgeoisie and suggested a route to economic modernisation via an authoritarian state.

Hence he saw the 'economic nationalism' of the Primo dictatorship as a response to the contradictions of Spain's economic development. Yet Primo's government served to alienate foreign capitalists because it represented an attempt to break free of their tutelage and thus end its semi-colonial relationship with the advanced countries. And Spain could not avoid the effects of the world crisis which began in 1929. Falling exports of key agricultural products and the subsequent industrial and financial crises were major contributing factors to the crisis of the old régime. It demonstrated that '[d]ue to its history, Spain finds itself faced with the urgent need to widen its internal market, to increase its productive capacity. This poses the problem of an agrarian revolution, a general redistribution of land and a rapid process of industrialisation'.[54] Even some of the very agrarian forces that had formerly supported the monarchy now appreciated that the entire edifice of the old régime and the economic

---

53    Maurín 1977b, pp. 43–6.
54    Maurín 1977b, p. 66.

foundations upon which it rested stood in the way of economic progress. It was significant, Maurín thought, that the Republican movement of 1930 and 1931 had been headed by Alcalá-Zamora, a *latifundista* from Andalucía.

While an interesting analysis of the Spanish bourgeoisie, Maurín's characterisation seems to lack a crucial ingredient that is evident in Nin's much briefer account and that forms an integral aspect of Trotsky's law of uneven and combined development. Maurín certainly stresses the unevenness of capitalist development in Spain, but he does not suggest that there existed an intimate relationship between different fractions of the bourgeoisie and the landed oligarchy. Hence, the notion of a combination of interests seems to be missing here. Although he makes much of the collaboration between the industrial bourgeoisie and the landed oligarchy, he believes its *raison d'être* lay simply in its fear of the working class. Maurín has a tendency to see the bourgeoisie as having objective interests that are squarely counterposed to those of the ruling 'agrarian interests'. Yet the notion of *combined* development suggests a bourgeoisie composed of various fractions whose interests are often contradictory. Rather than a divergence between industry and agriculture, combined development implies a structural convergence of certain capitalist interests with precapitalist forms within an archaic social and political framework. It also admits the crucial contradiction between those bourgeois fractions that require a modern capitalist state and society and those whose power and interests are bound up with the old régime. Such a conception is arguably more nuanced and subtle than that of a simple opposition between old and new forces.

### 'Democratic-Socialist' or Permanent Revolution?

At this point, it is important to take account of Maurín's particular conception of revolution. All of his writings during the years 1930 to 1936 are underpinned by a belief that Spain was about to experience what he terms a 'democratic-socialist revolution'.[55] The precise meaning of this formula appears to have undergone an appreciable change during the course of the Revolution. According to Maurín's initial use of the term, the bourgeois-democratic

---

55  It should be noted that although Maurín often uses the terms 'democratic' and 'bourgeois' interchangeably, he also imbues the former with a far more progressive quality. He did not believe that the bourgeoisie could be democratic; he shared Nin and Trotsky's conviction that true democracy could only come about under socialism. He also considered democracy's bourgeois form a mere cover for the bourgeoisie's class dictatorship: 'Democracy and bourgeoisie are antithetical terms. The bourgeoisie – monarchist or republican – is anti-liberal, dictatorial, absolutist'. Maurín 1977b, p. 106.

revolution, which the bourgeoisie could not carry out, would be the work of a revolutionary bloc led by the proletariat but also including the peasantry and the national liberation movement. The Revolution would witness both the solution of bourgeois-democratic tasks and the commencement of the socialist revolution. In this sense it would be both democratic and socialist.

Leaving aside for the moment the presence of the national liberation movement in the formula, it is worth examining the notion of 'democratic-socialist revolution' from the perspective of permanent revolution. As we saw in Chapter One, for Trotsky, the crucial element for a permanentist conception rests upon the denial of a *separate* democratic phase and the assertion of the proletarian revolution as the precondition for a full and complete solution to the democratic tasks. These tasks are never completed with their bourgeois class content intact, but instead *combine* with those of a socialist nature after, and as an inevitable consequence of, the proletarian seizure of power.

Maurín's various statements on the issue are certainly ambiguous. The following suggest a permanentist view:

> The democratic revolution is inseparable from the socialist revolution.[56]
>
> The democratic revolution, which has been retarded by the bourgeoisie, will not succeed other than by the proletariat taking power. Moreover, when power passes to the working class there is no separation between the democratic revolution and the socialist revolution.[57]
>
> To make the democratic revolution means to say to move onto the socialist revolution. In Spain, the democratic revolution will remain smothered or will triumph with the help of the labouring classes. In this case, the socialist revolution will be its logical continuation.[58]

The problem arises from the fact that Maurín also suggested that the democratic and socialist revolutions were different phases, albeit of a single process:

> [W]hen the democratic revolution has been carried out, the socialist revolution will be a natural process ... In those countries where the bourgeois revolution was not made at the proper time, the interval between the bourgeois revolution and the socialist revolution is much reduced, as has been shown by Russia.[59]

---

56    Maurín 1977b, p. 170.

57    Maurín 1977b, p. 163.

58    Maurín 1977b, p. 187.

59    Maurín *La Batalla*, 26 March 1931, quoted in Monreal 1984, p. 92.

Elsewhere, he states that the democratic revolution would, as in Russia, be made against bourgeois opposition with the working class taking power 'so as to finish the democratic revolution and then pass onto the socialist revolution'.[60] In these passages, Maurín implies that the bourgeois-democratic revolution was still to be made and that the proletariat would accomplish it not as a substitute for the bourgeoisie, but as a prelude to its own revolution. He suggests an interval, although 'much reduced', between the completion of the bourgeois-democratic revolution and the beginning of the socialist revolution.

For Trotsky, it was clear that the historical moment for Spain's bourgeois revolution had long since passed. Yet he clearly did not mean that he saw the democratic tasks of the Revolution as having been 'solved' or replaced by purely socialist tasks. His point was rather that the country's uneven and combined development had created a revolutionary dynamic that rendered the question of a *separate* bourgeois revolution or further stage of bourgeois development irrelevant. In the theory of permanent revolution, democratic and socialist tasks are combined. There is no point at which it is possible to say that democratic tasks are wholly completed independently of socialist ones. The very nature of a country's backwardness dictates that bourgeois-democratic tasks can only be properly addressed after the proletariat has taken state power. At this point, it is no longer meaningful to call them 'bourgeois' tasks, since the class interests of the proletariat are not those of the bourgeoisie. What might be labelled 'the outstanding historical obstacles to social and economic development' would now be overcome by passing beyond the limits of bourgeois legality. That is to say, they would be addressed via remedies of a socialist nature. Hence the term 'democratic-socialist revolution' had no meaning for Trotsky.

Viewed from this angle, it is possible to detect a subtle shift in Maurín's position that has been overlooked by his political biographer. Monreal argues that other than to give it a title, Maurín did not significantly alter his formulation of 'democratic-socialist revolution'.[61] Yet it seems that the Asturian Revolution of October 1934 did indeed provoke a modification in Maurín's thinking. In his 1935 book *Hacia la segunda revolución*, Maurín noted that the left Republican-Socialist coalition of 1931–3 had posed the problems of the Revolution but failed to resolve them.[62] The October 1934 Revolution, which he interpreted as

---

60    Maurín 'La revolución democrática', *La Nueva Era*, September–October 1931, in Nueva Era 1976, p. 108.

61    Monreal 1984, p. 95.

62    This work has been reprinted in 1966 under the title *Revolución y contrarrevolución en España*, Maurín 1966, p. 219. See also Maurín's article 'La marcha de nuestra revolución', *La Nueva Era*, June–July–August 1931 in Nueva Era 1976, p. 102, and Maurín 1977b, p. 106.

the workers' response to the bourgeoisie's inclination toward fascism, had taken on a distinctly socialist character in Asturias and Cataluña.[63] He referred to the events of October 1934 as the 'prologue' to a second revolution that would be socialist in nature.

It is necessary to highlight and then pass over an obvious contradiction in Maurín's thinking if we wish to make sense of his view of the Revolution. He referred to the socialist revolution as the second revolution. This implies that he saw the fall of the monarchy as the first revolution. But as Nin had already pointed out, the monarchy was not overthrown; it simply collapsed under the weight of its own contradictions. Maurín himself stressed that the Republic did not signify any fundamental alteration in the social and economic structure of Spain. April 1931 thus markedly failed to meet any of the criteria of a revolution as a Marxist might understand it. Thus it seems more consistent with the real substance and thrust of his argument if in place of the phrase 'second revolution' we were to read 'second phase of the revolution'. Even Trotsky was clear that revolutions unfurl in phases. But phases ought not to be confused with the separated, class-related 'stages' of orthodox Second International Marxism and Stalin's formulations.

After October 1934, Maurín thought it impossible to disconnect the democratic revolution from the proletarian seizure of power. He noted that Lenin had abandoned the formula of 'democratic dictatorship' in 1917 and effectively adopted Trotsky's theory of permanent revolution.[64] Maurín quotes Trotsky's statement to the effect that, in 1917, the dictatorship of the proletariat was only possible because the democratic revolution had not constituted an independent stage prior to the October insurrection. He also appears to accept Trotsky's point that the class that carries out the revolution does so, ultimately, in its own interests, and in doing so stamps its mark upon the revolution:

> Certainly the revolution was bourgeois, democratic, although *only in its initial phase*. Today the democratic revolution can only be made by the working class and for this very reason, the revolution will be converted 'ipso facto' into a socialist one.[65]

He affirmed that now there could only be socialist solutions to the agrarian and national problems:

---

63    Maurín, '¿Revolución democráticoburguesa o revolución democráticosocialista?', *La Nueva Era*, May 1936, in Nueva Era 1976, p. 266.

64    Maurín 1966, p. 116.

65    Maurín 1966, p. 90 (emphasis in original).

The taking of power by the working class will entail the realisation of the democratic revolution which the bourgeoisie is unable to make ... and at the same time will begin the socialist revolution ... Our revolution is at once democratic and socialist, given that the triumphant proletariat has to make a good part of the revolution that pertains to the bourgeoisie and, simultaneously, must begin the socialist revolution.[66]

In his article of May 1936, from which the last quotation is drawn, Maurín repeatedly states that the 'second revolution' would be socialist. In his opinion, the bourgeoisie had ceased to be democratic in any meaningful sense. This meant that all questions of a democratic nature now hinged upon the proletariat seizing power. He cites Trotsky and Rosa Luxemburg on the impossibility of separating questions of democracy from those of socialism.[67] Thus there seems little doubt that, by 1935, Maurín no longer envisaged a two-stage revolution and that his conception of the Spanish Revolution had become indistinguishable from that of permanent revolution.

## 3.4    Areas of Divergence and Convergence

Up until the two strands of Spanish dissident communism fused in September 1935, they had important points of agreement and disagreement over analysis of the revolutionary process and the tactics to be adopted. While the concrete experiences of the Asturian Revolution of October 1934 led to the subtle yet significant theoretical adjustment in Maurín's thought outlined above, there were still important points of political divergence with Nin. Perhaps the issue that most divided Maurín's BOC from Nin and the Spanish Left Opposition concerned the manner in which the democratic tasks would combine with the socialist aims of the Revolution. Although there was broad agreement over the content of the democratic revolution (broad political freedoms; agrarian revolution; separation of church and state; national liberation; women's emancipation), the relative importance and precise nature of some of these changes was hotly disputed. This was especially true of the centrepiece of the BOC's political programme: the struggle for national liberation.

Maurín's view of the centrality of the national question, which, in practice, constituted official BOC policy, stemmed from his perception of Spain's historical development according to which the progressive forces in Spanish

---

66    Maurín 1966, p. 271.
67    Maurín 1966, pp. 224–5.

society had shown a tendency to break free from the political centre. The permanent conflict between state and nation was, he argued, a consequence of the premature unification of Spain. It had been achieved through force rather than the economic unity associated with the development of capitalism. Maurín maintained that the struggle of Spain's national groups to escape the restrictive control of the absolutist state corresponded to the higher level of economic development in peripheral regions. This was especially the case in Cataluña, where the nationalist struggle had revived in the nineteenth century under the hegemony of the Catalan bourgeoisie.[68] Since the bourgeoisie had joined forces with the landed oligarchy rather than oppose them, leadership of the national struggle had duly passed to the petty-bourgeoisie. Maurín believed that this leading role could now be adopted by the Catalan proletariat.[69] He remarked that:

> The perspectives for socialist revolution in Spain are greatly improved by the presence of the national question. If it did not exist it would have to be created. It constitutes a powerful factor in the democratic revolution.[70]

However, Maurín took Lenin's dictum on the subject literally, advocating the separation of the Spanish nationalities on the basis of the perceived need to fragment first in order to unite later within a Union of Iberian Socialist Republics.[71] As he put it in a speech to the Madrid Athenaeum: 'We believe that Cataluña should separate; not from Spain, but from the state. When Cataluña, the Basque Country and Galicia have overcome the state, then the authentic national unity [of Spain] will be redefined'.[72] He thought that the struggle for separatism would radiate outward from Cataluña to most other regions and that regional nationalist conflicts would hasten the disintegration of Spain's centralised state. In this respect, he saw the national question as having equal importance alongside the struggles of the proletariat and the peasantry.

In criticising this perspective, Nin pointed out that by proposing separation, the BOC forgot Lenin's advice that recognition of the right to divorce did not

---

68    Maurín 1977b, pp. 118–124.
69    Maurín 1977b, p. 127, and Maurín 1966, p. 182.
70    Maurín 1977b, p. 128.
71    Maurín 1977b, p. 127.
72    Maurín, speech to the Ateneo de Madrid, in *La Batalla*, 2 June 1931, quoted in Monreal 1984, p. 130.

oblige one to carry out propaganda in favour of divorce.[73] He portrayed the BOC's stance on this issue as merely an opportunist attempt to win over the radical petty-bourgeoisie. Rather than attempt to convert them to communism, Nin noted, the BOC adapted its politics to the petty-bourgeoisie's own nationalist chauvinisms.[74] To advocate separatism meant to accept that the emancipation of the working class rested upon a successful outcome for the national liberation struggle. For Nin, the national question was simply one of the democratic tasks and would be resolved only after the proletariat achieved political power.

The two dissident communist organisations also differed over which parts of Spain had outstanding national questions. In addition to Cataluña and the Basque Country, the BOC considered Andalucía, Galicia, Murcia, Aragón and Morocco to constitute separate nationalities.[75] For their part, the Spanish Trotskyists recognised only Cataluña and the Basque Country as having convincing claims to a separate language and history, as well as fulfilling the criterion of more advanced economic development.[76] According to Nin, Galicia's claim was no more than 'regionalist babblings' issuing from purely cultural differences; he thought Morocco totally out of place in the BOC's list since its was a colonial struggle.[77]

In practice, the position the Spanish Trotskyists adopted toward the national question was not without inconsistencies. At their March 1932 congress, they affirmed the principle of self-determination, yet declared their opposition to Basque nationalism.[78] They did so on the grounds that the Basque Nationalist Party, the PNV, was supported by big industrial and financial interests, and was reactionary in character. This was in fact a departure from Trotsky's stated position on Spain's national question, which had affirmed the legitimacy of

---

73   Nin, '¿Adónde va el Bloque Obrero y Campesino?', *Comunismo*, September 1931, in Comunismo 1978, p. 448. See also Nin 1971, p. 76, and Nin 1977b, p. 142.

74   Comunismo 1978, p. 448.

75   Maurín, 1977b, p. 126; Jordi Arquer, 'El comunismo y la cuestión nacional y colonial', *La Nueva Era*, February 1931, in Nueva Era 1976, pp. 73–81.

76   Nin, 'El sindicalismo revolucionario y el anarcosindicalismo', *Comunismo*, October 1933, in Comunismo 1978, p. 423; Nin, 'El marxismo y los movimientos nacionalistas', *Leviatán*, September 1934, in Nin 1978a, p. 423.

77   Nin 1978a, p. 423.

78   See the resolution published in *Comunismo* in April 1932 (Comunismo 1978, pp. 74–9). The Spanish Left Oppositionists had affirmed their support for both Basque and Catalan independence movements at their congress in June 1931 (Comunismo 1978, pp. 46–9).

both Catalan and Basque claims.[79] Trotsky considered that the right of these nations to separate should be upheld. But this did not mean that it was the business of the communists to advocate separation. He condemned Maurín for doing so and remarked that this action displayed his 'petty-bourgeois', 'opportunist' and 'confusionist' politics. Trotsky thought that the reality of Basque and Catalan separation would be to turn the Iberian peninsula into another Balkans. This could only weaken and divide the forces of the proletariat. For that reason, separatism was not to be encouraged. Yet the struggle for national liberation from the imperialism of Madrid had to be supported by the communists with the aim not of separation, but of the creation of a Federation of Soviet Socialist Republics. Should separation still prove to be the democratically expressed will of the people, then the communists should campaign for a federation based upon economic unity.[80]

In practice, the Spanish Trotskyists' position on regional nationalism moved in the direction of the BOC's stance. On the Basque question, for instance, there was an important shift by September 1934 when, writing in the journal *Comunismo*, José Luis Arenillas noted that the conservative ideology and class composition of the PNV did not alter the fact that the local bourgeoisie sought to smash the feudal chains which restrained its economic development. In this sense, if no other, Basque nationalism did constitute a progressive force, he argued.[81] This is interesting in the light of the pro-Republican stance the PNV adopted during the Civil War. The strength of regional nationalism was clearly such a key aspect of the realities of Spain's political situation that both groups of dissident communists felt they needed to acknowledge it formally. In Cataluña, it formed an integral part of the BOC's political orientation.

Turning to another difficult area, the central importance of agrarian issues, both Nin and Maurín agreed that agrarian backwardness posed the main obstacle to economic development. They also concurred in anticipating that the Republic would be unable to radically transform what they described as semi-feudal rural social and property relations. At the heart of the crisis of the Restoration monarchy lay the overwhelming problems of a backward economy resting upon agriculture. The Republic did not embody an alternative economic system; Maurín thought that it represented a political adaptation

---

79    Trotsky, 'The Revolution in Spain', 24 January 1931 and 'The Spanish Revolution and the Dangers Threatening It', 28 May 1931, in Trotsky 1973a, p. 78 and p. 117.

80    Trotsky, letter to International Secretariat, 13 July 1931, in Trotsky 1973a, pp. 155–6; see also Trotsky's letter to Nin of 1 September 1931, in Trotsky 1973a, pp. 163–4.

81    José Luis Arenillas, 'El problema de las nacionalidades en Euskadi', *Comunismo*, September 1934, in Comunismo 1978, pp. 150–6.

designed to actively prevent a meaningful social revolution rather than bring one to a head.[82]

Maurín, in particular, argued that land redistribution would not in itself solve the agrarian question. Given the nature of much of Spanish agriculture, it was not enough to simply give the land to the peasants. They would require access to the means of turning it into truly productive land – that is to say, they would need modern machinery, irrigation, fertilisers, and other methods of increasing the fertility and productivity of the soil. Hence an agrarian revolution could not be separated from industrial modernisation.

> The agrarian revolution and the industrial revolution are two sides of the same coin. One cannot exist without the other. We are now touching fully upon the social revolution. The Spanish bourgeoisie is incapable of industrialising because this would mean a break with the capitalist world. Under bourgeois control, Spain will not emerge from its colonial situation. The bourgeoisie, be it monarchist or republican, is not daring enough to face the consequences of shaping a new nation. Republican Spain will go on 'basking in the sun' and decaying; eaten away by the same sickness it suffered under the monarchy.
>
> Spain can only save itself if, during the period of transition to socialism, the state is transformed into a great manager which, nationalising the land, the banks, mines, transport and communications in line with a scientific plan worked out beforehand, seeks to transform Spain from head to toe.[83]

The working class would be the leading agent of this transformation, in alliance with the peasantry. Maurín thought that the agrarian revolution, in the form of state-planned land nationalisation and collective farming, was a prerequisite for industrial development. Only the socialisation of agrarian production offered a viable economic future for Spain.[84]

Marino Vela expressed a Left Opposition perspective, arguing that, in spite of the ubiquity of feudal remnants, capitalist farming did exist in Spain. The presence of an increasingly organised and class-conscious rural proletariat attested to this fact. There was also evidence of a growing movement of poor tenant farmers for more land and an end to feudal practices. Vela argued that

---

82    Maurín 1977b, p. 146.

83    Ibid.

84    Maurín 1977b, p. 147 and pp. 148–9. See also Maurín's article 'El problema agrario en Cataluña', *Leviatán*, August 1934, in Leviatán 1934.

this presented the communists with a double task. First, they had to address those demands of the smallholding, poor, unemployed and landless peasants that belonged more to the bourgeois-democratic revolution than to the socialist revolution. And, second, the agrarian proletariat had to be guided toward collective occupation and common cultivation of the land. It was thus vital to present solutions of a socialist nature to the poor peasants and to formulate a programme directed against the power of the rich peasants. They needed to be shown that their interests lay in the collective occupation of land and that the realisation of this goal was inextricably bound up with the proletariat's struggle for power.[85] Once again this issue opened up aspects of the dynamics of Spain's Revolution that drew revolutionary Marxists onto terrain occupied by anarcho-syndicalism. To a large extent, this played out in the course of the summer revolution of 1936 and was reflected in the developing political positions and analyses of the dissident communists.

3.5     Conclusion

In drawing this chapter to a close, it is worth summarising the basic positions that Nin and Maurín adopted toward the revolutionary process which began unfolding in 1930. They were united in the belief that the coming revolution would be socialist in character due to the nature of the country's backward capitalist development. The bourgeoisie had proved incapable of carrying through a bourgeois-democratic revolution and now constituted a reactionary force in society. It would appear that Nin and Maurín differed somewhat over the precise reason for the bourgeoisie's failure and that, of the two, it was Nin who expressed the idea of a combination of modern and archaic social forms. Both identified the bourgeoisie's fear of a growing and organised working class, but it was Nin who added the argument that sections of the bourgeoisie were so closely linked to what he took to be feudal or semi-feudal forces that for the bourgeoisie to strike against these forces would be to undermine the basis of its own power. Rather than portraying Spanish society as a balance between feudal and bourgeois interests, as Maurín tended to do, Nin depicted a hybrid capitalism with a particular set of contradictions. Yet both of them agreed that the contradictions they identified were severe enough to predispose Spanish society toward a revolution of a socialist rather than bourgeois character.

---

85     Marino Vela, 'Fuerzas democráticas y fuerzas socialistas en el campo', *Comunismo*, May 1932, in Comunismo 1978, pp. 129–32.

REVOLUTIONARY MARXISTS IN SPAIN, 1930–1934

Hence, they agreed, the revolution would be socialist, but it would begin by addressing the unresolved democratic tasks of the bourgeois revolution. Since there would not now be a bourgeois-democratic revolution, these tasks would be addressed under the revolutionary leadership of the proletariat and would only be resolved by socialist means. This is clearly what Maurín intended by his formula 'democratic-socialist revolution', which he counterposed to the PCE's formula of 'bourgeois-democratic revolution'. We can see that Trotsky's objections to Maurín's prescription had to do with the tendency to use the terms 'democratic' and 'bourgeois' interchangeably. For Trotsky, it was tautological to combine the words 'democratic' and 'socialist', since he took it as self-evident that true socialism would be by definition democratic. 'Democratic' to him signified 'bourgeois'; he considered that Spain's bourgeois revolution had ended. Thus Trotsky interpreted the linking of the two words as a confusion of two different revolutions, the bourgeois with the socialist.[86] As we have seen, this was clearly not Maurín's intention. As he put it definitively in May 1936, 'In contrast to the Socialists and Communists, there is a Marxist sector, ours, which takes the view that we are in the presence not of a bourgeois-democratic revolution, but of a democratic-socialist or, more precisely, a socialist revolution'.[87]

Finally, it would appear that, while neither Nin nor Maurín expressly stated that their approaches to the problems of the Spanish Revolution were based upon Trotsky's theory of permanent revolution, their common adoption of a permanentist paradigm was more than coincidental. It is perhaps not surprising that Nin, through his involvement in the Left Opposition, his personal links with Trotsky and his translations of *The Permanent Revolution* and *The History of the Russian Revolution*, should have been very familiar with Trotsky's methodology and theory of revolution. As for Maurín, his writings of the 1930s contain only positive references to Trotsky's understanding of the dynamics of revolution. Only years later would Maurín claim that Trotsky's influence upon his political thought had been minimal.[88] This is not to say that Trotsky influenced both Nin and Maurín in equal amounts. As we have seen, only Nin

---

86    Trotsky's letter to a Spanish comrade of 12 April 1936, in Trotsky 1973a, p. 213.

87    Maurín, '¿Revolución democráticoburguesa o revolución democráticosocialista?', *La Nueva Era*, May 1936, in Nueva Era 1976, p. 261.

88    In his 'Preliminary Note' of December 1965 to the republication of *Hacia la segunda revolución*, Maurín states that the BOC considered itself a left socialist party that understood what was positive and negative about the Russian Revolution. It was 'ideologically influenced by Marx and Engels, by Lenin and Bukharin; [but] very little by Trotsky and not at all by Stalin' (Maurín 1966, p. 3).

identified the combined development of Spanish capitalism which underpinned the historic compromise of fractions of the bourgeoisie with the old
régime and proved a major obstacle to economic modernisation. Unfortunately
he did not have time to develop this theme into an extended analysis of Spanish
development. But, as we will see in the next chapters, the perspective outlined
above continued to inform his approach to the fundamental problems of the
Revolution. Yet Nin drew conclusions that diverged sharply from Trotsky's concerning the means by which the Spanish workers' movement could be influenced in a revolutionary direction. It is the growing convergence of Nin and
Maurín's political thought around the concrete conditions and events from
October 1934 onward that forms the substance of the next two chapters.

# CHAPTER 4

# The Threat of Fascism and the Challenge of Workers' Unity

Turning now to the Spanish dissident communists' approach to the key questions of unity and revolutionary leadership of the workers' movement, it becomes clear that the two dissident groupings' increasing convergence was driven by analysis of and reaction to events unfolding in Spain and across Europe in the early 1930s. However, it would be mistaken to assume that Nin's and Maurín's political analyses lacked deeper roots. Both recognised that the issue of working-class leadership was inseparable from the problem of how best to respond to the threat of fascism and dictatorship. Spain had already experienced a period of dictatorship under Primo de Rivera (1923–30) and the first two years of reformist Republicanism had been followed by increasing repression and the rise of a domestic fascist movement. This led many commentators to fear the coming to power of a Spanish variant of fascism. For those Marxists open to criticisms of Stalin's and the Comintern's responses to this growing authoritarianism, Trotsky's analysis of the nature of fascism and how to fight it constituted perhaps the single most influential strand of his political thought at this time. As outlined in Chapters One and Two, Trotsky considered fascism to be the last resort of capitalism in terminal crisis. It spelled the end of all that was progressive in bourgeois society. Most crucially, Trotsky argued that one of the prime objectives of fascism as a régime was the liquidation of the organised workers' movement. This signified that the historic mission of the working class to transform society had now become an immediate necessity. Proletarian revolution was the only guarantee of human civilisation. The choice facing humanity had been reduced to one of socialism or barbarism.[1]

Spain's dissident communists found no difficulty in accepting Trotsky's analysis that success in the struggle against fascism required the unity of working-class organisations at the national and international levels.[2] Since this was ultimately a revolutionary struggle, it was also necessary to establish revolutionary organisations. Until 1933, Trotsky believed this could still be achieved through the Third International and the national Communist parties affiliated

---

1 Many of Trotsky's key writings on fascism are to be found in Trotsky 1971. For a critical analysis of Trotsky's theory of fascism, see Kitchen 1976, pp. 76–80.

2 See, for instance, 'For a Workers' United Front against Fascism', 8 December 1931, in Trotsky 1971, pp. 132–41.

to it, by campaigning for a return to the principles of Leninism. But Hitler's victory caused Trotsky to abandon all hope of reforming the official Communist movement, and thereafter he urged revolutionary Marxists to enter the social-democratic parties and construct a new International.

Trotsky's influence upon the Spanish dissident communists in this respect tended to be theoretical rather than practical. As we will see, the Spanish Trotskyists, the BOC and even some on the left of the PSOE recognised the relevance of Trotsky's warnings when applied to the situation in Spain.[3] It was Maurín and the BOC who initially assumed responsibility for the task of building a united front against fascism by organising the Alianza Obrera (Workers' Alliance) in Cataluña. However, Trotsky's practical political advice had little impact beyond Nin's group; even the Trotskyists increasingly questioned the point of political work aimed at the official Communists. When Trotsky suggested the tactic of 'entryism', the majority of his Spanish followers rejected it on the grounds that it was inapplicable to Spain. They decided instead to join forces with Maurín's BOC and form a new party, the POUM, with the explicit purpose of unifying all Marxist elements in the workers' movement.

This chapter considers, from the viewpoint of the dissident communists, the question of the struggle for unity in the face of the threat of authoritarianism in Spain during the early 1930s. In order to understand why Nin, Maurín and their organisations proved unable to influence the official Communists in the PCE, were unwilling to work within the Socialist Party as Trotsky enjoined them to do and finally became convinced of the need to establish yet another political grouping, it is necessary to examine their analyses of the various workers' organisations. After this, attention is paid to Nin and Maurín's thoughts on the prospects for a Spanish fascism and the creation of an organisation both believed might best combat it, the Alianza Obrera. Particular consideration is given to Nin's understanding of fascism, since this constitutes the most original aspect of his Marxism. Although his conception of fascism is compatible with Trotsky's, he developed it independently during the 1920s, drawing heavily upon his own first-hand observations of Italy in the early 1920s. The chapter also returns to the issues surrounding the disagreements with Trotsky over 'entry' into the PSOE that led to a definitive organisational break with international Trotskyism.

---

3   See a discussion of this in Preston 1986, pp. 40–57.

## 4.1    The Spanish Workers' Movement

In his 1935 book *Hacia la segunda revolución*, Maurín comments upon the fact that the development of Spain's working-class organisations started in the 1860s and 1870s, yet even by 1930 they remained divided and unable to comprehend the realities of Spanish politics and society.[4] As he had suggested in a previous work, the workers' organisations proved unable to rid themselves of the deadweight of their past and had missed the revolutionary opportunities of 1930 and 1931. Unaware of the historic role of their class, the proletariat's representatives had simply not known how to place themselves at the forefront of what he calls the 'general liberation movement'. 'Lacking a proletarian theory', Maurín continues, 'our workers' movement has grown in an empirical fashion, at random'.[5] He notes that, for 60 years, the workers' movement had been dominated by the antagonistic forces of Madrid-based social democracy (PSOE-UGT) and an anarchist movement centred upon Barcelona. In spite of the revolutionary fervour of the period from November 1930 to the summer of 1931, the proletariat had remained under the influence of its traditional leadership. Indeed, the UGT and CNT had grown considerably in 1931, although the Socialists and anarcho-syndicalists had proved unable to see beyond a bourgeois republic. Republican illusions, he felt, had soon begun to fade – for CNT workers especially, although it seemed that the peasantry was in advance of the workers in forcing the pace of the Revolution. Referring to the strikes in Seville and Barcelona in June and September 1931, Maurín remarked:

> [In] Andalucía and Cataluña, the two epicentres of the revolutionary movement, the peasants and the proletarians, search for yet fail to find one another. And in 1931, as in 1930, it is in Seville where all the rural unrest of Andalucía is condensed; Seville which places itself at the forefront. Barcelona follows behind at a certain distance... The proletariat lags behind the peasant movement... when it ought to precede and guide it with a precise vision of the objective.[6]

The defeat of these strikes signalled the resurgence of bourgeois power and served to underline the weakness and political ineptitude of the working class's leaders. In the June elections, the workers had followed the advice of their leadership and voted to confirm the popularity of the petty-bourgeois–

---

4   Maurín 1966, pp. 84–7.
5   Maurín 1977b, p. 151.
6   Maurín 1977b, p. 157.

led Republic. This indicated to Maurín that the proletariat had so far only sought objectives of a democratic nature; the aim of a socialist revolution had yet to be raised.[7]

As mentioned in the previous chapter, Nin was less inclined than Maurín to apply the adjective 'revolutionary' to the events of 1930 and 1931. Indeed, he was critical of the FCCB-BOC for its initial political analysis that proclaimed the prospects of the proletariat attaining power in this situation.[8] Nin accused Maurín of ignoring the fact that democratic illusions were still very strong among the working class and that it simply possessed no agency for organising the assault on power.[9] In June 1931, Nin broke his links with the BOC and became highly critical of his friend Maurín's position.[10] While it is true that, in 1931, the politics of the FCCB-BOC were somewhat confused, the concrete reasons for the divergence of Nin's and Maurín's organisations had a great deal to do with the state of the workers' movement and, in particular, the crisis of the communist movement at home and abroad. Hence it is worth considering the relationships of both dissident groupings with the official Spanish Communists.

### Communism in Spain

The Partido Comunista de España (PCE) was founded as a result of splits within the Socialist PSOE over the question of affiliation to the Third International.[11] Inspired by the Bolsheviks' success and radicalised by the waves of worker and

---

7    Maurín 1977b, pp. 160–2.

8    The FCCB (Federación Comunista Catalano-Balear) officially joined forces with the PCC (Catalan Communist Party) in March 1931 and was thereafter known simply as the BOC. On the BOC, see Durgan 1996.

9    Nin, 'La huelga general de Barcelona. Algunas reflexiones sobre la huelga', Comunismo 5, October 1931, in Comunismo 1978, pp. 201–2.

10   For a discussion of Nin's break with Maurín, see Pagès 2011, pp. 196–200. There were several reasons for the rupture. It was partly to do with Trotsky's suspicions of the FCCB-BOC's political positions, which he thought tended toward petty-bourgeois Catalan nationalism, as well as its policy of reconciliation with the CNT. There was also the perceived need to establish a Spanish section of the Left Opposition in Barcelona as well as Madrid. Nin had been criticised for ignoring his Left Opposition comrades in favour of joint work with Maurín and appears to have taken this on board. Another reason had to do with the newly formed BOC's desire to maintain good relations with the Comintern and fears that Nin's links to Trotsky would obstruct this. See Nin's article '¿Adónde va el Bloque Obrero y Campesino?', Comunismo No. 4, September 1931, in Comunismo 1978, pp. 443–56.

11   Pagès 1978a, Chapter One.

peasant uprisings which swept Cataluña and Andalucía between 1919 and 1921, a minority of Socialists who favoured affiliation to the International abandoned the PSOE to create their own party.[12] The resulting Communist Party lacked any real influence among the working class and relied largely upon Moscow for political guidance. An initial membership of 500 had only increased to 800 by 1930; the Party was beset from the beginning by internal differences.[13]

Writing in August 1931, Juan Andrade, a founding member of the PCE who subsequently became a Left Oppositionist, argued that the weakness of Spanish Communism stemmed from a number of factors. In the first place, Spanish socialism lacked a strong theoretical tradition. The great debates of European Social Democracy found little echo within the PSOE. Second, the crisis of the Communist Party of the Soviet Union (CPSU) and Comintern during the 1920s had caused the Spanish Party to fragment at a time when it was already struggling to survive under the repressive conditions of the Primo dictatorship. Third, there was the fact that Marxist ideas had always found difficulty competing in the workers' movement with the notions of revolutionary syndicalism. Andrade also noted that the founders of the Spanish communist movement in 1920 and 1921 had brought with them a number of ideological legacies, ranging from libertarian and syndicalist notions to the mixture of reformist workerism and petty-bourgeois democratism known as *pablismo* (after the founder of the PSOE, Pablo Iglesias). All of these currents fused with Bolshevism in various ways, he argued. The splits of the 1920s gradually deprived the PCE of its theoreticians; those who gained control over the Party proved incapable of formulating their own policies. Hence they became dependent entirely upon directives emanating from Moscow.[14]

Moscow's directives proved to be a major handicap to the dissident communists, because the Comintern's supposed 'experts' were profoundly mistaken

---

12    For a time there were two Spanish Communist Parties. The Partido Comunista de España was formed in April 1920 by the first group to break away from the PSOE, the FJSE (Federación de Juventudes Socialistas de España). Among them were Juan Andrade and Luis Portela, both of whom would become prominent dissident communists. The second party, the Partido Comunista Obrero Español, was founded in April 1921 by the so-called *terceristas*, who supported affiliation to the Third International. With Comintern assistance, the two parties merged in September 1921.

13    See the account by Maurín, 'Sobre el comunismo en España', (1964), in the appendix to Maurín 1966, pp. 274–75.

14    Juan Andrade, 'La crisis del partido español como consecuencia de la crisis de la IC', *Comunismo*, June and August 1931, in Comunismo 1978, pp. 335–47. See also Nin's article, 'Por un gran partido comunista', *El Soviet*, 12 May 1932, in Nin 1978a, pp. 283–6.

about the significance of events in Spain. An example of this is the view of one of these 'experts' on the collapse of Primo's dictatorship:

> [I]n spite of a civil war which offers a way out of the revolutionary upsurge in Spain, the working class has only a modest role in this movement. In fact movements like this pass across the screen of history as mere incidents and do not leave a deep imprint on the minds of the working masses, nor do they enrich their experience of class struggle. Spain is not where the fate of the world proletarian revolution will be decided ... A single strike is of more importance to the international working class than this Spanish-style 'revolution' which has taken place without the Communist Party and the proletariat playing their historic leading role.[15]

Caught unawares by changes such as the fall of Primo and the monarchy, these agents responded by asserting that Spain was so backward that the Revolution could not pass beyond bourgeois limits. Charged with the task of ensuring that the PCE applied the famous 'general line', they seemed equally unable to grasp the nature of Spanish society or the political process they were witnessing.[16] Maurín notes that efforts on the part of the Spanish Party to apply Moscow's formulations were rewarded with reprimands for failing to play a leading role during the events of April 1931.[17] This came at the time of the Comintern's 'third period'. In line with the conclusions of the Sixth World Congress of the Comintern (July–September 1928) to the effect that world capitalism was entering a period of terminal collapse in which major opportunities for proletarian revolution would now open up, the PCE was ordered to build soviets with a view to completing the bourgeois-democratic revolution and preparing

---

15   D. Manuilsky, 'Statement to the Tenth Plenum of the Executive Committee of the Comintern', from *International Press Correspondence* No. 44, 1930. 523, quoted in Broué 1977, p. 153.

16   Some evidence of this can be found in the attitude of Jules Humbert-Droz toward the Comintern agents Duclos, Rabaté, 'Pierre', Stirner, Stocker and Purmann in Barcelona in January 1931. The PCE was almost non-existent in Barcelona at this time, having a paper membership of just 40. These agents were forced to do all of the political work themselves. Their private thoughts were that the PCE could do nothing in the present situation; they spent much of their time in idleness, as if on vacation. Most of their information, even concerning Barcelona, was gleaned from the foreign press. In March 1931, one month prior to the proclamation of the Republic, they communicated to Moscow their impression that 'republican and parliamentary illusions are disappearing' (Iglesias 1977, pp. 42–3).

17   Maurín 1966, pp. 282–3.

the way for a future socialist revolution. This meant that Communists were instructed to avoid any alliances with other political parties and to work to expose the supposedly 'counterrevolutionary nature' of the CNT and PSOE. The result was that the PCE leaders were unsure whether or not they were supposed to support the new Republic as the manifestation of the 'bourgeois-democratic revolution' – despite the fact that its government included the 'social fascists' of the PSOE – or embark upon adventurist actions against it. Attempting to formulate a constructive policy out of the confusions of Moscow's ideologues, and in the wake of the Sanjurjo coup attempt in August 1932, the local leadership finally decided to support the Republic against the threat from the Right. Moscow promptly condemned their action as opportunist and expelled the leaders Bullejos, Adame and Trilla.[18] Fernando Claudín suggests that this leadership team had in fact reached a similar conclusion to Trotsky: namely, that the coming period would be one of bourgeois parliamentarism and that the immediate task of the Communists was not to strive for power but to win over the masses.[19]

The attitudes of the BOC and the Trotskyists toward the official Communist Party were initially quite different. By the middle of 1931, Maurín's relations with the PCE had broken down; he and the FCCB-BOC (now simply calling itself the BOC) were expelled for, amongst other things, being allegedly pro-Trotskyist.[20] Thereafter, the BOC constituted the main communist organisation

18    The official party history criticises the rebellious leaders for failing to comprehend the bourgeois-democratic character of the 'republican' revolution. As the authors explain:
      'Their error was to have a false appreciation of the nature of power under the monarchy; closing their eyes to the feudal vestiges existing in the country and the political weight which the *latifundista* aristocracy still retained, considering that, within the governing bloc, the bourgeoisie and not the landowning aristocracy held sway. This is where the group's [Bullejos, Adame and Trilla's] conception that the revolution should be directed against the bourgeoisie came from, and hence its improvised slogan of 14 April: "Down with the bourgeois republic!"'
      The authors of this were among the new Moscow-approved leadership of José Díaz and Dolores Ibárruri (later to achieve fame as *La Pasionaria* during the Civil War) (Ibárruri et al. 1960, pp. 77–8).

19    Fernando Claudín argues that, by predicting in September 1932 that there would be no separate bourgeois-democratic stage under proletarian hegemony, Trotsky correctly anticipated the line of development of the Spanish Revolution (Claudín 1972, p. 5). In fact Trotsky said as much as early as January 1931 in his pamphlet *The Revolution in Spain*. Indeed, any other formulation would have been at odds with his theory of permanent revolution.

20    In his defence, Maurín affirmed his loyalty to the PCE and Comintern in the following manner:

in Cataluña up until the founding of the POUM in September 1935.[21] Although
it dissented from the official Moscow line, the BOC took a long time to break all
ties with the Comintern. It steered a course midway between the PCE and the
Spanish Trotskyists. Yet, unlike the Trotskyists, the BOC saw no reason to prolong the fiction of being a section of an official Communist movement which
barely existed in Spain and whose representatives they considered beyond
redemption. However, they were less willing to condemn the Comintern itself
and certainly never considered themselves 'Trotskyists' in any sense. While the
BOC was quick to criticise the Left Opposition and expel those sympathetic to
Trotskyism, Trotsky himself was usually viewed with respect.[22] At a time when
the BOC papers *La Batalla* and *L'Hora* frequently attacked Nin, they regularly
reproduced statements by Trotsky without criticism. The BOC's ideological
confusion can be seen from the fact that its press also carried Stalin's pro-
nouncements and referred to the PSOE as 'social fascist' up until 1932, although
Maurín does not seem to have used the term himself. Only after 1932 did the
BOC begin to seriously attack the policies of Stalin and the Comintern.

---

'As you know, I entered Spain to work in accordance with the line of the Comintern and
the resolutions of the Second Congress of the PCE. I wrote to you to this effect following
my stay in Moscow, and this was my true intention. The Executive Committee [of the
PCE] presents me as a Trotskyist. You know that this is totally false. I adopted a position
concerning Trotskyism in 1925 when the majority of the Executive Committee of the PCE
were Trotskyists. On the other hand, the Trotskyist organ *La Vérité* attacks me as the greatest danger to its project within the PCE. I very sincerely accepted the Comintern line and
always worked in accordance with it. You understand, I think, my total loyalty toward the
communist cause.'

Letter to the Comintern Secretariat, Barcelona, 8 July 1930, published in *International
Correspondence*, No. 65, 22 July 1931, p. 812, quoted in Broué 1977, p. 157. The FCCB maintained relations with the Comintern up until July 1931, the date of Maurín's formal expulsion (Pagès 1977a, pp. 44–5 n. 39).

21    There was a formal distinction between the FCCB and the BOC. The FCCB was a hard
core of Marxist militants who had broken with the PCE. The BOC was comprised of sympathisers whom the FCCB hoped would join it after gaining an education through political struggle. In practice, the name FCCB was dropped and the organisation was known
either as the BOC or the Bloc (Alba and Schwartz 1988, p. 25).

22    The attitude of the BOC toward Trotsky was contradictory. Although his political and
theoretical contribution to Marxist theory and practice was acknowledged and defended
against Moscow-originated slanders, the BOC never accepted his international position. However, in 1934, the BOC campaigned for Trotsky to be allowed to reside in Spain.
Yet its press also printed criticisms of a personal, even insulting, nature (Pagès 1977a,
pp. 250–1).

For its part, the Spanish Left Opposition, in accordance with Trotsky's advice, continued to call for a national congress of all Spanish communist groups with the aim of building a unified party based upon the principles of democratic centralism.[23] But as Giorgio Rovida has noted, the regionalist nature of Spain rather militated against the creation of centralised political organisations. Trotsky's entreaties against federalism in the party, although understood and acknowledged by Nin's group, were difficult to act upon.[24] The more advanced Marxists tended to gravitate toward the most politically advanced workers, which meant the industrial zones of Cataluña. Although the Spanish Trotskyists tried to resist this temptation and organised in most areas of Spain, they were ultimately drawn toward Barcelona. Later on, largely due to the weight of its Catalan members, the POUM's influence would be confined largely within Cataluña.

Given the Left Opposition's orientation toward winning over official party members, the virtual non-existence of the official Communist Party in Cataluña posed a major problem for Nin and his Catalan comrades. While they agreed with Trotsky that, in principle, the correct policy was to urge workers sympathetic to the Opposition to join the PCE, as was the practice in most of Spain, in Cataluña this was only possible in Barcelona. Only here was there an official PCE. In the rest of Cataluña, Nin informed Trotsky, the only practical solution was to advise them to adhere to the BOC. He explained that many of these people were new recruits to communism and would not wish to join the PCE. Inside the BOC these comrades would be able to work for communist unity and oppose the errors of the leadership, he reasoned.[25]

As noted in Chapter Two, Trotsky strongly disagreed with Nin over this. He insisted that while it was acceptable for individual activists to enter the BOC and attempt to build an opposition faction, it was utterly wrong to call upon workers in general to join its ranks. The policy of the International Left Opposition was, he stressed, one of winning workers over to the Comintern and its national sections, which in Spain meant the PCE. But this did not mean that the Opposition had merely to direct new recruits toward the official party. Such an action would be harmful because, once inside the Party, they would be taught that the Left Opposition was 'counterrevolutionary'. Trotsky's idea was rather that the Left Opposition in each country should constitute a faction

---

23    This policy was laid down in the document 'Nuestros propósitos', *Comunismo*, May 1931. It
        was formulated in the 'Proyecto de plataforma política de la OCE', *Comunismo* 1, May 1931.
        See Comunismo 1978, pp. 23–4 and pp. 37–46.
24    Rovida 1980, p. 1364.
25    Letter from Nin to Trotsky, 18 September 1931, in Trotsky 1973a, pp. 378–9.

within the communist movement and group around itself all those workers who were attracted by its arguments and actions. If this oppositional faction and those sympathetic to its platform grew in number, it might then be possible to discuss the unity of the communist ranks with the official party.[26]

Differences of approach within the Trotskyist movement to the key problem of how to unify the dispersed and mutually hostile elements of Spanish communism became more clearly defined during the Spanish Left Opposition's Third National Congress in March 1932. This congress ratified and extended the existing political platform and changed the name of the organisation to Izquierda Comunista de España (Communist Left of Spain). The decisions taken at the congress altered the political direction of the Spanish Trotskyist movement and plunged it into both internal crisis and conflict with the International Secretariat, the international Trotskyist organisation. In other words, this marked the beginning of the Spanish Left Opposition's rejection of Trotsky's international perspective and his tactical advice concerning the way in which a revolutionary communist party might be constructed in Spain.

The breach with the international Trotskyist movement was over the specific tactics to be applied in Spain, rather than matters of Marxist theory. Thus the 1932 congress did not alter the Spanish group's basic analysis of the course of the Revolution. Yet it did modify the Spanish Trotskyists' tactics and orientation toward the PCE. The Catalan delegates, Nin and Narcis Molins y Fábrega, proposed that participation in elections by the Left Communists should, in certain cases, now be independent of the PCE. The Asturian delegates opposed this on the grounds that the PCE, whose candidature the Trotskyists had backed in June 1931, had not degenerated to such an extent as to justify fielding independent candidates. Lacroix and Andrade also argued that the proposal deviated from the overall political strategy of the Left Opposition.[27] However, Nin found sufficient support to have his proposal adopted, thus altering existing policy and making possible the Left Communists' candidature independent of and in opposition to that of the PCE. This clearly challenged Trotsky's international perspective because it opened the way, in theory at least, to the creation of a second communist party.

Nin's delegation also proposed to change the name of the organisation to 'Spanish Left Communists' (ICE). This met with unanimous approval. However, it was stressed that this modification did not alter the organisation's status as the Spanish section of the International Left Opposition. Nor was there any suggestion of altering the relationship with the international organisation or

---

26    Letter to Nin, 27 November 1931, in Trotsky 1973a, pp. 164–7 and pp. 395–6.
27    Pagès 1977a, p. 124.

challenging broad Left Opposition strategy.[28] There was, however, more than a hint of ambiguity in the 'Thesis on the International Situation'. The Spanish section had, it stated, worked as if it were a faction of the PCE, in spite of its total exclusion from that party. But, the document continued,

> As great as the differences between the Communist Left and Stalinism may be, in practice the Opposition has no programme other than the 'reform of the party', which makes this reform a prior condition for the execution of its policy. The traditional attitude of the Opposition is totally insufficient in the actual circumstances, and by persisting in it the Opposition will not achieve a political solution in the decisive moments since any partial reforms that might be achieved in the International [i.e., the Comintern] would not substantially modify the nature of Stalinism.[29]

Members felt that a position of mere verbal criticism of the PCE had proved ineffectual and that the only way to put the Opposition's platform across to the advanced workers was to set an example by its own independent actions. Yet this 'Thesis' also acknowledged that the Opposition could not become a party without dissolving itself as a faction of the PCE, and there was no proposal to do this. Hence there is an evident contradiction between the Opposition's stated unwillingness to separate from the PCE and Comintern, which it said were not yet entirely beyond redemption, and its general pessimism concerning the value of its factional work. This indicates that the Spanish Trotskyists were caught between nostalgia for their historical links to the Russian Revolution and Soviet 'workers' state' and the growing realisation that, in Spain at least, they had to seek an entirely new direction.

In attempting to remain faithful to the international line and at the same time proposing a more independent role for the Spanish Opposition, the Spanish section perhaps unwittingly identified the fundamental flaw in Trotsky's strategy. This was the harsh reality that neither the Comintern nor its affiliated parties were ever likely to be persuaded by those who had been cast out of the ranks of official Communism to 'return' to the dissidents' understanding of Leninist internationalism and revolutionary Marxism. Members of the official Communist movement simply did not accept that they or the Soviet Union had departed from Leninism. Thus, however much the Left Opposition considered itself still a part of the Comintern, the reality was that its

---

28    'Tesis sobre la situación internacional y el comunismo', *Comunismo* 11, April 1932, in Comunismo 1978, pp. 79–84.
29    Comunismo 1978, p. 83.

supporters had been expelled without the prospect of readmission. Moreover, in relative terms, the ranks of the International Left Opposition were few in number – and at their head stood an isolated and stateless individual whose true historical role was in the process of being totally expunged from the annals of official Marxism. In view of this, and of the considerable ideological control exercised by Moscow over the national Communist parties, there was little chance of a dissident grouping being able to gain any influence. Though his Spanish comrades began the painful process of adapting to this reality in the concrete circumstances of Spain after the spring of 1932, it would be more than a year before Trotsky recognised the futility of trying to reform the Comintern and adopted a new strategy.

### Anarcho-Syndicalism

Turning now to the dissident communists' attitude toward the main representatives of organised labour in Spain, the anarcho-syndicalists (CNT) and Socialists (PSOE-UGT), we can see that the question of trade unionism was of the utmost importance for both Maurín and Nin. Unions were the main working-class organisations; in the relatively free political climate of the early years of the Republic, they grew rapidly. Yet the Spanish union movement was deeply divided between the UGT and the CNT.[30] Rather than greater unity, the main tendency in the Spanish workers' movement was fragmentation. During 1931 and 1932, the anarchists of the FAI (Federación Anarquista Ibérica) succeeded in gaining political control of the CNT and reversed the organisation's traditionally tolerant attitude toward affiliated unions led by Marxist elements such as the BOC. Many syndicalists also left the CNT or were forced out. In June 1932, the PCE established its own syndical body, the Confederación General del Trabajo Unitaria (CGTU, General Confederation of Labour).

Faced with this situation, the Spanish Trotskyists campaigned for syndical unity and the political autonomy of trade unions. Unlike the PCE or the BOC, the Trotskyists did not attempt to establish their own autonomous unions. Rejecting such a path, they argued that every union should recognise the CNT as the centre around which to organise joint action. They chose the CNT rather than the UGT because they considered the Socialist union to be tainted by class collaboration both with the Primo dictatorship and with Republican parties since 1930. The CNT, in contrast, had shown itself to be a revolutionary

---

30    These were organisations with sizeable memberships. The CNT comprised 511 syndicates
        (unions) with a total affiliation of well over 500,000 in 1931, rising to 1.2 million in the sum-
        mer of 1932. In Cataluña, there were some 300,000 affiliates. Broad numbers for the UGT
        are 287,000 in 1930, rising to more than a million members by October 1932 (Portuondo
        1981, pp. 101–2 and pp. 105–6).

organisation of prime importance during the 1920s. Thus the Trotskyists' tactic was to attempt to organise revolutionary groupings within existing unions with the aim of infusing their struggles with a revolutionary character. Unions would, they argued, play a key role in any future united front, as well as in the factory committees for which the Left Opposition was calling. In fact, Trotskyist militants were active in both CNT-controlled and UGT-controlled unions, and they achieved a certain degree of theoretical influence among the Socialist unions in Asturias, Madrid and Barcelona. In their newspapers and in *Comunismo*, the Trotskyists repeatedly criticised what they described as the 'putschist' tactics of the CNT-FAI; in 1933, Nin devoted an entire book to the syndical question.[31]

Maurín's attitude toward the CNT was somewhat different. He attributed even greater weight to the CNT than the Trotskyists did. Although he considered himself a Leninist and duly stressed the importance of dual-power organisations in the proletarian revolution, he did not think it possible to reproduce Russian-style soviets in Spain. Every revolution had its own specific 'national character', he argued. It was necessary to make the most of existing materials rather than attempt to create organisations artificially which had emerged out of very different historical experiences in other countries. In the Spanish case, he argued, the CNT was the only mass organisation with revolutionary potential: 'Anarcho-syndicalism is the first stage in the formation of a workers' movement which knows what it wants and where it is going'.[32] The CNT constituted a unique force in the European labour movement. It was 'an economic organisation, political party and revolutionary stronghold all rolled into one', he argued. As the embryonic organ of workers' power, this organisation could, as the Revolution unfolded, adopt new and previously unsuspected forms. Indeed, Maurín believed it would become the key organ of insurrection, the 'lever of power', as he put it in late 1931.[33]

Nin strongly disagreed with this assessment, arguing that the CNT could never achieve the broad democratic character of soviet-type organisations. It would never be a forum in which various tendencies could argue for their own policies and programmes. Consequently, he thought that Maurín's alternative organ of dual power would prove to be a narrow body which would only attract

---

31    Pagès 1977a, pp. 212–16. For a collection of articles on anarcho-syndicalism, see Comunismo 1978, pp. 401–42. Nin's book was *Las organizaciones obreras internacionales*, published in 1933.

32    Maurín 1977b, p. 162.

33    Maurín 1977b, pp. 167–9.

certain sections of the workers and peasants.[34] Given the hegemonic position of the FAI within the CNT after 1932 and the expulsion of all non-anarcho-syndicalist tendencies, Nin's point seems well made. As we will see, after 1933 Maurín switched his attention away from the CNT and focused instead upon building the Alianza Obrera as the broad united-front organisation which he believed would develop into the organ of dual power.

Despite their critical stance toward it, Nin and his comrades appreciated rather better than Trotsky the magnitude of the problem anarcho-syndicalism posed for the advancement of communism in Spain. They subjected it to lengthy scrutiny and criticism in the pages of their theoretical journal *Comunismo*.[35] Like Maurín, they viewed syndicalism as a revolutionary response to the reformism of the Second International. As such, it sought to combat the collaboration of reformist Socialists with the left bourgeoisie. Nin recalled that many former syndicalists like himself had progressed to communism under the inspiration of the Bolshevik Revolution. However, the syndicalist idea of overthrowing capitalism through the mechanism of the revolutionary general strike had ultimately proved unconvincing, especially after the Spanish experience of 1917 to 1923. Revolution required a political unity that could not be

---

34    Nin, 'Los comunistas y el momento presente: A propósito de unas declaraciones de Maurín', *El Soviet*, 22 October 1931, in Nin 1978a, p. 129. In fact, neither Trotsky nor Nin suggested that use of the slogan of 'soviets' (or *juntas* in the Spanish context) implied that the immediate struggle for power was beginning. They envisaged soviets initially as a means of unifying and organising workers around radical democratic demands, which would also be the basis for forging links with the peasantry. Nin spoke of *juntas* as formative organs of workers' democracy and a defence against the reactionary backlash he considered inevitable. For the views of Trotsky see letter to Nin, 12 December 1930 in Trotsky 1973a, pp. 64–5; letter to the Chinese Left Opposition, 8 January 1931, in Trotsky 1973a, pp. 65–6; letter to Nin, 12 January 1931, in Trotsky 1973a, pp. 66–7; 'The Revolution in Spain', 24 January 1931 in Trotsky 1973a, 85–6; letter to Nin, 13 March 1931 in Trotsky 1973a, 92–4; 'The Ten Commandments of the Spanish Communist', 15 April 1931, in Trotsky 1973a, pp. 104–5; 'The Spanish Revolution and the Dangers Threatening It', 28 May 1931, in Trotsky 1973a, pp. 127–9; letter to *Comunismo*, 12 June 1931, in Trotsky 1973a, p. 137; letter to Nin, 1 September 1931, in Trotsky 1973a, p. 162. Nin's views are to be found mainly in his 1932 pamphlet *¿Qué son los soviets?* in Nin 1987. Other texts by Nin which deal with the question of soviets are: 'Abstención y cortes constituyentes', 'Por unas cortes constituyentes revolucionarias' and 'La lucha contra la reacción', *L'Hora*, 11 February, 11 March and 23 April 1931, all in Nin 1978a, p. 60, p. 78 and p. 96.

35    Andrade, 'La revolución española, el partido comunista y el anarcosindicalismo', *Comunismo* 4, September 1931; and Nin, 'El sindicalismo revolucionario y el anarcosindicalismo', *Comunismo* 29 and 30, October and November–December 1933, in Comunismo 1978, pp. 401–8 and pp. 422–35.

achieved simply through the economic struggles of trade unionism. Unions were certainly key organisations, but they were not broad enough bodies to lead an alliance of revolutionary forces. Although the general strike was indeed a crucial means of mobilising the masses and stimulating class consciousness by education in struggle, it was not in itself an adequate revolutionary strategy and could never be a means of transforming society. In other words, general strikes might pose the question of power, but could not resolve it.[36]

Nin's Left Communist comrade Andrade tacitly acknowledged Maurín's point when he noted that the CNT's presence and weight within the workers' movement gave the Spanish Revolution a different character to that of any other. In sharp contrast to countries such as France and Italy, where the world war had signalled the end of syndicalist power, Spanish syndicalism had increased in strength since the start of the war.[37] Molins y Fábrega estimated that, between 1914 and 1918, the CNT's membership rose from 25,000 to 500,000. It now comprised the vanguard of the Spanish proletariat – which meant that the task of the communists was to win its members over to revolutionary Marxism.[38] This task had been made more difficult by the ascendancy of the FAI within the CNT. While the CNT had mistakenly pursued the policy of 'social peace' in the early days of the Republic, Nin felt its current tactics of 'putschism' and individual terrorism were futile and damaging to the workers' movement.[39] Andrade feared that the anarcho-syndicalists' lack of theory and revolutionary strategy and, in particular, their failure to see the importance of taking state power would lead to pointless adventures which might jeopardise the Revolution itself. In other words, the CNT left the proletariat without proper leadership and at the mercy of the petty-bourgeois politics of the Republicans and Socialists.[40]

The dissident communists' critique of the actions of the main labour organisations' leaders is of more than merely academic interest here. In many respects, they identified tendencies and behavioural traits that were to surface time and again during the course of the Spanish Revolution and Civil War. One example is Nin and Maurín's observation that, in April and June 1931, the CNT had given its support to the left Republican parties and effectively agreed not

---

36    Comunismo 1978, p. 431.

37    Andrade in Comunismo 1978, p. 401.

38    N. Molins y Fábrega 1933, 'La actividad negativa del anarcosindicalismo', *Comunismo* 30, November–December 1933, in Comunismo 1978, pp. 435–41.

39    Nin, 'La etapa de la revolucíon española y la táctica que se impone', *Comunismo* 14, July 1932, in Comunismo 1978, p. 213.

40    Andrade in Comunismo 1978, p. 408.

to cause problems for the new government.[41] They thought it an action typical of anarchists, insofar as it demonstrated a willingness to abandon principles in order to participate in the very politics they professed to despise.

Maurín, in particular, attempted to differentiate between what he considered to be the positive aspects of revolutionary syndicalism and the meaningless formulations of the anarchists. Since the late 1920s, he had contributed to an ongoing debate in the Marxist-oriented sections of the workers' movement around the emergence and popular appeal of anarchism in Spain.[42] Maurín dismissed the argument that anarchism had gained ground because it was the doctrine closest to articulating the traditional nature of popular protest in Cataluña. He pointed out that, up until the end of the nineteenth century, the UGT had been very influential among the Catalan working class. The Anarchist Federations had been able to win over much of this support because of the various shortcomings of the Socialists. He thought the Marxism of the PSOE lacked any revolutionary content and that, as reformists, its leadership worked easily alongside the Republican petty-bourgeoisie. It was also significant that the Socialists chose Madrid rather than Barcelona as a base, a fact which reflected the origins of the PSOE and UGT among the skilled working class of the capital. According to Maurín, the PSOE leadership, especially its father figure Pablo Iglesias, had been unable to see that the Barcelona working class was the key to a socialist future for Spain. They had effectively abandoned Cataluña to the chaos of anarchist and petty-bourgeois demagogues. Maurín concluded that, with the right leadership and programme, Spain's key industrial zone could have been won over to Socialism. Had this happened, he argued, there would have been a far more effective working-class challenge to the bourgeoisie and the Restoration régime.[43]

Maurín identified another reason for the strength of anarchist ideas among the Catalan working class which was more contentious than the previous point. He argued that anarchist notions were imported into Cataluña through the migration of workers from Extremadura, Galicia and Andalucía. As a consequence of this, he noted

---

41    See Nin's letter to Trotsky of 25 May 1931 in Trotsky 1973a, p. 375, and Maurín 1977b, p. 160.

42    'Socialismo y anarquismo: Pablo Iglesias y Anselmo Lorenzo', *L'Opinió* I, no. 9, 14 April 1928; 'Socialismo y anarquismo: El proletariado Catalan no es anarquista', *L'Opinió* I, no. 21, 7 July 1928; 'El anarquismo no es revolucionario', *L'Opinió* no. 30, 8 September 1928; 'Pablo Iglesias y el pabloiglesismo', *L'Opinió* no. 45, 22 December 1928. All reproduced in Balcells 1973, pp. 57–61, pp. 87–93, pp. 121–6 and pp. 155–61.

43    'Socialismo y anarquismo: Pablo Iglesias y Anselmo Lorenzo', in Balcells 1973, pp. 87–8, and Maurín 1977b, p. 154.

> The Catalan proletariat, upon whom history has conferred the grave responsibility of being the most important agent in the social transformation of Spain, has been prevented from forming a proletarian consciousness due to the constant immigration of Spanish peasants into Cataluña. The torrent of peasants flowing from Andalucía, the Levante and Aragón into Barcelona, has deformed the workers' movement. The proletariat has not been able to assimilate the influx. Those aspects which are characteristically proletarian have been submerged by this great mass.[44]

Maurín felt that the concept of libertarian communism corresponded to the mentality of the peasants, especially those from Andalucía, who had migrated to work in Barcelona. He believed that it reflected a simplistic belief in the absolute freedom of the individual and was the 'instinctive cry of the masses' lacking a socialist education. As such, it was a notion Maurín believed could never be shared by the 'true proletarian', the industrial worker who, because of the nature of his or her employment, tended toward collective, organised and disciplined actions. Yet, owing to the fact that Spanish industry was backward and small scale, the consciousness of the working class was still in the process of developing toward socialism. Maurín was effectively saying that the unskilled workers from outside Cataluña had effectively taken control of the CNT and that this explained the predominance of anarchist elements among its leadership.[45]

Entering into the debate from afar in 1928, Nin had agreed that peasant immigration into Cataluña brought a petty-bourgeois individualist ethos that was compatible with anarchism. He also accepted that the failure of the Socialists to organise had enabled anarchists to dominate the workers' movement. But he did not agree with Maurín's argument that immigration was the key factor determining the hegemony of anarchism within the Catalan workers' movement. Nin saw Cataluña's weak and incomplete capitalist development as the underlying cause of the relative failure of Marxism and success of anarchism. Although there were important industrial centres, the Catalan economy was more agrarian than industrial, he argued. Moreover, the predominance of small-holdings meant that a rural proletariat was almost non-existent. Industry was indeed relatively small in scale and technically backward. Most industrial workers had themselves come from the countryside. This had resulted in the Catalan workforce possessing a petty-bourgeois mentality – not because they were Catalan, but because of the social structure of the country. Had Catalan

---

44    Maurín 1977b, pp. 154–5.
45    Maurín 1977b, pp. 90–2.

industry been prosperous and concentrated, the unskilled workers would have been absorbed and transformed into modern proletarians. Since this did not happen, Catalan workers did not share the sense of co-operation and self-discipline instilled by concentrated factory production in more advanced countries. For Nin, this backwardness explained why Marxism had not found the resonance in Cataluña that it enjoyed in the Basque Country, where industry was much more concentrated. As capitalist industry developed in Cataluña, Nin predicted, Marxism would displace anarchism as the hegemonic doctrine of the workers' movement. Yet this was not an automatic process. It required a party to put forward revolutionary Marxist ideas.[46]

In his 1935 book *Hacia la segunda revolución*, Maurín summarised the activities of the CNT-FAI from 1931 to 1933. He argued that their lack of a theory of revolution led them to believe that in the next phase of the Revolution they would be able to achieve their goal of libertarian communism. Yet they were unaware that the Revolution had to begin with bourgeois-democratic tasks and would only become socialist as it developed. Because of this, the anarchists of the FAI could only see struggles for national liberation, such as that of the Catalan people, as reactionary. Although the CNT workers had been the objective revolutionary force during the early years of the Revolution, the leadership had not looked beyond what he termed 'putschist' and 'sectarian' actions, the most famous of which had been the rising in Casas Viejas in January 1933. By rejecting any collaboration with the Socialists and treating them as rivals for the leadership of the working class, he claimed, the CNT had greatly assisted the bourgeoisie by splitting the proletarian movement right down the middle.[47]

### Spanish Socialism

The attitude of the dissident communists toward the Socialists was to prove highly significant to the convergence of Nin and Maurín's organisations and their disagreements with Trotsky. Although this theme will be revisited later on, it is important to note here that neither the BOC nor the Spanish Trotskyists ever thought that the PSOE-UGT had the potential to become a revolutionary movement. Nin described its socialism as 'castrated', devoid of a theoretical base and at the service of petty-bourgeois Republicanism.[48] As collaborators with Primo and participants in the 1931–3 government, he thought that the Socialists shared responsibility for the violent suppression of worker and

---

46    Nin, '¿Por qué nuestro movimiento obrero ha sido anarquista?' and 'Las raices del anarquismo en Cataluña', *L'Opinió*, 11 and 25 August 1928, in Nin 1978a, pp. 23–31.
47    Maurín 1966, pp. 104–7.
48    Nin, 'El deber del momento', *El Soviet*, 15 October 1931, in Nin 1978a, p. 124.

peasant protest. Nin predicted that, once the Azaña government had completed its task of defusing popular discontent, the forces of reaction would demand that the PSOE leave the government and might even try to remove petty-bourgeois Republican politicians.[49] Maurín also noted the PSOE's reformism, suggesting that its brand of socialism was close to British Fabianism and that its leadership had modelled itself upon the British Labour Party. He characterised their overall strategy as one of participating in government and assisting in the completion of what they believed to be an unfinished bourgeois revolution. When the bourgeoisie opposed democratic reforms, the Socialists would bring their mass organisation onto the streets in order to force them through. In this way, Maurín argued, the PSOE believed it could become the dominant force in the workers' movement and would gradually be able to assume effective political control of the country without bitter struggles or recourse to violent revolution. In Maurín's opinion, precisely such policies were responsible for the repeated defeats of the European workers' movement during the 1920s and early 1930s, culminating in Hitler's rise to power in 1933.[50]

Given both dissident communist groupings' damning critiques of the Socialists, it is not difficult to comprehend the Left Communists' resistance to Trotsky's insistence after mid-1933 that they penetrate the ranks of Spanish Socialism, with the aim of winning militants over to revolutionary Marxism. Trotsky's change of tactic was a response to Hitler's rise to the chancellorship of Germany. In Spain, the election of a radical right-wing government in November 1933 also produced a major reorientation on the Left. Up until that point, during the first three years of the Republic, the dissident communists had been isolated and excluded from joint initiatives with other workers' organisations. As we have seen, the BOC had inclined toward the CNT, even to the extent of briefly advocating a syndicalist government. But its militants had been expelled from the CNT. The Trotskyists continued their efforts to influence the PCE through this period, without success.[51] They thought that the new leadership of the Party, which replaced the Bullejos-Adame-Trilla triumvirate in August 1932, might be more amenable to their calls for unity.[52] However,

---

49    Nin, interviewed for the book *El momento de España* by E. Marine, published by Aguilar in 1933, reproduced in Nin 1978a, p. 391.

50    Maurín 1966, p. 90.

51    Emilio Ruiz (Juan Andrade), 'Otra crisis en el partido comunista español', *Comunismo* 17, October 1932; The Executive Committee of the Left Communists, 'Resolución de la Izquierda Comunista', *Comunismo* 18, November 1932, both in Comunismo 1978, pp. 356–8 and pp. 359–61.

52    See Nin's 'Carta al partido', *Comunismo* 18, November 1932, cited in Pagès 1977a, p. 235.

the new team, headed by José Díaz, questioned Moscow's dictates even less than had its predecessor.

Relations between the two wings of dissident communism did not improve in this period either. Nin echoed Trotsky's criticisms of the BOC and suggested that it was caught between a tendency to follow aspects of the Comintern line and a practical orientation in the direction of the CNT. Not only did the BOC lack a policy regarding the Comintern, but its very name, the 'Workers' and Peasants' Bloc', suggested the intermediate stage of the revolution forecast by the Stalinists. Maurín's continued insistence upon the need to carry out the democratic revolution appeared to support this view. Nin also believed that the special conditions of the Spanish Revolution upon which Maurín insisted had led him, in practice, toward a syndicalist rather than a communist perspective.[53]

As has already been mentioned, the BOC did indeed lean toward the syndicalists at first and was slow in breaking with the Comintern. Yet, as noted in the previous chapter, it would be a mistake to think that Maurín and the BOC envisaged an intermediate workers' and peasants' revolution in Spain. Although the notion of a 'worker-peasant alliance' is often associated with Bukharin's position in the debates of the 1920s in the USSR, the BOC did not constitute a Right Opposition in Spain or advance such a perspective.[54] Bukharin had employed the term to mean a class alliance between workers and peasants, with the aim of winning the latter over to communism; Maurín and the BOC saw the tactic more as a mechanism for promoting the idea of democratic tasks. They saw the idea of a 'bloc' of workers and peasants as best suited to the peculiarities of the Spanish labour movement. In organisational terms, the FCCB, upon which the BOC was based, was organised along Leninist lines, with a democratic-centralist structure and functioning cells. While the idea of the BOC was that it would constitute a broader body of sympathisers that would include peasants, in practice it was synonymous with the existing FCCB.[55]

The point on which both dissident groupings could agree, and which became the basis of their fusion in 1935, concerned the need to unify the

53    See also the article by L. Fersen (Enrique Fernández Sendón), 'El congreso del Bloque Obrero y Campesino. Víspera de un congreso comunista', *Comunismo* 10, March 1932, and the ICE statement (written by Andrade), 'El congreso del Bloque Obrero y Campesino', *Comunismo* 26, July 1933, in Comunismo 1978, pp. 459–64 and pp. 465–9.

54    This contradicts the impression Les Evans gives in his introduction to Trotsky's writings on the Spanish Revolution (Evans 1973, p. 34).

55    Durgan 1989, pp. 69–70. Durgan notes that Maurín and the BOC seldom referenced Bukharin's ideas.

disparate Spanish workers' movement. The victory of the conservative coalition in November 1933 provided the necessary impetus for a united front. In the meantime, Nin considered the BOC to be an obstacle to unity. This was because he still believed unity could only be achieved through a strong communist party that could eliminate reformist and anarchist influences in the workers' movement. In this scenario, the Spanish Left Communists would constitute 'the vanguard of the vanguard of the proletariat'.[56]

## 4.2      The Threat of Fascism

The dramatic alteration of the political situation between November 1933 and October 1934 forced major changes in the dissident communists' strategy and tactics. The right-wing parties that triumphed in the November 1933 elections sought to reverse the modest reforms of the previous years and take away the political freedoms granted by the 1931 Republic. In the context of the emergence of organisations of the extreme Right, the new government appeared to many on the Left to be just a step away from a fascist régime. How, then, did the dissident communists understand the phenomenon of fascism? Did they believe that it could come to power in Spain?

### Nin's Theorisation of Fascism
Of the various Spanish Marxists who wrote about fascism, it was Nin who provided the most sustained, coherent and perceptive contributions. His analysis of fascism certainly coincided with Trotsky's, but it should be stressed that Nin's own ideas about the origins and nature of fascism were first elaborated in the 1920s and actually predate Trotsky's major writings on the phenomenon. Nin's writing, including his pamphlet and articles of 1923 and 1924 and his book devoted to contemporary dictatorships (*Las dictaduras de nuestro tiempo*, 1930), was supported by the first-hand experience of Italian fascism he gained as an agent of the Profintern.[57] Together with his work on the national question

---

56    Nin, 'La situación política española y los comunistas', *Comunismo* 22, March 1933, in
       Comunismo 1978, p. 223.
57    Nin's early writings on fascism include: Nin 1923; '¿El fascismo es un movimiento interna-
       cional?' *La Batalla* 33, 13 December 1923; and 'Los sindicatos y el fascismo', *La Batalla* 34,
       21 December 1923. His trip to Italy (January to March 1924) produced five articles: 'En la
       CGT italiana', *Correspondance Internationale*, 21 May 1924; 'La Italia actual', *Correspondance
       Internationale*, 28 May 1924; 'La Italia actual', *Correspondance Internationale*, 4 June
       1924; 'La Italia actual', *Correspondance Internationale*, 11 June 1924; and 'La Italia actual',

and trade unionism, it is arguable that his writings on fascism constitute Nin's most original and influential synthesis of Marxist theory.

In an early formulation of his thoughts on the nature of fascism, written for *La Batalla* in December 1923, before he had the opportunity to visit Italy, Nin suggested that

> fascism could be defined as a violent and illegal action on the part of cap-
> italism, supported by the industrial and agrarian petty-bourgeoisie, the
> 'lumpenproletariat' and 'déclassé' elements, so as to establish its domina-
> tion. Its methods are characterised by a contempt for all of the political
> formulas the bourgeoisie itself has created (democracy, law, freedom of
> assembly, parliament, etc.) and by the use of the most extreme violence
> against the workers' organisations and their revolutionary leaders.[58]

He stressed that fascism was a phenomenon that had developed since the world war and ought not to be confused with other forms of dictatorship. It was clear to Nin that the fascists' success in mobilising a mass movement comprised of ex-army officers and peasants meant that fascism posed a dire threat to the workers' movement. He warned that Mussolini's victory in Italy would lead to the growth of similar movements in other countries and that the bourgeoisie would not be slow to take advantage of them.[59]

Later on, in *Las dictaduras de nuestro tiempo*, Nin elaborated upon his earlier analysis in a more systematic way.[60] He emphasised the point that the origins of fascism were inextricably bound up with alterations in the nature of the capitalist world economy. These changes were mainly to do with the concentration of capital in the form of monopolies, the fusion of banking and industrial capital, and the international political alliances sought by govern-

---

*Correspondance Internationale*, 17 June 1924. In 1930 Nin published a book on contemporary dictatorships as a reply to a work by the leader of the Lliga Regionalista Catalan, Francesc Cambó. The book first appeared in a Catalan edition as *Les dictadures dels nostres dies* (Barcelona: Llibreria Catalònia, 1930). All references here are to the Spanish version, *Las dictaduras de nuestro tiempo*, first published in Madrid in November 1930 by Ediciones Hoy and later reprinted as Nin 1977a. The 1977 edition includes as appendices the two *La Batalla* and five *Correspondance Internationale* articles of 1923 and 1924 noted above.

58    '¿El fascismo es un movimiento internacional?', *La Batalla* 33, 13 December 1923, in Nin 1977a, p. 211.

59    Nin 1977a, p. 212. See also the very similar formulation in Nin 1923, p. 7.

60    It should be noted that *Las dictaduras de nuestro tiempo* was a comparative study of several forms of contemporary dictatorship: bourgeois, fascist and the Soviet dictatorship of the proletariat.

ments on behalf of their bourgeoisies with the intention of repartitioning the world.[61] Fascism was thus a product of capitalism in its imperialist phase. But it was also, Nin argued, a result of the post-war situation in Europe. He listed the key ingredients that had enabled fascism to emerge in the first place and to become the weapon of capitalism in crisis. First, the Russian Revolution had initiated a process of world revolution. The evidence for this was visible in the form of the various revolutionary uprisings and struggles for national liberation and emancipation from colonial domination that characterised the post-war period. This unrest had thrown imperialism into deep crisis. Second, Nin pointed to the ongoing rivalries between imperialist powers, most notably the economic competition between Britain and the United States. Third, he stressed the post-war rise in unemployment and the bourgeoisie's onslaught on the political, social and economic advances of the working class. Finally, of huge significance was the structural transformation of industrial capitalism, expressed via rationalisation, centralisation and new methods of mass production such as Fordism.[62]

It was evident to Nin that imperialism had proved incapable of resolving its post-war problems. The resulting political crises of the 1920s had been all the more intense because in many countries the working class had attained a high level of political maturity. Given the objective situation, it was only to be expected that any 'solution' to capitalism's problems would entail the suppression or destruction of the political power of the working class: its parties, trade unions and press. As he later expressed it, in a revolutionary situation such as the one Spain had entered in 1930–1, traditional methods of repression proved inadequate. The situation required a highly centralised state, ruled by a disciplined party with mass support. This state would be relatively free from the direct control of the economically dominant classes. Nin noted that '[a] country never finds itself as close to fascism as when it comes closest to proletarian revolution'.[63] In this sense, he thought that the Italian anarchist Fabri was correct to describe fascism as a form of 'preventative counterrevolution'.[64]

---

61    Nin 1977a, p. 53.

62    Nin 1977a, pp. 40–52.

63    Nin, *Reacción y revolución en España* (Ediciones Nuevo Surco, January 1934) in Nin 1971, p. 132. In two modern compilations of Nin's writings in which this pamphlet appears (Nin 1971 and Nin 1978a), the editors have added the subtitle 'La revolución de octubre de 1934'. One must presume that this is an error, given that the pamphlet was written in December 1933 and published the following month. Francesc Bonamusa concurs with this view (Bonamusa 1977, p. 250 n. 3).

64    Nin 1977a, p. 108.

Nin's writings on fascism carried the central message that it was vitally important for the workers' organisations to understand the specific character of fascism and not to confuse it with other forms of bourgeois repression and dictatorship. In other words, fascism differed from other forms of authoritarianism. In 1932 he noted that the Comintern and Spanish Communist Party had demonstrated the political costs of just such confusion when they mistakenly supposed the dictatorship of Primo de Rivera to be 'fascist'. The official Communists had stated that the dictatorship could only be overthrown by a worker and peasant insurrection. Yet Primo's resignation and replacement by General Berenguer forced them, by the logic of their own position, to say that nothing had changed. Thus they were taken completely by surprise when, a year later, Spain's old régime gave way to a bourgeois republic, something they had thought to be impossible. Nin did not doubt that in the period of 1930 and 1931 Spain had indeed displayed the objective conditions for proletarian revolution, but the subjective conditions had been missing. The PCE's mistaken conceptions had thus prevented the Party from anticipating a period of bourgeois democracy in which the Communists could neutralise or win over the petty-bourgeoisie through the use of radical democratic demands. Such errors underpinned the ultra-left position that saw proletarian revolution as imminent and blinded them from the reality that the European working class had been thrown on the defensive.[65]

Unlike fascism, which relied upon a mass social movement, Primo's régime had rested upon certain power factions: the army, the monarchy, the Church, the landed oligarchy and the big bourgeoisie. It had taken power by means of a nineteenth century-style *pronunciamiento* rather than a populist seizure of power. Nin acknowledged that the dictatorship had indeed assumed the function of suppressing worker and peasant unrest, but it took power when the workers' movement was tired and exhausted after the struggles of the years from 1917 to 1920. Rather than abolish existing workers' organisations and attempt to establish fascist unions, as Mussolini did, Primo encouraged the Socialists to collaborate with the régime. The political economy of the dictatorship was inconsistent and uncertain rather than aggressive and expansionist. Fascism made claims to be a radical and modernising force, whereas Primo

---

65    'La carta abierta de la IC y el congreso del partido', *Comunismo* 10, March 1932, in
      Comunismo 1978, pp. 347–56. Part of this article can also be found in English translation
      in Beetham 1983, pp. 225–59.

was merely a means of prolonging the Restoration monarchy.[66] Fascism, by contrast, was a modern phenomenon driven by the requirements of capitalism. It depended upon its radical appeal to a mass social base comprised mainly of the petty-bourgeoisie, a class which found itself squeezed between large-scale capitalist enterprises and the proletariat.[67] Lacking economic and political independence, this class was forced to follow either the workers' organisations or the parties of the bourgeoisie. Fascism offered the petty-bourgeoisie a sup-posedly independent alternative which combined opposition to socialism and communism with hostility toward big capital. In doing so, the fascists played upon the discontent, disenchantment and fears of a class that had been badly affected by post-war economic crises and was frightened by manifestations of proletarian militancy.

In *Las dictaduras de nuestro tiempo*, Nin explained that Italian fascism arose as a consequence both of the nature of Italian capitalism and of the post-war conjuncture. Italy had been a latecomer to industrialisation; its capitalist devel-opment had yet to overcome the country's agrarian backwardness and regional differences. Its dominant industrial sectors were textiles and the automotive industry. Heavy industry was not highly developed and, where it existed, relied upon imported raw materials, state contracts and subsidies. Nin argued that, in those countries where heavy industry played a predominant economic role, it tended to forge an alliance with finance capital. Jointly, these fractions of the bourgeoisie utilised their power to ensure that the state pursued policies that suited their interests. This was the economic imperative behind the build-up of military power and the aggressive pursuit of imperialism and colonialism. Yet, owing to the relative weakness of its heavy industry, Italian capitalism had little economic basis for imperialist expansion.

Nin observed that Italy had remained neutral at the beginning of the world war largely because its dominant economic sectors, the textile industry and the large landowners, had understood the advantages of non-intervention. Light industrialists also feared the war would afford heavy industry a chance to chal-lenge for dominance. But northern heavy industrialists, encouraged by French capitalists, campaigned for Italian participation in the war and, in 1915, they were successful. In the climate of social unrest, disenchantment and economic crisis of the immediate post-war years, fascism was able to make headway. It

---

66    L. Tarquin (Nin), 'La crise de le dictature militaire en Espagne', *La Lutte de Classes* 18, 14 January 1930. The version referred to here is the Spanish translation: 'La crisis de la dictadura militar en España', in Nin 1978b, pp. 21–8.

67    'La carta abierta de la IC y el congreso del Partido', in Comunismo 1978, p. 348.

was greatly assisted by the mistakes of the Socialists, whose reformist leaders, when presented with a revolutionary opportunity in 1920, had been afraid to make a bid for power and retreated. This left the way clear for the fascists, whose numbers had grown to about 300,000 by 1922, to attack the now-demoralised workers' organisations and, with the material assistance of the bourgeoisie and the complicity of the government, complete the counterrevolution.[68]

An important aspect of Nin's 1930 theorisation is his perceptive comment that, once it had attained power and formed a régime, fascism cast off its radical façade and displayed its true colours. Rather than the professed anti-capitalism of the rise-to-power stage, the fascist state demonstrated its true function as the armed guard of big business. This new capitalist state subsidised industry and facilitated the process of industrial, financial, agrarian and commercial concentration that was already underway at the end of the war. It employed extreme violence in repressing and liquidating workers' organisations and established a régime of slavery in the factories. Yet, even with such radical measures, fascism was unable to resolve the fundamental contradictions of capitalism and the specific problems of the Italian economy. Conflicts between agriculture and industry, on the one hand, and between light and heavy industry, on the other, remained. Fascism attempted to bolster the economy through militarism and a policy of aggressive imperialist expansion. While heavy industry welcomed many of these policies, the cost had to be met by those who constituted fascism's mass base. Finally, since fascism did not represent a social revolution, it could never eradicate the essential class conflict between the proletariat and the bourgeoisie. Nin predicted that this would prove to be its ultimate downfall, although he did not rule out the possibility of the fascist régime being succeeded, briefly, by parliamentary democracy.[69]

It is possible to detect elements of a conception of uneven and combined development within Nin's analysis. He certainly considered fascism to be a phenomenon associated with countries whose capitalist development was backward, but he also saw a significant level of industrialisation as a prerequisite. Commenting upon the Turkish dictatorship, Nin observed that it would not become 'fascist' in character because Turkey was still emerging from its

---

68    Nin 1977a, pp. 110–18. Daniel Guérin acknowledged the influence of Nin's book upon his own understanding of fascism. He noted the emphasis Nin placed upon the different roles of light and heavy industry and the reasons why big business required a strong state of a fascist kind more than other economic interests did (Guérin 1973, p. 18).

69    Nin 1977a, pp. 119–37.

semi-feudal past.[70] This suggests that Nin saw fascism as a possibility only in countries that had passed beyond the phase of bourgeois revolution. Indeed, he stressed that fascism only became a serious option for the bourgeoisie once the objective conditions for proletarian revolution were present.[71]

In the presence of just such conditions during 1930 and 1931, Nin remarked, the Spanish workers' movement had failed to develop its revolutionary potential and now found itself on the defensive. In response to the failure of the revolutionary general strike called by the CNT for 8 January 1933, Nin employed Lenin's concept of revolutionary crisis.[72] Despite being profound in character, the strike failed to spread to the key industrial regions of Asturias and Vizcaya and did not radicalise the UGT or bring in rural workers and peasants. The anger that the petty-bourgeoisie and working class felt toward the Republic, Nin suggested, had yet to predispose them toward revolutionary action. Bourgeois power, based upon Republican illusions, still remained strong in Spain. Only as the bourgeoisie became demoralised and unable to control the political situation was there any danger of it seeking fascist solutions. And only if a large section of the population came to support the revolutionary party, or if the proletariat proved capable of at least neutralising the petty-bourgeoisie, would one be able to speak of a revolutionary situation in which victory was possible. In the absence of workers' councils (soviets) and a revolutionary communist party, Nin concluded, the Spanish working class might be unable to successfully oppose the imposition of another authoritarian régime.[73]

Until late in 1933, Nin tended to think that, while fascism was not yet an immediate danger in Spain, some form of Bonapartist dictatorship was possible.[74]

---

70   Nin 1977a, p. 106. Here, Nin is referring to the Turkish Revolution of 1920, led by Mustafa Kemal. This began as a nationalist uprising and led to the founding of a republic in 1923.

71   *Reacción y revolución en España*, in Nin 1971, p. 135.

72   See the discussion of Trotsky's use of the concept of 'revolutionary crisis' in Chapter One. The labour unrest of January 1933 was the context for the massacre of very poor rural workers in Casas Viejas in Cádiz province. This event proved to be highly damaging to the reformist Republican government, contributing to the break-up of the left Republican-Socialist coalition and further alienating anarchist workers from the Republic. It also gave the radical Right ammunition in its political attacks upon the reformist Republicans. These factors contributed to the electoral victory of the right-wing coalition in November 1933 (Preston 2006, pp. 61–5).

73   Nin, *La huelga general de enero y sus enseñanzas* (Editorial Comunismo, March 1933), reprinted in Nin 1971, pp. 105–16.

74   Nin, 'La situación política española y los comunistas: Notas al margen de la actualidad' and 'Las posibilidades de un fascismo español', *Comunismo* 22 and 23, March and April 1933, both in Comunismo 1978, p. 225 and p. 229.

The right-wing coalition's electoral victory in November suggested that fascism was now a real possibility. The new government of Alejandro Lerroux might easily be followed by an interim dictatorship similar to that of Salazar in Portugal, Nin warned. Owing to the inadequacy of such a régime from a capitalist point of view, a strong, centralised and disciplined fascist party with a mass base might develop, given favourable conditions.[75] Nin felt that the petty-bourgeoisie's social weight in Spanish society provided the raw material for a fascist movement. And Lerroux was a possible future dictator.[76]

### Maurín and the Alianza Obrera

Maurín's response to the dangers of authoritarianism was more at the level of practical politics than Marxist theory. His characterisation of Primo's régime had been of a military dictatorship that 'bordered on fascism'.[77] In his books *Los hombres de la Dictadura* and *La revolución española*, he did not offer a theoretical analysis of fascism, but warned that the Republic's failure to restructure the old state and its coercive apparatus made possible a coup attempt by the head of the Guardia Civil.[78] General Sanjurjo fulfilled this prediction to the letter in August 1932. In late 1931, Maurín still thought that the conflict between agrarian and industrial interests, the strength of democratic hopes and Spain's regional nationalist struggles all militated against the emergence of a strong fascist movement. He argued that the bourgeoisie was likely to look toward a military solution again.[79] While he modified and extended this assessment of the dangers of authoritarianism in his 1935 book *Hacia la segunda revolución*, Maurín did not add anything to Nin's general analysis of fascism. He still felt that fascism of the Italian and German variety had not yet gained much ground in Spain. Those elements often labelled 'fascist', such as Gil Robles and the CEDA, in reality represented the forces of the pre-1931 traditional order. Although Maurín never ruled out the possibility of a fascist-type movement developing, he thought that it was liable to be based in the military. In this sense, Maurín's surmise that a future dictatorship would take the form of a 'military-fascist régime', perhaps led jointly by Gil Robles and General Franco or Calvo Sotelo and General Goded, proved rather closer to the actual course of

---

75    Nin, *Reacción y revolución en España*, in Nin 1971, p. 144.
76    Nin, '¿Qué significa Lerroux en la política española?', *Comunismo* 30, November–December 1933, in Nin 1971, pp. 127–30.
77    Maurín, 'La marcha de nuestra revolución', *La Nueva Era*, June–July–August 1931, in Nueva Era 1976, p. 101.
78    Maurín 1977b, pp. 176–7.
79    Maurín 1977b, p. 299.

events than Nin's prognosis.[80] Maurín was also an originator and prime mover in a major effort to build unity among the disparate and fragmented Spanish workers' movement in the face of a political shift to the authoritarian Right.

By 1933, it was clear to many in the labour movement that it was imperative to respond to the growth of right-wing political militancy. Faced with the possibility of a CEDA government and the growth of fascist groups such as the Falange Española and Juntas de Ofensiva Nacional-Sindicalista (JONS, or Unions of the National-Syndicalist Offensive), the left wings of the Socialist PSOE and UGT became increasingly radicalised.[81] The anarcho-syndicalists of CNT-FAI also became more belligerent. In December 1933, various groupings on the Catalan Left signed a political agreement, including the local UGT and PSOE, the BOC, the Left Communists (Trotskyists), the Rabassaires' Union and the various syndicalist organisations. They agreed to construct a Workers' Alliance (Alianza Obrera) with the aim of safeguarding the gains made by the working class and opposing any attempt at a coup.[82] However, the CNT and PCE remained aloof from this attempt to build a united front. In 1934, the Alianza spread beyond Cataluña to other regions of the country, but only in Asturias did the local CNT participate. In September 1934, the PCE, hitherto hostile to the Alianza Obrera, changed tack and decided to participate. This complete turnaround in attitude in some ways foreshadowed the Comintern's move toward the Popular Front tactic. Yet the Spanish Popular Front was to prove far more a product of the internal dynamics of Spanish political conditions than is often assumed.[83] This debate is dealt with in greater depth in Chapters Five and Six.

As a founder and vigorous campaigner on behalf of the Alianza Obrera, Maurín had a very definite notion of the role that this broad workers' front might play. He conceived the Alianza as a new form of proletarian organisation that would exist over and above single parties or trade unions.[84] The threat of fascism, or a new dictatorship imposed by the army as in Poland and Portugal, demanded a workers' anti-fascist alliance. However, Maurín did not see it as a purely defensive organisation. He argued that the Alianza embodied the working class's unity in action on its way toward socialist revolution.[85] He came to see it as the Spanish alternative to the Russian soviet, growing organically out

---

80    Maurín 1966, pp. 404–19.

81    See the Appendix to this volume for more on the CEDA and the political situation in 1933.

82    See the 'Manifiesto de presentación de la Alianza Obrera de Cataluña', 10 December 1933, in Alba 1977, p. 189.

83    See the important revisionist perspective of the Spanish Popular Front in Graham 2002.

84    Maurín, 'El movimiento obrero en Cataluña', *Leviatán*, October 1934, p. 23.

85    Maurín, 'Alianza Obrera', Barcelona 1935, in Alba 1977, p. 238.

of the existing workers' organisations. He envisaged the Alianza beginning as a united front and becoming the instrument of insurrection, then the organ of proletarian power.[86]

Maurín's conception of a united front differed fundamentally from the version the official Communists advocated. For them, the united front had to be constructed from the base of the workers' organisations – because they assumed that the leadership, especially that of the social-democratic parties, would always betray the rank and file. Maurín rejected this assumption and argued that, had there been united action based around genuine agreement between the leaders of the German workers' organisations, Hitler would not have been able to take power. Although Maurín's initiative was a massive advance upon the then-sectarian view of the Comintern, the intractable problem facing the Alianza Obrera was the half-hearted, even hostile attitude adopted by the PSOE-UGT and CNT-FAI. Except in Asturias, the CNT refused to participate meaningfully in the Alianza. As Maurín himself noted, the PSOE-UGT's support for it was variable and reflected its general reluctance to cooperate with other workers' organisations.[87]

For his part, Nin had signed the manifesto of the Catalan Alianza Obrera on behalf of the Left Communists in December 1933 and now served on its Regional Committee. Like Maurín, he believed its formation marked the beginning of a genuine united front which would quickly spread across the entire country and enjoy the active support of all working-class organisations. In an interview with the workers' daily *Adelante* about the newly formed Alianza, Nin described it as one of the most important events in the international workers' movement since the 1920s. It marked an end to what he called the 'absurd' policy of the Stalinists that had proved so damaging. Nin also argued that the Alianza demonstrated the working class's readiness to fight independently for the completion of its historic task, the social revolution. He asserted that the rabassaires' participation in the Alianza showed that the peasants realised that their demands could only be satisfied through the proletarian revolution.[88] However, Nin was evidently mistaken on this point, since the rabassaires left the Alianza before long and returned to the more familiar political terrain of the Catalan nationalist organisation, the Esquerra.

As the Alianza Obrera spread to Valencia, Asturias and Madrid in 1934, the Left Communists participated fully in its local committees. Although it would be true to say that the Left Communists drew closer to the BOC in organisa-

---

86    Alba 1977, p. 241.

87    Heywood 1990, p. 136.

88    Nin, interview in *Adelante*, 16 January 1934, in Nin 1978b, pp. 179–80.

tional terms through their joint work in the Alianza, this did not imply a shared perspective on the revolutionary role of the Workers' Alliance. The Trotskyists rejected Maurín's argument that the Alianza could become the Spanish version of the soviet. They acknowledged that, in Russia, soviets had been created with relative ease from the very base of the working class because of the absence of mass working-class organisations. However, the Alianza was a united front established through a pact between existing organisations that did not show any signs of being prepared to relinquish their own control and set up a new revolutionary organ.[89] In other words, the Trotskyists did not share Maurín's optimism that the Alianza would play a role in the Spanish Revolution equivalent to that of the soviets in 1917.[90] This did not stop them from viewing the Alianza as a massive step forward; they subjected the CNT and PCE to sustained criticism for initially rejecting it.[91] Andrade also questioned the PSOE leaders' conviction and presented them as the main internal brake upon the Alianza's development.[92]

The greatest success of the Alianza Obrera came during the events of October 1934. The Left interpreted the CEDA deputies' entry into the government as a movement toward fascism. The wave of strikes that greeted this event reached the proportions of an insurrection in the two regions where the Alianza was strongest. In Cataluña the Alianza Obrera organised a revolutionary general strike in the face of FAI opposition. Following the declaration of a Catalan republic in Sabadell and a Socialist republic in Vilanova, the Alianza called upon the Generalitat to proclaim a Catalan state, but this was a short-lived affair that was easily suppressed by the army. In Asturias, where the Alianza uniquely enjoyed the support of all workers' organisations, including the local CNT and PCE, resistance to government forces continued for two weeks.

Reflecting upon what he called 'the lessons of the October insurrection', Nin noted that, in spite of the immaturity of conditions, the workers could not have done other than they did. To have avoided a conflict would have been a sign of weakness and would have deprived workers' organisations of a valuable

---

89    L. Fersen (Enrique Fernández Sendón) cited in Pagès 1977a, pp. 178–9.

90    Maurín stated that 'what the soviet was for the Russian Revolution, the Alianza Obrera is for the Spanish Revolution' (Maurín 1966, p. 119).

91    See the various articles from *Comunismo* on the Alianza Obrera in Comunismo 1978, pp. 300–1; see also Nin's article 'Hacia la Alianza Obrera Nacional', *La Antorcha* 1, 1 May 1934, in Nin 1978b, pp. 181–2.

92    Emilio Ruiz (Andrade), 'Los partidos y organizaciones obreras ante el frente único', *Comunismo* 32, February 1934; and 'El frente único, los stalianos y las Alianzas Obreras', *Comunismo* 37, August 1934, in Comunismo 1978, pp. 304–10 and pp. 319–25.

education. In Cataluña and Asturias, the insurrection had been motivated by the workers' desire to take power. In Asturias especially, Nin thought, events provided an important lesson in organising a Red Army, revolutionary committees and other actions peculiar to the initial stages of a proletarian revolution. This would not have been possible without the Alianza, Nin concluded.[93]

Maurín agreed that the remarkable force of the Asturian Revolution had been generated largely by the feeling of strength and unity fostered by the Alianza, as well as the specific political and economic situation in Spain at the time. In Cataluña, the absence of the CNT had proved the decisive weakness. Nevertheless, he believed that events had vindicated his hopes for the Alianza and made its elevation to a national scale with a central body a task of supreme importance. Had the Alianza been stronger in other areas, he suggested, the outcome might have been very different. Yet Maurín recognised that the Alianza would not be sufficient on its own. The concrete experience of October 1934 suggested that it was also necessary to build a united revolutionary socialist party. Under the guidance and leadership of such a party, the Alianza could become what Maurín called a 'supra-organisation, over and above the political and syndical organisations'. But it also had to become an instrument of insurrection, guided and led by a single revolutionary Marxist party. Maurín thus saw confirmation of his earlier prognosis that these events demonstrated the Alianza's potential to perform the same role as the soviets in 1917: once power had been taken, it would develop into the organ of proletarian power with all workers' and peasants' organisations represented in it.[94] Yet it still left unresolved the problem of how to construct a united revolutionary Marxist party.

## 4.3    Entryism or Fusion?

This brings us to the controversy that signalled the definitive break between the Spanish Trotskyists and Trotsky and his international organisation. It is also the issue that facilitated the process of fusion between the Left Communists and the BOC. As noted in the previous chapter, in June 1934 Trotsky proposed that his French followers enter the Socialist Party (SFIO) in order to take advantage of the recent radicalisation of a significant section of that organisation and as a means of breaking out of the political isolation in which the Trotskyists

---

93    Nin, 'Las lecciones de la insurreción de octubre. Es necesario un partido revolucionario del proletariado', and 'Derrotas demoralizadoras y derrotas fecundas', *L'Estrella Roja*, 1 December 1934 and 16 February 1935, in Nin 1978b, p. 446 and pp. 451–3.

94    Maurín, 'Alianza Obrera', Barcelona 1935, in Alba 1977, pp. 244–5.

found themselves. He believed that this would allow them to place the revolutionary programme of the Fourth International before a mass working-class
audience.[95] The Spanish Left Communists reacted to the French section's
adoption of this proposal by stating that this contradicted the very principles
Trotsky himself had laid down. The key objective should rather be to build a
united front, they argued, but this could not be done at the expense of losing
what they termed 'the organic independence of the proletarian vanguard'. In
order to maintain this principle of independence, they were prepared to risk a
formal rupture with Trotsky.[96]

It seems clear that the events of October 1934 provoked a change in the attitude of many Left Communist leaders toward the new tactic of 'entry' into
social-democratic parties. Trotsky condemned what he called the 'passivity'
of the Spanish section and argued that its position in the workers' movement
would have been more favourable had it entered the PSOE in the build-up to
Spain's October Revolution.[97] One of those who had previously been hostile
to entryism, Enrique Fernández Sendón, had since become an advocate of it
following discussions with Socialist Youth leaders in prison.[98] Meanwhile, in
Cataluña, Nin began talks over the question of unity with the BOC and several
other left groups, including the Catalan Federation of the PSOE. Political differences, as usual, soon reduced the spectrum of groups involved to just the
BOC and Left Communists. The Executive Committee of the Left Communists
now proposed a compromise solution whereby its local sections outside of
Cataluña would try to enter the PSOE. In Cataluña, however, the PSOE was
very weak and the possibility of fusion with the BOC appeared the best way
to build a revolutionary party.[99] This compromise, which Trotsky might just
have accepted, was in practice rejected by the majority of rank-and-file Left
Communists. They did not believe in the possibility of influencing the Socialist
Party and feared being absorbed by it, losing all political independence. They
now sought to participate in a new revolutionary party which, although based
in Cataluña, would spread to all parts of Spain via the existing Left Communist

---

95    Deutscher 1963, p. 271.

96    Editorial in *Comunismo*, No. 38, September 1934, cited in Pagès 1977a, p. 276.

97    Trotsky's letters to International Secretariat, 1 November and 16 December 1934, in Trotsky
      1973a, p. 202 and p. 206.

98    See L. Fersen (Enrique Fenández Sendón), 'Boletín interior de la ICE', No. XII, 25 April
      1935, cited in Pagès 1977a, p. 277. *Comunismo* was banned after October 1934 and never
      appeared again. This must have added to the Left Communists' feelings of isolation and
      impotence.

99    'Boletín interior de la ICE', No. XII, 25 April 1935, reproduced in Trotsky 1977, pp. 259–63.

groups. The Executive Committee accepted the majority's wish, finally opening the way for the creation of the POUM in September.[100]

The following chapter deals with the formation and significance of the POUM, but it is worth considering briefly the realistic prospects for 'entry' into the PSOE in 1934 and 1935. Pierre Broué has argued that, in proposing the Left Communists' temporary entry into the Socialist Party, Trotsky was primarily concerned with winning over the youth movement. He notes that from September 1933 the Socialist Youth were influenced by Trotskyist ideas, even engaging in a debate around the project of building a Fourth International.[101] They viewed the Trotskyists as seeking the same ends as themselves: namely, to break with the Second International's revisionism and the Comintern's Stalinism. Yet they were ambivalent over the question of a new International, anxious not to be seen as attacking either official or dissident communists.[102] Socialist Youth leaders such as Santiago Carrillo, who became a severe critic of Trotskyism only months later, expressed admiration for Trotsky and the Fourth International and were critical of the PCE. In the Alianza Obrera and the Banking Federation of the UGT, the Trotskyists and Socialist Youth worked alongside each other, yet these ideological and circumstantial convergences were never transformed into a formal political partnership.[103] Outside of the Alianza, the only real collaboration between the Trotskyists and left Socialists came in the form of Nin's articles for the journal *Leviatán*.[104] However, it soon became clear to Nin and his comrades that Largo Caballero's radicalism derived from a need not to appear to lag behind the rank and file. Fernández Sendón described Largo Caballero's 'conversion' to Marxist-Leninism as a ploy to gain control of his own Socialist Party.[105] No one doubted that there were genuine revolutionary currents within the PSOE, but the Trotskyists felt that

---

100  A minority disagreed with this and some key figures left to 'enter' the PSOE. These were Fernández Sendón, Esteban Bilbao, Grandizo Munis and two others. According to Andrade, they took between six and eight other militants with them. Juan Andrade, 'Carta a un camarada americano', 29 June 1935, in Trotsky 1977, p. 272. For a defence of the tactic of 'entryism' by one of its Spanish exponents, see Munis 1977, pp. 213–18.

101  Broué 1983, p. 26 n. 23.

102  Extracts from articles by Federico Melchor in *Renovación*, the Socialist Youth paper, are to be found in Pagès 1977, pp. 255–6.

103  Pagès 1977, pp. 256–7.

104  The brainchild of the Socialist intellectual Luís Araquistáin during a brief flirtation with revolutionary Marxism, *Leviatán* was one of three serious theoretical journals to emerge from the Spanish Left of the 1930s. The other two were *Comunismo* and *La Nueva Era*, both produced by the dissident communists. See Preston 1986, pp. 40–57.

105  Fernández Sendón 1934a, pp. 377–81.

the prospect of another left Republican government might weaken these currents' radicalism.[106]

Thus there seems little reason to doubt that the 800 or so Left Communists had the opportunity to break out of their isolation by joining forces with the left Socialists.[107] It could be argued that this might have given Nin and his comrades the chance to utilise the very quality that had earned them a measure of respect out of all proportion to their numerical weight, namely their superior Marxist theoretical analysis. Within the Socialist Youth alone, they could have reached some forty thousand by April 1936.[108]

Further evidence that the Socialist Youth sought concrete links with the dissident communists rather than the PCE came in 1935. Speaking in June, at which time the BOC and Left Communists were discussing fusion, Carrillo lamented the fact that what he termed 'the Bolshevisation of the Socialist Party' was taking place without the participation of 'all authentic Marxists'. He feared that, without the aid of Nin and Maurín's groups, the Socialists' efforts would prove 'sterile'.[109] In August and September, Carrillo wrote three articles in which he suggested that Maurín and his comrades might enter the PSOE.[110] In reply, Maurín rejected Carrillo's case for two main reasons. First, he did not think that the PSOE could be converted into Spain's Bolshevik Party. Its reformist tradition ruled this out. Indeed, no existing force could play this role. He believed that the revolutionary party would be constructed by unifying all revolutionary Marxist forces within an organisation that did not yet exist. His second reason was that he simply did not believe it would be possible for the dissident communists to successfully enter the PSOE. Those French Trotskyists who had entered the SFIO now faced expulsion. The same would happen in Spain. In addition, he noted that the PSOE's regulations required a probationary period before new members were able to enjoy full rights in the party. All of this would entail a step backwards for the dissident communists who were on the brink of creating a new organisation. Maurín claimed this new party, the

---

106  Fernández Sendón 1934b, pp. 248–52.

107  The membership figure of 800 is suggested by Pagès. Estimates vary between 200 (Víctor Alba) and 2,000 (Grandizo Munis). However, much of the material on the Left Communists, the BOC and the POUM was written by participants in them and must be handled with care. Pagès, on the other hand, bases his figure upon a study of surviving documentation of the various local groups and weighs this alongside the contemporary figures of 700, given by Jean Rous, and 800, by Andrade. See Pagès 1977, p. 94.

108  Heywood 1990, p. 175.

109  Santiago Carrillo, 'Habla el secretario de la Juventud Socialista', *La Batalla*, 28 June 1935, quoted in Broué 1983, p. 43.

110  Two of Carrillo's and three of Maurín's articles are to be found in Alba 1977, pp. 52–71.

POUM, would correspond to the changing situation in Spain in a way in which existing parties, weighed down by their traditions, could never do.[111] In other words, Maurín thought that, rather than bury themselves in an outmoded organisation, the dissident communists' task was to form the pole of attraction toward which all genuine revolutionary elements would be drawn.

Broué has argued that Maurín failed to comprehend what was really at stake in the internal struggles of the PSOE, namely the independence of the main working-class party from the bourgeois Republicans. On the Right of the Socialist Party, Indalecio Prieto sought to renew the alliance with the Republicans broken by the events of 1933. The left Socialists, led by Largo Caballero, opposed any such collaboration with the bourgeoisie and proclaimed the need for a proletarian revolution. Disarmed by the limitations of their own political comprehension, in particular their ignorance of the nature of Stalinism, Broué argues that they were open to the influence of those who appeared to embody the authority of the Russian Revolution. For him, therefore, this was a missed opportunity that, if taken, might have altered events significantly. In the event, impressed by the new Comintern policy of the 'Popular Anti-Fascist Bloc', the left Socialists were increasingly drawn toward the official Communists and, in April 1935, the Socialist Youth fused with the Communist Youth to become the Unified Socialist Youth.[112] This afforded the PCE the mass base it had always lacked.[113] Broué's point is that if the two wings of dissident communism had taken the opportunity to enter the Socialist Party and furnish it with the revolutionary clarity and guidance it desperately lacked, their warnings about the 'mistakes' of the Stalinists might have been heeded. It might be objected that such a view resides within the realms of the 'if only' school of history that often marks historical and political writing on the Spanish Civil War. Yet it does indicate, supported by some primary-source evidence, the possibility of a different constellation of forces on the revolutionary Marxist Left in the run-up to the Civil War period.

---

111   See Maurín's first article in response to Carrillo in Alba 1977, pp. 58–61. All of these articles were first published in *La Batalla* at the time and then subsequently collected in a pamphlet, *La polémica Maurín-Carrillo*, published in 1937 by Andrade's Barcelona-based Editorial Marxista.

112   Broué 1983, pp. 43–4.

113   In November 1936, many of the Socialist Youth leaders went the full distance and joined the PCE.

## 4.4     Conclusion

As we have seen, the major disagreements between Trotsky and the Spanish dissident communists revolved around the question of how best to achieve unity and create a revolutionary organisation within a deeply divided labour movement. Even with the advantage of hindsight, it is impossible to state with any certainty which course of action would have produced the best results. However, it is important to underscore the strengths and weaknesses of the dissident communists' analysis and actions up until the POUM's founding in September 1935.

In practice, if not in theory, both the BOC and the Left Communists appear to have anticipated Trotsky's conclusion that it was impossible to influence the official Communists in a revolutionary direction. Since the BOC included most of those who had made up the Catalan Federation of the Communist Party, the requirement to 'win them over' clearly did not really apply in Cataluña anyway. The Trotskyists, organised upon a national basis, did attempt to influence the PCE, but without success. From March 1932, their political activities increasingly contradicted their supposed status as an oppositional faction within the PCE. It would appear that their influence was far greater among the Socialist Youth and the left wing of the PSOE than among the Communists.[114] We have seen that this reality led the leaders of the Left Communists to accept the principle of entering the PSOE in all regions other than Cataluña, although they failed to win enough members to this policy. It is, then, perhaps ironic to note that one of the main arguments deployed against entryism and in favour of fusion with the BOC had to do with preserving the Left Communists' political independence. Logically, both actions involved some degree of sacrifice of independence. Chapter Five examines the extent to which partisans of the prevailing 'fusion' perspective were able to maintain their 'political independence' within the POUM.

It is clear that the BOC pursued policies mainly oriented toward the situation in Cataluña.[115] The question of Catalan nationalism was a central aspect of its political programme. Indeed, one of the original causes of the splits within the PCE concerned the official Party's failure to campaign on the national question. Over this issue, the BOC found itself closer to the petty-bourgeois Esquerra than to the PSOE-UGT or the anarchist elements in the CNT. Yet there

---

114     See Pagès 1977, p. 73 and pp. 253–8.
115     However, the BOC did have small groups of sympathisers in Asturias, Madrid and Valencia (Alba and Schwartz 1988, p. 47).

was considerable support for Catalan nationalism among the rank and file of the CNT, some of whom were also members of the Esquerra. The BOC conducted much of its political work within the trade unions and enjoyed a large measure of success among union members. But Maurín and the BOC's major achievement was undoubtedly the creation of a united-front organisation. The Alianza Obrera represented the only serious attempt to unite the workers' movement. It achieved remarkable, if brief, success in Asturias. After October 1934, however, the Alianza faded into the background due to the indifference of both the Socialists and the anarcho-syndicalists.

As we have seen, Nin arrived early on at a sophisticated understanding of the phenomenon of fascism. Neither he nor Maurín underestimated the dangers of a similar movement developing in Spain; both realised that a potential petty-bourgeois mass base existed. Yet, despite an awareness of the potential support for fascist-style movements among the peasantry, it is notable that the dissident communists devoted surprisingly little attention to working out how to win their support for radical tactics such as land seizures.[116] Like Trotsky, they tended to assume that revolutionary action had to be focused upon industrial centres. They overlooked the more proletarian character of rural workers in Spain. When claiming that the influx of peasants from Andalucía and elsewhere to Cataluña had 'deformed' the workers' movement, Maurín suggested that these peasants had been totally impervious to Socialist propaganda.[117] Yet this was written at a time when the Socialist Landworkers' Federation (FNTT), which was part of the UGT, was undergoing a massive increase in membership, especially in the south.[118] In other words, it was a major tactical and theoretical error to overlook or downplay the land question.

---

116    Heywood is certainly right to note that the dissident communists paid insufficient attention to the agrarian question (Heywood 1990, p. 142). He is inaccurate, though, when he states that in its 38 issues *Comunismo* carried only three articles devoted to agrarian matters. There were in fact six articles: Roberto Mariner, 'Proyecto de tesis agraria', *Comunismo* 2, June 1931; Luís García Palacios, 'Comentarios al proyecto de reforma agraria', *Comunismo* 4, September 1931; Luís García Palacios, 'Las perfidias del proyecto de reforma agraria', *Comunismo* 9, February 1932; Marino Vela, 'Fuerzas democráticas y fuerzas socialistas en el campo', *Comunismo* 12, May 1932; Emilio Ruiz (Andrade), 'La contrarrevolución agraria en Salamanca', *Comunismo* 26, July 1933; and L. Fersen (Enrique Fernández Sendón), 'Crítica de la reforma agraria', *Comunismo* 27, August 1933.

117    Maurín 1977b, p. 154.

118    Between June 1930 and June 1932, membership in the FNTT rose from 36,639 to 392,953. In 1930, only 13 per cent of UGT members were rural workers, but by 1932 they made up 38 per cent of a larger total membership (Preston 1983, p. 54 and p. 166).

Finally, it is worth stressing the extent to which Maurín and the BOC moved away from positions that bore traces of the Comintern line. Chapter Three argued that, as a result of the Asturian Revolution, Maurín's view of the Spanish Revolution became unequivocally permanentist. He similarly clarified his attitude toward the USSR. If the BOC had ever taken Stalin's conception of 'socialism in one country' seriously, Maurín totally dismissed it in his 1935 book *Hacia la segunda revolución*.[119]

> The victory of Stalin over Trotsky is the victory of Russian socialism over international socialism. Between 1917 and 1924 Russia had oriented itself toward the question of revolution in other countries. But upon witnessing the failure of attempts at workers' revolutions in Hungary, Austria, Germany and Bulgaria, it lost confidence in the European proletariat and concentrated upon itself. Stalin invented the myth of 'socialism in one country'. Yesterdays' internationalists were transformed into fervent nationalists.... The consequences were inevitably felt in the international workers' movement. The Communist International changed from being the centre of world revolution into an instrument at the service of the Soviet State.[120]

Maurín stressed that Stalin's argument was that Russia had to be defended at all costs and by all means while international capitalism decayed. Only then would international socialism be a real possibility. But this meant it was no longer in Stalin's interests to promote a revolutionary policy. As Maurín pointed out:

> Moscow, precisely because of its Russian policy, fears and shrinks away from a workers' revolution in another European country for two reasons. In the first place, because a workers' revolution could destroy the current 'status quo' and precipitate a war, something Russia needs to avoid at all costs. Russia comes first; everything else is secondary. In the second place, because a proletarian revolution in another European country would be bound to lose Russia the influence it has held over the proletariat up until now.[121]

---

119    The possibility that they did is noted in Durgan 1989, pp. 69–70.
120    Maurín 1966, p. 108.
121    Maurín 1966, p. 110.

Maurín proposed building a united revolutionary Marxist party out of the elements who had rejected Stalin's abandonment of Leninism. But he stressed that Lenin had succeeded because he knew how to adapt Marxism to Russian conditions. The dissident communists were now faced with performing the very same task, but under quite different circumstances. Their efforts to do so are examined in the next chapters.

# CHAPTER 5

# Marxist Unity: The Creation of the POUM

The last three chapters of this study examine the political ideas and main activities of the POUM in the context of the immediate background to the Civil War: the 'summer revolution' of 1936, participation in the Catalan government, the campaign against the POUM and the crisis of May 1937. A full history of the POUM lies beyond the scope of this study and is to be found elsewhere in any case. The intention in the present chapter is to address a number of political questions concerning the party's approach to the fundamental problems of the Spanish Revolution. Chief among these is the key problem of revolutionary agency. Why did the two main groups of dissident communists join forces in the autumn of 1935 and how did the new entity, the POUM, set about building a revolutionary party in a situation radically different to the one faced by the Bolsheviks in 1917? To what extent did the POUM constitute a compromise between the political ideas of Nin and Maurín? Was its programme informed by a permanentist perspective? Chapter Six looks at the question of the POUM and its participation in the Popular Front electoral pact. Why did the POUM sign the pact in the first place? Did its later decision to participate in the Catalan government, the Generalitat, contradict its revolutionary theory? How did the POUM leaders rebuff the fierce criticisms Trotsky and his international organisation aimed at them? Chapter Seven addresses the question of the extent and manner of the POUM's participation in the revolutionary transformations from July 1936. How did the party approach the question of political power at the local and national levels? What was its attitude to the military question and what role did its militias play in the Civil War? How did the POUM warn the revolutionary workers of the onset of the counterrevolution and what steps did they take to combat it? Finally, how might the events of May 1937 and after – the destruction of the POUM, the murder of Nin and the attempt at a 'show trial' of surviving leaders – be understood by historians today?

As we have seen in earlier chapters, it is important to take Trotsky's attitude toward events in Spain into account because of his continuing influence over the dissident communists' positions. While, in general historical studies, the POUM is often mistakenly referred to as a 'Trotskyist' party, there are good reasons to add a rider when correcting this error. Although the POUM diverged from Trotsky over questions of strategy and tactics, its political practice was still informed by a conception of revolution consistent with the theory of permanent revolution. That is to say, the POUM leaders never doubted that the coming revolution would witness the combination of democratic and social-ist tasks within a single, uninterrupted process. They thought the revolution would begin by addressing the outstanding 'democratic' issues the bourgeois Republicans had been unable or unwilling to resolve, but by virtue of the class base of those making the revolution – workers and peasants – the 'solution' to these questions would be of a socialist nature. Hence, one might argue that while, in organisational terms, the POUM was certainly not in any sense Trotskyist, in its theoretical perspectives and many of its political positions Trotsky's influence loomed large.

The current chapter examines the organisational convergence of the dissi-dent communists in 1935, outlining and exploring their stance toward political conditions in Spain and their efforts to build international Marxist unity. It starts by examining the political basis upon which the Left Communists and BOC merged and the programme of Marxist unification the new party adopted.

## 5.1     Fusion or Absorption?

The Left Communists formally merged with the BOC to form the Partido Obrero de Unificación Marxista (POUM, Workers' Party of Marxist Unification) in Barcelona on 29 September 1935. Its programme was the outcome of nego-tiations between Maurín and Nin during which it was agreed that the new organisation would be completely independent of all other groupings and that there would be no contact with Trotsky.[1] Looking back on the fusion pro-cess many years later, Maurín noted that he considered the merger with Nin's organisation to have been more of a 'confluence' than a fusion. He argued that Trotsky had been correct when he said that the Left Communists had rallied to the BOC. Indeed, Maurín continued, the only concession the BOC had made was over changing the name to the POUM.[2]

We might conclude from Maurín's recollections that, rather than two organ-isations fusing based upon agreed principles, the Spanish Trotskyists were

---

1   This is according to Maurín's letter to Víctor Alba of 29 February 1972, quoted in Alba and Schwartz 1988, p. 90. The negotiations between leaders of the Left Communists (ICE), BOC, Unió Socialista de Catalunya, Partit Comunista Català (PCC), Catalan Federation of the PSOE and Partit Català Proletari (PCP) began in January 1935, but by the late spring only the ICE and BOC were still talking. For a detailed account of the ICE's role, see Pagès 1977, pp. 260–88.

2   Maurín, letter to Pierre Broué, 18 May 1972, in Pagès 1977, p. 91.

simply incorporated into the BOC. But this is far from the truth of the matter in terms of political theory. In the previous two chapters, it was noted that Maurín modified his ideas significantly in response to the events of October 1934. The BOC became increasingly critical of the Comintern and rather less critical of the Left Communists as they collaborated in the Alianza Obrera. In a letter to an American Trotskyist, Juan Andrade expressed his opinion that Maurín had completely corrected his point of view and was now in agreement with the Left Communists.[3] If this was stretching things somewhat, the reality was that after October 1934 the leaderships of both organisations had shifted position over many of the issues that had previously divided them. It is evident both from the programme of the new party and from the manner in which it was formulated that the POUM was really a synthesis of Nin's and Maurín's political ideas at a particular stage of the Spanish Revolution. According to Nin's July 1935 article, the common ground between the two organisations made fusion possible without either party sacrificing its principles or tactics.[4]

Perhaps the clearest expression of the political convergence of the two dissident communist groups can be seen in the programmatic document ¿Qué es y qué quiere el POUM? ('What Is the POUM and What Does It Want?').[5] In this explanation of the purpose and nature of the new organisation, written jointly by Nin and Maurín, the POUM is placed squarely in the context of Spain's political development from 1931 to the end of 1935. As the opening sentence states: 'The current phase of the revolution taking place in Spain is one of transition between fascist counterrevolution and the democratic-socialist revolution'.[6] As with all revolutions, if Spain's was to succeed it would require a revolutionary party. Indeed, the main reason for the failure of the insurrections in Asturias and Cataluña in 1934, the authors argue, had been precisely the absence of this indispensable revolutionary ingredient. Hence, the POUM was designed primarily to promote and facilitate the process of unifying all revolutionary Marxist elements.

---

3   Andrade, letter to an American comrade (A. González), 29 June 1935, Trotsky 1977, p. 273.

4   Nin, 'Un pacto de unificación firme y sincero', 19 July 1935, in Nin 1978a, p. 459. Andrew Durgan also notes that, in spite of the numerical superiority of the BOC inside the POUM, the new party cannot be seen as a continuation of the BOC under a different name with the absorption of the Left Communists (Durgan 1989, p. 249).

5   ¿Qué es y qué quiere el POUM? Written in late 1935 and early 1936, reproduced in Alba 1977, pp. 29–51.

6   Alba 1977, p. 30.

The Workers' Party of Marxist Unification, resulting from the merger of the Workers' and Peasants' Bloc and the Left Communists, thinks that it can provide the focal point that will enable the joining together of all Marxists in a single resolute party. The problem is not one of entryism or absorption, but of revolutionary Marxist unification. A new party must be formed through the fusion of revolutionary Marxists.[7]

This raises the question of whether the POUM itself was intended to constitute the new revolutionary party or whether it was the means of creating a revolutionary Marxist party. According to the founders, it seems clear that the POUM was intended to establish the conditions for broader unification of all revolutionary Marxists.[8] Though its title included the word 'party', the POUM itself would not necessarily constitute the revolutionary party. Such a party would be the final result of a broader process of unification that would encompass all genuine revolutionary Marxist elements from the PSOE, PCE and other groupings outside of the POUM. Nin insisted that unification must take place upon the basis of revolutionary Marxist principles and a non-sectarian programme.[9] The POUM's practical task was therefore to win all like-minded elements over to this point of view and to convoke what he called a 'congress of revolutionary Marxist unification'.[10] *¿Qué es y qué quiere el POUM?* outlined a clear political programme that the new party advanced as a potential basis upon which unification could take place. In other words, the POUM's function was to provide the revolutionary Marxist political theory for Spain's revolutionary forces.

## 5.2     The POUM's Programme

The programme began by describing the current phase of the Spanish Revolution, from late 1935 to early 1936, as finely balanced between a possible fascist counterrevolution against the Republic and a potential 'democratic-socialist revolution' that would take matters beyond the limits of bourgeois democracy. It seems clear that the authors ruled out the continuation of the Republican status quo. They argued instead that, since the bourgeoisie was

---

7     Alba 1977, pp. 33–4.
8     Nin, 'Hacia la unidad marxista', *La Batalla*, 23 August 1935, in Nin 1978a, p. 469. Maurín was also clear that the POUM was never intended as a fully formed party. See his letter to Joan Rocabert, 11 October 1971, reproduced in Fundació Andreu Nin, 1989a, p. 13.
9     Nin, 'Hacia la unidad Marxista', in Nin 1978a, p. 470.
10    *¿Qué es y qué quiere el POUM?* in Alba 1977, pp. 34–5.

no longer even nominally democratic, the working class remained the only guarantee of democracy. By defending truly radical democratic demands, the actions of working-class organisations would bring Spain to the brink of a socialist revolution. Within this context, it would be possible to establish the framework for a meaningful democracy – a workers' democracy. Their prognosis was that either the counterrevolutionary forces of the big bourgeoisie and the remaining semi-feudal interests would succeed in establishing a dictatorship of a fascist nature 'or it will be the working class that is victorious, installing the dictatorship of the proletariat that will bring to a head the democratic revolution that had been truncated when in the hands of the petty-bourgeoisie, so as to pass without interruption onto the socialist revolution'.[11]

Although this conception was couched in the terms of Maurín's 'democratic-socialist revolution', of which Trotsky was highly suspicious, it was clearly a permanentist perspective. Nin and Maurín contrasted their conception with that of the Socialist Party. Whereas the PSOE considered the Spanish Revolution to be merely democratic,

> we have said that the proletarian revolution – and the example has been set us by the Russian Revolution – will triumph as a democratic-socialist revolution. In the current historical period, there can no longer be revolutions that are exclusively democratic nor, in a certain sense, revolutions that are exclusively socialist. The revolution has to be democratic-socialist in its initial phase.[12]

The workers would take state power, they insisted, and address the democratic tasks that the bourgeoisie had failed to confront. Yet the key point was that workers' 'solutions' to questions of democracy, justice and equality would not be those of the bourgeoisie. Rather, they would reflect their own class project and thus prove socialist in nature. The transition from democratic to socialist revolution would, they said, be 'uninterrupted' ('sin solución de continuidad').[13] It is hard to see this as anything other than a restatement of Trotsky's version of the theory of permanent revolution.

In their programmatic document, Nin and Maurín affirmed that the proletariat, by which they really meant its representatives, needed to become the strongest advocate of radical democratic demands, including wider democracy,

---

11   Alba 1977, p. 30. Also Maurín, 'El año crucial de nuestra revolución', *La Batalla*, 3 January 1936, reproduced in Fundació Andreu Nin, 1989a, p. 4.

12   *¿Qué es y qué quiere el POUM?* in Alba 1977, p. 32 and pp. 41–2.

13   *¿Qué es y qué quiere el POUM?* in Alba 1977, p. 30.

the solution of the agrarian question, national liberation, restructuring the state, women's liberation, destroying the power of the Church and improving the workers' material situation.[14] The national question, previously a major source of disagreement between them, now received a theoretical treatment that was closer to the one outlined by the Left Communists than the position the BOC had hitherto maintained. The POUM programme recognised three regions with realistic claims to national liberation: Cataluña, the Basque Country and Galicia.[15] In addition, its manifesto did not actively seek to promote separatism, although it affirmed the right of nationalities to self-determination, up to and including formal separation.[16] This change of policy by the BOC leadership in the course of negotiations with Nin's group was a major cause of the break-away by the more nationalist-minded elements around the Catalan-language weekly *L'Hora*. Most of this group gravitated toward the Catalan Federation of the Socialist Party.[17]

With respect to the agrarian question, Nin and Maurín predicted that, at the beginning of the revolution in the countryside, the peasants would take control of the land. As they stated, the revolutionary slogan would have to be 'The land for those who work it!'[18] In gaining control over the forces of production, the peasants would attack not simply the remaining feudal and semi-feudal elements, but also the big bourgeois interests that were closely linked to them. The democratic and socialist aspects of the revolution would thus combine in the following way:

> The process of this revolution is dual: while on the one hand, the peasants will undermine the feudal-bourgeois fortress by their actions, the proletariat, on the other hand, will begin to nationalise large industries such as mining, transportation, the banks, etc.; that is to say, they will begin the socialist aspect of the revolution. The bourgeois revolution in the countryside and the socialist revolution in the cities will coincide.[19]

---

14    *¿Qué es y qué quiere el POUM?* in Alba 1977, p. 31.

15    Durgan 1989, p. 244. *¿Qué es y qué quiere el POUM?* makes reference only to the Basque and Catalan cases.

16    *¿Qué es y qué quiere el POUM?* in Alba 1977, p. 42.

17    For a discussion of this Catalanist grouping, whose members always opposed merging with the Left Communists, see Durgan 1996, pp. 368–72.

18    *¿Qué es y qué quiere el POUM?* in Alba 1977, p. 40.

19    Ibid.

Once the workers had taken power, Nin and Maurín anticipated that the land would be nationalised. Here they assume the inception of a workers' state that would initially grant peasants the right of use but not outright ownership of the land. As a second phase in the socialisation of agriculture, the government would help peasants to convert the large estates into cooperatives and collective farms and promote the modernisation of agrarian production.[20] The proletarian revolution could not succeed in a backward country like Spain unless the great mass of the peasantry came to identify their own interests within it, they argued.

As we noted in the previous chapter, Nin in particular thought that the prospect of a Spanish form of fascism exploiting the discontent and fears of the petty-bourgeoisie made the anti-fascist struggle a matter of life and death for the workers' movement. Since the petty-bourgeoisie, according to Nin's analysis of fascism, tended to provide the key mass support for authoritarian parties, this social class would need to be either won over to the revolution or neutralised in political terms. Yet, in order to achieve this outcome, he did not think the revolutionary party should enter into permanent alliances with petty-bourgeois parties. Such a tactic appeared close to the recent 'turn' in the Comintern policy toward building cross-class 'people's fronts'. However, the POUM programme did state that it was permissible to reach what it called 'circumstantial pacts' with the left petty-bourgeoisie; it made an appeal to the authority of Lenin in this respect.[21] Maurín had previously noted that the once-radical Esquerra had demonstrated its conservatism in October 1934 by deserting the revolutionary movement in Cataluña.[22] He thought that the Esquerra would soon disintegrate and that the workers' movement would be able to gain hegemony over the Catalan national liberation movement.[23] This was one way in which he envisaged the revolutionary party being constructed in Cataluña and then spreading to the rest of Spain.[24] In *¿Qué es y qué quiere el POUM?*, Nin and Maurín argued that as soon as the petty-bourgeois Republican and nationalist parties realised that the deepening of the democratic revolution, particularly in regard to the national and agrarian questions, meant moving closer to the goals of socialism, they would abandon their radicalism. This had indeed occurred in Cataluña in October 1934, they noted, once it became clear that leadership of the national struggle was likely to pass into the hands

---

20   *¿Qué es y qué quiere el POUM?* in Alba 1977, p. 41.
21   *¿Qué es y qué quiere el POUM?* in Alba 1977, p. 32.
22   Maurín, *Alianza Obrera* (1935), reproduced in Alba 1977, p. 241.
23   Maurín 1966, p. 184.
24   Durgan 1989, pp. 223–4.

of the working class. At this point, the Esquerra had retreated from the scene in order to retain control over the nationalist movement.[25] Hence a key task of the POUM in the coming period would be 'to work for the displacement of the petty-bourgeoisie from the leadership of the national movement so that the proletariat itself can take control and provide a solution that will lead to the construction of an Iberian Union of Socialist Republics'.[26]

If the POUM could be criticised for focusing too much of its attention upon Cataluña and failing to take full advantage of the foundations the Left Communists had laid for a national party, it should be stressed that a major aspect of its proposed programme for revolutionary Marxist unity was the creation of the truly national Alianza Obrera. Coupled with this ambition was a proposal for trade union unification. Nin and Maurín believed that the only way to overcome the major historical weakness of the Spanish workers' movement, especially the division between the UGT and CNT, was by creating a single centre around which to organise. They thought that, if syndical unity could be created in Cataluña, the rest of the country might follow.[27] In May 1936, with precisely this purpose, Nin was instrumental in setting up a Workers' Federation of Trade Union Unity, the Federació Obrera d'Unificació Sindical (FOUS).[28] The new organisation operated in Cataluña in an attempt to consolidate the Alianza by unifying the various union federations. However, the PSOE's, CNT's and PCE's effective opposition to the Alianza Obrera and the continuing hostility between the UGT and CNT nullified all of the POUM's best efforts to unify the trade union movement. Indeed, outside of Cataluña, POUM affiliates tended to join the UGT.

Another important aspect of the POUM's political theory that had always been central to both Left Communist and BOC thinking, although perhaps more prominent in the literature of the former, was its commitment to revolutionary internationalism. On this point, the dissident communists shared Trotsky's belief that a socialist society could only be built after the success of proletarian revolutions in several major capitalist countries. If revolutions were essentially national in terms of the conquest of power, a socialist economy could only succeed on the basis of an international division of labour. Hence, the POUM concurred with Trotsky that all proletarian revolutions were necessarily connected and interdependent parts of a wider process of 'world revolution'. An

---

25    ¿Qué es y qué quiere el POUM? in Alba 1977, pp. 42–3.

26    ¿Qué es y qué quiere el POUM? in Alba 1977, p. 43.

27    ¿Qué es y qué quiere el POUM? in Alba 1977, pp. 38–9.

28    Nin, 'La Federación Obrera de Unidad Sindical', La Batalla, 15 May 1936, in Nin 1978a,
      p. 513.

international revolutionary strategy was also the only guarantee against the spread of fascism and another imperialist war, as well as the best defence of the Soviet Union.[29] In this respect, the POUM programme mirrored Trotsky's criticisms of the Comintern, arguing that it was no longer a revolutionary force and now pursued a policy of class collaboration in capitalist countries. Where the POUM differed profoundly from Trotsky was over the question of building a new Marxist international. Nin and Maurín stated that:

> The POUM forms part of the International Committee for Revolutionary Socialist Unity, whose centre is in London and whose adherents are the independent socialist and communist parties that find themselves outside of the Second and Third Internationals. The International Committee for Revolutionary Socialist Unity is not the germ of a new international, but the centre around which all of those revolutionary socialist parties that are struggling for the reconstruction of world revolutionary unity upon new foundations can converge.[30]

This was a clear rejection of the international Trotskyist project of constructing a Fourth International. In terms of its rationale, it follows the logic behind the creation of the POUM itself. In other words, the 'London Bureau', as the International Committee for Revolutionary Socialist Unity was known, was not itself the new international organisation but rather the mechanism for constructing revolutionary Marxist concord. Over the question of affiliation to the London Bureau, it would seem that Maurín was correct to state that the Left Communists accepted an existing BOC position. The BOC took the view that it was premature to speak of setting up a new international in the absence of a powerful and successful revolutionary party that could provide the impetus and inspiration that Lenin and the Bolsheviks had given to the Third International. Maurín also thought that a new international would almost certainly fall under the influence of either Trotskyism or the numerically strong left Socialist parties.[31] In other words, the POUM sought to occupy

---

29      *¿Qué es y qué quiere el POUM?* in Alba 1977, p. 44.

30      *¿Qué es y qué quiere el POUM?* in Alba 1977, p. 48.

31      The International Committee for Revolutionary Socialist Unity was a grouping of independent socialist and communist organisations which neither believed that the Second and Third Internationals could be rescued nor accepted the possibility of constructing a new international. The London Bureau, as it became known, included the British Independent Labour Party (ILP), the French Workers' and Peasants' Socialist Party (PSOP), the German Socialist Workers' Party (SAP), the Communist Right led by Brandler, the BOC, and a few

a new political space in the communist constellation with political affiliations to neither Stalin nor Trotsky.

This had not been the Left Communists' position prior to the creation of the POUM. In April 1935, when discussions between the BOC and Left Communists were already under way, Nin and his comrades had resolved that 'the most urgent task of the moment consists ... in creating revolutionary parties in all countries and a new international which is able to absorb the rich experience of recent years'.[32] But it would appear that the question of international orientation was not a 'make or break' issue in the negotiations between Nin and Maurín.[33] In June 1935, Andrade assured his American comrade that it had been agreed the new party would work toward 'the creation of a new revolutionary Marxist International'. He believed that, in reality, this could only mean the Fourth International.[34] Nin himself gave a similar impression in his reply to the International Secretariat of the International Communist League:

> It is true that the Fourth International is not mentioned explicitly in the adopted resolution, although it is recognised tacitly. What else can be meant by: 'to reconstruct the international revolutionary unity upon a new basis', especially after having affirmed the bankruptcy of the Second and Third Internationals? Naturally an explicit recognition of the need for a Fourth International would have been more satisfactory. But when they [the BOC] refused to accept the text most satisfactory to us, would we not then have had to break off relations, thus ruining the chance to quickly win the new party over to the movement for the Fourth International? In any case, we can assure you that the representative of the new party in a future international conference will not speak of the 'sectarian idealism of the supporters of the Fourth International' ... Adherence to the London-Amsterdam Bureau is due not so much to pressures coming from the BOC, but more to our own opinion that we ought to intervene in this movement. The intention is not to declare our solidarity with the centrists who are behind this movement, but rather for us to take advantage of the opportunities this offers to put forward our principles, in the same

---

others. Maurín attended the initial conference in August 1933 (in Paris) on behalf of the BOC.

32    'Resolución del CE de la ICE.' *Boletín interior de la ICE*, No. XII, 25 April 1935, quoted in Pagés 1977, p. 278.

33    Durgan 1989, p. 248, and Durgan 1996, p. 364.

34    Andrade, in Trotsky 1977, p. 273.

way that the Bolshevik-Leninist groups which entered the sections of the
Second International are doing.[35]

In his report to the International Communist League on the creation of the
POUM, Jean Rous accepted that Nin and his comrades believed that the BOC
had moved toward the idea of a new International. Indeed, Rous understood
from his discussions with the Left Communists that they believed the fusion
would not only lead to the creation of a revolutionary party, but that this party
would constitute the Spanish section of the Fourth International.[36]

Whatever the line produced for the consumption of the international
Trotskyist movement may have been, it is difficult to believe that Nin really
expected the BOC to change its mind over the question of the Fourth
International. He must have been only too aware that a major reason behind
Maurín's opposition to that project was his virtual certainty that the new body
would be dominated by Trotsky. Joining such an organisation would have been
unacceptable to a large proportion of the BOC's membership. Thus we may conclude that this question was of secondary importance to the Left Communists
and that they were not prepared to allow disagreement over it to jeopardise
their fusion with the BOC.[37]

---

35  Executive Committee of the ICE (signed by Nin), letter to the International Secretariat of
    the International Communist League, 21 June 1935, in Trotsky 1977, p. 284. The International
    Communist League was the name the International Left Opposition adopted in 1933 after
    abandoning its policy of attempting to influence the official Communist Parties and the
    Comintern.

36  Jean Rous, 'Informe sobre la fusión de la Izquierda Comunista de España (sección espa-
    ñola de la LCI) y el BOC (Bloque Obrero y Campesino, Maurín)', October 1935, reproduced
    in Trotsky 1977, pp. 287–295. Its acceptance of Rous's report suggests that the ICL still
    viewed the Spanish comrades as linked to the international Trotskyist organisation and
    open to its influence. The implication is that the POUM might be won over to the project
    to build a Fourth International and divested of its 'centrist' tendencies.

37  Alba states that, although it is possible Nin thought he could influence the new party in the
    direction of the Fourth International, he did not attempt to do so either prior to or during
    the Civil War. Alba suggests that the truth of the matter was that Nin and most of the Left
    Communists were not convinced of the viability of Trotsky's project (Alba and Schwartz
    1988, p. 94). This may be so, but the fact remains that the Left Communists did not make
    this public and led the International Secretariat of the International Communist League
    to believe that they still supported its efforts to build a Fourth International. Clearly, they
    were not prepared to make a complete break with Trotsky's organisation.

5.3     Conclusion

Maurín's recollection toward the end of his life that, in political terms, it was
Nin's organisation that moved over to the positions of the BOC is clearly not
borne out by the primary-source evidence. If the Left Communists made
political compromises, especially over the question of international affiliation,
then the BOC also moved toward Nin in terms of political theory. By 1935, as
witnessed by the formulations in his book *Hacia la segunda revolución* (discussed in Chapter Three), Maurín's conception of revolution seems to have
become pretty much indistinguishable from Trotsky's version of permanent
revolution. This was confirmed in his joint authorship of *¿Qué es y qué quiere
el POUM?* and other writings of this period. Thus Andrade's 1935 reference to
Maurín correcting his political perspective is broadly accurate with respect to
his conception of the nature of Spain's revolutionary process.

     As we have seen, the possibility of a political merger was itself the product
of both the internal disagreements in the international Trotskyist movement
and the specifically Spanish political crisis that developed from October 1934.
As Pelai Pagès has pointed out, the difficult relationship between Trotsky and
Nin was never repaired and soon worsened over the question of the Spanish
Popular Front. The Left Communists, like the international Trotskyist movement, failed in their bid to influence the official Communists. As with the
other national groupings they remained essentially a political sect rather than
a party, with a respected theoretical profile but little political influence apart
from their work within the Alianza Obrera.[38] After rejecting Trotsky's tactical switch toward entry into the Socialist parties, it is hardly surprising that
Nin's group sought to increase its political weight by joining forces with a larger
organisation. But it is also important to stress that this course was not taken in
a defensive or pessimistic spirit – quite the opposite. Nin's assessment of the
political situation in Spain after October 1934 exhibits great optimism for
the chances of creating a revolutionary Marxist party and of syndical unity via
the Alianza.[39]

     In the context of a labour movement dominated by the twin pillars of the
PSOE-UGT and the CNT-FAI, the POUM's creation could be viewed as a logical fusion of one marginal organisation with a medium-sized party that had
real weight within Cataluña, although not in the rest of Spain. Given their very
similar political orientations, the practical reasons for uniting were certainly
compelling for both. The BOC, by far the larger organisation with perhaps 5,000

---

38   Pagès 2011, pp. 239–40.
39   Pagès 2011, p. 243.

members compared to the 800 or so Left Communists, had so far failed to organise effectively beyond Cataluña. Fusing with the Left Communists established
a national organisation overnight, in theory at least. For Nin's group, which had
been better known for theoretical interventions in debates than meaningful
political activities, a key advantage was the increase in size of organisation and
profile. They now had access to a weekly paper (*La Batalla*) with a circulation
of up to 10,000. In January 1936, the POUM revived the monthly theoretical
journal *La Nueva Era* under Nin's editorship. To replace *L'Hora*, now in the
hands of the opposition group that left the party at the end of 1935, a new
Catalan-language weekly appeared under the title *Front*.[40]

At the level of political theory, it seems clear that the POUM adopted a political programme that can only be described as one of revolutionary Marxism,
drawing heavily upon Leninist organisational principles and underpinned by
a permanentist conception of the revolutionary process. However, it would
be a mistake to assume that Nin and Maurín's joint formulations wholly capture the political character of the POUM. Most of the new party's militants
had been members of the BOC; many had come from anarcho-syndicalist or
Catalan Republican political backgrounds. The BOC had both urban industrial
supporters and peasant affiliates. Hence it was, as Pagès notes, a diverse and
complex party over which Maurín exercised considerable charismatic leadership.[41] Its pluralism and the hugely important personal role Maurín played
in the first ten months of the POUM's existence became crucial issues in the
radically altered situation of war and revolution after July 1936. Maurín was
caught in the Nationalist zone and, for a long time, was assumed to have been
killed. Unresolved tensions within the POUM, where a number of ex-BOC
militants had deep misgivings over the merger with the Trotskyists, were to

---

40    Alba and Schwartz 1988, p. 95. Alba puts POUM membership in September 1935 at 7,000.
      By March 1936 this had risen to 9,000; the party controlled unions with perhaps 60,000
      members. In his 'Informe sobre la fusión de la Izquierda Comunista de España (sección
      española de la LCI) y el BOC (Bloque Obrero y Campesino, Maurín)', of October 1935, Jean
      Rous estimated the ex-BOC members to have been between 5,000 and 6,000 strong and
      the ex–Left Communists to have been 700 in number (see Trotsky 1977, pp. 287–288 and
      p. 290). In his detailed study of the BOC, Andrew Durgan notes the difficulty of obtaining
      reliable figures but observes that the BOC claimed a membership of over 5,000 in 1934. By
      the summer of 1936, he estimates that POUM membership in Cataluña was about 6,000.
      Insofar as its trade union influence is concerned, he notes that at the founding congress
      of the FOUS in May 1936, representatives of 50,000 union members were present (Durgan
      1989, p. 284, p. 303 and p. 349). See also Durgan 1996, pp. 437–57, for a detailed breakdown
      of membership of the BOC, POUM and FOUS.
41    Pagès 2011, pp. 244–5.

present political difficulties in the context of war and revolution. Long after the end of the Civil War, Víctor Alba and others who had been members of the BOC reflected upon the 1935 fusion as a mistake that allowed the official Communists to label the POUM 'Trotskyists'. However, this would seem to owe much to hindsight, given the POUM's subsequent history during the Civil War and its political destruction by forces within the Republican side. At the end of 1935, the newly unified dissident communists' expectations were high that they could provide the true pole of attraction for all revolutionary Marxists in Spain. The process of unification was described as a 'spiral', to be achieved through 'unity in action'.[42] But, when unity finally did infect the Spanish workers' movement, it took the form of an electoral pact with the left Republican parties rather than a united front of workers' organisations. Chapter Six looks at the POUM's signing of the Popular Front agreement, an act Trotsky considered nothing less than a betrayal of the working class.

---

42      Durgan 1996, p. 249.

CHAPTER 6

# The POUM and the Popular Front

When attempting to assess the POUM's role in the Spanish Popular Front
and Trotsky's heavy condemnation of Nin's and the new party's actions, it is
important to realise that one is entering both a political and historical controversy. Much of the debate around the Popular Front, then and now, has centred upon the role of the official Communists and, especially, the influence of
the Comintern. As noted in Chapter Two, Trotsky saw the alliance as a class
betrayal of the workers, a Menshevik strategy that had nothing to do with
Lenin's tactic of a workers' 'united front'. He condemned the POUM for what
he saw as adopting the 'centrist' policy of the Comintern's Seventh Congress. If
the fusion with Maurín's BOC had been a tactical mistake, this was full-blown
'treachery'.[1]

Trotsky's perspective has achieved the status of orthodoxy among sympathetic commentators and often forms the basis of a wider explanation of
the role played by official Communists in the War and Revolution in Spain.
The argument runs as follows: Stalin's 'turn' away from the 'class-against-class'
policy of the 'third period' and toward the class collaborationist tactic of the
'Popular Front' was driven by a desire to defend the Soviet Union against inevitable attack by Hitler. By defending democracy, albeit bourgeois democracy,
against fascism, Stalin sought a strategic alliance with Britain and France
against Nazi Germany. This tactic was jeopardised by the genuine social revolution that erupted in response to the military rising in Spain in the summer of
1936. In order to avoid alienating the democracies, it is claimed, Stalin crushed
Spain's Revolution using local Communists, Comintern agents and the GPU
(Soviet secret police).[2]

This is a powerful thesis in many respects and has received support from
some specialist historians working in the field.[3] However, it does contain the
assumption that because the Comintern adopted the idea of the Popular Front
in January 1935 and then the Seventh Congress endorsed it in July–August, it

---

1  Trotsky, 'The Treachery of the POUM', 23 January 1936, in Trotsky 1973a, pp. 207–11.
2  A summary of this argument is to be found in North 2010, p. 86. North is criticising Thatcher's
   explanation of Trotsky's position regarding the Popular Front tactic. See Thatcher 2003,
   pp. 202–3. In reality, Thatcher's is an accurate outline of Trotsky's thoughts on the matter.
3  Most notably from Carr 1984. See also the impressive collection of documents from the Soviet
   archives contained in Radosh, Habeck and Sevostianov 2001.

was a specifically and uniquely 'Communist' policy. As will be seen, the Spanish Popular Front was mainly the product of domestic conditions and the broad demands for united action against growing authoritarianism. In the Spanish case, at least, it is difficult to view the electoral pact of February 1936 as an official Communist initiative. Concerning the broader thesis on the crushing of the Revolution, there are serious questions over the extent to which Moscow, regardless of intentions, was capable of playing the role often ascribed to it in shaping Popular Front government policies and actions during the Civil War. In this matter, once again, the spotlight has increasingly been thrown back upon the role of Republicans and Socialists in ending the Revolution.

This chapter deals with the genesis of the 'Popular Front' pact, to which the POUM became a signatory, and considers the POUM's political orientation up to the military rising in July 1936. It then turns to the POUM's analysis of and participation in revolutionary events and military operations during the summer and autumn of 1936. This includes a discussion of the reasons behind Nin's entry into the Generalitat. Once again, relations with Trotsky need to be taken into account, given the depth of his critique of the POUM. However, the Norwegian government's restrictions upon his political communications meant that Trotsky was severely constrained in expressing his views during the critical period of the Spanish Revolution, August to December 1936. The starting point is a brief historical assessment of the Popular Front's emergence in Spain.

## 6.1    The Coming of the Popular Front

The origins of the Spanish Popular Front electoral pact lie in the left Republican-Socialist alliance of the first two years of the Second Republic, rather than in a simple adoption of the Comintern's policy. It is worth noting at the outset that the term 'Popular Front' is more of a convention than an accurate description of the agreement that was signed in January 1936.[4] Unlike the example of the French Popular Front, which stemmed from a 1934 alliance between Socialist and Communist parties which was then extended to include the bourgeois Radical Party, the Spanish version was largely the work of two figures: the left Republican Manuel Azaña and the moderate Socialist Indalecio Prieto. It has

---

4   As a key historian of the Spanish Frente Popular has noted, formal committees of that name only emerged after the beginning of the Civil War in July 1936. In relation to the electoral agreement between various political organisations and the associated political programme, though, 'the use of the term is entirely misplaced' (Juliá 1989, p. 24).

been argued that the main role of the Spanish Communists was to help persuade the left Socialist leader Francisco Largo Caballero to join the coalition.[5] Others, however, have argued that Largo Caballero arrived at his changed position independently and that he sought to exert some control over the PCE by suggesting they be included within the electoral pact.[6]

The context for the initiative to reconstruct the original reformist Republican-Socialist alliance lies in the growing power of both the 'legalist' and fascist Right and the erosion of civil and political freedoms over the course of the *bienio negro*, the two years of conservative government beginning in November 1933. This rightward drift found its most extreme expression in the government's response to the October 1934 rising in Asturias. This insurrection consisted of a protest headed by miners against three CEDA politicians considered 'fascists' entering the government and against the continued reversal of Republican reforms at a time of deep economic crisis. The government suppressed the revolt with extreme brutality, including torture and extra-judicial executions. It suspended civil and political rights, closed left-wing newspapers, arrested and imprisoned 30,000 militants and initiated mass sackings of left-wing activists and union members. The damage to left-wing political and union organisations was considerable and proved traumatic for many of its leaders, several of whom were imprisoned in late 1934, including Azaña himself. Prieto escaped into exile and corresponded for months with Azaña over the proposed electoral coalition. Thousands of activists remained in prison throughout 1935; the call for a full amnesty proved to be the key demand of the electoral alliance as it developed.[7]

The failure of the October rising delivered a severe blow to those who advocated proletarian revolution; it constituted a short-term victory for the Right. Franco and the Army of Africa had been employed to crush the Asturian miners, demonstrating to Prieto and Azaña the crucial need for political control over and reform of the state apparatus. The debate within the Socialist Party was over the means of achieving this. Prieto advocated the parliamentary road, whereas Largo Caballero, later dubbed the 'Spanish Lenin' by the Communists, rejected the collaborationist politics of the early Republican years and still talked of a coming Russian-style revolution. He dominated the left wing of the Socialist movement, comprised of the PSOE's Federación de Juventudes

5   Preston 1987, p. 102.
6   Heywood 1990, p. 166; Juliá 1979, p. 108 n. 74.
7   See also Graham 1986, pp. 19–20. For a fascinating study of Azaña and Prieto that includes detailed commentary upon their political relationship, see Preston 1999, pp. 212–21 and pp. 255–7.

Socialistas (Socialist Youth Federation), the Madrid PSOE group and several powerful trade union federations of the UGT. By contrast, Prieto's wing of the Socialist Party continued to argue that state power could only be won via the ballot box and that achieving this would require another electoral pact with the moderate Republican parties.

In the spring and autumn of 1935, Azaña spoke at a series of open-air rallies designed to promote the renewed idea of Republican unity. These began long before a concrete coalition had come into being or an election had been announced. His immensely popular speeches pledged that a new Republican government would go beyond the reforms of the first two years, offering a radical democratic message based upon strengthening the Republic and ensuring economic prosperity. His speeches, which attracted crowds of up to half a million, reaffirmed a liberal commitment to civil and political rights and promised amnesties for political prisoners and the reinstatement of workers sacked after October 1934.[8] Azaña sought to appeal across social and party divisions to workers, peasants and the middle classes alike. Largo Caballero's eventual conversion to the 'people's front' idea, as opposed to the purely proletarian front he had been advocating, would have much to do with these manifestations of mass support for the Azaña-Prieto idea.[9]

It is easy, when appraising Azaña's publicising of the idea of Republican unity, to play down the depth of radical feeling among his audiences. His moderation was not shared by hundreds of thousands of impatient proletarians who sought rapid results and whose expectations were raised by the mass rallies and increasingly polarised national and international politics of this period. As Preston puts it, faced with the approbation of the crowds and their clenched fist salutes, 'like the sorcerer's apprentice, the mild liberal politician was taken aback by the fervour of proletarian passion'.[10]

Prieto's role in the building of a Republican-Socialist coalition was largely to do with convincing the radicals in the PSOE/UGT that a circumstantial pact encompassing moderate Republican parties and extending to the Left in general was a more realistic electoral prospect than a purely proletarian bloc. He argued that the aim should be to attack the Radical-CEDA government and avert the prospect of José María Gil Robles, an admirer of Hitler widely regarded as a fascist, becoming prime minister. It is certainly the case that Largo Caballero's left Socialists presented a major obstacle to the Azaña-Prieto parliamentary initiative, given the power he wielded in the trade union movement.

---

8    Preston 1987, pp. 61–4.
9    Preston 1987, p. 64.
10   Preston 1987, p. 100.

They remained hostile to the Popular Front until quite late in 1935. But, while the Caballeristas talked of revolution, in reality, they lacked a practical programme and proved increasingly responsive to the general clamour among workers and wider society for unity in the face of the threat of fascism. In this respect, it would be true to say that the change in the Comintern 'line' came at an opportune moment, allowing the numerically small PCE to campaign for cross-class unity and influence significant numbers of the left Socialists, especially the UGT and Socialist Youth. The Communists' growing profile, despite their small numbers, was certainly one factor influencing Largo Caballero's change of attitude.

In summary, it has been argued that there were four main reasons for the switch in the UGT leaders' thinking.[11] First, the evident popularity of the renewed Socialist-Republican project – especially the overwhelming clamour for an amnesty – suggested that failure to support it could leave the left Socialists politically isolated. Second, the manifest weakness of the government in late 1935 meant an election was imminent; there was a chance that with their popular appeal, Prieto and Azaña might fill the power vacuum themselves.[12] Third, it would seem that Largo Caballero was impressed by the arguments in favour of the unification of Marxist forces. Yet he tended to look toward the official Communists, with the authority of the Soviet Union behind them, rather than to other forces on the Left. Finally, Largo Caballero was influenced by the Comintern strategy of a Popular Front against fascism that coincided with the Azaña-Prieto initiative in Spain. It seemed likely that an electoral coalition against the Right would emerge and that the Communist Party would join it. This would again leave the left Socialists politically isolated. Hence, in November 1935, Largo Caballero made clear that he accepted the electoral pact with Azaña's Republicans and suggested that the PCE be invited to join as well.[13] Hence it may well be that Largo Caballero's 'turn' to

---

11    Under pressure from the Prieto wing of the PSOE, Largo Caballero resigned from the national executive on 16 December 1935. Thereafter he associated himself wholly with his UGT leadership role. The union was his power base and remained so until May 1937, constituting, in effect, a second Socialist leadership that refused to engage with the Electoral Committee (Juliá 1989, pp. 32–3).

12    Indeed, the end of the *bienio negro* came as a result of a deep political crisis caused by financial scandals and divisions among the right-wing parties. With the government unable to function, Alcalá-Zamora called a general election for 16 February 1936. During the run-up to this, all of the workers' organisations, with the exception of the CNT, reached a formal agreement.

13    Heywood 1990, pp. 164–6. Helen Graham argues that Largo Caballero's participation in the pact was 'conditional' upon the PCE being included. Graham 2002, p. 64.

the Popular Front idea had much to do with his fear of losing ground to Prieto and the PCE.

The outcome of the bargaining and negotiation process was officially announced a month before the election on 15 January 1936. The pact was signed by Azaña's Left Republicans, the Unión Republicana, the Socialists (PSOE/ UGT and Juventudes Socialistas), the PCE, Ángel Pestaña's Partido Sindicalista and the POUM.[14] The CNT was the main organisation refusing to participate. Although there was never a joint meeting of the signatories to the Frente Popular, there was a manifesto that promised an amnesty for all 'social and political crimes' committed before 15 November 1935. It also outlined a series of specific and more general policies including the defence of the Republican Constitution and social and economic reforms. However, the Popular Front, a title Azaña never acknowledged, was far from being a renewal of the 1931 Republican-Socialist coalition, whatever Prieto's and Azaña's ambitions may have been in that direction. In reality, the main aim of each party to the pact was to preserve the independence of its organisation rather than form a governing coalition. Hence, the Popular Front proved merely a means to an end: a joint ticket facilitating the election of candidates, many of whom would afterward go their separate ways. Far from representing the Popular Front parties that narrowly triumphed in the February election, the new government was a wholly Republican affair comprised of Left Republican and Unión Republicana ministers.

### *The POUM and the Popular Front Pact*
In order to understand why the POUM felt that it had no choice but to sign the electoral pact, it is worth recalling the dissident communists' assessment of the political situation toward the end of 1935. The years 1931 to 1933 had confirmed their argument that the petty-bourgeois Republicans would be unable to create a stable political democracy and address the democratic tasks. Events in the rest of Europe since 1933 and the experience of right-wing government in Spain led them to conclude that the choice was now between socialism and fascism. But, if petty-bourgeois politicians had failed, they realised that the petty-bourgeoisie as a class could not be overlooked. Unless this social layer could be won over to the socialist project, it might easily provide the mass base that fascism had hitherto lacked in Spain. According to the POUM, the only way to appeal to them was by demonstrating in practice that the aspirations of the petty-bourgeoisie could only be met under socialism. It was necessary to put

---

14    Casanova 2010, p. 123 For the full text of the 'Programa electoral del Frente Popular', see
       Broué 1977, pp. 184–93.

THE POUM AND THE POPULAR FRONT

forward a programme of concrete demands that clarified the common ground between the proletariat and the petty-bourgeoisie, especially the peasantry.[15] It is clear from the publications of both dissident communist groupings during the merger process and those of the POUM from September that there was no difference between their critique of the Comintern's Popular Front tactic and Trotsky's. However, it was difficult to resist the reality of Azaña's mass rallies and the political attractions of securing an amnesty.[16] Moreover, the BOC had been open to joint political action, up to and including fusing with other organisations in Cataluña, for some time.

On the question of alliances between workers' parties and petty-bourgeois forces, the POUM programme quoted Lenin to the effect that circumstantial agreements were permissible.[17] Indeed, prior to fusion, the BOC had collaborated with the Esquerra in the United Pro-Amnesty Committee for prisoners taken in October 1934. Efforts to find common ground with the Unió Socialista de Catalunya (USC), the second largest independent Catalan socialist party, had been made but failed. Joan Comorera's USC then embarked upon a journey that ended in a merger with the official Communists.[18] Ongoing discussions over fusion with Nin's Left Communists looked promising. However, by the summer of 1935, Maurín was speaking of the need for a much broader tactical pact with the left Republicans and other political forces. His openness to a transitory electoral pact came in response to the resurgence in popular support for Azaña and the mass rejection of the parties of the legalist Right. He made it clear, as the POUM would after September, that any circumstantial agreement with the left Republicans would take place in the context of a prior accord between workers' organisations. To this end, in November 1935, the POUM approached the PSOE and PCE to propose a broad Workers' Coalition as the basis for an electoral agreement. When this initiative received no response, it became clear to Maurín and Nin that the Socialists and Communists were about to make a deal with Azaña. *La Batalla* announced that the POUM would only support such a pact if it was transitional and had the aim of defeating the Right, securing a full amnesty for political prisoners and reviving the Statute of

---

15    See José Luís Arenillas, 'Las clases medias en su relación con el proletariado', *La Nueva Era* 2nd epoch, year 1, No. 6, July 1936, Nueva Era 1976, pp. 331–9.

16    Writing with the benefit of hindsight in June 1936, Gorkín insisted that the masses who attended Azaña's open air rallies were not simply Republicans but rather 'revolutionary workers'. Julián G. Gorkín, 'Retrato político de Azaña', *La Nueva Era*, 2nd epoch, year 1, No. 5, June 1936, in Nueva Era 1976, pp. 298–9.

17    *¿Qué es y qué quiere el POUM?*, in Alba 1977, p. 32.

18    See the discussion in Graham 2002, pp. 66–7.

Catalan Autonomy.[19] But it is clear that, just as with Largo Caballero, they were very concerned at missing out on a key political initiative.

Despite its willingness to participate, the POUM was excluded from discussions over the nature and content of the national Popular Front pact and programme. This was, of course, in common with all the signatories besides the Socialists and Republicans, to whose pact the others were simply invited to subscribe. Faced with the prospect of being left on the side-lines, Juan Andrade signed the pact on behalf of the POUM in the full knowledge that his party had not been allowed any say in its drafting.[20] Strictly speaking, the Popular Front did not cover the entire country. Cataluña had its own version, negotiated during 1935. This produced the Front d'Esquerres (Left Front), announced just two weeks before the election. It encompassed bourgeois Catalan nationalist, Republican, communist and socialist parties, although the locally dominant CNT's refusal to participate deprived working-class parties of the same weight they enjoyed in the Popular Front beyond Cataluña. The Catalan version was rather less committed to specific reforms than its national counterpart, simply demanding amnesty, renewal of the statute of autonomy and restoration of the social legislation of 1931–3 and the Law of Agricultural Contracts.[21] Nor did the Front d'Esquerres promote the moderate Republican programme of the Madrid pact. In this respect, there was some reflection of the POUM's ability to reach an agreement with all the Catalan workers' parties and petty-bourgeois nationalist parties, including the most important party, the Esquerra. Undoubtedly this owed much to its relative weight as the major Catalan socialist organisation.

Following the electoral victory of the Popular Front coalition and the formation of an exclusively Republican government, the POUM leadership felt obliged to defend its signing of the pact. It also immediately distanced itself from what was now being referred to, highly inaccurately, as the Popular Front government. The POUM programme – written by Maurín and Nin in late 1935 and early 1936 and published in March 1936 – argued that on the one hand,

> [t]he results of the Popular Front have already been experienced in our country. In 1931–3, the Socialist Party practiced the politics of the Popular Front, whose second edition is now being enthusiastically encouraged

19    *La Batalla*, 15 November and 27 December 1935. See Durgan 1989, pp. 261–5.
20    Juliá 1979, pp. 118–9. Andrade said later that signing the pact was a mistake and that he had not been in favour of doing so at the time. He was instructed to do so by the POUM leaders in Barcelona (Fraser 1981, p. 560).
21    Esenwein and Shubert 1995, p. 27.

by the Communist Party. The collaboration between Republicans and Socialists led to the triumph of the counterrevolution in November–December 1933. The outcomes would now be even more catastrophic if the position of the official Communists, who are more radical-socialist than communist, were to prevail.

But on the other:

> Our interpretation of the Popular Front does not contradict, as one might suppose, the fact that the POUM signed the document which served as the basis for the general elections of 16 February 1936. Then it was a matter of a simple pact of an electoral nature, having the amnesty as its principal goal. The POUM then developed its propaganda in a wholly independent manner, pointing out that the established pact could not be interpreted as more than a purely and exclusively electoral undertaking. The POUM – as has been indicated above – does not reject contacts and alliances with the petty-bourgeoisie, but these pacts and alliances must always be around concrete and circumstantial questions.[22]

Thus the POUM portrayed the pact as a passing alliance that had ended as soon as the specific objective of securing an amnesty had been achieved. It proclaimed that the only acceptable 'front' was the workers' united front.[23]

It is certainly true that, in its press and political propaganda, the POUM had opposed the very notion of a Popular Front since the Comintern's adoption of the policy at its Seventh Congress. Nin, for instance, noted that the Congress marked a turn in the Comintern toward the reformism of the Second International. He also linked the Popular Front policy to the notion of 'socialism in one country' and the abandonment of proletarian internationalism.[24] In an article published in January 1936, Jordi Arquer argued against the Popular Front tactic on the grounds that it not only subordinated the interests of the

---

22    *¿Qué es y qué quiere el POUM?* in Alba 1977, p. 38.

23    Some historians have incorrectly suggested that the POUM supported the Popular Front alliance after the February elections. One example appears to be Graham 2002, p. 235, although it is unclear about which dates precisely she is talking. As can be seen from the current discussion, this was not the case. Indeed, the POUM press increasingly attacked the Popular Front in terms very similar to Trotsky's.

24    Nin, 'El congreso de la IC y los socialistas de izquierda', *La Batalla*, 30 August 1935, Nin 1978a, p. 473. See also Maurín, 'El VII Congreso de la Internacional Comunista', *La Batalla*, 23 August 1935, in Fundació Andreu Nin 1989a, p. 2.

international working class to those of the Soviet state, but also tied them to those of the bourgeoisie. Since fascism was, in essence, the last resort of the bourgeoisie, the only effective means of defeating it was to destroy the socio-economic system to which it corresponded: capitalism.[25]

The dissident communists thought that only a workers' united front could defeat fascism and that the new Republican government was just another bourgeois régime, but they signed a far broader pact. What did they hope to gain from doing so? Without repeating all of the points made in Chapter Two, it would appear that the main advantages were the release of political prisoners, the opportunity to campaign widely under the auspices of the Popular Front banner, and Maurín's election to the Cortes. At the end of December 1935, *La Batalla* explained that the ideal way forward had been that of a workers' front based around the Alianza Obrera. However,

> our interpretation, although undoubtedly finding a favourable echo among the working masses, was not accepted by the other workers' parties.
>
> ...
>
> For our part, today we still lack the electoral force of the Socialists and would not be opposed to an understanding with the left Republican parties. We believe that such an understanding, should it be reached, must have the following objectives:
> First. To defeat the counterrevolution in the elections.
> Second. To obtain an amnesty.
> Third. To re-establish the Catalan Statute.
> Once these three objectives have been secured, the workers' movement and the petty-bourgeois parties should consider this circumstantial pact ended and freely continue on their different ways.
> That is our position. It is upon this that we will act in the following days.[26]

As discussed in Chapter Two above, Trotsky responded by roundly condemning the POUM's actions. As he expressed it: 'Electoral *technique* cannot justify the *politics* of betrayal, which a *joint programme* with the bourgeoisie

25    Arquer, '¿Frente popular antifascista o frente único obrero?', *La Nueva Era*, 2nd epoch, year 1, No. 1, January 1936, in Nueva Era 1976, pp. 156–64.

26    'El momento politico: Ante las próximas elecciones', *La Batalla*, 27 December 1935, quoted in Pagès 2011, p. 258.

amounts to'.[27] Even Andrade later said that the POUM's association with the bourgeois electoral programme had been a mistake.[28] All of the four Front candidacies promised to the POUM outside of Cataluña were in practice blocked by the PCE and Republicans. Thus the only POUM candidate was Maurín, who stood successfully in Barcelona under the Catalan Front d'Esquerres.[29] The POUM's considerable interest in securing parliamentary representation in early 1936 might be seen to indicate the ambiguity of its political analysis at that moment. In practice, the POUM utilised every opportunity to promote revolutionary Marxist propaganda, yet its very presence in the Cortes via Maurín tended to contradict the message that the parliamentary phase of the Spanish Revolution had ended.[30] Trotsky had no doubt that Spain had entered 'an acute revolutionary period'.[31]

Even more damaging, insofar as the POUM was concerned, was the high profile the Popular Front afforded the official Communists. February 1936 constituted the PCE's first major political success and greatly increased its standing with the very left Socialists the POUM had hoped to win over. Its power and influence within the Spanish labour movement increased massively. At the end of 1935, the Communist trade union, the CGTU, had been taken under the UGT umbrella. In April 1936, the Socialist and Communist Youth fused to form the Juventudes Socialistas Unificadas (JSU, Unified Socialist Youth) and progressively adopted the political positions of the official Communists. In Cataluña, the Socialists and the official Communists sought unity. Following the military rising in July, their Catalan organisations merged to form the Partit Socialista Unificat de Cataluña (PSUC).[32] In other words, unity had indeed been achieved between the left Socialists and official Communists upon the basis of the Popular Front, a tactic underpinned in theory by the notion

27    'The Treachery of the POUM', in Trotsky 1973a, p. 210n.

28    Andrade, in Fraser 1981, p. 560.

29    In theory, the POUM was allocated Teruel and Cádiz as well, but it had few supporters in those places and the putative candidates, Nin and Gorkín, decided to withdraw. For a discussion of the manner in which the POUM was denied the opportunity to field candidates by some of the other signatory parties to the pact, see Durgan 1996, pp. 407–8, and Pagès 2011, pp. 260–1.

30    See, for instance, Maurín's four speeches in the Cortes, reproduced in Alba 1977, pp. 75–87.

31    Trotsky, letter to a Spanish comrade, 12 April 1936, in Trotsky 1973a, p. 212.

32    Formed on 25 July 1936, the PSUC was a fusion of the Catalan branch of the PCE, the Unió Socialista (Catalan federation of PSOE), the Partit Comunista de Catalunya and the Partit Català Proletari. It had a membership of between 2,500 and 3,000, compared to the POUM's 6,000 in July 1936 (Durgan's figure). However, the PSUC's trade union audience was larger, at 80,000 (Durgan 1989, p. 284).

that the Spanish Revolution was bourgeois-democratic. It represented a convergence of the stagism of the Comintern and the reformism of the Second International Social Democracy that constituted the theoretical basis of the PSOE's Marxism. The advent of what became known as the Spanish Popular Front thus signified the eclipse of the Alianza Obrera and effectively neutralised a major part of the POUM's political programme of Marxist unification. Yet it has to be said that this would probably have mostly been the case even if the POUM had not signed the electoral pact.

### *The Popular Front in Power*

What was the POUM's attitude to the new political situation that arose as a result of the February elections? The editor of the newly revived theoretical journal *La Nueva Era* declared the electoral victory of the Popular Front to be 'an important phase in the Spanish Revolution'. Nin predicted that this period would see the working class free itself from all 'democratic illusions', afford a massive impulse to the Alianza Obrera and provide conditions in which the revolutionary party could finally emerge.[33] The contradictions between the proletariat's aspirations and the Republican government would soon come to a boil again, he thought: the great desire for change that had produced the Popular Front victory would now propel the workers beyond the limits of bourgeois democracy and toward a socialist revolution. The experience of the previous five years, especially of October 1934, had proved an invaluable education for the workers' movement. Had the PSOE become a revolutionary force after 1934, he suggested, the Republicans would not have gained hegemony in the struggle against the counterrevolution; that struggle would now be taking place upon a different basis. However, Nin insisted, the working class had actually shown itself to be stronger than the Republicans; even if the workers were underrepresented in the Cortes. He predicted that the moderate Azaña government would seek to contain the Revolution and would again fail to address the democratic tasks. If the question of workers' power was not yet on the agenda, it soon would be. As he noted: 'The conditions are not mature enough for the working class to be able to take power today, but it must prepare properly now to be ready to take it shortly'.[34]

As we saw in Chapter Two, this was rather different to Trotsky's view of the situation. Although Nin accepted that the revolution had developed a great

---

33   Nin, 'Comentarios', *La Nueva Era*, 2nd epoch, year 1, No. 2, February 1936, in Nueva Era 1976, p. 176.

34   Nin, 'Después de las elecciones del 16 de febrero', *La Nueva Era*, 2nd epoch, year 1, No. 2 February 1936, in Nueva Era 1976, p. 187.

deal since 1931, this did not seem to Trotsky to be reflected in Nin's own political actions. If part of the PSOE had taken up revolutionary positions after October 1934, why had Nin and his comrades not sought to channel these energies toward a coherent revolutionary strategy? It was all very well to lament the dissipation of the Socialists' radicalism when faced with the populism of the Popular Front, but the fact remained that Nin had not grasped the nettle and sought a mass audience for his undoubted theoretical and oratorical skills among the Socialist Left. It appeared to Trotsky that Nin was incapable of initiating any creative political moves of his own. He seemed condemned to merely respond to events in a totally inappropriate manner. Why, Trotsky asked, was it opportunist to enter temporarily into the PSOE but perfectly acceptable to enter an alliance with the representatives of the bourgeoisie?[35] This act was even more perplexing given that, by 1936, the situation was clearly revolutionary. Of what value was it to assist the left bourgeoisie and PSOE in recreating the 1931 coalition government?[36]

It is quite clear that neither Nin nor Maurín possessed an obvious answer to the question of how to achieve revolutionary leadership. Neither believed that the so-called Popular Front government would be in power for very long. Both argued that the bourgeois-democratic revolution no longer corresponded to Spain's political realities and that the situation in 1936 was objectively revolutionary.[37] Yet they did not think the workers' movement was prepared for a power struggle because it still lacked a mass revolutionary party. Speaking to the Cortes in April 1936, Maurín warned the Azaña government that the only remaining defenders of democracy were the workers. The bourgeoisie had

---

35  Trotsky, 'The Treachery of the POUM', in Trotsky 1973a, p. 209. Written on 23 January, this article was published in the organ of the American Workers' Party, the *New Militant*, on 25 February 1936, the eve of the Spanish elections.

36  Nin's position is indeed inconsistent if one is looking solely at his political writings. In August 1935 he noted that the bourgeoisie required another 'left' bourgeois government to neutralise the discontent of the masses. However, he realised that such a government would be even less radical than the 1931 government. Azaña now represented not the petty-bourgeoisie, as he had five years before, but the big bourgeoisie; Nin thought he would perform the role of a Spanish Thiers. One might reasonably wonder, therefore, why the Left should assist a bourgeois candidate (Nin, 'La evolución del Republicanismo pequeño-burguesa', *La Batalla*, 2 August 1935, in Nin 1978a, pp. 465–7).

37  Nin, 'Reformas inmediatas y revoluciones sociales', *Imant*, 21 December 1935, in Nin 1978a, p. 492. Maurín stated that the 'historical phase of bourgeois revolutions corresponds to the eighteenth and nineteenth centuries' ('¿Revolución democráticoburguesa o revolución democráticosocialista?', *La Nueva Era*, 2nd epoch, year 2, No. 4, May 1936, in Nueva Era 1976, p. 265).

abandoned the parliamentary road and was embracing fascism. The true vic-
tors in the February elections had not been the Republicans but the workers,
who now looked beyond bland reformism and sought to transform society.[38]
It was paradoxical, Maurín noted, that the working class clamoured for socialism, yet the Socialist and Communist parties had no idea what practical steps
to take. The PSOE and PCE believed that socialism would not enter the agenda
until after the fulfilment of the bourgeois revolution.[39] This had led to the
bizarre situation of the workers' parties defending bourgeois democracy after
the bourgeoisie itself had deserted this particular sinking ship. The POUM
believed that this obdurate position threatened to detain the revolutionary
movement within a framework that no longer corresponded to the actual situation. Parliamentary democracy had to give way to workers' democracy in the
form of the Alianza Obrera.[40]

If his analysis of the political situation was astute, Maurín unfortunately
had no answer to the question 'and what if the workers do not support the
Alianza?' Indeed, it is difficult to see why they should suddenly have taken
the advice of a small, mainly Catalan party with one lonely representative in
the Cortes. Even those elements within the PSOE most open to revolutionary theory had demonstrated that they did not possess the level of political
sophistication required to distinguish between the Marxism of the dissident
communists and that of the Stalinists. It might be argued that Trotsky's tactic of 'entryism', improvised as it was in an emergency situation, at least had
the merit of recognising that revolutionary Marxism had to be taken to the
revolutionary workers. The POUM's belief that the mountain had to come to
Muhammad might be seen as at best optimistic and at worst conceited.

Maurín was also well aware of the imminent threat from the extreme Right,
particularly in the form of a military coup, and the fragility of the Republican
government.[41] As he noted in a rather prophetic speech to the Cortes:

> What did the German and Austrian Social Democrats do, socialist com-
> rades, in believing they could establish a democratic republic, but give
> time to the fascist organisation to prepare itself to take power? If we do

38 Maurín, speech in the Cortes, 15 April 1936, in Alba 1977, p. 77.
39 Maurín, '¿Revolución democráticoburguesa o revolución democráticosocialista?', in Nueva
   Era 1976, p. 268.
40 Maurín, '¿Revolución democráticoburguesa o revolución democráticosocialista?', in Nueva
   Era 1976, pp. 268–70.
41 Maurín, '¿Revolución democráticoburguesa o revolución democráticosocialista?', in
   Nueva Era 1976, p. 271. Also, speech in the Cortes, 16 June 1936, in Alba 1977, p. 80.

exactly the same in Spain, within one, two or three years – I can't give an exact date – we will follow Italy, Hungary, Germany, Portugal and several other countries in having a fascist regime presided over by Gil Robles, Calvo Sotelo or some other aspiring 'Führer' or 'Duce'.[42]

Nor did the POUM underestimate the mood of the masses, which appeared to be in advance of the leadership of the workers' parties. Both Nin and Maurín commented upon the way the workers had moved to free jailed workers before the 'Popular Front' government had done so, as well as upon the industrial action the workers had taken to force employers to reinstate those sacked for political reasons. These strikes had been called against the wishes of the PSOE-UGT leaders.[43] The Madrid building strike, for example, was brought about by the CNT in the Socialists' home city. Maurín even thought the PSOE leadership's hegemony had been undermined by this radical action.[44]

Maurín and Nin's analysis of the political situation in the spring and early summer of 1936 seems a pretty accurate one. It was clear that Spain was indeed faced with both a revolutionary crisis and what Maurín called a 'pre-fascist situation'. The Republican government proved unable to address popular expectations of social and economic reforms far greater than those of April 1931. The left Socialists opposed the PSOE's participation in government and in May blocked Prieto's attempt to become prime minister after Azaña agreed to run for president. Largo Caballero opposed any Socialist participation in what he assumed to be the 'bourgeois-democratic revolution' being carried out by the Republicans. He awaited the opportunity to lead the socialist revolution once the necessary bourgeois stage had been completed.

In reality, the left Socialists were already being overtaken by events as agricultural workers, despairing of empty promises of reform and suffering high unemployment and immense hardships, began to occupy large southern estates. Up to 60,000 rural workers in Extremadura took over some 3,000 estates beginning in March, forcing the government to accelerate agrarian reforms. Landowners took refuge in towns and cities, often becoming ever more committed to supporting forces of the extreme Right.[45] But government action came too late; the rural unrest was overlaid with urban strikes and even

42   Speech in the Cortes, 15 April 1936, in Alba 1977, pp. 77–8.

43   Maurín, speech in the Cortes, 20 April 1936, in Alba 1977, pp. 79–80; Nin, 'Comentarios', *La Nueva Era*, 2nd epoch, year 1, No. 3, March–April 1936, in Nueva Era 1976, p. 208.

44   Maurín, 'Ante una situación inquietante', *La Batalla*, 17 July 1936, in Fundació Andreu Nin 1989a, p. 10.

45   Esenwein and Shubert 1995, pp. 98–9.

factory occupations. The CNT-FAI was busy forming militias and led a general strike on May Day. As already mentioned, some 100,000 construction workers in Madrid went on strike in June. Attacks upon churches, a traditional outlet for popular anger and frustrations, increased; political violence escalated.[46]

Here the far Right of the political spectrum, the Falange and the CEDA youth movement Juventud de Acción Popular (JAP), became increasingly active, stockpiling weapons and contemplating armed insurrection. *Arriba*, the Falange's newspaper, was banned in March; the government then moved to ban the party. Stanley Payne has stressed the moderation of José Antonio in the early months of 1936.[47] However, tit-for-tat killings continued, with the Falange leader almost certainly authorising some of the reprisals.[48] Early March witnessed a wave of such murders involving victims from the Socialist Left, Communists, Carlists, Falangists and even a policeman. The government arrested Falangist leaders in an attempt to avoid the Italian and German experiences, in which fascism had achieved power partly through legal means.

After a lull, political violence involving paramilitary organisations increased around mid-April. From February to mid-July 1936, there were some 300 political assassinations. The leaders of the Falange remained in prison, but now money flowed into the clandestine party's coffers and José Antonio continued to direct the party's affairs and operations secretly from his Alicante jail cell. His activities included playing a role in the military conspiracy during June and the first half of July.[49] He was even able to publish a newspaper containing lists of enemies which, as Payne remarks, was surely an incitement to murder in the circumstances.[50] Despite José Antonio's claim to have 150,000 members in June 1936, no one really knew the true figure – although it was certainly several times the 8,000 of the beginning of 1936.[51]

The military and civilian Right coming together with fascist and other authoritarian organisations certainly constituted a bid to destroy the Second Republic through armed insurrection. Even within the Cortes, self-proclaimed 'fascist' deputies like José Calvo Sotelo were calling openly for military intervention against left-wing organisations. Actions of a revolutionary nature by

---

46   Attacks upon church property were far fewer in number than has often been claimed in the months prior to the Civil War. Nor were there any politically motivated killings of clergy in this pre-war period (Durgan 2007, p. 28).

47   Payne 1999, pp. 185–7.

48   See Preston's essay on José Antonio in Preston 1999, pp. 75–108, especially pp. 96–8.

49   Preston 1999, pp. 100–1.

50   Payne 1999, p. 191.

51   Payne 1999, p. 199.

significant elements of the labour movement also suggest that, on the Left, what the POUM referred to as 'parliamentary illusions' had largely dissipated.[52] Workers and peasants were attempting to carry out the transformations that the Popular Front, by virtue of its class nature, could not. Nin stressed that only the historic mission of the working class offered a solution to the country's backwardness and agreed with Maurín that Spain's economy could not develop other than through socialism.[53] But, if the radical Right was increasingly organised for action around elements in the army, the Left still lacked an agency for revolution. Thus it is hard to maintain the argument that Spain really was on the brink of revolution in July 1936. The fact that, in certain areas of Spain, there was about to be a social revolution of considerable depth has much to do with the temporary eclipse of central government and the strength of local responses to the military rising.

## 6.2    Military Rising and Revolutionary Response

The military rebellion began among elements of the colonial army in Spanish Morocco on 17 July 1936 and spread to many provincial garrisons in mainland Spain the following day. This appeared to confirm the POUM's predictions of the imminent collapse of the Republic amidst a revolutionary crisis. It elicited what appeared to be a spontaneous response from large numbers of Spanish workers and sections of the lower middle classes. Thousands of workers mobilised and were rapidly organised into militia units. These militias, together with loyal Assault Guards, police, some Civil Guard units and significant sections of the military that remained loyal to the Republic, successful resisted the rebellion in many of the major cities. Hence the military rising, supported by right-wing paramilitary groups with general approval from the most conservative-traditionalist forces in Spanish society, was only partially successful on the mainland.[54]

Although the insurgent Nationalists launched their rebellion against the Republic with the intention of forestalling a social revolution, their actions

---

52    However, many of the strikes in the weeks and months prior to the Civil War were designed to put pressure upon the government to restore the labour conditions of the *bienio reformador* (1931–3) and reinstate workers sacked after October 1934 (Durgan 2007, p. 28).

53    Nin, 'La acción directa del proletariado y la revolución española', *La Nueva Era*, 2nd epoch, year 1, No. 6, July 1936, in Nueva Era 1976, pp. 327–78.

54    Preston 2006, pp. 102–15.

in practice led directly to the very thing they most feared. Paralysing the Republican state apparatus allowed a transfer of power on the ground to work-ers' parties and unions organised in Anti-Fascist Militia Committees. Aragón, the Basque Country and Asturias all became largely independent of Madrid; power remained decentralised for several months. However, as Durgan points out, the situation never approached the 'dual power' experience of Petrograd in 1917. Power was instead fragmented among committees rather than focused in an alternative revolutionarily organ.[55] The composition of these commit-tees reflected the strength of the workers' organisation in each particular local-ity. In some areas, they included Republican and regional nationalist parties as well.

The Anti-Fascist Militia Committees attempted to deal with both military matters and the business of governance in a manner influenced by their partic-ular social, economic and political perspectives. Hence, in areas where the CNT, left Socialist (UGT) and POUM militants held political control, a high degree of social and economic change began taking place in the summer of 1936. In Cataluña and Aragón, the CNT, informed by its 'libertarian communist' ideol-ogy, drove through the collectivisation of industry, services and agriculture as well as many social and moral reforms.[56] Valencia had both anarcho-syndical-ists and left Socialists in control for a time. The parts of Castilla and Andalucía that remained outside of Nationalist control for any length of time saw collec-tivisation driven by the UGT. Madrid, traditionally a Socialist city, very quickly became the major war front; military requirements and the growing influence of the official Communists severely limited the impact of the social revolution there. The isolation of Asturias, owing to the Nationalists' early success, meant that social revolution was heavily constrained. In the Basque Country, the con-servatism of the nationalist PNV, which took the Republican side because of its support for regional autonomy, meant that there was no social revolution.[57]

With Maurín caught in the Nationalist zone by the military rising, Nin was now the most prominent figure in the POUM leadership; he occupied

---

55    Durgan 2007, p. 79.

56    Among the many books dealing with these transformations from a sympathetic perspec-
      tive are Peirats 1990; Leval 1975; and Alexander 1999. For a very different approach that
      challenges a collectivist perspective from solid historical research, see Seidman 1991,
      available in electronic format at http://ark.cdlib.org/ark:/13030/ft5h4nb34h/ (accessed
      27 August 2012), and Seidman 2002.

57    The early phases of the war and revolution are covered particularly well and in a nuanced
      way by Graham 2002, pp. 79–130.

the post of political secretary.[58] The POUM took a leading role in organising armed opposition to the military, especially in Cataluña. It participated in the Anti-Fascist Militia Committee which, for a brief period, substituted for the Generalitat.[59] As a consequence of its high profile, party membership rose to an estimated 30,000 in the space of just two weeks.[60] However, the question of political power was addressed only on a local and haphazard basis. Factory committees and defence committees sprang up overnight without any coordinated direction from political organisations. Even in Cataluña, where expropriation and experiments in workers' democracy reached their height, the CNT and POUM did not attempt to prevent the Generalitat from reasserting its political control. The POUM lacked the power to act on its own; the CNT lacked the desire to install a proletarian dictatorship.

In the context of fast-moving events in Cataluña, the POUM Executive Committee soon outlined its immediate programme of demands. These included a 36-hour week, higher pay, strike pay, lower prices, unemployment relief, workers' control of factories, division of the large estates among the poor peasants, progressive revision of the Catalan statute of autonomy, soldiers' and militias' committees, and immediate trial of the leaders of the 'fascist insurrection'.[61] Yet, in the ongoing social revolution, driven largely by the anarcho-syndicalists, these appear to have been fairly moderate demands. This may well indicate the degree to which even the POUM was taken by surprise at the depth of the changes occurring. Of course, it is important to note here that

---

58    Maurín was attending a conference in Galicia when the military rising took place. Unable to return to Barcelona, he was detained by pro-Franco Guardia Civil while attempting to make his way to the French border. His disappearance was a serious blow for the party, which was deprived of its most charismatic and popular figure. Nin was never fully accepted by many of the ex-BOC militants and thereafter the leadership was much more of a joint affair. For a long time it was believed that Maurín had been executed by the Nationalists. In fact, he survived even after his true identity became known and spent the next ten years in Nationalist prisons. For details of his post-1936 life, see the obituaries collected in Fundació Andreu Nin 1989a, pp. 16–27; Bonamusa 1973; Portela 1973 (a reply to Bonamusa); Bonet 1973; and Iglesias 1974a.

59    On 20 July, after the popular defeat of the military rising in Barcelona, the Catalan president, Lluís Companys, offered power to the CNT-FAI. However, the anarcho-syndicalist leaders rejected the notion of a proletarian dictatorship and decided the Generalitat should remain in office, with a Central Committee of Anti-Fascist Militias comprised of five CNT-FAI members, three UGT, and one each from the PSUC, POUM, Esquerra, Unió de Rabassaires and Acció Catalana (Catalan Action) (Casanova 2010, pp. 239–40).

60    Alba and Schwartz 1988, p. 114. The POUM's membership grew to 40,000 within a few weeks of the outbreak of war (Fraser 1981, p. 340).

61    *Avant*, 24 July 1936, quoted in Pagès 2011, p. 272.

Cataluña's distance from the war at this time was a major factor allowing such profound transformations to take place. Another factor was Barcelona's urban nature and industrial periphery, which made its proletarian cultures unique in 1930s Spain.[62]

Although the POUM was a little slow in realising the depth of the revolution taking place, by early August *La Batalla* was announcing its 'Manifesto' for the creation of a planned socialist economy organised by a workers' government.[63] The party's early assessment of the revolutionary situation and the potential development of workers' power was highly optimistic, not to say misleading. Nin summarised it well in a speech that September, proclaiming that all of the Revolution's problems had been resolved. The bourgeois-democratic Republic had been circumvented and now represented no one; in five days, the workers and peasants had achieved what the Republic had failed to begin in five years; feudal vestiges and the capitalist economy had been overthrown in one go; the peasants had taken over the land and the workers now controlled the factories; Cataluña was a fully autonomous state, its national question resolved; the army had been dismantled and replaced by workers' militias in order to defend the revolutionary gains. All of this had occurred as the POUM had foreseen, he added. In answering fascist aggression by immediately implementing socialist measures, the working class had demonstrated that the struggle was between fascism and socialism rather than between fascism and democracy. He concluded that it was this organic connection between fighting fascism and building socialism which made the questions of the War and the Revolution inseparable.[64]

The idea that a successful revolution would guarantee victory in the War was a key point of connection between the POUM and the anarcho-syndicalists. Both could agree that any army created must be a proletarian revolutionary army and must be formed out of the militias created by the workers' organisations in response to the military rising. They also concurred, as did all factions, that a unified command was needed. But there could be no question of rebuilding a bourgeois army with its oppressive hierarchy. Their ideal was the creation of a Red Army along the lines of the army Trotsky created during the Russian Civil War.[65] POUM militants had been on the front lines from the very beginning of resistance to the military rising; the party had formed its own

62    See Ealham 2010.

63    Cited in Pagès 2011, pp. 274–5.

64    Speech by Nin at a POUM meeting in the Gran Price, *La Batalla*, 8 September 1936, in Nin 1978a, pp. 525–30.

65    The POUM's perspective on the military situation was outlined in Granell 1937.

militias under the banner of the 'Lenin Battalion'. They fought mainly on the Aragón front alongside the CNT-FAI, a zone of the war that, after the first three months, remained relatively quiet, until the June 1937 Huesca offensive. POUM units also played a role in the defence of Madrid and on the central front.[66]

In economic and social terms, Pagès notes that the programme to which the POUM adhered throughout the Spanish Revolution defended rural and urban collectivisations as intermediate platforms for the full socialisation of wealth. Yet, in practice, the POUM showed a willingness to respect petty-bourgeois interests, as it did during debate in the Economic Council over the level at which collectivisation might take place. The POUM accepted a minimum level of fifty workers in an enterprise, against the 250 advocated by the PSUC and Catalan Republican parties. The actual 'Collectivisation and Workers' Control' decree of 24 October stipulated 100.[67] The POUM also supported collectivising the large estates rather than simply dividing them among the workers. However, La Batalla and other POUM publications rejected using force to intimidate small peasants who resisted collectivisation.[68]

Until becoming minister of justice, Nin played an important role on the Economic Council in Cataluña during the height of the revolutionary summer and early autumn. The Council, comprised of all representatives from the revolutionary, left Republican and regional nationalist parties and trade unions, produced a 'Plan for the Socialist Transformation of the Country' in mid-August. The existence of this council corresponded to the CNT's perception of the Revolution as developing by virtue of popular control of the economy through factory committees and collectives and by controlling the

---

66  On the POUM's military contribution between July 1936 and June 1937, see Durgan 2004 and Tosstorff 2009, pp. 155–96. The POUM militia amounted to some 10,000 and included as many as 700 foreign volunteers from 28 countries, the most famous of whom was George Orwell. Durgan notes that many of the ex-Trotskyists from the ICE were located in zones that were overrun by the Nationalists early in the war: Galicia, Salamanca, Extremadura and Sevilla. Others were stranded in areas cut off from the core of the core Republican zone: Asturias and the Basque Country.

67  Pagès 2010, p. 275. As Pagès notes, in the relatively small-scale Barcelona textile industry, 100-plus workers meant larger businesses. Firms of 50 or fewer workers were the norm; most of the medium-sized bourgeoisie sided with the military insurrection.

68  Between November 1936 and April 1937 the POUM's Economic and Technical Council studied the economic situation and published a report 'La guerra y la revolución en Cataluña en el terreno económico'. It was written by J. Oltra Picó, a POUM representative on the Economic Council who had also published a pamphlet, 'El POUM y la colectivazión de industrias y comercios', in late 1936. These and other articles by Oltra Picó and Rafael Sardá are to be found in Alba 1977, pp. 191–268.

military through the militias. Some observers even saw the Anti-Fascist Militia Committee itself as an organ of dual power.[69] Yet the Generalitat still existed – and the CNT resisted the POUM's entreaties for it to seize state power in Cataluña. Although the Communist PSUC had declared the Generalitat to be the proper organ of power, for the moment it did not publicly declare that the Militia Committee should be divested of its powers. But, in September 1936, the Catalan president, Lluis Companys, suggested that the organisations comprising the Committee join the Generalitat, thus fusing the two bodies.

Thus it was premature to declare, as Nin did in early September, that 'in Cataluña, we can affirm that the dictatorship of the proletariat exists'.[70] To say this was to give the impression that the question of power had been resolved in favour of the Catalan workers and that the revolutionary gains were irreversible. Nin was well aware that the 'new institutions', which he believed would replace the Republican government and the Generalitat, did not yet exist. The POUM might well call for a workers' and peasants' government purged of all bourgeois representatives, but, in Cataluña, where the PSOE was weak, it was evident that such a government could only be formed by the CNT-FAI. It appears that Nin wrongly believed that the anarcho-syndicalists had abandoned their apoliticism and a dual-power organisation could now be created. When the CNT did decide to participate in government, it chose to enter the Generalitat and the Popular Front government of Largo Caballero rather than continue to insist upon the exclusively workers' government for which the POUM was calling.

### The Largo Caballero Government

Early September 1936 saw the formation of a new government under Largo Caballero that can genuinely be described as a Popular Front, since it included Socialists, Communists, left Republicans and moderate Republicans. The impetus behind this move was the need to create a unified military and political structure in the face of a civil conflict that was rapidly transforming into an international war. In addition to the logistical and strategic imperatives, those involved perceived a need to bring the middle classes over to the defence of the Republic in order to avoid alienating the democracies and persuade them to lift the embargo on war materials.[71] The fact that the new government sought to put aside or even end the social revolution certainly resonated with the

---

69    Pagès 2011, p. 280.
70    Speech by Nin at a POUM meeting in the Gran Price, *La Batalla*, 8 September 1936, in Nin 1978a, p. 530.
71    Graham 2002, pp. 128–9.

moderate Socialists and left Republicans, who had never sought to move beyond the bourgeois-democratic reforms of the 1931–3 Republican governments. The official Communists' aim was to reconstruct a cross-class Popular Front against fascism. Largo Caballero's appointment as prime minister furthered this cause, since he appeared to be the only figure able to unite the entire workers' movement. The new cabinet was comprised of six Socialists, four Republicans and two Communists from the PCE, who were soon joined by a Basque nationalist (PNV) representative. Its purpose was to re-establish the Republican state under what might be widely accepted as working-class leadership.

Two days after the formation of the Largo Caballero government, Nin commented:

> The current government undoubtedly represents a step forward compared to the previous one. Yet it is a Popular Front government, a government that corresponds to the situation prior to 19 July; that is to say, when the workers' uprising had yet to happen. In this sense, then, compared with the previous government it signifies a step forward but in relation to the present situation a step backward. The slogan of the working class in the days to come is: 'Down with the government of bourgeois ministers and long live a government of the working class!'[72]

Unfortunately for the POUM, though, events were moving in the opposite direction. At the end of September came the decree creating the Popular Army and the introduction of conscription. This meant that the militias were converted into units of a regular military force under a unified command, although they retained their existing officers. The new army was a more conventional force in terms of its hierarchy and discipline. It was certainly far removed from the POUM's or CNT's conception of an egalitarian workers' army, although the political affiliations of the militias were also transferred to the new units. The Soviet influence was reflected in the creation of political commissars inside the Popular Army.[73]

The immediate context for the military reform was the seemingly unstoppable advance of Franco's formidable Army of Africa toward Madrid. The reform proved a major success for the Communists, who had argued for just such a militarisation led by professional officers. The PCE built its own militia, the Fifth Regiment, along these conventional military lines; it was heralded as a template for the new Popular Army units. As in other aspects of organising the

---

72    Quoted in Pagès 2011, p. 281.
73    Durgan 2007, p. 35.

war effort, the Communists were beginning to win the approval of more conservative, middle-class social elements that often possessed the needed professional abilities. Graham has argued that the PCE's remarkable political success
lay in its ability to increase its working-class membership significantly while
also rebuilding the cross-class Popular Front idea that had been destroyed by
the military rising.[74] To appeal across the class divisions to Spaniards who nevertheless supported the Republic, it increasingly shed most of its recognisably
'Communist' discourse and articulated a pragmatic 'people's war' propaganda.
Although its growing strength has usually been attributed to the material
assistance and military advice the Republic received from the Soviet Union, it
seems clear from recent historical research that this explanation is in need of
serious revision.[75] More credit may be due to the Spanish Communist leaders
themselves, who were not mere ciphers for the transmission of the Moscow
'line'.

## 6.3      The Generalitat

In the context of the altered political and military situation, the CNT reversed
its position of hostility to the Republican state; four of its leaders joined the
Popular Front government on 4 November 1936. This came after its proposal
to form a National Defence Council with the UGT while retaining Azaña as
president was rejected.[76] Now the lure of state power, in the midst of the prac-
ticalities of fighting the war, proved too great to resist. In fact, the CNT's decision to join Largo Caballero's cabinet came some time after some of its leaders
took ministerial posts in the Generalitat and accepted the dissolution of the
Anti-Fascist Militia Committee in Cataluña. Both moves represented significant changes in the balance of forces within the Republican zone.

For its part, the POUM followed the CNT into the Generalitat on
24 September, joining the Catalan nationalist parties and the Communists. Nin
became minister of justice, giving up his place on the Economic Council to
do so. He defended his entry on the grounds that his party had only agreed to

---

74      Graham 2002, p. 183. PCE membership increased from about forty thousand in July
        1936 (itself the result of the recent incorporation of the Socialist Youth) to 250,000 by
        December.

75      Two important studies of the Soviet involvement in Spain that challenge many of the tra-
        ditional perspectives are Rees 1998 and Kowalsky 2001, also available online: http://www
        .gutenberg-e.org/kod01/frames/fkod23.html [accessed 20/08/2012].

76      Graham 2002, p. 136.

participate if two conditions were fulfilled: that workers' representatives remain a majority in the Catalan government and that the Generalitat should immediately implement measures of a socialist nature. Nin argued that this decision was the product of a 'transitory situation' which brought together all of the workers' organisations in Cataluña. They now constituted a majority inside the government. Nin accepted that the central Republican government, which had just moved to Valencia, was also comprised of both workers and petty-bourgeois parties, but in Cataluña there was a major difference:

> It is evident that in Cataluña the working class exercises an influence which is far more considerable, far more revolutionary, than in the rest of Spain. Here the Revolution has a much more accelerated rhythm. Thus in spite of the fact that in social composition the Valencia government and that of Cataluña are analogous, there is an undeniable difference in shade between them. In the government of Cataluña is reflected the revolutionary pressure of the mass of workers. In the Valencia government, the petty-bourgeois tendency predominates and working-class representation is subordinate to it.[77]

Nin maintained that the POUM's task would be to ratify and deepen the revolutionary transformations the workers had already achieved. As minister of justice, his own charge would be to defend socialist gains and limit the excesses that threatened to discredit the Revolution.[78] He rejected the suggestion that the Generalitat was simply a Catalan version of the Popular Front. Although he acknowledged that it did include some petty-bourgeois elements, Nin nevertheless believed it to be a radical government genuinely committed to socialist objectives. But, if these characteristics changed, he assured his audience, the POUM would leave.[79] In the event, the POUM was not given the luxury of a choice in the matter. It was forced out of the Catalan government in December 1936 through pressure from the PSUC and the Soviet consul in Barcelona, Vladimir Antonov-Ovseyenko.

---

77    Taken from Nin's report on the political situation to an enlarged Central Committee meeting of the POUM held in Barcelona between 12 and 16 December 1936. Published in the POUM's Internal Bulletin No. 1, 15 January 1937, and reproduced under the title 'El POUM y los problemas de la revolución' in Nin 1978b, p. 226.

78    From a talk given by Nin on Radio POUM about the Popular Tribunals and revolutionary justice, *La Batalla*, 17 October 1936, in Nin 1978a, pp. 537–9.

79    Speech by Nin to a meeting in the Gran Price in honour of Maurín, 27 October 1936, in Nin 1978a, p. 546.

Why had the POUM entered a government containing petty-bourgeois parties, something absolutely ruled out by its own hostile position toward the Popular Front? In his biography of Nin, Pelai Pagès notes that many POUM militants who had come from the BOC saw Nin as having decided to join the Generalitat without consulting the party. Pagès argues this was clearly not the case since the POUM's Central Committee had decided to enter the government on 15 September; La Batalla published the resolution three days later.[80] The real criticism of this action lies in the fact that the POUM felt compelled to abandon its earlier strongly held position. Wilebaldo Solano, the leader of the POUM youth movement Juventud Comunista Ibérica (JCI, Iberian Communist Youth), later explained that the simple reality was that the POUM was too weak to resist the Anti-Fascist Militia Committee's liquidation once the CNT abandoned it. He argues that refusing to join the Catalan government would have given the Stalinists a pretext to outlaw the POUM. The party would then have been denied access to the materials with which to maintain its military units. The POUM's leaders felt that, given the official Communists' increasingly virulent attacks, they were safer alongside the CNT.[81] Yet the notion that there was safety in numbers was soon shown to be false when the CNT still refused to address the question of political power or form a bloc with the POUM inside the government. When the POUM was expelled three months later under PSUC and Soviet pressure, the CNT refused to intervene in what it considered a quarrel between Marxists.[82]

Not all of the POUM's leaders had agreed with entering the Generalitat. Andrade, who had come from the ICE rather than the BOC, privately concurred with Trotsky's later accusation that it amounted to collaboration with the bourgeoisie.[83] In an editorial for La Batalla, he condemned the formation of a new Popular Front government, led by Largo Caballero and in which the PCE

---

80    Pagès 2011, pp. 283–4.

81    Wilebaldo Solano, in Fraser 1981, pp. 341–2.

82    Fraser 1981, p. 342.

83    Trotsky's personal situation in Norway prevented a contemporaneous response to the
       POUM's entry into the Generalitat. However, his 19 February 1937 interview with the
       French news agency Havas makes clear that he saw no imperative behind the POUM's
       actions. Fighting the war alongside the Republicans was one thing, but colluding in a
       government that safeguarded bourgeois interests meant the POUM could not advance
       the 'audacious social reforms' for which the working masses would be prepared to fight
       (Trotsky 1973a, pp. 242–4).

participated, as 'counterrevolutionary'.[84] Although the Generalitat now adopted a radical programme that accepted the need for collectivisation, nationalisation and workers' control, it did begin to reverse some of the achievements of the Revolution. On 9 October, it dissolved the workers' committees that had taken on the functions of local government after July 1936 – committees the POUM had seen as the very organs with the potential to become soviets.[85] What had been working-class committees were now replaced by administrative bodies with the same political composition as the Generalitat. In November, the government abolished 3,000 official posts in revolutionary bodies, thus destroying the entire structure of workers' power in Cataluña.

### Nin as Catalan Minister of Justice

Against this very substantial erosion of revolutionary gains since July, the POUM's achievements in the Generalitat appear modest and transitory. During Nin's brief period as minister of justice from 26 September to 17 December 1936, he set up Popular Tribunals in a serious effort to stem the extra-judicial 'justice' that had been meted out to those considered to be 'fascists', Nationalist spies, saboteurs or some other sort of class enemy. The Generalitat passed the decree establishing seven tribunals in Cataluña on 13 October. It outlined specific types of crimes, from 'armed rebellion' to 'false accusations', and formalised the composition of the tribunals, drawn from parties represented in government. The president of each tribunal was to be qualified in law.[86] The system was designed to ensure quick and fair trials based upon due process. Guilt or innocence would be determined by concrete evidence; the accused would have the right to a defence counsel. Nin stated on Radio POUM that the tribunals 'would guarantee the integrity of the proletarian achievements that were contributing to victory in the war'.[87] Well aware of the repression in the Republican zone over the summer, Nin was concerned to limit the use of the death sentence. He realised that Nationalist propaganda was using the issue,

---

84    This earned Andrade a ban on writing editorials for *La Batalla* (Fraser 1981, p. 184 and p. 341). See also Andrade's introduction to the collection of Nin's writings (Andrade 1971, p. 30). Francisco de Cabo, another POUM veteran, notes in a letter to Ignacio Iglesias of 7 December 1973 that it was a mistake to enter the Generalitat, but doubts that would have made much difference one way or the other (Fundació Andreu Nin, 1989b).

85    *La Batalla* of 27 September 1936 declared that power should transfer to the workers' committees (cited in Alba and Schwartz 1988, pp. 137–8).

86    For an outline of Nin's work as minister of justice, see Pagès 2011, pp. 289–310.

87    POUM Radio talk, Nin 1978a, pp. 537–9.

which had then been picked up by the international press. Hence all death sentences would be passed on to the Generalitat for a final decision.

The Popular Tribunals started work toward the end of October; initially, they dealt with the backlog of civilians charged with collaboration with the military rebels in July. Much of the work was undertaken by the four Barcelona tribunals. In the period from November 1936 to February 1937, 48 death sentences were passed, of which 40 were carried out. However, the majority of trials ended in freeing the prisoners.[88] Elsewhere in Cataluña, the tribunals for Girona and Tarragona passed more than twenty death sentences each, but the majority were commuted. It seems that the Lleida tribunal was the most punitive, passing 83 death sentences. However, Pagès notes that overall, at least ninety death sentences were commuted through the review system Nin set up.[89]

Thus it would appear that Nin had a significant impact upon reducing the violence of the so-called 'uncontrollables' in the Catalan rear-guard. He began the process of reforming the penal system and appointed a woman as director of the Barcelona women's correctional establishment. He also introduced civil marriage and a system of adoption that took account of the rights of the child. Divorce and abortion were all legalised and contraception made available. The age of majority was reduced to 18 years, acknowledging young Spaniards' massive commitment to the war effort and the new responsibilities this entailed. Young men could, after all, be expected to fight from the age of 18. This also addressed the voting age, which had been set at 23 in 1931 – in a country where more than 20 per cent of the active population was under 20 years old. The importance of youth movements during the Republican years suggests that there was indeed a huge appetite for political participation among the young.

It should be noted that Nin's reform of the judicial process was not without opposition, particularly from more radical anarchist elements who viewed 'popular justice' as their territory. Indeed, much of the tension between the CNT-FAI and the POUM had to do with the mutual suspicions generated by their overlapping social base and areas of interest and power.

Apart from Nin's useful work as minister of justice, the major success in which the POUM participated was the legalisation of collectives with more than a hundred employees, mentioned earlier. Yet, as Víctor Alba has pointed out with some justification, the real history of the POUM during this period has little to do with the workings of the Generalitat or the 'legalisation' of aspects of the Summer Revolution. It really concerns their activities in local

---

88    See the details of these trials in Pagès 2011, pp. 299–300.
89    Pagès 2011, p. 302.

government and economic and military organisation.[90] A Maurín Institute was established to promote education. The important role of women in the Revolution was reflected in the work of the POUM Women's Secretariat and women's involvement in politics, economics, the military, journalism and medicine.[91] The POUM also played an important part in helping to resolve the housing crisis and run public services. But the area in which the dissident communists continued to attempt to play a decisive role was in the formulation of economic policy through the autumn and winter of 1936 and 1937.

Unlike the CNT, which had long possessed a vision of what a libertarian communist society should look like, the POUM developed its economic policy as the Revolution unfolded. As has been noted earlier, in July 1936 it had not been clear to POUM leaders that the massive working-class response to the military rising signified more than a defensive reaction. The slogan of 'workers' control' had therefore appeared initially as a means of preventing the bourgeoisie from sabotaging military organisation. The industrial and agrarian collectives did not come about under guidance from the POUM, but often emerged as a logical consequence of the workers taking control and many owners fleeing. However, the CNT often practised forced collectivisation, especially in the countryside, a practice the POUM condemned with reference to the effects of Stalin's agrarian policy in the Soviet Union. The POUM also discussed the benefits of collectivising small enterprises. Some contributors to the debate thought that it was pointless to deprive the petty-bourgeoisie of its economic power while permitting it to retain political power, since it would employ the latter to undermine the Revolution. Yet, as we have seen, the POUM lacked the means to act independently of the CNT. In broad terms, the POUM's literature makes it clear that it did not view collectivisation as, in itself, the 'solution' to the Revolution's economic problems. Yet it does seem to have been considered a necessary phase on the road to the socialisation of the economy. But, unlike the anarcho-syndicalists, for whom collectivisation *was* the revolution, the dissident communists were well aware that the final step in this process could

---

90    Alba and Schwartz 1988, p. 140.

91    On the question of health, see Dr. Mina, *El problema sanitorio ante la revolución proletaria*, (Barcelona: Editorial Marxista, 1937); on women and the revolution see María Teresa Andrade, *La mujer ante la revolución*, (Barcelona: Editorial Marxista, 1937). Both pamphlets are reproduced in Alba 1977, pp. 271–87 and pp. 290–301. Among the accounts by foreign women who were connected with the POUM, see the chapters by Mary Low in Low and Breá 1979. Other accounts are Etchebehere 1976; Landau 1988; Cusick 1979; and Ensner and Thalmann 1983. For a discussion of foreigners' involvement with the POUM, see the chapter by Stephen Schwartz in Alba and Schwartz 1988, pp. 280–99, and Durgan 2004.

only be taken after the issue of state power had been decided in favour of the proletariat.[92]

Not surprisingly, perhaps, a key area of disagreement that surfaced in the Generalitat from September 1936 concerned the composition and command of the army. As has been noted, the POUM's initial position was to defend the militia system. It even supported its position by publishing Trotsky's *Red Army Manual* and, ironically as it turned out, an old pamphlet by Vladimir Antonov-Ovseyenko which extolled the virtues of militias over regular armies.[93] But, in the context of early defeats and the opening of the 'battle for Madrid', it was clear to most observers that a unified army was essential. With the arrival from early October of Soviet military assistance, pressure from Moscow to create a unified army was becoming irresistible. In this changing context, the POUM took the view that this should be a workers' revolutionary army under the command of working-class organisations; hence, it did not see the militias as sacrosanct.[94] Behind the POUM, CNT and left-Socialist argument was the contention that only the prospect of fighting for meaningful social achievements, enshrined in the revolutionary changes of the summer, would provide the morale for a people's army to fight against the ruthless professionals of Franco's Army of Africa. Clearly, this was yet another area in which the revolutionary voices lost the argument to the Republicans, moderate Socialists and Communists, although it was not yet evident that revolutionary gains were being rolled back. Of course, it took time to create the new Popular Army. It began with merging the highly

---

92  See documents in Alba 1977, pp. 191–268. For a discussion of the POUM's role in the social and economic revolution see Tosstorff 2009, pp. 125–54; Alba and Schwartz 1988, pp. 143–50; and Pagès and Virós, 1971.

93  Nin translated this pamphlet. Vladimir Antonov-Ovseyenko, the old Bolshevik who led the storming of the Winter Palace in 1917, was appointed Soviet consul to Barcelona in August 1936. Although he had known Nin in Russia, the consul always pretended not to recognise him when they met at official functions.

94  In a letter to Francisco de Cabo, Iglesias argues that the impression Pierre Broué gives that the POUM counterposed the defence of the militias to the creation of a unified army was false. The point to be made was rather that the POUM sought a truly revolutionary army, something the PCE opposed. Iglesias also rejects Broué's contention that dissolving the revolutionary committees was an anti-democratic act. These committees only corresponded to the immediate requirements of the situation caused by the military rising, he argues. They were not democratically elected and tended to act independently of one another. The need to organise an effective defence meant that political and military unity was essential. However, the error of the Negrín government (after May 1937) was to think that the war could be won without the Revolution (Letters to Francisco de Cabo of 5 November and 7 December 1961, in Fundació Andreu Nin 1989b).

disciplined Communist Fifth Regiment into 'mixed brigades' that combined militia units with loyal regular army units. This established a template, but the process took months to complete.[95] There were 15 mixed brigades by the end of 1936, including the largely Communist-organised International Brigades, but the process continued into the spring of 1937. As Beevor notes, in addition to other motives was the perceived need to impress the democratic powers that the Republic was a normal state with a regular army.[96]

### Nin's Expulsion from the Catalan Government

Political tensions between those who wanted to continue and deepen the social revolution and those who portrayed it as a barrier to prosecuting the war deepened toward the end of 1936. In Cataluña, this conflict played out between the PSUC and the POUM and, in this phase of the War, culminated in Nin's expulsion from the Generalitat. The question of the intense conflict between the official Communists and the revolutionary parties has been subject to serious historical revision in recent years.[97] There is now greater focus upon the rivalries between the POUM and the newly formed PSUC and the similarities between the pre-war forerunner organisations in terms of their social base and Catalanism. While there certainly were bitter pre-war divisions with deep local roots, it is a mistake to play down the part played by wider political conflicts. In November, the POUM was barred from representation on the Madrid Defence Council as a result of Soviet diplomatic pressure channelled through Marcel Rosenberg, the Russian ambassador. Even Graham accepts that this was an example of the Soviets employing their veto power by virtue of the military support they were giving the Republic.[98] But, as Durgan points out, it is important not to underestimate the importance of the anti-'Trotskyist' campaign being waged around the Moscow show trials.[99]

August 1936 had seen the public trials of leading old Bolsheviks accused of being traitors and agents of fascism. While many political organisations involved in the various Popular Fronts chose to play down or even ignore the Moscow trials, the POUM newspaper *La Batalla* covered them in depth and offered an analysis and explanation that differed little from Trotsky's – that

---

95   On the Aragón front, CNT and POUM militias still existed as such in March 1937, at which time the authority of the War Ministry in Valencia was finally accepted (Graham 2002, p. 314).

96   See Beevor 2007, pp. 138–43 and pp. 229–31.

97   See Graham 2002, Chapters Three and Five, and Kowalsky 2001.

98   Graham 2002, p. 198.

99   See Durgan 1996 and Durgan 2007, p. 94.

is to say, the paper portrayed the trials as a move by Stalin to eliminate rivals and place the blame for the Soviet Union's failings upon convenient scapegoats. The executions of Kamenev, Zinoviev and others at the end of August were denounced as 'a monstrous crime that has just been perpetrated in Moscow'.[100] The POUM also defended Trotsky against the Moscow allegations while also signalling their disagreements with him, although elements of the old BOC membership were wary of further souring relations with the official Communists.

## 6.4    Conclusion

In Madrid, the POUM was very small and further weakened by the heavy losses in the early defence of the capital; its exclusion from the Madrid Defence Council was a simple and uncontroversial matter. However, the POUM's voice was much louder in Cataluña: here, it responded to the PSUC's increasing attacks with heavy criticism of Stalin, the Comintern, the Madrid Defence Council and the Republican government in Valencia. *La Batalla* criticised the Comintern for subordinating the Spanish Revolution to the requirements of Soviet foreign policy. This criticism offered sufficient grounds for the PSUC to insist that the POUM be expelled from the Catalan government. It was clear to Companys that the POUM's presence was a provocation to the Soviets, whose military support was vital. But it was also convenient for both the Esquerra and the PSUC to diminish the POUM's political weight and target one of its support bases among the Catalanist lower middle classes. The CNT was persuaded not to defend the POUM on the Generalitat by allowing it to retain its own defence committees. Hence, the new cabinet that emerged from this political crisis on 16 December did not include a POUM member. Nin was replaced as justice minister by one of the PSUC leaders, Rafael Vidiella.[101]

---

100    Quoted in Alba and Schwartz 1988, p. 132.

101    Vidiella was followed as minister of justice by the top PSUC leader, Joan Comorera, in April 1937. Comorera set out to end Cataluña's legislative independence and introduce the same measures as in the rest of the Republican zone. In the case of the Popular Tribunals this meant transferring oversight to the Valencia government. The summer of 1937 saw the creation of new 'special' tribunals dedicated to espionage and treason. This signalled a new phase of political repression that gave free rein to the political police. It was very far from Nin's ideas as minister of justice; indeed, he would become one of the victims of this repression (Pagès 2011, p. 309).

Speaking that day on Radio POUM, Nin explained the situation in the following terms. The PSUC and UGT leaders had wanted a government with full powers, a council of war and the postponement of socialist measures. By accusing the POUM of attacking the USSR and refusing to carry out Generalitat dictates, the PSUC had been able to secure his expulsion from the government. But the POUM still existed and would defend the Revolution at the front and in the rear.[102] Eleven days later, Nin declared, more prophetically than he could have known, that 'we may have been eliminated from the government; but as we have said already and repeat today: in order to eliminate us from political life, it would be necessary to kill all of the militants of the POUM'.[103]

---

[102]   Broadcast by Nin on Radio POUM concerning the situation created by the crisis in the Generalitat, *La Batalla*, 16 December 1936, in Nin 1978a, pp. 553–5.

[103]   Speech by Nin at a meeting in the Teatro Olympia in Barcelona on 27 December 1936. Printed in *La Batalla* No. 128, 29 December 1937 and reproduced under the title 'Los avances de la contrarrevolución', in Nin 1978b, p. 244.

# CHAPTER 7

# Defending the Revolution

The POUM's exclusions from both the Madrid Defence Council and the Catalan government were stages in a wider process of centralising power and reversing the revolutionary achievements that would reach its climax a few months later in Barcelona. It was accompanied by a campaign of vilification and slander against the POUM, organised by the PCE, the Comintern and other national Communist parties, that accused its members of, among other things, being 'Trotsky-fascists'. May 1937 witnessed the playing out of a civil war within the Civil War that involved the POUM and other revolutionary forces in a desperate attempt to defend the social revolution. The inevitable failure of this resistance was swiftly followed by the Republican government outlawing the POUM, Andreu Nin's disappearance and murder by the official Communists and Soviet agents, and the arrest of many militants involved in the 'May Days'. Some of those arrested were tried by the Republican government the following year. Today few historians would take issue with this summary of the POUM's fate. However, explanations for the propaganda assault and the causes and nature of the May events and Nin's murder are matters of considerable historical and political debate. Much disagreement surrounds the roles played by the official Communists, Soviet agents and other forces; the culpability or otherwise of the POUM leaders; and whether or not the vilification campaign was connected to Soviet foreign policy, whose logic – it is argued – dictated terminating Spain's social revolution and the forces supporting it.

This chapter considers these questions, beginning with Nin's response to the Communist campaign against the POUM. It then turns to the pivotal events of May: their causes, nature and outcome. What was the POUM's role in defending the revolutionary advances? How did Nin evaluate the significance of his political organisation? How, why and by whom was he removed from the scene shortly after the May crisis? What does this episode reveal about the nature of Soviet intervention in the politics of the Republic? The chapter ends with a reflection upon the POUM's theory and practice during the Spanish Revolution and considers how its position might be understood in the context of recent historiography.

## 7.1      The Campaign against the POUM

In early January 1937, *La Batalla* signalled its appreciation of the dangers facing its organisation by reproducing a quote, which it attributed to the Soviet
press organ *Pravda*, announcing the hope that 'the cleaning up of the Spanish
Anarchists and the Trotskyists in Cataluña will be carried out with the same
energy as in the USSR'.[1] Even if, as is most likely, this was not an accurate quotation from any of the Soviet news sources (*Pravda* appeared in several different
editions), it nevertheless can be seen to express the POUM's perception of the
Communists' intentions. After all, attacks upon the POUM and other avowedly
Marxist organisations critical of Moscow or connected in any way with Trotsky
were hardly new or unusual.[2] Thus the POUM's perspectives at the time of
Nin's expulsion from the Generalitat display the slow dawning of an appreciation of the seriousness of the situation facing them. Much had occurred on
the international stage since the spring of 1936, especially the first Moscow
'show trial', in which Trotsky, *in absentia*, was the main accused. In Spain, the
official Communists' growth in power, influence and popularity was due not
merely to the crucial military assistance the USSR was providing, but also to
the apparently moderate and pragmatic political stance the PCE had adopted.
The POUM could, with some plausibility, be portrayed in Communist propaganda as marginalised extremists who were linked to 'convicted' enemies of
the Soviet Union.[3]

Nin was well aware that what he termed a 'counterrevolution' was in progress. In response, he proposed that the POUM call for dissolving what they considered to be a bourgeois parliament and assembling a congress of workers,
peasants and militia representatives. A pressing task was to convince the CNT

---

1    *La Batalla*, 5 January 1937, quoted in Esenwein and Shubert 1995, p. 220. This quotation has
     been widely reproduced in studies of the Communist movement in Spain and is usually
     attributed to *Pravda*, 17 December 1936. See, for example, Pagès 2011, p. 331. However, it is
     clear from Esenwein's research that this is an unreliable attribution. Yet the case is perhaps
     not wholly clear-cut, as shown by the exchange between authors in Schwartz, Esenwein and
     Horowitz 1989, pp. 153–7.
2    Durgan notes that in April 1936 the Comintern was advocating intensifying the campaign
     against Spanish 'Trotskyists', quoting recognition of these attacks by the POUM's paper, *La
     Batalla*, from 10 and 17 April 1936. This came in the context of the ongoing fusion of the
     Socialist and Communist youth organisations, the USC and Catalan PCE (Durgan 2007, p. 94,
     and Durgan 1996, pp. 432–4).
3    The August 1936 Moscow trial was by no means immediately and unanimously condemned
     by the foreign press or many Russia 'experts' (see Conquest 2008, pp. 469–70).

leadership to make common cause with the POUM in defending revolutionary gains against the PSUC and the Esquerra.[4] However, it is less clear either from Nin's report to the POUM Central Committee or from the resolutions passed at the plenum held between 12 and 16 of December 1936 that the POUM was completely aware of the nature and extent of the Republican-Communist threat to the Revolution and to those groups most closely associated with it. Nin noted that the USSR's intervention had denied the POUM any representation on the Madrid Defence Council. He also referred to accusations that the members of the POUM were fascists.[5] But although the POUM leaders certainly appreciated that the official Communists sought to confine the Revolution within bourgeois-democratic limits and saw the POUM and CNT as obstacles to this, in December 1936 they still seemed to lack Trotsky's understanding of the lengths to which Stalin was prepared to go in order to silence them.[6] It may be that they considered the ongoing attacks on their party largely a propaganda response to the POUM's earlier very public condemnation of the Moscow trials and Comintern policy toward Spain.[7] There is little indication in the Executive Committee resolutions that they appreciated the degree of their isolation within the Republican camp or that verbal attacks would soon become physical ones. Of course, this may also reflect an underestimation of the extent of Soviet political influence at this time.

For *La Batalla*, the focus was primarily upon the official Communists. The paper noted the parallels being drawn by Communist newspapers between the defendants in the Moscow trials and the POUM. The Communists had brought the same charges of 'Trotskyism' and 'agents of fascism' against the POUM. Yet, the paper noted: 'Fortunately, Spain is not Russia, but an attempt is being made

---

4   Speech by Nin at a meeting in the Teatro Olympia in Barcelona on 27 December 1936. Printed in *La Batalla* No. 128, 29 December 1937 and reproduced under the title 'Los avances de la contrarrevolución' in Nin 1978b, p. 244. See also Nin's report on the political situation to an enlarged POUM Central Committee meeting held in Barcelona between 12 and 16 December 1936 in Nin 1978b, p. 227.

5   Alba and Schwartz 1988, pp. 172–3.

6   Following Kirov's assassination in December 1934, Trotsky had predicted that Stalin would increase his attacks upon communist dissidents on a 'world scale'. Trotsky's family members, friends and comrades were soon to suffer from the terror initiated by Stalin. In *The Revolution Betrayed*, completed in August 1936, before the Moscow trials but after the outbreak of the war and revolution in Spain, Trotsky compared Stalinism and fascism thus: 'Stalinism and fascism, in spite of a deep difference in social foundations, are symmetrical phenomena. In many of their features they show a deadly similarity' (Trotsky 1972a, p. 278).

7   On 28 August 1936 the POUM Executive Committee condemned the Moscow trials and the execution of Lenin's old comrades. See editorial in *La Batalla*, 28 August 1936.

to place Spain under Russian domination which we will oppose with all our energy'.[8] Nin warned in a speech to the JCI that the slogan 'first win the War and the Revolution will follow' – a slogan derived from the notion that the Spanish struggle was between democracy and fascism – actually amounted to a call to reverse the Revolution itself. By slandering the POUM, he explained, the Stalinists hoped to destroy the Revolution in the same way they had liquidated the old guard of the Bolshevik Revolution. Echoing Trotsky, Nin also warned that the failure of the Spanish Revolution would only serve to hasten the onset of another imperialist war; a war for which the international proletariat and the USSR would pay the human cost.[9] In other words, the POUM's response to the campaign against it remained rhetorical and theoretical.

Identifying a growing counterrevolution in the Republican camp aimed against the CNT and the POUM led Nin to pose the question of power with far greater urgency. Failure to complete the social revolution by seizing political control had given the bourgeoisie, assisted by the Stalinists and reformist Socialists, the chance to reconstitute itself and launch an offensive against the revolutionary gains. But, by responding immediately, Nin believed the revolutionary workers' organisations could rectify this 'profound error'. What form should their response take? Nin answered that because the specific weight of the revolutionary workers and peasants was so great and their revolutionary advances so profound, in addition to the fact that they had retained their arms, it was still possible to take power 'without recourse to armed insurrection'. By forming a Constituent Assembly of delegates from the factory committees, peasants' organisations and those fighting at the front, the present attempt to reconstruct the bourgeois state could be resisted simply by creating a workers' and peasants' government to fill the power vacuum. Such a government would, he said, be based upon extending and consolidating the Revolution.[10]

However, as Nin knew only too well, the main obstacle to taking action remained the failure of the CNT-FAI to recognise the need to conquer state power and accept that a workers' and peasants' government was the missing revolutionary ingredient. Nin was convinced that recent experiences had demonstrated this necessity to the CNT-FAI leadership. Had they not already participated in both the Popular Front government and the Generalitat? Indeed, he remained confident that the anarcho-syndicalists would join a Workers'

8    *La Batalla*, 27 January 1937, cited in Alba and Schwartz 1988, p. 174.
9    Speech by Nin to the POUM youth (Juventud Comunista Ibérica), 30 January 1937, reported in *Juventud Comunista* and reproduced in Nin 1971, p. 185.
10   Nin, 'La concepción marxista del poder y la revolución española', *La Batalla*, 14 March 1937, in Nin 1971, p. 197.

Revolutionary Front with the POUM which, at least in Cataluña, would realise the political revolution. Today it was still possible to achieve power peacefully; tomorrow it would only be possible through violent struggle, he stressed.[11] This analysis revealed the problem presented by CNT participating in government yet failing to draw the necessary lessons from it. By entering the state apparatus, the CNT leaders had effectively turned their backs on a revolutionary path and were, whether they admitted it or not, complicit in any actions the government might take. The May events would reveal precisely this reality to the revolutionary anarcho-syndicalist rank and file, who would struggle to comprehend the stance taken by CNT leaders Juan García Oliver and Frederica Montseny. It was a crisis from which the CNT would never really recover.

If Nin had previously underestimated the threat from the Republicans and the Communists, its magnitude became more apparent in early 1937 as the campaign against the POUM intensified and the process of centralising power in the hands of the Valencia government accelerated. Comorera's PSUC had grown quickly in Cataluña during the autumn and winter, with control over the mass Socialist trade union and the UGT and considerable influence among the rabassaires and some white-collar workers, small businessmen and other lower-middle-class Catalans.[12] It had forged a crucial alliance with Companys' Esquerra Republicana de Catalunya (ERC).[13] Both Communists and Catalanists could agree that the Revolution needed to be curtailed and the Popular Front economic régime, in which small and medium-sized property rights were respected, quickly restored. Undoubtedly, the main target of the Communist-Esquerra alliance was the CNT, the dominant revolutionary force with a truly mass base. But they seemed far too strong to take on at this point.

Here, the influence of the Soviet Union upon the process of centralisation was significant. In December 1936 Antonov-Ovseyenko, the Russian consul in Barcelona, used the bargaining chip of Soviet military help in Cataluña to exert pressure upon Lluis Companys to exclude the POUM from the Catalan government and accept a unified Republican political and military command.[14]

---

11      Speech by Nin at the Teatro Olympia on 10 April 1937, published as '¿Qué clase detenta el poder?', *La Batalla*, 11 April 1937, in Nin 1971, pp. 199–200. See also Nin, 'Primero de Mayo de 1937', *La Batalla*, 1 May 1937, in Nin 1971, p. 205.

12      The PSUC had, over the war months, outstripped the POUM in membership to become the largest Catalan socialist party. By March 1937 its membership stood at 50,000 compared to the POUM's claimed membership in December 1936 of 30,000 (Graham 2002, p. 238 n. 92). The PSUC's control of the UGT gave it effective sway over hundreds of thousands of Catalan workers.

13      Esenwein and Shubert 1995, pp. 218–19.

14      Graham 2002, p. 239.

The second of these offended many Catalan nationalists' sense of superiority over the rest of Spain, rooted as it was in the region's relative economic dynamism. Despite the brief successes of the battles of the Jarama and Guadalajara, in which the International Brigades played important roles, the realities of the poor military situation, the serious problems posed by the Non-Intervention Committee, and the fall of Málaga in February all contributed to a sense of crisis in the Republican zones. As Anthony Beevor notes of this period, 'Stalinist spy mania was reaching its peak. Suspicions in Spain and suspicions back in the Soviet Union fed upon each other.'[15] Soviet political and military advisers were looking for people to blame for the failure to inflict a decisive defeat upon the Nationalist forces threatening Madrid. The prime target was Largo Caballero, who was both prime minister and war minister. He had already proved resistant to the 'advice' emanating from Moscow. In December, Stalin stressed the need to avoid alienating the peasantry and 'petty and middle urban bourgeoisie' by protecting their property rights. Azaña's Republicans should be supported in order to avoid the impression abroad that Spain was a 'Communist Republic'.[16] Largo Caballero was, however, less convinced of the importance of the Republican parties and sought cooperation with the other great syndical force, the CNT. This placed him on a collision course with the official Communist PCE, which hoped to merge the moderate and left Socialists with its own organisations. A crisis might lead to a change of government, to one more favourable to the Communist project. This motive has often been mentioned in support of the contention that Communist forces manoeuvred a confrontation between the groups defending the Revolution and those of the Republican state, so as to provoke a major political crisis.

In Cataluña, the PSUC had intensified its bid to divest the anarcho-syndicalists of their political and economic power by employing its alliance with the Esquerra in the Generalitat to dissolve the revolutionary committees controlling food distribution and to create a single police force beyond the control of the CNT-FAI. Since the Revolution's inception, *patrullas de control* and other armed workers' committees had dealt with local policing; the CNT-FAI exercised considerable sway in these. Both CNT-FAI and POUM papers, *Tierra y Libertad* and *La Batalla*, had attacked the PSUC's stance in print. By the end of April, the situation had moved beyond rhetoric and degenerated into violence, with

---

15    Beevor 2007, p. 246. He quotes the Soviet aviator A. Agaltsov reporting to Moscow that 'the fascist intervention in Spain and the Trotskyist-Bukharin gangs that are operating in our country are links of the same chain' (Beevor 2007, p. 247).

16    Stalin, Molotov and Voroshilov, 'Letter to Caballero', 21 December 1936, in Carr 1984, pp. 86–7.

the killing of a PSUC official and what was seen as the revenge killing of a prominent anarchist in Puigcerdá.[17]

Secret communications from Soviet agents, published after the opening of Russian archives in the 1990s, have been cited as primary-source evidence to support the thesis that the official Communists, with the Comintern and Moscow's connivance, conspired to provoke the internecine conflict of May 1937.[18] Documents in the collection *Spain Betrayed*, edited by Ronald Radosh, Mary Habeck and Grigory Sevostianov, appear to demonstrate a consistency in the ways in which Comintern, GRU and NKVD agents refer to the CNT-FAI and the POUM. The language used is reminiscent of the Moscow trial, including phrases such as 'putschists', 'strike-breakers of the struggle against fascism', 'Trotskyists', 'fascist-anarchists', 'counterrevolutionary Trotskyists' and 'subversives'.[19] For instance, Nikonov, the deputy head of the GRU in Spain, stated on 20 February that he was attempting to rid the army of 'traitorous elements' involved in counterrevolutionary activity that he blamed for the fall of Málaga. He spoke of an anarchist plot to overthrow the Popular Front government, but reserved his most extreme vitriol for the POUM:

> Even worse scum is the small group of counterrevolutionary Trotskyists, mainly in Cataluña and in part of the Basque Country, who are carrying out vile anti-Soviet activity and propaganda against the VKP(b) [Communist Party of the Soviet Union], its leaders, the USSR, and the Red Army. With the connivance of the 'orthodox' anarchists, the Trotskyists (POUMists) at the beginning of the war had their own special régiment with two thousand rifles on the Catalan front. This has now increased to thirty-two thousand men and has received weapons from everyone. This régiment is the rottenest unit in the entire Republican army, but has nonetheless existed up to now and received supplies, money, and ammunition. It goes without saying that it is impossible to win the war against the rebels if these scum within the Republican camp are not liquidated.[20]

---

17    Esenwein and Shubert 1995, p. 221. This incident was more complex than this summary suggests since it was tied into the ongoing conflict over control of the Franco-Catalan border posts and the Esquerra's efforts to establish a non-union/non-party police force against the CNT's control committees (Graham 2002, pp. 261–2).

18    See, for instance, Pagès 2007.

19    Radosh, Habeck and Sevostianov 2001, p. 8, p. 48, p. 132 and p. 139. The GRU was the Soviet military intelligence agency and the NKVD was the secret police service.

20    Radosh, Habeck and Sevostianov 2001, pp. 132–3.

Marchenko, the Soviet plenipotentiary in Spain, devoted a whole section to the POUM in his report of 22 February entitled 'On the Political Situation in Spain'. He argued that the POUM was dangerous because it had several thousand activists and was seeking to draw CNT members into its sphere of influence, especially the youth movement. This was 'sabotaging' the PSUC, he complained.

> Under the pretext of defence, the POUM is actually carrying out a savage offensive against the party, in deploying, especially lately, the vilest, most slanderous campaign against the USSR … [O]nly the utter political defeat of the POUM (since police measures alone are not enough) will establish the conditions for a protracted collaboration between the party and the CNT, for the POUM is the headquarters of the provocations, and it has its tentacles in every organisation and especially in the CNT and the FAI.[21]

In a March report probably written by the French Communist André Marty, who was chief political commissar of the International Brigades and a Comintern agent, the general staff of the Republican army is blamed for the fall of Málaga and accused of 'treason'.[22] Largo Caballero is condemned for his wish to form a syndical unity between the CNT and UGT that would exclude the Communists and the Republicans. Toward the end of the report there is a rather mystifying reference to a 'systematic, ever increasing flirtation' between the Socialists and the 'Trotskyists (POUM)'. The author continues:

> One can sense the growth of a dirty campaign by socialists from other countries, along with the Trotskyists and along with the Gestapo against the Comintern, against the USSR, against the Spanish Communist Party … Then – the censors, who crossed out in articles of the *Frente Rojo* [a Communist paper] every attack on the Trotskyists, especially the arguments that show the counterrevolutionary work, the fascist wrecking done by these people in Spain. Then – the proposal by the UGT (whose president is Caballero) to convene that international conference from which the Communists were excluded and which, according to the intentions of the leaders of the UGT, should have some anti-Communist imprint.[23]

---

21  Radosh, Habeck and Sevostianov 2001, p. 140.
22  Radosh, Habeck and Sevostianov 2001, p. 156.
23  Radosh, Habeck and Sevostianov 2001, p. 163.

When assessing the import of these primary sources, a note of caution should be sounded. Their use of terminology needs to be explored and questioned in greater depth than the editors of these documents attempt in their commentaries. For instance, while the meaning of the terms 'wrecker' and 'Trotskyist' might appear self-evident, during the Soviet purges of the mid-1930s they were labels applied to a wide range of supposed offences, from actual criminality to failing to fully endorse the 'general line' of the moment.[24] The terms were in reality anything but precise and appear to be deployed here in a formalistic manner. It is highly probable that agents filing reports from Spain felt obliged to employ particular words and be seen to indulge in the type of political abuse that had become common currency in the Soviet Union. Failure to do so might leave them open to suspicion.[25]

In reference to the Catalan situation in the early spring of 1937, an undated report from a GRU operative identified as 'Cid' stresses the local strength of the anarcho-syndicalists.[26] It notes the CNT-FAI's demands to be given more power in the Catalan government and warns of the possibility of an attempted 'seizure of power'.[27] Agent Cid suggests the motivation for this was the Communists' growing success in winning over members of the UGT and the Rabassaires' Union. In other words, the document is describing a struggle for influence within the Catalan working class and peasantry – one the CNT-FAI was losing. In response, the report states, 'preparations for an armed action' were going ahead, including setting up machine-gun posts in Barcelona.[28] Military inaction on the Aragón front is attributed to the anarchists' unwillingness to fight and preference for making the Revolution first. (Yet the strength of their forces suggested they would be in a good position to move to take power in Barcelona.) For their part, the Esquerra's military forces are also said to be unwilling to engage the enemy because they were keeping their powder dry in order to protect their regional nationalist gains. The POUM are labelled 'yes-men for the extreme anarchists on all the main questions' and enemies of the Soviet Union, the Popular Front and the 'Spanish democratic revolution'.[29]

---

24    '[A]nyone who had belonged to any oppositional movement was labeled a "Trotskyist", a universal name for absolute evil in the Stalinist cosmos, quite independently of actual political positions adopted' (Schlögel 2012, p. 79). See also Getty and Manning 1993.

25    As in Russia, toeing the line was no guarantee of avoiding the gulag or worse. Many of the Soviet political, military and secret service personnel who served in Spain would become victims of the terror on their recall to the USSR.

26    Radosh, Habeck and Sevostianov 2001, pp. 178–84.

27    Radosh, Habeck and Sevostianov 2001, p. 178.

28    Radosh, Habeck and Sevostianov 2001, p. 181.

29    Radosh, Habeck and Sevostianov 2001, p. 182.

While the report is somewhat confused, it seems reasonable to conclude that Cid was warning of the likelihood of a CNT-led insurrection in the near future.

Studying the secret communications in *Spain Betrayed* certainly provides intriguing and important insight into some of the concerns of Soviet advisers, diplomats and secret police operatives present in Spain, though it is less clear that this yields any new information. The documents certainly require broader contextualisation and interpretation than the editors of the volume provide.[30] There is no doubt that some of the documents offer evidence to support the contention that Soviet agents sought to end the POUM's role in the political, social, economic and military spheres. It is very clear that they freely used the same terminology encountered in the 1936 Moscow trial, obsessed as it was with treasonous conspiracies against the Soviet Union. Yet there is a danger of elevating the importance of this issue above other Soviet concerns in Spain. An example of this tendency is the significance Radosh, Habeck and Sevostianov attribute to another report dated 28 March 1937. It was passed by Dimitrov, head of the Comintern, to Marshall Voroshilov in Moscow on 15 April and is said to offer an answer to the historical debate around a Communist 'provocation' designed to offer an excuse to finish off the Revolution in Cataluña and liquidate the POUM.[31]

The document in question is a lengthy report of some five thousand words, translated from French and marked 'Top Secret'. The editors suggest that it may have been written by André Marty and the language certainly contains evidence of his trademark paranoia about 'fifth columnists'.[32] Dimitrov notes in his covering letter that it 'also expresses the mood, opinion and circumstances of the CC Politburo' of the PCE. The report deals with the general political situation in the Republican areas in the context of what the author describes as an 'imminent government crisis'.[33] Again, Largo Caballero is the prime target, said to have come under a barrage of criticism for his conduct of the war.

> From all directions they [people from the front] are demanding a quick end to the sabotage, negligence, incapability, and bureaucratic tyranny that reign in the war ministry. At the same time, among the broader

---

30  Many of the documents display considerable confusion, misunderstanding and internal contradictions over both the political situation and official Communist policies. For a critical review of the volume, see Graham 2004, pp. 364–9.

31  Radosh, Habeck and Sevostianov 2001, p. 174.

32  See Beevor 2007, pp. 180–1.

33  Radosh, Habeck and Sevostianov 2001, p. 185.

masses a dissatisfaction with the economic and administrative policies of the government is growing – a dissatisfaction that attests to the growing discrediting of the experimental syndicalist policies – policies that the government at times not only supported but encouraged.[34]

Once again, the left Socialist newspapers' attacks upon the Communists are noted and mention made of what the author describes as Largo Caballero's 'real crusade against the Communists'. This reveals the fear that the prime minister was closer to the CNT than other forces in the Popular Front and sought a UGT and CNT government that excluded both Communists and Republicans. Other claims made in the report relate to the Communists' surge in popularity owing much to their role in the defence of Madrid, as well as to the charge that socialising industry and agriculture was undermining the war economy. Here, the customary references to 'sabotage, traitors and incompetents' are made. It is proposed that the PCE accept a leadership role in both military and economic matters:

> Lately, especially after the Málaga catastrophe, which exposed the weaknesses of the government, the eyes of the soldiers, as well as the eyes of the greater part of the civilian population have turned toward the Communist Party. They are waiting for the party: what will it say, what will it do? The party spoke. The party pointed out the path that had to be taken. The party brought forward the tasks and pointed out the measures that had to be adopted. Later, in the critical days, when real danger threatened Madrid – the party again saved the situation. Ought the party to be silent now? Can't the party, to avoid a ministerial crisis, repulse the crusade directed against it, against its best officers and political commissars? Can the party be silent when it sees that all heavy industry, all the factories that might produce the best shells, are replaced by the production of toys and beds? Can the party be silent, seeing the hundreds of facts just like these, be silent before acts that even during peacetime deserve the most severe punishment? Can the party be idle when officers and soldiers, not Communists, people of very great value, absolutely dedicated to the people's cause, hold out their hands to it [the party] and openly declare that the head of the War Ministry is conducting policies to destroy the army? Can it be silent just to avoid a ministerial crisis?
>
> ...

34    Radosh, Habeck and Sevostianov 2001, p. 186.

Everyone here agrees that the directives and advice of the Comintern are absolutely correct on every question; only one question has already been overtaken by events, this is the question concerning the possibility of finding a common language with Caballero. Here everyone agreed to recognise that further agreement is impossible, that every possibility has been exhausted, that the leading position must be seized, to force Caballero to relinquish the post of minister of war and, if it becomes necessary, the post of chairman of the Council of Ministers.[35]

Much of this report, as with several others cited, is taken up with a tirade against Largo Caballero and what is termed his 'bitter campaign against the Communist Party'. The claim is that the prime minister feared military victory because achieving it required the Communists, whose political position in Spain would be greatly strengthened by the kudos such a victory would earn them. It was, then, a question of political rivalry, pure and simple. The prime minister's position is connected with what the author believes are British fears of a Republican victory leaving Spain with deep ties to the Soviet Union. While Britain did not want a fascist victory, he argues, neither did it want a Communist-influenced outcome. Hence, the British sought a negotiated compromise; the suggestion is that Largo Caballero shared the same perspective, a view shaped by the growing strength of the Communists.[36]

The document concludes with a summary of the PCE leadership's position at the end of March that appears somewhat contradictory in places. On the one hand, the Communists continued their policy of unification with the Socialists via a press campaign calling for a 'united party' and joint union. But, on the other, they also waged a publicity campaign to mobilise mass opinion in favour of purging the military apparatus and the general staffs and replacing them in a 'unified command' with officers 'who come from the people'. Other aims would be to rationalise economic and military organisation, production and distribution; 'ensure order in society'; and maintain and deepen links with the Republican parties and President Azaña; but also attempt to forge better relations with the anarchist unions. Above all, the Communists and their sympathisers would be kept informed of Largo Caballero's policies, and would be ready for 'possible changes in the makeup of the government'.[37] The overall policy appears to have been to make friends with the Socialists and perhaps the CNT, but prepare to jettison Largo Caballero and 'his circle'.

---

35    Radosh, Habeck and Sevostianov 2001, pp. 191–2.
36    Radosh, Habeck and Sevostianov 2001, pp. 192–3.
37    Radosh, Habeck and Sevostianov 2001, p. 194.

Thus, at the core of the strategy set out in this document, was a proactive 'critical campaign' against the Caballeristas, who had removed Communists from military positions and who apparently sought to split the Socialist Youth movement (which had earlier fused with the Communist Youth organisation). The author declares, in summary, the need,

> [i]n a word, to go decisively and consciously to battle against Caballero and all of his circle, consisting of some leaders of the UGT. *This means not to wait passively for a 'natural' unleashing of the hidden government crisis, but to hasten it and, if necessary, provoke it, in order to obtain a solution for these problems*; not to wait for an attack at the critical moment at the front, then to beat one's breast, tear one's hair out, and reproach oneself that one ought to have foreseen it and known earlier, and to have freed oneself in good time from the people who were leading [the country] to defeat. The leadership of the party is more and more coming to the conviction that with Caballero and his circle the Republic will be defeated, despite all the conditions guaranteeing victory. The comrades are more and more coming to the conviction that Caballero and his circle are a government group to which all the elements that are afraid of victory and desire the defeat of the Republican army are attaching themselves, elements that oppose putting into effect all the measures necessary for the successful conduct of war.[38]

The italicised passage is taken by the editors of *Spain Betrayed* and other commentators as proof of the existence of a Communist plan, hatched at the highest levels, to provoke a confrontation with the forces defending the Revolution.[39] Yet it could equally well be read simply as further evidence that the principal target was the Largo Caballero government. It has been known since the time that the Communists wanted to be rid of Largo Caballero and to see him replaced by a Socialist better disposed toward them. It may be that 'hastening the crisis' did indeed mean indulging in provocations, but there is no specific plan of action mentioned – only a general statement of intent. For a convincing historical analysis, further explanation for the May events is required.

---

38    Radosh, Habeck and Sevostianov 2001, pp. 194–5 (emphasis added).

39    This passage is also cited in Schwartz 2010, pp. 113–31.

## 7.2    May 1937

The extent to which Nin was wrong to imagine that a violent struggle over state power to defend the Revolution could be avoided was soon demonstrated by the May events in Barcelona. Nin and others had made the mistake of believing the position of the revolutionary workers of the CNT and POUM to be stronger than it actually was in Cataluña. In late April, he again declared that the forces of 'counterrevolution' sought to disarm the workers and would succeed unless the CNT participated in creating a workers' and peasants' government.[40] Here, Nin was, in fact, describing the existing situation. Outside of Cataluña, the POUM and CNT papers were being closed down or heavily censored. At the front, PSUC units were refusing to coordinate military actions with POUM units. From January, official Communist press organs had stepped up their propaganda campaign against the POUM, labelling them 'Trotskyite traitors', 'Franco's accomplices', 'Gestapo agents' and 'uncontrollables'.[41] Sporadic violence had already broken out between the CNT and UGT forces. In Barcelona, the regular police force was disarming workers' patrols. *La Batalla* was warning of an imminent government provocation designed to elicit a reaction from the POUM that would offer an excuse to close down its press.[42] On 3 May, this is in effect what happened when a PSUC-led police unit attempted to take control of Barcelona's central telephone exchange, which the CNT had held since the beginning of the War. This event sparked four days of street fighting in Barcelona and effectively marked the beginning of the end of the Spanish Revolution.

While a simple conspiratorial explanation for the events of May seems attractive, the social, economic and political background is rather more complex than is often appreciated. While the immediate cause of the violence was indeed the attempt to eject CNT militants holding the Telefónica building, the longer-term context needs to be appreciated in order to make sense of the situation that developed. The social and economic conditions in Cataluña in general and Barcelona in particular had steadily deteriorated, owing to a

---

40    Speech by Nin at the Principal Palace, Barcelona, 25 April 1937. Published in summary form in *La Batalla*. Reproduced under the title 'El problema de poder en la revolución' in Nin 1978b, pp. 271–7.

41    In papers such as *Mundo Obrero, Frente Rojo* and *Treball*. For examples see Alba and Schwartz 1988, pp. 171–85. Also see examples in Pagès 2011, pp. 32–6.

42    Nin had warned that the bourgeois state was poised to 'totally disarm the working class'. Nin, 'La concepción marxista del poder y la revolución española', *La Batalla*, 14 March 1937, in Nin 1971, pp. 195–8.

major refugee crisis that exacerbated existing problems of food distribution.[43] The result was that shortages and rationing were having a big impact upon working-class and lower-middle-class areas of the city, leading to street demonstrations in early 1937. The response of the PSUC to this was to argue that 'strong government' and 'order' were required.[44] The PSUC, UGT and Esquerra identified the largely CNT-FAI – dominated collective enterprises as key problems. When factory committees sought to protect their resources from outside interference, it was a simple matter to accuse them of damaging the war effort, a charge that was taken extremely seriously given industrial Barcelona's crucial role in the wartime economy. As Casanova comments, 'the desire to control industry unleashed a brutal struggle among revolutionary syndicalism, the UGT and the Generalitat.'[45] The PSUC and Catalan UGT attracted white-collar workers and some lower-middle-class supporters who tended to endorse the Communists' criticisms of the socialised factory system and rather liked their assurances of protection for small property owners. The financial power of the Generalitat, no longer dominated by the CNT, meant that it could withhold credit from collective enterprises. By April 1937, the Catalan government was even refusing to certify the factory councils' ownership of exported goods that were tied up in foreign ports and where the former owners had lodged legal suits.[46] Thus, by early 1937, there had been serious reversals of what the CNT, POUM and some left Socialists considered the economic advances of the Revolution. 'Bourgeois order' had been restored to some considerable extent, as the accounts of several foreign observers who knew Barcelona at its revolutionary zenith bear witness.[47]

Graham argues convincingly that policing in Cataluña was a key issue that provoked deep resentment and strong resistance. The *patrullas*, or workers' patrols, constituted the nearest thing to a revolutionary police force. While they had already been effectively outlawed in Madrid and Valencia, in Barcelona and some other Catalan towns, a very different dynamic persisted. Here deep-seated antagonisms surrounded popular perceptions of the

---

43 As Borkenau noted on his second visit in early 1937, 'the big problem of Barcelona is not bombs: the problem is food. And the food problem is inextricably involved in political antagonisms' (Borkenau 1963, p. 177).

44 For a detailed account of the social and economic background to the May events to which the current summary owes a great deal, see Graham 2002, pp. 254–9.

45 Casanova 2002.

46 Graham 2002, pp. 263–4.

47 First-hand accounts of Barcelona that note the contrast between the earlier revolutionary period, July–December 1936, and that of spring 1937 include Orwell 1979, pp. 106–8; Low and Breá 1979, pp. 212–5; and Borkenau 1963, pp. 175–7.

repressive state apparatus. In short, many working-class communities had always viewed the police with great suspicion and hostility, associated as they were the rule of dominant élites.[48] Now the Communists, Esquerra and other Catalanist Republican parties sought to tighten up police discipline by recreating a centralised police force loyal to the government rather than the workers. This move was distinctly unwelcome to those who had become used to policing their own communities for the first time in their history. It was bound to be resisted.

In early 1937, the Assault Guards and National Republican Guards were merged into a single Catalan police corps whose members were prohibited from belonging to political parties or trade unions. This effectively delegitimised the *patrullas* and caused an open conflict between workers' committees and the state. CNT members of the Catalan cabinet withdrew after being unable to prevent an order to disarm the workers' patrols being issued in March. A three-week crisis ensued, out of which emerged a new cabinet that was not so dissimilar to the old one, except that the Esquerra representatives now sought to push the policing issue further. By mid-April, the police were disarming workers on sight in Barcelona. This action met with considerable approval from many white-collar workers and the lower middle classes, who welcomed what they saw as a restoration of social order and protection of private property. Many police officers joined the PSUC after July 1936, attracted by the party's stance on order and discipline. As Graham notes, the PSUC came to be 'closely identified with liberal state building and the economic establishment – not least by the police operatives who joined it'.[49]

The Generalitat's moves to enforce state-controlled policing in Cataluña, disarm workers and obstruct the functioning of collective enterprises added to rising social and political tensions and were important contributing factors to the violence that erupted in early May. Owing to a heightened level of social unrest, the traditional May Day labour demonstrations were suspended across the whole of Cataluña. The police raid on the Telefónica two days later thus needs to be understood as part of an ongoing bid to restore the full authority of the Catalan government. It must also be viewed in the context of the PCE/PSUC's desire for a crisis that might lead to the end of the Largo Caballero government and suppression of the POUM. While the figure in charge of the raid – Commissar-General of Public Order Eusebio Rodríguez Salas – was indeed a PSUC member, the raid was authorised by Artemi Aiguader, the Home Office/Security minister in the Generalitat, who was from the Esquerra.[50] Burnett

---

48    For a detailed account of working-class cultures in Barcelona see Ealham 2010.

49    Graham 2002, p. 265.

50    Casanova 2010, p. 258.

Bolloten notes that, given the very real problem posed by the monitoring of government functionaries' calls, it is likely that this raid had the approval of most of the non-CNT Generalitat ministers.[51]

Responding to the raid on the Telefónica and its CNT occupiers' armed defence of the building, central areas of Barcelona witnessed a spontaneous reaction not dissimilar to the one that had greeted the military rising in July. Without orders from either the CNT-FAI or the POUM, barricades were erected, work stopped and armed workers engaged police units in fire-fights. Other working-class districts and the industrial satellites of the city firmly backed the militants. At the core of this resistance were neighbourhood and factory CNT committees, the surviving *patrullas* and militant workers who had engaged in local labour conflicts before.[52] Activity focused upon the central areas of the city, where the political and economic hub of power sat uneasily in close proximity to one of the poorest, most radicalised and, hence, volatile working-class districts. Here, militants of the CNT channelled the city's long history of class conflict through its own political ideology of anti-statism, popular direct action and hostility to all authority. In the context of wartime hardships, this deep-seated culture of working-class resistance was roused by the alien impositions of what Graham refers to as 'liberal Cataluña', represented by the Esquerra and PSUC.[53] In certain respects, then, this was class politics as usual in the revolutionary city, with the Communists firmly on the side of 'law and order'.

Neither Companys and the Generalitat nor the workers in the streets proved willing to climb down. The CNT-FAI leadership, desperately seeking to curtail the confrontation, was initially unable to influence its own militants. Fearful of losing sight of the broader picture of the Civil War and aware of the CNT's weaker position outside of Cataluña and Aragón, the anarcho-syndicalist leaders appealed for a ceasefire. They were also well aware that the Valencia government, to which they belonged, was likely to intervene if CNT militants made a bid for state power in Barcelona. Thus the resistance to Catalan government police came from local groups; it was not supported by the main CNT leaders or by all of the organisation's military units in positions around the city.

---

51   Bolloten 1979, p. 404.
52   Ealham has written eloquently about 'revolutionary urbanism' in Barcelona and the need to set this within the cultural politics of the *barrios* (districts) over a 100-year period (Ealham 2005, pp. 111–32).
53   Graham 2002, p. 268.

The POUM leaders also tried to keep front-line forces out of the conflict in Barcelona.[54] It would seem Nin and his comrades were trying to be pragmatic after failing to convince CNT leaders to support their own militants on the barricades and recognising the hopelessness of the situation. However, POUM militiamen and women, including those on leave from the front, did fight alongside CNT workers in what was essentially a defensive action.[55] There was no attempt to seize power in the city, nor any realistic prospect of doing so. The aim of the POUM leaders throughout was to negotiate an end to the crisis, securing safeguards against reprisals and some gains for the workers if possible.[56]

Although the CNT troops in the Telefónica were forced to surrender on 5 May, skirmishing continued in the city centre for another couple of days, with perhaps 400 killed and 1,000 wounded.[57] Among the dead were some well-known figures, like the Italian anarchist and former philosophy professor at Florence University Camilo Berneri, and Antoni Sesé, the Catalan UGT leader who had just been appointed as a Generalitat minister. In an attempt to address what it viewed as an insurrection, the Valencia government embarked upon a two-pronged approach. First, it sent a delegation of two CNT ministers, the secretary of the CNT's National Committee and a Caballerista UGT Executive member to negotiate. At the same time, they despatched thousands of Republican paramilitary police and two warships to Barcelona in anticipation of the failure of talks – and also to secure the safety of President Azaña, who was trapped for a time in the Catalan parliament building. Elsewhere in Cataluña, in Tarragona and Lérida for instance, CNT and POUM offices were easily taken over by government forces and police. On 7 May, the Valencia government's Assault Guards entered Barcelona and resistance fizzled out.

The effects of the events of May 1937 were far-reaching within the politics of the Republican zone. The process of centralisation of political and economic power and the reversal of the Revolution could continue more systematically and with less internal opposition and criticism. Barcelona was at the heart of the Republic's war economy, and this had been disrupted by the May crisis.

---

54    Although some 2,000 CNT and POUM troops there did disobey their own leaders by leaving the front and marching toward Lérida, where they were confronted by air force troops. After negotiations, they returned to the front (Casanova 2010, p. 259).

55    Orwell's account of the fighting gives a good sense of the confusion and lack of purpose of the conflict in Barcelona (Orwell 1979, pp. 116–43).

56    Graham 2002, pp. 274–5.

57    These were the official figures (Graham 2002, p. 260). Other sources put casualties higher. 500 were killed and 1,500 wounded according to Alba and Schwartz 1988, p. 195.

Now the aim was to secure it against further disruption. To this end, the Generalitat rescinded its earlier decree allowing for the socialised control of industrial production. However, Companys's powers were diminished as a result of the Valencia government's intervention. He had hoped to resolve the trouble in Cataluña using local police forces, thus enhancing the Generalitat's legitimacy in the face of a central government poorly disposed toward regional devolution. But the Valencia government now took charge of public order and security, depriving the Catalan government of key powers over the army and police. This was a blow to Companys and the nationalists, although his government retained its other powers.

The major revolutionary force, the CNT, never fully recovered from the contradictions of having a foot in both camps, so to speak – being represented in government while many of its militants actively participated at the barricades. Faith in its leadership was shaken; the old internal divisions between the more anarchist-minded and those who viewed the War as the priority deepened. The CNT was excluded from Negrín's first cabinet, announced on 17 May, and its Catalan ministers never returned to sit on the Generalitat. But the POUM received the main blame and paid the highest price for what the Communist and Republican press presented as an insurrection. The POUM's publications, especially *La Batalla*, defended the workers on the barricades and sought to make sense of the situation from a revolutionary perspective. Before considering the reasons and nature of the POUM's suppression after May, it is worth briefly considering its political secretary's assessment of the significance of this episode.

### Nin's Analysis of the May Days

Responding to the defeat of CNT and POUM militants in May, Nin attempted to draw up a balance sheet for the whole revolutionary period. Contrary to the revolutionary 'theory' of the PCE and the Socialists, Nin reiterated that only the proletarian revolution 'would resolve the problems of the bourgeois-democratic revolution and simultaneously open the way to the socialist transformation of society'.[58] The working class's gains since July 1936 had passed

---

58    Nin (ed), 'El significado y alcance de las "jornadas de mayo" frente a la contrarrevolución', in Nin 1978b, p. 208. See also the 'Political Thesis' edited by Nin and entitled 'La situación política y las tareas del proletariado', in Nin 1978b, p. 217. This thesis was intended for discussion at the POUM national congress scheduled for 19 June 1937, but the repression of the POUM prevented the conference from taking place. The text is partly available in English translation in Beetham 1983, pp. 229–36. It should be noted that, in this version, the reference to the revolution as 'social-democratic' on page 229 is an incorrect and mis-

beyond the tasks associated with bourgeois-democratic revolutions. Contrary to the Stalinists and reformists, who claimed that the military struggle was in defence of the Republic, Nin argued that what was being defended both at the front and in the rear-guard was a genuine social revolution. Why else, he asked, would the working class make such enormous sacrifices if all they were defending was the existing bourgeois state of affairs?

Nin went on to note that the official Communists had claimed that the Republic under the Popular Front was somehow more progressive than other bourgeois democracies; that it was a 'popular' republic 'over and above class interests'; that the material base of fascism had disappeared from it. Nin ridiculed these notions, pointing out that, from a Marxist perspective, capitalism was the material base of fascism and that the Popular Front government was defending bourgeois interests. History had shown that the bourgeoisie was prepared to dispense with democracy when threatened by proletarian revolution. It followed that to defend even the most 'democratic' of bourgeois states in a period of revolutionary crisis would be to prepare the ground for disarming and repressing the workers. This was precisely what the slogan 'first win the War and then make the Revolution' amounted to – namely, disarming the workers whose key weapon had been the Revolution. Hence, the POUM believed that its own task was to fight fascism at the front and defend the Revolution in the rear-guard. This meant protecting and deepening revolutionary gains and creating an efficient war economy.

Nin presented the barricades in Barcelona not as an insurrection but as a defensive response to attacks upon revolutionary achievements. As the weaker of the two truly revolutionary organisations, Nin thought it logical for the POUM to be the initial target for the attack by the counterrevolution. Even before May, its leaders had been labelled as fascist agents by the PCE and PSUC press. He explained that physical and verbal attacks upon the POUM and CNT and attempts to dismantle the revolutionary achievements had produced a climate of uncertainty and anxiety among Catalan workers. The attack on the Telefónica building was a deliberate provocation by the Stalinists, to which Barcelona workers had reacted spontaneously by taking to the streets in order to prevent further incidents. In such a situation, the POUM's response could not have been other than to give unconditional support to this mass action and attempt to offer it a direction, he argued. While they had been fully aware that the time was not propitious for such an insurrection, Nin maintained that

leading translation. The original reads 'democrática socialista' which should be rendered as 'democratic socialist' and not 'social democratic'. See the Spanish version cited above.

it had been their duty to ensure that certain failure did not turn into a decisive defeat.[59]

On the question of seizing power, there was a certain ambiguity in Nin's stated position that is worth drawing attention to. The POUM had long been calling for the formation of a workers' and peasants' government, in Cataluña at least. When the moment that might have provided an opportunity to take power in Barcelona presented itself, the erstwhile students of the Bolshevik action in Petrograd did not attempt to reprise Lenin and Trotsky's leading role. Nin explained that the absence of clear revolutionary leadership from the CNT-FAI made it utopian to think of attempting to take power. Yet he felt certain that, had the CNT leaders shared the POUM's conception of revolution, state power could have been taken in Cataluña in May 1937.[60] As a minority party, for the POUM to have launched an insurrection on its own would have been fatal. Once the CNT leaders had called on their militants to return to work, the only responsible course of action open to the POUM had been to limit the damage and make a strategic withdrawal.[61] Yet, given the deep knowledge Nin possessed of CNT-FAI perspectives and the compromised status of its most prominent leaders, was it not equally utopian to think that the anarcho-syndicalists were likely to realise the error of their ways and provide leadership? Given the very strong support the POUM's press had provided to the Barcelona workers, it was very difficult to deny any responsibility for the resistance to the government forces after the event.

Nin clearly felt obliged to continue to offer an optimistic prognosis, despite the utter disaster this defeat represented. He still expressed the belief that a workers' revolutionary front could be built.[62] Because revolutionary workers still occupied strategic positions, a workers' and peasants' government might still attain power without an armed insurrection. The War could be won, but only if the revolutionary power of the workers and peasants could be harnessed. Victory, Nin affirmed, would have a massive impact upon the proletarian struggle against fascism in other countries. It would lead to a surge in the world revolution comparable to that caused by October 1917.[63]

By June, all of this sounded very hollow, even fanciful. Nin provided no answer to the problem of how the non-violent transfer of political power of

59    Nin (ed), 'El significado y alcance de las "jornadas de mayo" frente a la contrarrevolución', in Nin 1971, pp. 207–15.

60    Nin 1971, p. 212.

61    Ibid.

62    Nin, 'La situación política y las tareas del proletariado', in Nin 1971, p. 229.

63    Nin 1971, p. 230.

which he spoke was to be carried out. He outlined the mechanism through which revolutionary power might be wielded: an assembly of delegates drawn from the trade unions and those fighting at the front. But how could such an assembly be convened? Who would be represented besides the CNT-FAI and the POUM? More to the point, what was going to force the present government to relinquish power to such a body? Was it not now demonstrating its intention to crush all elements refusing to acknowledge its legitimacy? Nin did not have time to even attempt to formulate answers to these questions.

## 7.3    The Suppression of the POUM

Not surprisingly, the POUM's close association with the Barcelona barricades was now used against it by both the official Communists and the Republican government, although for different reasons and in different ways. The government was entering another crisis in the second and third weeks of May which would see Largo Caballero resign and Negrín take over as prime minister. It sought to make an example of the POUM and demonstrate the restoration of liberal constitutionality by holding its leaders to account for the May unrest. The fact that Largo Caballero opposed banning the POUM was certainly one of many charges against his continuing as prime minister and war minister. However, there were other reasons why not only the Communists wanted rid of him. The Republican parties and President Azaña needed a prime minister with international appeal who grasped the requirements of the situation, who encapsulated the liberal-democratic values of the Republic and who would not frighten the bourgeois democracies away at a time when there were diplomatic moves to end the Non-Intervention Committee's embargoes upon war materials purchased by the Republican government on the open market. A firmer hand at home was also needed, they felt: someone willing to crack down on 'fifth columnists' and 'saboteurs', even if this meant upsetting the unions. Azaña chose Socialist finance minister Juan Negrín, who offered many of these qualities.

When examining the suppression of the POUM, it has been argued that it is vital to differentiate between the government's interest in placing the leadership on trial with full due process and the illegal and unconstitutional actions of the official Communists.[64] Graham warns against assuming that the motivation for violent actions against the POUM and other left-wing critics of Moscow was always to do with transferring the culture of the Moscow show trials onto

---

64    Graham 2002, p. 284.

Spanish soil. There were home-grown motives for many Spanish Communists' participation in the persecution that unquestionably took place over the following months. Moreover, it seems there were simply not enough Comintern and NKVD personnel in Spain at any one time to facilitate a systematic purge of dissidents.[65] Once again, attention is drawn to the police, who arrested the entire POUM Executive Committee on 16 June. Orders for the arrests came not from the government itself but from director general of security and former Carabinero officer Antonio Ortega. Graham speculates that the motives for this arrest may have had much to do with the old antipathies of the police toward labour militants.[66] Yet, as she points out, the security police concerned were themselves Communists sent from Madrid and ordered to bring their prisoners back to the besieged capital. However, Andrade and his comrades survived this ordeal, owing, perhaps, to the concerns of some astute Republican officials who realised the potential for their permanent disappearance if they fell unsupervised into the hands of Soviet agents. Nin, who had been arrested separately, was not so fortunate.[67]

Over the intervening years, the question of Nin's kidnapping and murder has been surrounded by a good deal of controversy and speculation, some of which was dispelled after the partial opening of Soviet archives in the 1990s. There is now little doubt that central to the 'operation' was Aleksandr Orlov, the NKVD station chief who was primarily involved in running small Republican secret-police units aimed at countering internal opposition to the state, generally referred to as Special Brigades. One of these brigades was active during the May Days and was probably responsible for the murder of several foreign anarchists and Trotskyists. It seems that foreign Communists involved in these NKVD-organised groups were tasked with dealing with foreign dissident leftists, leaving the POUM to the Spanish police. Orlov appears to have been the prime mover behind the conspiracy to destroy the POUM leadership, using forged documents to incriminate the party in a known fifth column

---

65    Graham notes that the Comintern was neither a well-resourced nor especially efficient organisation. There were a few dozen Comintern agents of whom perhaps 30 were high-ranking operatives and only a handful of whom were present at one time. Other Soviet personnel in Spain numbered some 3,000 over the whole period of involvement in the war and only between 600 and 800 at any one time. Of these the vast majority were military personnel (Graham 2002, p. 285 n, 129).

66    Graham 2002, p. 287.

67    Payne 2004, p. 227.

organisation involving Falangists.[68] Nin was taken by Spanish police to Madrid, where a Special Brigade officer questioned him several times. After this he was transferred to a hotel in Alcalá de Henares, not far from Madrid, where he made four written declarations to the police.[69] On the night of 22 June he was kidnapped by a group of armed men and possibly taken to a chalet elsewhere in Alcalá, where he was held under Orlov's supervision.[70] It remains unclear whether or not he was tortured, although many accounts insist that he was. If so, then the aim was to force him to sign a 'confession', as in the Moscow show trials. Yet Preston doubts this because Nin could have been brought to trial in a Republican court based upon a confession. But there would need to be no evidence of torture. With no confession extracted through normal inter-rogation, Preston argues, Orlov decided to have him killed.[71] Of course, this is also supposition, since one might equally conjecture that torture was used but failed to secure a confession and then Nin was murdered. Indeed, it is hard to believe that Orlov had any intention of delivering Nin back to the legitimate police authorities for trial.

The perceived need to add further 'evidence' of Nin's association with fas-cists may explain the elaborate circumstances of his kidnapping. In the staged 'raid' on the hotel where Nin was being held, his guards were tied up. Some of the raiders spoke German and left 'evidence' to link the kidnappers to the Nationalists and sustain the fiction that Nin had in fact been rescued by German agents. Nin was then driven away and, at some point later, was almost certainly shot somewhere outside of Alcalá de Henares. Yet it is not really clear what happened after the kidnapping, although, as already noted, several accounts suggest that Nin was taken to a chalet belonging to the chief of the Republican

---

68    Preston 2012, pp. 406–13.

69    Nin's testimony was recorded and is published as 'La última declaración de Andreu Nin ante la policía' on the website of the Fundación Andreu Nin, http://www.fundanin.org/nin7.htm [accessed 13/9/2012].

70    This account is taken largely from Pagès 2010.

71    Preston 2012, p. 412. Preston cites Jesús Hernández's book *Yo fui un ministro de Stalin* (Mexico, 1953) for some very precise details of Nin's murder. Hernández was a Communist minister in the Republican government between 1936 and 1938. He became disillusioned with the USSR and wrote a 'revelatory' book about Stalin's manipulation of the Spanish Republic. Preston notes that his account is reliable on some matters but not on others, such as the allegation of torture.

Air Force and tortured.[72] Others contend that he may have been murdered up to a month later, but the evidence for this is flimsy, to say the least.[73]

Few commentators on these events doubt that instructions for Nin's murder came from Moscow and not from the Republican government. The international outcry at his disappearance was precisely the sort of publicity the government wanted to avoid. Orlov himself soon defected to the United States with his family, in the not-unreasonable belief that he would himself be purged on return to the Soviet Union. Stanley Payne, who interviewed Orlov via a questionnaire in 1967 and then in person in 1969, seems to accept his claim that Stalin issued a handwritten order to kill Nin and that this remains in the KGB archives.[74] If this is the case, then it has yet to be declassified.[75] However, the Soviet archives have yielded proof that documents used against Nin were forged by Russian agents; they provide evidence of Orlov's deep personal involvement. Orlov's report of 24 July entitled 'Operation Nikolai' offers some indications of his role. A note in his personal file appears to reveal the location of Nin's execution and names members of the death squad, among them Orlov himself and two or three Spaniards.[76]

Nin's fate was almost certainly determined in Moscow, and probably had as much to do with his past as a Profintern functionary and member of the Left Opposition during the 1920s as it did with his role as political secretary for the POUM. His connections with Trotsky and other key defendants in the Moscow trials linked Nin to the wider concerns of Stalin's domestic and foreign policies. Yet his murder was not ordered simply out of malice. It was geared to a very real purpose. It was crucial to the credibility of Stalin's accusations against the Bolshevik 'old guard' that similar rings of supposed fascist agents

---

72    See the television documentary on Nin's murder, Genovès and Ferri 1992. It was based upon previously known evidence and newly unearthed documents from the archives of the Comintern and KGB. See also Company 1992; Solano 2008; and comments in Graham 2001, pp. 287–9.

73    See the lengthy account and discussion of various theories in Pagès 2011, pp. 378–89.

74    Payne 2004, p. 228. A transcript of Payne's interview is to be found in Anexo I of Zavala 2005, pp. 438–70.

75    Orlov is also an unreliable witness, since he had pressing reasons to distance himself from association with such activities. Initially, he denied any knowledge of Nin's fate because he was seeking permanent residence in the USA and was under FBI investigation. When Payne interviewed him he changed his story, placing all the blame on the Spanish Communists. Payne himself describes Orlov as revealing 'a strange mixture of exactitude over events, half-truths, exaggerations and obvious lies' (Payne 2005, pp. 19–20).

76    Genovès and Ferri 1992. It needs to be noted that this account and some of the evidence it uses have been challenged by others (see Pagès 2010).

could be shown to be masquerading as revolutionaries in other countries. As a leading dissident communist linked in the past to Trotsky, Nin fitted the bill perfectly. Establishing this fiction tied in with Stalin's concern not to offer the Western democracies any excuse to favour Germany in a conflict with Russia. By demonstrating the Soviet Union's hostility to socialist or libertarian communist revolution in Spain, Stalin believed he might even be able to construct an alliance with France and Britain.[77] As we have seen, such a policy required the Revolution to be halted and bourgeois legality restored. It also meant rewriting recent history to deny that a social revolution had taken place.[78] Theoretical justification for this was drawn from the Comintern 'analysis' that Spain was too backward to be ready for socialism.

Of course, it is one thing to highlight Stalin's aims and intentions in Spain, but quite another to claim these were achieved in reality on the ground. As Daniel Kowalsky's study suggests, Soviet intervention in Spain was an unmitigated disaster in spite of the considerable volume of military aid despatched in the first full year of the war.[79] Stalin made a huge, if somewhat belated, effort to help the Republic win but became increasingly pessimistic about the prospects of victory later in 1937. The ideological agenda in Spain proved a massive distraction, as Soviet operatives' attentions were often focused upon promoting the Communist profile and attacking political rivals on the Left rather than the Nationalist enemy. While the POUM and CNT militants can be criticised for adopting positions that at times detracted from the war effort, it often seemed that the Communists were waging their own internal war in the Republican zone. Soviet military and secret service personnel sometimes acted with gross incompetence and, as we have seen, criminality. This internal war cannot be separated from ongoing events in the Soviet Union. Moscow committed fewer than 3,000 personnel to Spain over the course of its intervention, but mistrust of its own operatives meant they were often sent for very short periods and withdrawn at inconvenient moments that disrupted consistency and proved strategically damaging. Relations with Republican politicians and civil servants were also handled poorly, displaying considerable arrogance on the part of many Soviet advisers and political personnel. As Kowalsky puts it:

---

77   For Stalin's Spanish policy after 1935, see Carr 1984.

78   This rewriting of history, encapsulated in Orwell's statement that 'history stopped in 1936', underpins much of the political argument of *Homage to Catalonia* and is surely a forerunner of those found in *Animal Farm* and *1984*.

79   Kowalsky 2001.

Moscow's policy toward Spain was rarely altruistic, almost always self-aggrandising, and sometimes counterproductive. Many Spanish Republicans, meanwhile, were suspicious of Moscow's presence from the start, and accepted Stalin's help only to stave off immediate annihilation.[80]

It would seem from this important study of Stalin's involvement in Spain that it is wrong to say that he lacked a genuine desire for a victory in Spain or adopted a purely manipulative policy. Stalin desired victory for his own foreign and domestic policy ends, but, in reality, he controlled little about the Spanish war. The Soviet Union was simply not a great military power in the mid-1930s; abroad, as at home, it was capable of displaying considerable incompetence and ineptitude. Moscow was very distant from Madrid, making supply and communications extremely difficult. Contrary to the impression given by many first-hand accounts, often those of International Brigaders, the Russians were not omnipresent in Spain, although their contribution was necessary to the Republic's war effort. Faced with German and Italian assistance to the Nationalists, Soviet aid allowed the Republic to prolong the War, but it could not provide the wherewithal to win it.

Thus it is important not to overstate the case for the efficacy of Soviet operations in the Republican zone during the War. Soviet agents were almost certainly responsible for murdering Nin and several other dissident communists, but the POUM was proscribed and its leaders brought to trial by the Republican government (which, of course, included the official Communists). The Republican government in no way desired Nin's death or *checas* in Spain, despite the complicity of some Communist police officers.[81] Other leading POUM figures, including Andrade, were detained by police after the party was outlawed, and were released and then re-arrested by Communist police. Intervention by government ministers probably saved them from a fate similar to Nin's. Whatever the pressures upon the Negrín government to comply with a Soviet agenda, it is clear that the prime minister was intent upon prosecuting the POUM leadership for what he considered rebellion against the Republic in May 1937. Despite Negrín's personal hostility to the POUM, it was of vital importance to the credibility of the Republic that due process be seen to be done. In 1938 the POUM leaders were convicted by a special tribunal on the

---

80    Kowalsky 2001, Conclusion.

81    However, from the summer of 1937 the Republic developed its own counter-espionage police force, the Servicio de Investigación Militar (SIM), which did become a political police and took over many of the existing *checas* that had been run by some political organisations.

charge of 'rebellion against the constitutional order'. The charges of treason and espionage were dismissed by the court.[82]


## 7.4    Conclusion

This book has attempted throughout its course to present and examine the political thought and practice of the Spanish dissident communists and to place it in historical context. It seems clear that the political analysis of its key intellectuals, Nin and Maurín, made a significant contribution to political debate on the socialist Left during the Republican period. Moreover, it is evident that the POUM was far from being a peripheral player in the Revolution and Civil War in Cataluña between July 1936 and May 1937. However, it cannot be said that the POUM was a successful political organisation. Indeed, it might be argued that the ease with which the party was wiped off the political map in May and June 1937 was symptomatic of its leadership's belated grasp of political realities. But was its vulnerability simply the product of a failure to appreciate the extent of Communist influence within the government, or were there other factors at play that have to do with the strategic implications of its theory of revolution?

It is hard to read Nin's repeated assertions that the revolutionary workers could take power without recourse to violent struggle as anything other than the last of a series of political miscalculations based upon overestimating the strength of revolutionary forces in Cataluña. By 1937, there had been no 'dictatorship of the proletariat' or 'dual power', even during the heady days of the Summer Revolution in 1936. The Generalitat had never truly constituted a workers' government, even with CNT and POUM participation, nor had it been a purely bourgeois or petty-bourgeois government either. The reality was that, by early 1937, the official Communists (PCE/PSUC) had gained a great deal of prestige and political leverage, leading to remarkable membership growth. This cannot simply be attributed to the boost afforded by Russian military assistance but must also be seen as recognition of the popularity of their political positions. The implication of Nin's argument, that the revolutionary workers must seize power, was that power would have to be taken from a government enjoying the support of significant sections of the Catalan working class as well as the lower middle classes. Trotsky may have been correct to say that power could only have been achieved through a civil war within

---

82    For details of the trial, documents and contributions by POUM veterans see Fundació Andreu Nin 1988; Gorkín 1973; Iglesias (as Suárez) 1974b; and Revol 1979, pp. 121–32.

the Republican zone, but such a conflict would have been fought primarily between workers' organisations. In the context of the War, this could only have weakened the Republican side. Neither Trotsky nor Nin addressed this uncomfortable fact. However, it is important to stress that, through its actions, the POUM demonstrated that, together with the tiny grouping still loyal to Trotsky, it was the only Marxist party prepared to defend the social revolution.[83]

If the POUM's final actions demonstrate that, in practice, it was a revolutionary Marxist party, it is important to understand why the leadership adopted positions that at times conflicted with the party's own revolutionary principles. Trotsky criticised POUM leaders for wavering between revolutionary politics and reformism. However, the charge of 'centrism' rests upon the supposition that Nin and Maurín were not wholly convinced by the theory of revolution to which they subscribed, or that they feared the practical implications of this theory. Yet the POUM's support of the Barcelona working class in May 1937, despite appreciating the hopelessness of the situation, and the fate of its leaders offer sufficient grounds to refute Trotsky's accusation. Trotsky himself acknowledged Nin's revolutionary credentials and referred to the POUM's political honesty after Nin's disappearance in June. Yet it appears to have become commonplace in Trotskyist circles to describe the POUM as 'inveterate centrists'.[84] In order to reveal the real reasons the POUM signed the Popular Front pact and entered the Generalitat, one needs to recall the history and composition of the POUM and appreciate the weakness of its position in the Spanish labour movement.

As we have seen, the POUM was an amalgam of Catalan Marxists and Spanish Trotskyists in which Maurín's supporters enjoyed overwhelming numerical superiority. It was noted in Chapter Five that the political positions the new party adopted reflected a shift toward the Left Communists rather than a continuation of BOC policies. However, this left a legacy of uneasiness among the ranks of the POUM's former BOC members over issues such as the national question and fears that they were adopting Trotskyist positions that would leave them vulnerable to the attacks of their political rivals in Cataluña. With the loss of the party's main leader, Maurín, at the outset of the War, the majority of former BOC members tended to be suspicious of Nin and the other

---

83    This refers to the very small group of Left Communists who refused to merge with the BOC in September 1935. They formed the Sección Bolchevique-Leninista de España (SBL). Their organ was *La Voz Leninista*. See the account of one of its leaders: Munis 1977. Other references to the SBL are found in Low and Breá 1979.

84    For example Frank 1979, p. 52.

former Trotskyists.[85] Notwithstanding post-war recriminations by surviving POUM militants over its tactical decisions, it is clear from the primary sources that both Nin and Maurín shared a conception of revolution that can only be described as one of permanent revolution. The party's programme explicitly counterposed a permanentist conception to the Socialists' belief that the next stage of Spain's Revolution would be bourgeois-democratic. They contrasted their view of the Spanish situation as a struggle between fascism and social-ism with that of the official Communists, to whom it was a conflict between fascism and democracy. A shared appreciation of the socialist character of the Revolution and common criticisms of the Comintern and the Soviet bureaucracy's degeneration under Stalin constituted key points of political concurrence between Nin's and Maurín's organisations. This undoubtedly facilitated their fusion in September 1935. The POUM's position on the USSR seems indistinguishable from Trotsky's and was certainly informed by his powerful criticisms of Stalinism. After the Austrian Socialists, the POUM had been the first workers' party to condemn the Moscow trials and defend Trotsky and the other Bolsheviks accused with him. Trotsky's portrait hung alongside Lenin's at POUM political meetings and his articles occasionally appeared in the party's publications.[86]

The POUM is often described as a largely Catalan party; most of its members did indeed come from the BOC. However, it genuinely attempted to establish itself as a truly national party. Maurín modified his original position concern-ing the relative importance and scope of the national question; the party adopted the more orthodox Leninist view favoured by the Left Communists. It is important to note that the POUM had only been in existence for 10 months when the War broke out. Franco's territorial gains would reduce the party's zones of activity to Cataluña, Madrid and Valencia. Only in Cataluña, and, to a much lesser extent, in Valencia, did the POUM enjoy the kind of influence in the workers' movement that allowed it to play a real part in the Revolution. The fact that the CNT had such weight among Catalan workers was also some-thing many supporters of the POUM who had arrived at Marxism via revo-lutionary syndicalism must have welcomed. Given this history, not least the political backgrounds of Nin and Maurín, it is not difficult to understand why the party believed it would be possible to work with the CNT leadership and convince them of the need to take state power. However, the reality was that during the revolutionary response to the military rising, the CNT-FAI did not

---

85    Durgan 1991, p. 47.
86    Maurín wrote an article defending Trotsky in *La Batalla*, 1 May 1936, the title of which translates as 'I am not a Trotskyist but ...' (cited in Durgan 1991, p. 46).

see the need to alter its rejection of state power. As far as many of its leaders and militants were concerned, the summer and autumn of 1936 witnessed the Revolution in practice via collectivisation. Its main leaders presented joining the government as simply a way of ensuring these social transformations were protected, although it also expressed some leaders' recognition of the practical demands of the military situation. It also indicated serious divisions within the anarcho-syndicalist movement between 'governmentalists' and those elements holding local power.[87] The CNT-FAI also had a dangerously inflated opinion of its own strength in Cataluña, underestimating that of its rivals, the Catalan UGT and Communist PSUC, both of which grew at an alarming rate after July.[88] The fluid nature of working-class political affiliation in Cataluña meant that several organisations contended for the support of the same social groups. In this struggle and in the context of the War, the newly formed PSUC proved capable of winning over not just workers but also lower-middle-class Catalans. Many of these were UGT and Socialist youth whom the POUM might reasonably have expected to recruit. In other words, the POUM had to confront the reality that, with the Popular Front policy being so vigorously promoted by the Communists and backed by Socialists, Catalan nationalist and Republican parties had a very strong political appeal in wartime.

Doubts and disagreements within the POUM concerning the wisdom of some leadership decisions have already been mentioned. In an important introduction to a collection of articles by Nin, Juan Andrade notes that the ex-Trotskyists (Left Communists) formed a minority faction within the party that was not always in agreement with the ex-BOC majority. After Maurín's disappearance, Nin became the best-known public exponent of his party's politics, but he never enjoyed Maurín's popularity inside the party and his opinions were sometimes rejected by those who considered themselves 'Maurinists' and who suspected Nin's sympathies still lay with Trotsky.[89] Andrade refers to Trotsky's criticisms of the POUM and claims that the former Left Communists decided not to enter into a debate with Trotsky for fear of damaging their new party. This was in line with Nin's agreement to break all remaining links with Trotsky in order to facilitate fusion with the BOC. It was felt that a polemic with Trotsky's organisation might be interpreted by the Maurinists as factional activity. Andrade adds that Trotsky's attacks upon him and Nin always failed to take account of the fact that the ex-Left Communists were a minority in the POUM:

---

87    Ucelay-Da Cal 2005, p. 104.

88    Fraser 1981, p. 182.

89    Andrade 1971, pp. 7–8.

For Trotsky, continuance in a group or party always depended solely upon whether the points of view of the militants who assumed the functions of leadership, and above all those of the 'boss', were entirely acceptable. The least discrepancy would give rise to a split, as the whole history of Trotskyism's development has demonstrated insofar as it has been a continuing series of break-aways.[90]

This may support the suggestion that Nin and some of the ex-Left Communists had doubts about joining the Popular Front pact. Certainly, the signing in Madrid was delayed while a highly sceptical Andrade conducted a telephone discussion with party leaders in Barcelona, who instructed him to sign.[91] It may well be that the ex-Trotskyists felt unable to object to the POUM's participation in the Popular Front agreement for fear of splitting the new party. But they must have been aware that supporting an electoral strategy that was designed to secure another bourgeois Republican government directly contradicted their conception of 'democratic-socialist revolution' and understanding of the dynamics of fascism. According to the POUM's stated position, outlined in ¿Qué es y qué quiere el POUM?, the only way to prevent the petty-bourgeoisie from being drawn toward fascism was to mobilise its support for proletarian revolution by posing demands that went beyond those of bourgeois democracy. Their claim was that only the democratic-socialist revolution could bring the petty-bourgeoisie over to the side of the workers. Another bourgeois régime would simply leave this class dissatisfied and open to fascist influence. Since the government that arose from the February 1936 election was a wholly bourgeois Republican affair, it could be argued that, by signing the pact, the POUM contributed in a practical way to creating just the situation against which its theoretical declarations warned. Divisions over the attitude toward the Popular Front within the POUM certainly arose in the context of the war situation, with the Valencia section tending to support the governing Popular Front alliance. However, Graham is mistaken in stating that, after the February 1936 election, the POUM as a party supported the Popular Front.[92]

Turning to the issue of the dissident communists' theoretical originality (or otherwise), Antonio Elorza has suggested that in formulating the POUM's strategy, Nin rigidly applied a pre-determined schema modelled upon October 1917 which Maurín, had he not been captured at the outbreak of hostilities, would

---

90    Andrade 1971, p. 28.

91    According to Andrade's own testimony in Fraser 1981, p. 560.

92    Graham 2002, p. 235. See the discussion of the POUM and the Popular Front in Chapter Six above. See also Pagès 2011, p. 257 and pp. 262–3.

not have accepted. Elorza contends that in spite of the break with Trotsky, Nin remained loyal to a Bolshevik strategy that sought to subordinate the War to the Revolution.[93] This argument not only exaggerates the differences between Nin and Maurín, but also fails to take account of the fact that, due to its weak position, the POUM knew that it was unable to play a leading role. Elorza supports his counterfactual assertion that Maurín's actions would have differed from those of Nin with a quote from a letter to Víctor Alba in which Maurín states that by placing the Revolution before the War, the POUM committed a fundamental error. However, this letter was written in February 1973, long after Maurín had abandoned revolutionary Marxism in favour of democratic socialism. Given Maurín's political positions up until July 1936, explored in some depth in previous chapters, it would seem reasonable to assume that had he not disappeared he would have sought to defend the Revolution in much the same way as Nin.[94]

The main difficulty with Elorza's argument rests upon the fact that the POUM proved unable to develop a revolutionary strategy. It had, it is true, a theory of the course that the Revolution would take and what a revolutionary party ought to do in order to take political power. Yet, by the outbreak of War, the POUM had already failed in its bid to facilitate the creation of a revolutionary party capable of attracting radicalised workers. Those revolutionary Marxist elements in the PSOE-UGT whom the POUM had sought to unify around its programme had been persuaded by the Popular Front argument of the defence of the democratic Republic against fascism. After this, the Alianza Obrera was, to all intents and purposes, redundant as a potential united work-

---

93    Elorza 1987, pp. 119–36.

94    In a letter to Alba of 11 February 1973, Maurín writes: 'It is very possible that if I had been there, the leadership of the POUM would have committed errors and oversights, but never the unspeakable *stupidities* that you mention. I would never have consented to *La Batalla* appearing adorned at its head with the Soviet insignia, the hammer and sickle; nor that the POUM executive should ask the Generalitat to admit Trotsky to Cataluña. Trotsky was a permanent factor of disorder and, supposing he had reached Barcelona, the POUM would have been the first to experience his disorganizing spirit, something it had combated, was combating and continued to combat. Moreover, to invite Trotsky was like a challenge to Moscow. Moscow accepted this challenge and counter-attacked . . . The POUM executive never understood that the first thing was to win the War. It placed the Revolution before the War and lost the War, the Revolution and itself.' It is interesting to note that in one publication in which an extract from this letter appears, the editors have wittingly or otherwise printed beside it the header from *La Batalla* of Friday, 23 August 1935, complete with its hammer-and-sickle logo (Fundació Andreu Nin 1989a, p. 17). It does not seem clear that Maurín objected to this at the time.

ers' front. Once it was clear that the response to the military rising had adopted a revolutionary character, the POUM took the view that the Revolution could not be separated from the War and sought to collaborate with the only other organisation that took this perspective, the CNT. But the POUM's relatively weak position, even in Cataluña, consigned it to a fruitless strategy of lobbying the CNT on behalf of a revolutionary Marxist conception of the need to take political power. In reality, the POUM was only able to react to events and attempt to defend any influence it possessed. The opportunity to participate in the Generalitat seemed to offer the party a chance to affect events. Its involvement in the May events cannot be seen as an insurrectionary move to overthrow the Republican government, as Elorza maintains. Rather, it was a desperate attempt to defend the Revolution. The attack upon the Telefónica, if not a calculated provocation by the Communists, was nevertheless symbolic of the counterrevolution and reassertion of central state power already taking place.[95] Yet the barricades were erected by the workers themselves, not upon the direct orders of the CNT or POUM. Just as in July 1936, the support Barcelona workers gave the POUM was a response to events rather than to the attempt of a vanguard party to shape events.

Although the Spanish dissident communists cannot be accused of viewing the Spanish Revolution as a carbon copy of the Russian experience, it would be equally wrong to accept the suggestion that they developed a new theoretical approach uniquely tailored to its problems.[96] It is, however, true to say that they were able to devise new organisational forms such as the Alianza Obrera that took account of the particular barriers to united action within the Spanish workers' movement. The formation of the POUM – which, it will be recalled, was not envisaged as necessarily *the* vanguard party but rather as a vehicle for creating one – and the syndical organisation, the FOUS, also represented creditable attempts to build revolutionary unity around a political programme sensitive to the specific problems of the Spanish Revolution. On its own terms, then, the POUM's key project was a failure: the Spanish Revolution had no vanguard party.

Of the two key Marxist intellectuals, Nin was the more inclined to think that a general formula derived from 1917 might be adapted to fit the particular conditions of any country. However, he predicted no more than that Spain's Revolution would share the same basic similarities with the Russian case that

---

95    As noted above, it seems more likely that the clashes that broke out in May 1937 provided a fortuitous opportunity for the Communists to realise the project of unseating Largo Caballero and getting rid of the POUM at the same time.

96    That they did is one of the contentions of the article by Rovida 1980, pp. 1355–401.

the bourgeois revolutions had shared with one another. Maurín, on the other hand, believed the Revolution would adopt a national character and that there could be no question of trying to construct either a Bolshevik-style party or dual-power organisations in the image of the soviets. It could be argued that, to some extent, the actual course of the Revolution vindicated both positions. The nature of Spain's historical development was such that, as in Russia, there was no successful bourgeois-democratic revolution. When local power fell into the workers' and peasants' hands, they initiated actions that passed far beyond the bounds of bourgeois democracy. Yet it is arguable that the particular character of the social revolution that did take place owed much to the peculiarities of Spanish society, not least its backward rural capitalism, the extent of which was greatly underestimated by everyone, including the dissident communists. Spain's strong workers' organisations also meant that there was little room for a vanguard party to develop. The dissident communists were thus consigned to the role of providing theoretical guidance and promoting the cause of workers' unity. They were never faced with the task of revolutionary leadership. Under such difficult conditions, it is perhaps remarkable that the POUM was able to play as great a role as it did.

# Conclusion

This book has argued that the theory of permanent revolution constitutes the main thread connecting Trotsky's political thought with that of the Spanish dissident communists. Though the germ of the idea that socialist revolutions can occur in less developed capitalist countries is to be found in some of Marx's writings and those of a few early Marxists, it was Trotsky who formulated a coherent theory of socialist revolution based upon the structural disparities of these societies. For Trotsky, the uneven and combined character of development in backward capitalist countries predisposed them toward revolutions of a socialist nature. As an explanation of Russian historical development up until 1917, Trotsky's account has proved influential. But it is important to recognise that he explicitly extended his theory of revolution to encompass all backward capitalist countries within a conception of world revolution. As we saw in Chapters One and Two, this theoretical analysis is integral to all of his political writings of the 1920s and 1930s, not least those dealing with Spain. This study has argued that the Spanish dissident communists' political thought owed a great deal to the influence of Trotsky's theory of revolution, although rather less to his specific political advice. By way of conclusion, the components of the argument will be drawn together, summarised and reflected upon. How should Nin's and Maurín's contributions to revolutionary Marxism in both theory and political practice be assessed? Finally, the sense in which the Spanish Revolution might be viewed through the optic of the law of uneven and combined development and the theory of permanent revolution will be considered.

The relentless propaganda campaign against the POUM launched by the official Communists at the end of 1936 was designed to convince the world that these dissenters from the Moscow line constituted a 'fifth column' inside the besieged Second Republic. They alleged that the POUM was controlled by Trotsky, a figure who, as everyone knew, had already been condemned through legal process as a 'counterrevolutionary' and a 'fascist'. Although historians have seldom been taken in by these pernicious allegations, some of the first serious histories of the Revolution and Civil War did perpetuate the myth that the POUM was a Trotskyist organisation.[1] Even quite recent studies repeat the mistaken idea that Nin was once Trotsky's secretary.[2] As we

---

1   Perhaps the most prominent of these is the influential study by Thomas 1986. In later editions of this book the error was rectified.
2   For instance: Graham 2005, p. 65; Casanova 2010, p. 267.

have seen, the truth of the matter was quite different. Not only was the POUM completely unconnected with the international organisation that became the Fourth International, but Trotsky subjected its strategy and tactics to sustained and withering criticism. Although it would be incorrect to label the POUM 'Trotskyist' in terms of its organisational affiliations, there is a strong case for arguing that its Marxism was deeply influenced by Trotsky's conception of revolution as well as his specific comments upon Spain's historical development. George Orwell, who perhaps came closer than most foreign observers and participants in Spain to understanding the real situation, noted that the POUM could only be described as Trotskyist in the sense that, like Trotsky, it advocated world revolution and opposed the notion of 'socialism in one country'.[3] Orwell also stressed the crucial difference in Marxist theory separating the dissident communists from the official Communists; that is to say, the conviction that the Revolution was essentially socialist rather than bourgeois. This book has argued that, in order to understand how the POUM's most prominent theorists came to share Trotsky's analysis, it is necessary to go beyond the organisational history of the two major dissident communist groups and consider their intellectual conceptions of the dynamics of Spanish historical development. In Maurín's case, this theoretical analysis was not tied up with any bonds of personal or political loyalty to Trotsky.

In terms of Trotsky's understanding of capitalist development, Chapter One established that the idea of 'combined development' describes the way in which the coexisting archaic and modern social forms identified by the 'law of uneven development' are united. Trotsky maintained that this combination imbued backward capitalist countries with specific inconsistencies over and above the fundamental contradictions of capitalist development identified by Marx. It is important to stress that, by extending the law of uneven development in this way, Trotsky avoided the pitfalls of dualism. Rather than two more or less separate sectors – one feudal or semi-feudal, the other capitalist – he identified an articulation between precapitalist and capitalist forms and practices. The result of this articulation could not be described as the sum of the component parts, but rather as a new socio-economic formation dominated by the logic of capitalism. Trotsky thus rejected the notion that there could be a universal model of capitalist society that was valid for each country. He stressed, instead, that the specific features of each national capitalist society resulted from the operation of the highly variable law of uneven and combined development. The particular characteristics of any given national capitalism were therefore the product of an original combination of changeable social,

---

3   Orwell 1966, p. 169.

economic, political and cultural forms. The nature of this combination can have a decisive importance for the revolutionary potential of each country.

This book has argued that, in their historical analyses of Spain, both Nin and Maurín employed a conception of uneven development. However, only Nin appears to have been influenced by the law of combined development. This may well have been prompted by his translating some of Trotsky's writings, not least *The History of the Russian Revolution*, where this concept is applied to Russian history. As a consequence, it was argued, Nin was able to recognise the additional contradictions thrown up by the amalgamation of archaic with modern social forms in twentieth-century Spain. Maurín, on the other hand, could get no further than the conflict between landed interests and those of the industrial bourgeoisie. Nevertheless, both Nin and Maurín agreed that Spain was a capitalist country that had left the stage of bourgeois revolution far behind. But this did not mean that there were no precapitalist remnants or that the tasks of the bourgeois revolution had been fully resolved. They all, Trotsky included, had a tendency to overestimate the extent and importance of these residues. However, Trotsky and Nin recognised that while agrarian production often took on a feudal or semi-feudal appearance, it was actually articulated to the wider capitalist economic system. Large landowners were tied to world capitalism through the market and through finance capital; the industrial and financial bourgeoisie were also bound up with agrarian and foreign interests.

Since the 1970s, many social and economic historians have confirmed the view that Spain was indeed a capitalist society by the middle of the nineteenth century. They stress that in addition to the development of modern industry, Spain's agriculture underwent a major transformation that enabled an agrarian bourgeoisie to emerge. These changes, which could be said to constitute Spain's bourgeois revolution, involved freeing land for sale through disentailment; establishing the notion of labour power as a moveable commodity; abolishing the majority of gratuitous and coercive practices; lifting restrictions on trade and industry; returning jurisdiction to the realm of the state; and altering the form of the state from one which defended precapitalist interests to one which protected and favoured bourgeois ones. The historical essay contained in the Appendix to this volume refers to the historiography surrounding this. Suffice it to say, therefore, that it would seem that Trotsky and the dissident communists were justified in seeing the relative backwardness of Spanish historical development less as a question of its degree of capitalist development and more in terms of the particular nature of Spanish capitalism.

Even those historians who argue that Spain experienced a bourgeois revolution in the middle decades of the nineteenth century would not go so far as to say that all of the 'tasks' of this revolution were fully completed. They stress that although the 'revolution' cleared the way for the emergence of an agrarian bourgeoisie, it did not significantly alter the structure of landholding. This meant that radical agrarian reform remained the main precondition for capitalist agriculture to take off. Spanish absolutism's failure to complete the task of national unification meant that the national questions in Cataluña and the Basque Country were left unresolved. The intimate relationship between church and state also remained at the centre of political conflict. Although there were attempts to liberalise the Spanish political system in the nineteenth century, these ended in failure. The parliamentary arrangement established under the Restoration monarchy was a grotesque parody of the British system. To this list might be added a 'democratic task' that stemmed from the peculiar nature of Spain's capitalist development – namely, political and economic emancipation from foreign capital's domination of sectors of the national economy.

Trotsky, Nin and Maurín considered all of the above points to be unresolved problems stemming from the incomplete nature of Spain's bourgeois revolution. However, their particular assessments of the national bourgeoisie differed. Unlike Maurín, Trotsky and Nin viewed its class formation as a process of combination rather than strict differentiation. Maurín emphasised the opposition between landed interests and the industrial bourgeoisie, whereas Trotsky and Nin identified a convergence of interests as well as a contradiction. According to the latter conception, fractions of the industrial and financial bourgeoisie had become so bound up with agrarian interests and the existing political arrangements that completing the bourgeois-democratic revolution was contrary to their own interests. The combination of bourgeois interests with those of the large landowners had produced a conservative agrarian bourgeoisie wedded to the old régime and resistant to modernising forces. This fraction of the bourgeoisie formed the social base upon which the Restoration régime rested. It remained resolutely opposed to the Second Republic, especially its early attempts at agrarian reform. Yet the agrarian bourgeoisie was not the only conservative fraction. The Catalan industrial bourgeoisie, whose objective interests would have been served by completing the bourgeois revolution, also played a reactionary role.

Maurín stressed that one of the major reasons for the de facto alliance between Catalan industrialists and the agrarian bourgeoisie was a common fear of the organised working class. Cataluña, with 40 per cent of the industrial proletariat, witnessed a period of intense class conflict between 1917 and 1920. Terrified by this experience, Catalan industrialists abandoned their radical pretentions and welcomed the dictatorship of Primo de Rivera. By 1930 the

Spanish industrial working class had grown so much in size and organisation that the bourgeoisie had legitimate reason to fear it. To Trotsky and the dissident communists, it was evident that all fractions of the bourgeoisie would resist any attempts to address what they identified as the outstanding democratic tasks as long as the working class remained a potentially revolutionary force.

It was also clear to Trotsky and Nin from the beginning of Spain's revolutionary period, and became so to Maurín after October 1934, that, if the proletariat succeeded in taking state power and began to address the democratic tasks, the logic of its own class domination would push it beyond bourgeois limits. The very fact that the bourgeoisie would play a counterrevolutionary role would force the working class to take control of the means of production and distribution. In this respect there is no doubt that Maurín's conception of 'democratic-socialist revolution' – which became the POUM's stated position – was entirely consistent with the theory of permanent revolution. Maurín even supported his position with favourable references to Trotsky's position in 1917. Had this theoretical convergence not taken place, it is unlikely that there would have been sufficient common political ground to fuse Nin's and Maurín's organisations. The central thrust of the POUM's political thesis was precisely that the Spanish Revolution had begun as a democratic revolution but could only be completed as a socialist one. There could be no intermediate revolution, no 'democratic dictatorship of the proletariat and peasantry'. The Revolution would either succeed as a socialist one or the forces of counterrevolution would triumph. In the Europe of the 1930s, the consequence of failure was liable to be the imposition of a military-fascist dictatorship.

It is clear that the dissident communists, both those who had been in Maurín's BOC and those in Nin's ICE, also understood the Spanish Revolution to be part of a process of world revolution that had begun with the triumph of the Bolsheviks. A victory for the Spanish working class would not only provide a massive boost to this process but would also hasten the demise of fascism in Europe. Working toward this end, they argued, was the best way to defend the gains of October 1917. There can be no doubt from what was said in the early chapters that this was the internationalist position of which Trotsky was the supreme champion.

While there is ample evidence to confirm that Trotsky's Marxism had a fundamental impact upon the dissident communists' historical and political analysis, it still remains to underline the ways in which they differed with him over questions of strategy and tactics. But, before doing this, it is necessary to emphasise another key proposition of the theory of permanent revolution upon which the dissident communists were in complete agreement with

Trotsky. They took it as axiomatic that the revolution could only be led by the proletariat, at whose head stood the revolutionary communist party. Neither the peasantry nor the petty-bourgeoisie could pursue an independent policy. These social layers – or the political forces emanating from them – would be forced to choose between supporting the bourgeois counterrevolution or the proletarian revolution. As discussed in the later sections of Chapter One, this aspect of Trotsky's theory has been seriously undermined by the actual development of revolutions in backward capitalist countries. Indeed, the experience of the Spanish dissident communists in Cataluña highlights some of the problems associated with a strategy based upon such a premise.

It ought not to surprise us that the dissident communists' understanding of their own working-class organisations was, in many respects, superior to Trotsky's. Nin correctly predicted as early as December 1930 that the revolutionary party would be built outside of the official Communist Party. In hindsight, it might have proved more productive if Trotsky had encouraged the Left Opposition to join forces with the BOC at this early stage. But, if Trotsky's policy toward the Comintern was flawed, it remains the case that Nin and Maurín had significant political differences that continued to divide them until after the Asturian Revolution of October 1934. Hence, the idea that Nin's loyalty to Trotsky was the key factor preventing the creation of a united party before 1935 is not convincing.[4] The argument is even less persuasive if one considers that the origins of the political differences with Trotsky can be traced back to the Spanish Left Opposition's 1932 Congress. Even after the break with Trotsky over the issue of entryism, it would be another year before the POUM was created. In Chapter Five we saw that fusion was only possible on the basis of the political convergence of the two organisations. This concordance was a product of their joint experiences of revolutionary struggle, most notably through collaboration in the Alianza Obrera and the lessons of the Revolution of October 1934.

In practice, if not in theory, the POUM's creation signified the final emergence of a revolutionary Marxist party in Spain. Yet it is significant that from the outset this new party did not insist that it was *the* revolutionary party, but rather argued that it would serve to facilitate the creation of such a party by bringing together all revolutionary Marxists. In other words, it constituted the vanguard of the vanguard of the Spanish working class. This curious reluctance to stake a claim as Spain's Bolshevik Party is undoubtedly the result of the dominance of the Socialist and anarcho-syndicalist movements. However,

---

4   See the exchange of letters between Iglesias and Francisco de Cabo, reprinted in Fundació
    Andreu Nin 1989b.

in a fluid situation such as the one created by the military rising, political allegiances changed rapidly, as the success of the official Communists of the PCE
and PSUC demonstrated. Trotsky remarked both before and after the liquidation of the POUM that the party had repeatedly failed to respond to the urgency
of the circumstances in which it found itself.[5] It looked to other forces to take
the initiative, especially the CNT, thus failing to offer leadership. For him, the
'treachery' of the POUM lay not in any deliberate torpedoing of the Revolution
by its leaders, but rather in its failure to apply the most basic lesson of revolutionary Marxist theory – namely, that, in a class struggle, no accommodation
with the enemy is possible. The party, in signing the electoral pact, entering
the Generalitat and coat-tailing the anarcho-syndicalists displayed a failure to
attack the bourgeoisie.[6] Unwittingly and unintentionally, perhaps, the POUM
became just another member of the 'coalition' that 'paralysed the socialist revolution, which the Spanish proletariat had actually begun to realise'.[7]

Given the centrality of the vanguard party's role in his political approach,
it is curious to note that, at the time of the POUM's formation in September
1935, Trotsky did not believe that, this new party represented the best means of
influencing the Spanish workers' movement in the direction of revolutionary
Marxism. It could be argued that given factors such as the nature of the Spanish
workers' movement, the extent of the left Socialists' radicalisation and the relative organisational insignificance of the dissident communists, Trotsky's project of entering the Socialist Party might well have proved the most effective
tactic. At the very least, it might have prevented the loss of the Socialist Youth
to the official Communists. Yet the Socialist Party's history of reformism and
collaboration with first the Primo régime and then the Republicans led the
dissident communists to discount Trotsky's advice. Instead of entering another
party, they felt it more productive to maintain their political independence
and attempt to win over revolutionary Marxist currents from other groups and
parties by virtue of a superior political programme. By establishing the POUM,

---

5   For instance: 'Is Victory Possible in Spain?', written 23 April 1937, published in the *Bulletin of
    the Opposition*, Nos. 56–57, July–August 1937, in Trotsky 1973a, p. 261. Trotsky tellingly com-
    mented of the POUM that 'it is necessary to teach them to trust in themselves', by which he
    meant to trust in the working class but, by the same token, have confidence in their own
    power to influence events (Trotsky 1973a, pp. 262–3).

6   One of the articles left unfinished at his death was entitled 'The Class, the Party, and the
    Leadership: Why Was the Spanish Proletariat Defeated? (Questions of Marxist Theory)',
    20 August 1940, in Trotsky 1973a, pp. 353–66. It contains a section headed 'The Treachery of
    the POUM'.

7   Trotsky 1973a, p. 365.

then, it might be thought that they had created a classic vanguard party. But, as noted above, this is clearly not the way they thought of their new organisation. Trotsky felt that, owing to the unique composition of the Spanish workers' movement, the tactic the POUM proposed was unlikely to bear fruit. He also deeply distrusted Maurín and the ex-BOC majority, whom he considered petty-bourgeois Catalan nationalists. Of course, it could be argued that his alternative tactic, entryism, was itself an admission of the impracticality of the Leninist conception of a vanguard party in countries whose labour movements were already well developed. However, it is equally clear that Trotsky did not view things this way and thought that the end point would always have to be a vanguard party. He clearly did not believe that what he understood to be the social base and policies of the BOC would provide the foundation for such an agency.

In building its organisation, the POUM was forced to look first to the left Socialists and later to the anarcho-syndicalists and the Esquerra for recruits. But the problem of winning mass support proved insurmountable even in Cataluña. The party was unable, and perhaps unwilling, to challenge the hold of petty-bourgeois regional nationalism and anarcho-syndicalism over the masses. It even proved incapable of establishing a solid base among Catalan industrial workers. Party membership was drawn largely from white-collar workers. Although there is evidence that the BOC and POUM gained support in rural areas of Cataluña, it has to be said that the predominance of small property owners and various types of tenant farmers did not favour its development.[8] Graham has suggested that the conflict between its revolutionary political stance and the need not to alienate its more conservative social base was at the heart of the POUM's problems after July 1936.[9] She conjectures, as many former POUMists later did, that, had Maurín not been caught in the Nationalist zone at the outbreak of War, his political experience and understanding of the requirements of the party's Catalan supporters would have provided a more successful leadership. Once again, this owes much to the benefit of hindsight. As we have seen, whatever Maurín's differences with Nin may have been, his understanding of the socialist dynamic of the Revolution was no different to Nin's and Andrade's. In fact, Nin did not succeed Maurín as the party leader, as Graham seems to think, although he was certainly the best-known figure in the POUM. He held the post of political secretary in a joint leadership. Moreover, if one accepts that the party's constituency

---

8   Durgan has researched and compiled detailed membership figures for the various dissident communist organisations. Durgan 1989, pp. 338–42, and appendices to Durgan 1991.

9   Graham 2002, pp. 235–6.

significantly overlapped with and was in places identical to that of the PSUC, it is hard to imagine the conflict playing out very differently between these rival communist organisations. It is unlikely, simply if one considers the history of bitter animosity between them, that the POUM would have joined the official Communists in supporting the Madrid/Valencia government.

Given the POUM's limited ability to influence events, it may well be the case that the political acts which earned it Trotsky's condemnation had minimal impact upon the course of the Revolution. Had the POUM not signed the Popular Front pact, it is unlikely that this would have altered the outcome of the February 1936 election. It is equally improbable that, by remaining outside of the electoral bloc, the party would have won many new converts. By the same token, it is hard to think that Maurín's presence in the Cortes held much significance given the increasingly polarised mood of the country in the spring and early summer. The real importance of the POUM's action lay in the effect upon its own perception of the political situation. This appeared to be ambiguous. While the notion of an electoral alliance with bourgeois parties contradicted the POUM's revolutionary theory, this clearly did not mean the party now considered the Revolution to be a bourgeois-democratic one. Yet, by accepting that it was important to secure the return of a left-bourgeois government, it would seem that they underestimated the extent to which the revolutionary process had progressed since 1933. Nin's prognosis in early 1936 was that democratic illusions would now dissipate and the revolutionary party could be built. It was already evident to Trotsky, however, that the Revolution had moved beyond this point. The question of seizing power was not waiting to be posed, as Nin thought, but was actually on the agenda. The land occupations that began barely a month after the February 1936 election and the growing number and intensity of strikes illustrated Trotsky's point.[10] However, the POUM continued to believe that the situation in the spring and early summer of 1936 was pre-revolutionary. If the subjective conditions for proletarian revolution were absent, then the objective conditions suggested to many on the extreme Right that a preventative military coup was necessary to forestall a workers' revolution. As Nin himself had observed in the past, a country is never as close to fascism as when it is on the point of a proletarian revolution. Yet it seems that he was slow to appreciate that this point had now been reached.

It could be argued that the workers' and peasants' response to the military rising would not have been as radical as it proved to be if the country had not already been poised on the brink of social revolution. The depth of the revolutionary response took the leaders of the various workers' organisations by

---

10    See Fraser 1981, pp. 92–7.

surprise. But the POUM, assisted by its understanding of the dynamics of the Revolution, realised that once begun, it would either continue as a socialist revolution or be defeated. However, Nin appears to have greatly overestimated the extent to which the workers' organisations held real political power in Cataluña. In entering the Generalitat, he clearly believed that this government represented working-class power and would be able to implement socialist measures. In this respect, Trotsky was perhaps justified in condemning Nin's action as opportunist.[11] Although the Generalitat passed some radical decrees, such as the one legalising collectivisation, some argue that these were actually designed to limit and codify the direct control taken by the workers after July 1936.[12] Nin certainly underestimated the power of the PSUC and its Soviet backers and believed the relative strengths of the CNT and the POUM to have been greater than they were. After his expulsion from the Generalitat, Nin condemned its counterrevolutionary role, yet he continued to state that power lay in the hands of the Catalan workers and peasants. In this he was clearly mistaken.

It was noted in Chapter Seven that some commentators have detected originality in certain aspects of the Spanish dissident communists' Marxism. In terms of theoretical concerns, such as a conception of historical development, the theory of revolution and the question of the party, we have seen that this is not the case. Yet there are aspects of Nin's and Maurín's political thought that certainly do merit serious consideration. Nin's writings on fascism are interesting examples of an early attempt at a Marxist analysis of the phenomenon, based upon the Italian case. Maurín's extended writings on Spanish history also deserve closer investigation. At the level of organisation, the Alianza Obrera was a serious attempt to create a genuine united front organisation. However, it would be more accurate to view the Spanish dissident communists' Marxism as essentially a synthesis of the revolutionary ideas of Marx, Lenin and Trotsky.[13] Despite its intentions, the POUM was ultimately a Leninist party rather than a qualitatively new form of revolutionary organisation.

In terms of the Spanish Revolution's general course, it seems reasonable to argue that it could be characterised as a process of permanent revolution. The Second Republic proved unable to address most of the democratic issues it targeted in the reforms of 1931 to 1933. The revolutionary events triggered

---

11    Trotsky, 'A Test of Ideas and Individuals through the Spanish Experience', 24 August 1937, published in the *Internal Bulletin*, Organizing Committee for the Socialist Party Convention, No. 1, October 1937, in Trotsky 1973a, p. 271.

12    Richards 1972, p. 108.

13    This is certainly the view of Nin's biographer (Pagès 2011, p. 410).

by the military rising offer evidence to support Trotsky's argument that, once the workers and peasants held power, they would not be bound by the limitations of bourgeois legality. However, there are certain peculiar features of Spain's Revolution that should be underlined. Workers took political power at a local level, but the question of state power remained unresolved. Arguably, the reason for this was the absence of a central organisation capable or willing to constitute a revolutionary authority. Yet the fragmentation of power, especially the disintegration of the state's coercive military and police apparatus in the summer of 1936, permitted the widespread socialisation of production in many areas, involving large numbers of people and spreading to industry, services and agriculture alike.

The anarcho-syndicalists' experiment in libertarian communism was a unique feature of this revolution. The fact that the peasantry played a key role in collectivisation tends to undermine Trotsky's argument that it was only able to follow the proletariat's lead. As discussed in Chapter One, peasants played key roles in all the other successful post-1917 revolutions that adopted socialist complexions. It is also worth noting that rural collectives were not confined to a single region of Spain, were not solely inspired by libertarian communism and did not just involve a single layer of the peasantry. Agrarian collectivisation, both forced and voluntary, occurred in Aragón, Cataluña, the Levante, Castilla and Republican areas of Andalucía. Supporters of the Socialist Landworkers' Federation (FNTT) and UGT took part in collectivisation. It is possible that up to one and a half million peasants and workers were involved in this social transformation, ranging from those with small and medium-sized holdings to landless rural proletarians. Perhaps as many as 1,500 rural collectives existed at the height of the social transformation. The 750,000 or so rural workers who toiled on the large estates and who had played such a prominent part in rural class struggles became highly radicalised as a result of the Popular Front electoral victory. The mass land occupations of mid-1936 demonstrated that their expectations of radical land redistribution had been raised to fever pitch. It may thus be reasonable to say that, had many key areas of *latifundia* not been occupied early on in the War by the Nationalists, the extent of rural collectivisation would probably have been far greater. In addition to the land question, socialisation of industry and services took place – most pronouncedly in Barcelona – as did experiments in a range of areas, from providing social services to women's rights.

It would seem, then, that the concrete experience of the Spanish Revolution permits us to separate the strategy of the proletarian vanguard party from the theory of permanent revolution itself. It is hard to see how such a party could have exercised a decisive influence unless it could draw support from the ranks of the Socialist trade unions and youth movement. However, the theory of permanent revolution possessed great validity as a general explanation of the dynamics of revolution in a backward capitalist country like Spain. The Socialists remained trapped in a conception of revolution that required them to complete the democratic revolution on behalf of the bourgeoisie before the socialist revolution became a possibility. Yet the actions of large numbers of Socialist industrial and agrarian workers demonstrate the Spanish Revolution's 'growing over'. In practice, they were not detained at a bourgeois-democratic 'stage' but sought to socialise both economy and society. The left Socialists' awareness of their theoretical poverty had left them open to the influence of other political forces. If there was a point at which the dissident communists might have filled this theoretical vacuum, by the spring of 1936 the attractions of the Soviet-backed official Communists were proving seductive. Yet, as we have seen, the PCE/PSUC were bound not simply by a stagist view of the Spanish Revolution that was very similar to that of Socialist intellectuals, but also by their relationship with the Comintern and Moscow. It is certainly possible to exaggerate the degree of control Soviet agents exercised over the republican government, but it is impossible to ignore the resonance of their political advice, especially after May 1937. It is not enough to register that the policies of reversing the social revolution, eliminating the POUM and neutralising the CNT-FAI were driven by Moscow's own foreign policy requirements. They were driven, in reality, by the left republican, moderate Socialist, regional nationalist and official Communist coalition. The Negrín government's primary concerns were ending Non-Intervention, re-establishing central control and 'order', and building the Republican army. These aims coincided with those of Stalin. However, in believing that by presenting a moderate, democratic and distinctly non-revolutionary Spanish Republic, they were likely to persuade the governments of Britain and France to abandon their 'malevolent neutrality', both Negrín and Stalin proved equally deluded.

# Historical Essay

This brief overview of modern Spanish history up until the end of the Spanish Civil War in April 1939 is designed to furnish the reader with some relevant historical background and to highlight the historical and contemporary problems to which Trotsky and the dissident communists addressed themselves. It also suggests a framework for evaluating their solutions to some of these questions in the light of historical controversies. What follows is thus included for reasons of clarity and does not attempt to advance any original historical arguments or interpretations.

This essay has three sections. The first looks at the development of capitalism in Spain. It begins with a summary of competing historical interpretations of this process and goes on to sketch an outline of the country's development from the so-called 'reconquest' (*reconquista*) to the eve of the Second Republic. The second section considers the development of the workers' movement up to 1930; the final section offers a brief outline of the Second Republic, the Revolution and the Civil War.

## Spain's Transition to Capitalism

Perhaps the most fundamental of the many contentious issues facing students of modern Spanish history concerns the nature of the country's transition from feudalism to capitalism. Disagreements over this process's form, timing and degree of completeness have given rise to a number of very different interpretations. For those influenced by Barrington Moore, Spain's path to modern capitalist society was the result of a 'revolution from above' rather than a bourgeois-democratic revolution with popular support. According to this version, the old structures of the absolutist state were not overthrown and replaced by meaningful parliamentary institutions capable of responding to the needs of developing capitalism. The development of the Spanish state is often compared to that of Prussia, a crucial difference being that in Spain industry remained underdeveloped. By the end of the nineteenth century, the argument concludes, Spain was governed by a conservative coalition consisting of a dominant political oligarchy of the monarchy, large landowners and the Church on the one hand and, on the other, a politically weak commercial and industrial bourgeoisie.[1]

---

1 Two historians who share this view are Preston 1981, pp. 336–7, and Heywood 1990, p. 3. In his seminal work, Barrington Moore has little to say about Spain other than to suggest it had a semi-parliamentary régime which carried out an economic and political revolution

Another view considers Spain's bourgeois revolution a failure. Referring to the various liberal revolts of the nineteenth century, this school of thought argues that the resulting disentailment of land failed to lead to the dynamic development of capitalist agriculture. The fact that the structure of landholding barely altered is seen as a material, legal and psychological obstacle to capitalist development.[2] It has also been argued that rural feudal relations of production were not transformed into capitalist ones enough to enable us to call nineteenth-century Spain a truly capitalist society. Rather than becoming bourgeois, the argument runs, the old feudal aristocracy retained its traditional conservative ideology and assimilated the new business élite. The bourgeoisie is thus considered to have sacrificed its own 'bourgeois-democratic revolution' in favour of collaboration with the political oligarchy. It is argued that this stifled any prospect of dynamic modernisation of industry or agriculture. Even in the most industrially oriented region, Cataluña, the local bourgeoisie is seen to have abandoned any democratic aspirations and allied itself with agrarian and financial interests out of fear of the political power of a growing industrial proletariat.[3]

Historical studies dealing with the subject of bourgeois revolutions in Europe have often pointed out certain problems with interpretations such as the aforementioned. It is argued that these versions often seek to measure the success or failure of a bourgeois revolution against a set of predetermined criteria such as a developed industrial base; the transformation of large estates into capitalist farming enterprises; the emergence of the bourgeoisie as the politically dominant class; and the emergence of representative democracy as the natural political form of modern capitalism. Those who are critical of such an approach often suggest that it is not necessary to see the bourgeoisie as a class taking political control in order to identify a successful bourgeois revolution. However, they also accept that such a revolution cannot simply be reduced to the triumph of capitalist relations of production. The general thrust of much literature on the subject is to suggest that in order to speak of a 'successful' bourgeois revolution we must be able to detect a process resulting in both structural changes, whereby the capitalist mode of production becomes predominant, and transformations or modifications of social, political and legal practices and institutions in favour of the requirements of capitalism. Indications of this change include a free market in property and labour; the unrestricted movement of labour; trade and industry unhampered by restrictions such as the guild system; and a political system in some way representative and protective of capitalist interests. But, it is argued, this need not entail a popular revolution against the ruling oligarchy, carried out with the bourgeoisie at

---

from above. This revolution failed to take Spain very far along the path to modern capitalism (Moore 1966, p. 438).

2   This was the opinion of the leading French historian Pierre Vilar (Vilar 1977, cited in Shubert 1990, p. 2).

3   See Tuñón de Lara 1977.

the helm of a coalition of classes. Nor does this transformation require conditions of bourgeois parliamentary democracy.[4]

Drawing upon the more recent conceptions of bourgeois revolution and basing his interpretation upon the work of post-Franco Spanish historians, Adrian Shubert has criticised those who present Spain's revolution as curtailed, distorted or a failure. He argues that the essence of Spain's nineteenth-century bourgeois revolution is to be found less in economic changes than in the undoubted transformation of the legal structures of Spanish society. Although the pattern of landholding remained little changed – that is to say, there was no expropriation of the *latifundios* (estates) – the Church and municipalities did lose their lands and a great deal of land changed hands as a consequence of abolishing restrictions on its sale. Shubert also argues that, from 1834, there existed a definite commitment to political liberalism, albeit one which fell far short of meaningful democracy. The social base for Spanish liberalism was the new class of landowners created by this 'liberal revolution', which found its key expression in the *turno pacífico*.[5] It was this 'symbiosis of bourgeois and former seigniorial lords' that would form the hard core of opposition to the agrarian reforms of the Second Republic and support for the military rising.[6]

The issues that arise out of these very different interpretations of Spanish development are, of course, far from new and are encountered in the discussion of Trotsky and the dissident communists running through the present volume. In order to understand why Spain's history has given rise to such conflicting views of its capitalist development up to the 1930s, it is necessary to focus upon questions such as the nature of its absolutist state; the persistence of profound regional disparities; the debate over the degree to which Spanish society was feudal; the issue of Spain's bourgeois revolution; the character of its economic development, in particular the pattern of industrialisation; the role of foreign capital; Spanish colonialism; and the political crises of the nineteenth and early twentieth centuries. All of these issues will be encountered in the following pages.

One of the most frequently cited dates in early modern Spanish history is 1492. That year witnessed both the completion of the supposed *reconquista* of Spain from the Moors by the united kingdoms of Castilla and Aragón and the 'discovery' of America by Columbus. It also marked the opening of a period in which Castilla, already enjoying hegemonic power within the new Spain, established a single state under the rule of an absolute monarchy. During the sixteenth century, Spain became the first early

---

4   See the influential work on Germany, Blackbourn and Eley 1984. For an assessment of the theoretical importance of their arguments see R. Evans 1985, pp. 67–94. Another example of historical writing in this vein is Mooers 1991.

5   The *turno pacífico* was an electoral agreement whereby the Liberal and Conservative parties of the constitutional monarchy (1875–1923) took office by turns.

6   Shubert 1990, pp. 5–6.

modern European great power. Its formidable economic and military might and the immense wealth of the American colonies suggested that it could look forward to a dynamic future. However, the duration of Spain's 'Golden Age' can be measured only in decades. In the seventeenth century, its power in Europe waned and its economy declined. By the Industrial Age, Spain, having squandered its early advantages, had been reduced to the ranks of the more politically and economically backward countries of Western Europe.

Historians often place much of the blame for this rapid fall from imperial greatness upon the particular type of absolutist state that emerged from the process of the *reconquista*. It is argued that the new state's outward appearance of power belied the reality of its internal disunity and structural weakness. Although the 1469 marriage of Isabel of Castilla to Fernando of Aragón laid the basis for a united kingdom, this was not seen to require a single legal and constitutional system or a unified economy. Quite the contrary: both kingdoms retained their traditional systems of law and taxation. Aragón's provinces, Cataluña and Valencia, retained their own parliaments. Traditional Catalan liberties were preserved; that region was largely left to administer its own affairs.[7]

Nor was the economy of the new state any less decentralised. There was no common currency and the old customs system remained in place, with the effect that goods incurred heavy duties as they crossed from one region to another. Castilla, with an economy based on wool and grain production and on control over the exploitation of the New World, looked westward and northward. Aragón, by virtue of its commercial centres, Barcelona and Valencia, looked toward the Mediterranean. Catalan merchants were even prevented from direct trade with America because of the monopoly granted to Sevilla. This was symptomatic of the way in which economic regionalism fuelled the centrifugal tendencies of the new state.[8]

---

7   The account in the following paragraphs draws heavily upon Elliot 1963 and Anderson 1974, pp. 60–84.

8   As Marx asked in 1854,

> "how are we to account for the singular phenomenon that, after almost three centuries of a Habsburg dynasty, followed by a Bourbon dynasty – either of them quite sufficient to crush a people – the municipal liberties of Spain more or less survive? That in the very country where of all the feudal states absolute monarchy first arose in its most unmitigated form, centralization has never succeeded in taking root? The answer is not difficult. It was in the sixteenth century that were formed the great monarchies which established themselves everywhere on the downfall of the conflicting feudal classes – the aristocracy and the towns. But in the other great states of Europe absolute monarchy presents itself as a civilizing center, as the initiator of social unity. There it was the laboratory in which the various elements of society were so mixed and worked as to allow the towns to change the local independence and sovereignty of the Middle Ages for the general rule of the

The sixteenth century witnessed a series of European wars in which Spain participated at a huge economic cost, initially offset by domestic taxation but increasingly drawing upon the riches of the colonies. Reliance upon this external revenue removed any immediate pressure for Spain to follow the example of other European powers which were unifying their financial and bureaucratic institutions. Moreover, American bullion imports were actually damaging the economy. Their initial impact was to stimulate exports to the colonies of textiles, olive oil and wine. This, together with the monarchy's encouragement of wool production at the expense of grain, led to an alteration of land use away from cereal production and toward sheep farming. The result was that Spain became a regular grain importer for the first time toward the end of the sixteenth century. Manufacture was also affected as high inflation made textile production extremely expensive and uncompettyive.

In spite of the evident need to consolidate the gains afforded by the New World and use them to develop the domestic economy, the state chose to equip its military machine for even greater foreign adventures. While Spain's colonial bounty undermined the domestic economy, the very European campaigns it helped finance led to a decline in the power of Spanish absolutism. Under the Habsburgs, sixteenth-century Spain was linked dynastically to the Low Countries, Naples and parts of Germany. It acquired Mexico, Peru, the Philippines, and Portugal and its dominions by conquest. At the head of an empire between 1517 and 1556, Spain was drawn into a series of European conflicts with the Turks, with the French, with German Protestant princes and in Italy. Placing the country on a constant war footing inevitably stunted its economic growth. Despite the parlous state of royal finances, this pattern continued into the second half of the sixteenth century. After this point, Spain looked to its American empire to fund its imperial exploits.

The economic growth and naval power of England and the commercial strength of the Dutch, who freed themselves from Spanish control at the end of the sixteenth century, all contributed to the collapse of Spanish dominance in Europe. The following century proved catastrophic as the country suffered military defeats in Europe; domestic bankruptcy; the loss of Portugal, Naples and Sicily through local rebellions; revolt in Cataluña; and the near dissolution of the monarchy. Indeed, the fact that in the 1640s Spain came very close to reverting to the twin kingdoms of the mid-fifteenth century

---

middle classes and the common sway of civil society. In Spain, on the contrary, while the aristocracy sunk into degradation without losing their worst privileges, the towns lost their medieval power without gaining modern importance ... Thus the absolute monarchy in Spain, bearing but a superficial resemblance to the absolute monarchies of Europe in general, is rather to be ranged in a class with Asiatic forms of government'."

Karl Marx, *New York Daily Tribune*, 9 September 1854, in Marx and Engels 1975, pp. 25–6.

indicates the structural weakness of Spanish absolutism. As Perry Anderson remarked, 'It had expanded too fast too early, because of its overseas fortune, without ever having completed its metropolitan foundations'.[9]

The French Bourbon dynasty's victory over the Habsburgs in the War of the Spanish Succession could be said to have rescued Spanish absolutism. Employing the methods of the French monarchy, the Bourbons reorganised the Spanish state on a centralised basis, remodelling and professionalising the army and rationalising the colonial system. Only in the eighteenth century was Spain recognisable as a unitary state in any meaningful sense. However, its social and economic decline had been too severe to provide the foundations for industrial development similar to that of England or France. Even if the revitalised state had not itself declined toward the end of the century, the authority of the monarchy was so tempered by the power of the nobility and the Church that it would have been unable to offer an adequate political basis for modernisation. This brings us to the question of the social and economic organisation of Spain under its absolutist régime.

Whether or not post-*reconquista* Spain can be described as 'feudal' is a major historical debate which cannot be adequately summarised in the space of a few lines. However, it is possible to indicate some of the historical problems that have a bearing upon the political debates of the 1930s. For those influenced by Marxism, attempts to define feudalism have often resulted in a tendency to reduce the phenomenon being studied to the simple formula of 'surplus extraction through extra-economic coercion'. But if it is true that Marx understood the feudal economy to be characterised by social relations of production through which feudal lords extracted a surplus from direct producers by means of coercion, he did not claim this was unique to feudalism. Marx understood *all* pre-capitalist modes of production in class societies to be based upon extra-economic coercion. As Rodney Hilton has noted, if this defines feudalism, then feudalism can be seen to have existed in many parts of the world at many points in history.[10] Such a definition thus fails to capture the elements that differentiate European historical development from that of the rest of the world.

---

9    Anderson 1974, p. 81. Elliot remarks that, during Spain's 'Golden Age', the prospects for economic development and the will of the 'business classes' were as good and as strong as in other European countries. The reasons for the lack of dynamic capitalist development were partly a worsening economic and social climate and partly the state's failure to encourage domestic economic development. He notes, 'There was no attempt at systematic exploitation of the resources of the New World other than those of the mines, and almost nothing was done to develop in the New World an economy which might complement that of Castile'. Colonial industries developed without regulation and came to challenge those of Spain. American silver was not utilised to improve the domestic economy. Elliot 1963, pp. 198–9.

10   Hilton 1984, p. 85.

The European feudalism of the Middle Ages had specific features that were political and legal as well as economic. It has been argued that the feudal mode of production was characterised by a 'chain of parcellised sovereignties' in which economic extraction and political power were united.[11] The ruling class was itself a hierarchy of monarchs, dukes, counts and knights within which fiefs were granted in return for loyalty and military service. Political authority was decentralised, with local lords enjoying rights of jurisdiction over specified areas. The economy was based upon agrarian production both within the peasant household unit and, to a lesser extent, on the lord's estate. Peasants produced both their own subsistence and the bulk of the surplus, on holdings over which they had effective possession but seldom owned. The lord extracted a rent from the peasants that might take the form of payment in labour service, in kind or in money. Marx insisted that the latter, money rent, was not the same as capitalist ground rent because, under feudalism, peasants had the right of access to and use of the land in order to subsist. Under capitalism, land could be bought, sold or rented; its monetary value was subject to the fluctuations of the market. The payment of feudal rent, on the other hand, was entirely dependent upon the ability of the lords to extract it and the capacity of peasants to resist. The fact that peasants could and often did refuse to comply meant that local jurisdiction was essential if lords were to enforce their feudal powers.

Under feudal law, some peasants were bound to the land as serfs. Others, although legally free, had to respect seigniorial jurisdiction. This might involve paying a variety of dues and taxes and paying to use such facilities as the lord's mill or wine press. We might conclude from this that feudalism so defined does not necessarily entail serfdom. What does seem essential to a Marxist definition is that peasants have access to land in order to subsist and that surplus extraction is based upon the actual or potential threat of physical violence.[12] It has been argued that this fundamental class relationship, according to which peasants could effectively reduce or withhold the feudal levy, provided the essential conditions in which agrarian capitalism could develop out of feudalism.[13] According to this process, peasants accumulate capital through selling their surplus and eventually become owners of the land they work. They can then dispose of this land as they see fit.

---

11     Anderson 1974, p. 19.

12     Serfdom has received a broader definition than that of legal bondage to the land. For Kohachiro Takahashi, serfdom is the social existence form of labour power in feudal society. In all its many forms, then, the extra-economic coercion that underpins the transfer of surplus from peasant to lord is seen to define the producer as a serf; see Takahashi 1978, p. 70. Hilton shares this broad definition. See also Introduction to Hilton 1984, p. 14.

13     Hilton 1984, p. 92.

Serfdom in Spain, where it existed at all, was officially abolished in most territories held by the Crown of Castilla in 1480 and in Cataluña in 1486. However, if it is true that the legal status of peasants tended to improve as the authority of the monarchy was extended into the countryside, it should not be forgotten that, even by the beginning of the nineteenth century, only about one-third of Spain fell under royal jurisdiction. Half of the country was still under the control of the nobility and one-sixth under that of the Church.[14] This meant that a large number of peasants were governed by noble and ecclesiastical jurisdiction and subject to a range of tithes, dues, taxes and local monopolies. The extraction of this surplus ultimately depended upon the threat or use of physical violence on the part of the landlords.[15]

Other aspects of precapitalist land tenure that are often considered to be feudal concerned the entailment of land held by the nobility and the inalienable status of Church and municipal land. From the fourteenth century, many nobles had established entails based upon primogeniture. Known as *mayorazgo*, this was a means of consolidating large landed estates, retaining them within the family and protecting them against the encroachment of market relations. Land held by the Church and municipalities was likewise protected against sale or transfer. It has been estimated that perhaps as much as 60 per cent of productive land was held either in *mayorazgo* or in mortmain.[16]

Some historians cite the various forms of emphyteutic land tenure as further evidence of the presence of feudalism in Spain up until the nineteenth century.[17] By that time, land tenure in the north and east of Spain was typically small-scale often on the basis of share-cropping. These *minifundios* were often subject to leases of a feudal character such as the *foro* in Galicia and Asturias, and *rabassa morta* in Cataluña.[18]

---

14    Shubert 1990, p. 57.

15    The *señorío*, the Spanish form of seignior, dated from the twelfth and thirteenth centuries. Combining both local sovereignty and property, it afforded the landlord jurisdiction over the land he owned and, in the seventeenth century, over some that he did not. This gave him control over local administration and the courts as well as the right to exercise certain monopolies and exact dues. The extent and scope of this jurisdiction tended to vary greatly and is often seen to have reached its zenith in Valencia.

16    Shubert 1990, p. 57.

17    See García Sanz and Garrabou 1985a, pp. 7–99, and Clavero 1976, p. 185 ff.

18    The *foro* was a highly complex relationship which became a hereditary lease carrying a fixed rent but no restrictions on land use or threat of eviction. Wide subletting eventually conferred the same security of tenure upon the subtenants. This led to conflict when, in the nineteenth century, the title-holders purchased the land from the Church. The subtenants could not be evicted, thus confounding the principle of absolute property ownership. This dispute was still unresolved in the 1930s. *Rabassa morta* describes a form of lease peculiar to the vine growers of Cataluña, the *rabassaires*. These leases lasted the lifetime of the vine and rents were paid in kind. Other rights and practices that survived

It is often noted that the large estates of southern Spain were not feudal; this has to do both with the Moorish invasion, which halted the development of feudalism, and the manner in which these areas were later 'reconquered', colonised and resettled.[19] However, these *latifundios* were usually entailed and their owners were seldom interested in developing the productive capacity of the land by introducing new technology. Landowners tended to be absent from their estates and either leased their land

---

well into the nineteenth century were the *censo*, a hereditary emphyteutic lease often taking the form of a fixed annual payment to the landowner, and *diezmo*, a tax of 10 per cent of produce levied by the Church.

19    Edward Malefakis has noted that the timing and the process by which areas were 'reconquered' tended to be reflected in the patterns of land tenure that emerged. The lateness of the reconquest of the south, the form it took, and the manner in which the resident population was assimilated and new settlement occurred, all determined the form of land tenure that developed there, which was very different from those areas 'reconquered' earlier. By and large, the conquest of central Spain, which occurred between the ninth and eleventh centuries, was not carried out under royal control. Since the region was depopulated and the Moors had withdrawn further south, settlers were able to lay claim to this land. The form of land tenure to emerge was thus in the nature of free landholding. Even those who took leases on land originally claimed by nobles or the religious orders enjoyed effective possession of the land. Malefakis argues that the tradition of a relatively independent settler population meant that feudalism did not develop in the way it had in other parts of Europe. Instead, a particular form of relationship between the lord and the peasants who sought his protection emerged. Under the *behetría*, peasants could replace the lord if his exactions became too heavy. More southerly *reconquistas* in the centre of Spain often took place under Crown influence. However, colonisation took the form of small properties and was organised by municipal councils or *consejos*. So, here too, the tradition of settlers with effective control of the lands was continued.

Further south, however, the *reconquista* came up against strong Moorish resistance; in the late twelfth century, military orders were established to continue the push south. This created a strong military caste that demanded payment in land for its services. Although the major cities remained under royal control, via municipal councils, most of the countryside fell under the control of the military orders, individual nobles or the Church. Property in Andalucía was thus concentrated in vast *latifundios*. In order to ensure their property remained in the hands of the family, many nobles established *mayorazgos*. Land was further concentrated through marriage. In Valencia the Crown had far greater control over the process of colonisation and repopulation; consequently, the land was divided into much smaller units which were settled by Catalans and Agragonese (Malefakis 1970, pp. 50–9).

Perry Anderson also stresses that in the sixteenth century the rural social structure of Castilla and Andalucía was quite unlike any other Western European country. Perhaps 60 or 70 per cent of the rural population were agricultural labourers or *jornaleros* (Anderson 1974, pp 72–3). Elliot notes that, in the Castilian kingdom of the late fifteenth century, a mere 2 to 3 per cent of the population owned or controlled 97 per cent of the land. More than half of this land was held by a few noble families (Elliot 1963, p. 113).

to one or more tenants or employed local administrators to manage it.[20] Agricultural labour was often performed by wage labourers hired by the day. These landless *jornaleros* and *eventuales* comprised a rural proletariat which, by 1930, constituted two-thirds of the southern peasantry. Low wages, high unemployment and frequent seasonal layoffs meant that these rural workers and their families existed in conditions among the poorest in Western Europe.[21]

## Spain's Bourgeois Revolution

Between the 1760s and the 1850s, Spain underwent a complicated and highly uneven process of transformation which fundamentally altered the legal basis of property ownership and firmly established the notion of labour power as a commodity. This is the period in which Spain's bourgeois revolution, successful or otherwise, is usually located. These years witnessed the abolition of most of the gratuitous and coercive practices that had survived from the Middle Ages, as well as the disentailment of land and the restoration of jurisdictional rights to the state. The majority of precapitalist agrarian property relations were transformed into freely disposable commodities. Under the impetus of its severe indebtedness, the Crown freed most Church and municipal land for sale on the open market. The estates of the nobility were also disentailed and all rights that did not stem from property ownership annulled. After 1836, those nobles whose lands had been entailed were free to dispose of them as they wished. The *señoríos* were simply converted into the property of those who held them. Feudal dues, the collection of which had become so difficult that the nobility faced economic ruin, were recognised as property and then reimbursed by the state.[22]

If it is accepted that these legal changes laid the basis for capitalist agriculture, it is still necessary to explain why this proved to be insufficient to stimulate a dynamic development of the agrarian economy. A possible answer to this question lies in the peculiar nature of Spain's bourgeois revolution, of which the changes just outlined form such a vital ingredient. The term 'bourgeois revolution' can be said to describe,

---

20    When leasing to tenant farmers did occur (Castilla, León, Extremadura, Andalucía, the Basque Country, Navarre and Aragón), it was often on the basis of short-term contracts of up to ten years.

21    On the capitalist nature of social relations of production on the *latifundios*, see Giner and Sevilla 1977, p. 50. Elsewhere, Giner has cited the census of 1860, according to which Spain's total working population stood at 6,391,000, of whom 37 per cent were rural workers. Small peasant proprietors made up 22 per cent of the total, more than 10 per cent are listed as 'artisans', 13 per cent were servants and less than 3 per cent were industrial workers (Giner 1973, p. 6).

22    Shubert 1990, pp. 57–9.

first, a structural change that establishes land and labour as commodities and lifts restrictions upon trade and industry and, second, a transformation of the form of the state from one protective of precapitalist interests to one favourable to those of bourgeois society. Nineteenth-century Spain experienced just such changes. However, it has been argued that the manner in which this revolution was carried out profoundly affected the nature of Spanish capitalism. The results of this process have led commentators to the conclusion that either a bourgeois revolution did not happen at all, or that it was a 'failed' or 'distorted' revolution.

Early attempts to liberalise Spanish society and politics by drawing upon the ideals of the French Revolution met with only partial success. It was the crisis of the absolutist monarchy in the 1830s that provoked real change. The previous decade had witnessed the collapse of Spain's American empire. This deprived the state of a major source of revenue and robbed Spanish manufacturing industry of its colonial markets just when other European countries were expanding theirs. The economic penetration of Spain by industrialising countries also placed pressure upon the state to adapt to the requirements of domestic capitalist development. The civil war of 1833 to 1839 represents a crucial phase in the process of disentailment. In order to finance the war against the Carlists, the Mendizábal government disentailed and sold off Church and monastic lands. It has been argued that this initiated the transformation of the nobility from a feudal or semi-feudal class into an agrarian bourgeoisie.[23] This altered the very social foundation upon which absolutism rested and signified the emergence of a

---

23    As Bartolomé Clavero argues:
      "Entailed property, as we have said, is an element which belongs to the developed feudal economy; *disentailment means the fulfilment of the bourgeois revolution in the sphere of property rights*. Entailment permitted . . . the reproduction of feudal rent; disentailment corresponds to its abolition . . . disentailment *appears as one of the basic aspects of the bourgeois revolution*, which in Spain occurred at the end of the third and beginning of the fourth decade of the nineteenth century."
      Clavero, quoted in Acosta Sánchez 1975, p. 74; (emphasis in original).
      Clavero argues that, even if titles survived disentailment and property remained in noble hands, this does not prevent us from seeing the landowners as capitalists:
      "*Disentailment means the transformation of property rights, not necessarily the transfer of property* . . . Capital's historical imperative lies in the abolition of the entailment of land, of the means of production or labour power . . . in order for capital to appropriate production *it was necessary for all the elements of the production process to be constituted as goods in the market; for this to occur it was enough that feudal relations as a whole be abolished, among them the form of property known as* 'mayorazgo'. *Yet for the establishment of capitalist relations of production the identity of the person who effectively held those goods which had been transformed from feudal to free property was a matter of indifference.*"
      Clavero, quoted in Acosta Sánchez 1975, pp. 74–75; (emphasis in original). See also the excerpts in Aracil and García Bonafé 1976, p. 185.

new power bloc distinct from and opposed to the remaining palace nobility and their supporters in the army.

Between 1836 and 1895, about 30 per cent of the country's land surface changed hands as a result of disentailment. It is striking, however, that this did not fundamentally alter the structure of land ownership. Nevertheless, the argument seems very convincing that this change brought into being a new agrarian class that was in the process of becoming an agrarian bourgeoisie. This new class in the making included commercial and industrial capitalists who had purchased land; wealthy tenants who could now buy the land they cultivated; and those nobles who had become absolute owners of their estates and may have even acquired Church, Crown and municipal land. For the nobility, the new arrangement was a compromise whereby they retained the social status and political power afforded them by land ownership yet accepted the legal and institutional changes introduced by liberal governments and the purchase of land by the urban bourgeoisie. The fact that many financiers, merchants, industrialists, politicians and top military officers received titles, bought land and tied themselves to the old landed nobility through marriage has led some historians to speak of the incorporation of the bourgeoisie into the old nobility.[24] However, one could equally point to the participation of some of the old nobility in banking, railways, hydroelectric schemes and many other decidedly bourgeois activities.[25] Therefore it may be more accurate to say that after the middle of the nineteenth century the old landed nobility formed a fraction of the Spanish bourgeoisie, at least in terms of material interests if not ideology.

The fact that the structure of landownership – as opposed to the social composition of landowners – did not radically alter meant that the question of agrarian reform remained unresolved; it would not receive serious attention until the 1930s. Yet it is important to note that some historical research has suggested that the traditionally accepted view of Spanish agriculture as hopelessly backward, wholly resistant to innovation and a dead weight holding back industrial development requires some revision.[26] But it still seems fair to say that agriculture, in which the great majority of the population was in some way involved, did not experience dynamic capitalist

---

24   For instance, Tuñón de Lara 1977, p. 103. He rejects the notion that the feudal nobility was transformed into an agrarian bourgeoisie, on the grounds that its ideology did not change simply because the status of its property had. On the contrary, the big bourgeoisie became integrated with the nobility by ennoblement, marriage and the purchase of land. Rather than contributing to pressures for a liberal, bourgeois-democratic political system, Tuñón de Lara sees this absorption of new elements by the old as favouring authoritarian government.

25   Shubert 1990, pp. 66–7.

26   See the articles in García Sanz and Garrabou, 1985b.

development and did not create conditions conducive to the rapid growth of manufacturing industry. As always, the picture varies from region to region, with Cataluña, Valencia and the Basque Country as the more advanced and prosperous and Andalucía and Extremadura as the most backward and poorest. A prevalent feature of Spanish agriculture was the poverty of those who performed the manual labour. Only a minority of them benefited at all from the liberal revolution; the resulting rural protest reached its highest point during the revolution of 1936 and 1937, as many peasants and rural workers sought a radical solution to the agrarian problem.

By the middle of the nineteenth century, the two broad phases of Spain's bourgeois revolution overlapped each other. The years 1854 to 1856 mark both the culmination of disentailment, as municipal lands were brought onto the market, and the freeing of industry and commerce from the restrictions that had stifled their development. The power of the guilds had been broken in 1836. This created the conditions of 'free' and mobile labour which were essential for capitalist industrial development. But perhaps the most important stimulus to industrial growth and diversification came from a series of legal changes that opened the door to foreign capital. The Railways Act of 1855, the banking and limited societies laws, and the Mining Law of 1856 all did much to shape the course of Spanish industrialisation. It has been argued that these changes created a legal framework that overcame the domestic problems of low levels of capital accumulation, technology and production by offering very favourable conditions to foreign investors and industrialists. This led to a process of industrialisation tailored more to the requirements of foreign capitalists than those of the indigenous bourgeoisie.[27]

Industrialisation was confined largely to Cataluña and the Basque Country. It began in the late eighteenth century with the cotton textile industry in Cataluña. With Barcelona at its core and wage labour as the dominant relation of production, this industry took off in the period between 1840 and 1860. Yet in spite of mechanisation and considerable growth, the textile industry, like most other industries in Cataluña, remained notable for its smallness of scale. The Basque province of Vizcaya witnessed more rapid industrialisation based upon iron mining and the metallurgical industry. The latter, which grew quickly after 1875, was centred on Bilbao and attracted migrant workers from other regions. The neighbouring province of Guipúzcoa also experienced industrial development based upon metallurgy and textiles, although this tended to be less concentrated and smaller in scale, with a slower rate of growth.

Outside of Cataluña and the Basque provinces, the most significant industrial activity took place in Asturias, where coal mining began on a major scale in the 1860s. However, up until the boom period of 1914 to 1918, during which the workforce more than doubled due to an influx of workers from other parts of Spain, most miners

---

27    Acosta Sánchez 1975, pp. 84–6.

combined mining with agricultural work, as did the copper miners of Huelva. These mixed industrial-agricultural workers posed problems for mine owners precisely because they did not form a true proletariat deprived of access to the means of subsistence. This severely diminished the owners' control over workers and, it was argued at the time, held back the development of the mining industry. In reality, geological obstacles and low wages were more likely culprits.[28]

Elsewhere, industrial development was still in its early stages even by the 1930s. Madrid, for example, was not a significant industrial city, although it did produce consumer goods and had a handful of large factories. Its local economy was based mainly upon very small businesses such as retail and food. However, the 1920s witnessed growth in the construction industry, dominated by large companies which undertook major public works schemes during the Primo de Rivera dictatorship.

With the noted exception of Catalan textiles, the dynamic force behind Spanish industrialisation was external rather than internal. Railway construction took off in Spain during the 1860s. It has been argued that this absorbed capital that could have been better invested in manufacturing. However, the financial institutions set up in the 1850s were often foreign-dominated and, as Jordi Nadal notes, 'the foreigners had railways very much in mind'.[29] Railways presented a convenient and secure investment and provided a means by which extracted minerals could be transported, often out of the country. It is not surprising, therefore, that the key railway companies were controlled by the very foreign capital (French, English and Belgian) which also dominated mining. The power of foreign interests also ensured that the native iron and steel industry, which ought to have benefited heavily from railway building, had to compete with imported materials that paid no duty. By the early twentieth century, North American and German capital had joined that of the other industrial powers and underpinned transportation, shipbuilding and new industries such as hydroelectric power, chemicals and telephones.[30] Insofar as its industry was concerned, Spain

---

28     See Shubert 1987.

29     Nadal 1972, p. 551. Nadal points out that by the mid-to-late nineteenth century, Spain was the second-largest debtor country after Russia. High proportions of French and British foreign investment in securities were directed toward Spain: 35 per cent of the Paris Bourse in the period from 1816 to 1851, and 23.8 per cent of the London Stock Exchange between 1869 and 1873 (Nadal 1972, p. 543 and pp. 547–9).

30     All of these modern sectors were either dominated by or heavily reliant upon foreign capital. Canadian and German investment was prominent in electrical power generation. International Telephone & Telegraph (ITT) was granted the telephone monopoly under Primo's régime in the 1920s. There was French, Belgian and British capital in transportation, French capital in the chemical industry, and British capital in shipbuilding. Although the mining industry was more Spanish than foreign-owned, the 165 foreign companies (out of a total of 464 in 1913) accounted for just under half of the capital in the mining

fulfilled the function of a peripheral economy that was subordinate to and dependent upon advanced capitalist economies. It provided a market for foreign capital, certain industrial goods and machinery and was also a source of raw materials for competing economies.

Foreign capital also played an important part in the political transformation of the Spanish state. Since the 1830s the monarchy had sought a compromise with the conservative wing of Spanish liberalism. This fraction, which included the agrarian bourgeoisie and later the financial-speculative bourgeoisie, would dominate the state from the 1850s until 1931. Only the revolutionary periods 1854 to 1856 and 1868 to 1874 proved exceptions to this rule. The financial-speculative bourgeoisie benefited from railway bonds, the expansion of the cities and public debt. As part of the power bloc, they had a vested interest in collaborating with foreign capital and opposing those who sought greater political democracy and social modernisation.[31]

The modernising liberals were presented with an opportunity to alter the conservative character of Spain's capitalist development during the period from 1868 to 1874. Queen Isabel II went into exile in 1868 in the face of an economic crisis, mounting social conflict and a military *pronunciamiento* (uprising). But the following years, which included a short-lived republic, merely demonstrated the weakness and disunity of the progressive liberal bourgeoisie. At this point, it is worth mentioning the Catalan industrial bourgeoisie, a force which might have led a full bourgeois-democratic revolution.[32]

It is notable that as the only truly 'national' fraction of the bourgeoisie, the Catalan industrialists remained politically isolated throughout the nineteenth century and, despite brief manifestations of radicalism, played a fundamentally conservative role. Cataluña had long been the most economically dynamic region of Spain, as well as possibly the only region to experience the full weight of feudalism. It began to cast this burden off just as Castilla was reinforcing its apparently feudal power structure. However, the Catalan economy experienced periodic crises that hampered capital accumulation and prevented the continuous growth of capitalism. Its bid for independence (the Catalan revolt of 1640) failed and the region was subdued by the forces

---

industry. The mainly British-owned Río Tinto mining company was the major producer of iron and copper pyrites in the world by 1884. In 1912 they produced 44 per cent of the total world output. Sixty-six per cent of this came from their Spanish operations in Huelva. By the 1930s, Germany's involvement in mining gave it a key economic stake in the Civil War; German aid to Franco was repaid in Spanish minerals. Germany was to receive 60 per cent of Río Tinto production and a 40 per cent stake in a mining consortium. See Broué and Témime 1970, p. 33 and p. 51; Nadal 1972, p. 570 and 576; Fontana and Nadal 1976, p. 502; and W. Carr 1972, pp. 69–70.

31    Acosta Sánchez 1975, p. 89.

32    Acosta Sánchez 1975, pp. 141–2.

of Spanish absolutism. Economic prosperity in the eighteenth century enabled the Catalan bourgeoisie to build upon earlier advances and forced Madrid to accept the economic aspirations of the periphery. Catalan merchants thus gained access to Spanish colonial markets just as they were being exploited by other European countries. However, most of Spain's colonies were soon to separate from the metropole.

The nineteenth century also saw a re-emergence of the historical conflict between Castilla and Cataluña, this time in the form of a battle between different fractions of the bourgeoisie. The hegemony of the agrarian and financial bourgeoisies within the power bloc left Catalan industrialists excluded and without political representation or influence. They were powerless to challenge their foreign compettyors, even within their own national boundaries. Until 1898, the Catalan bourgeoisie did not even possess a coherent political organisation capable of representing its interests. This meant that it was unable to adequately confront the opposing agrarian, financial and commercial bourgeoisies, which were politically organised. Nor did it have the means to seek an alliance with the urban petty-bourgeoisie, a social layer that was becoming increasingly radical and which found representation initially in the Democratic Party and the Republican movement.[33] Hence the Catalan industrial bourgeoisie had the political profile of a mere pressure group, with no influence upon state policies. In concrete terms, this meant that agrarian interests, because of their weight, enjoyed protection from foreign imports. Meanwhile, Spanish industry had to survive as best it could in the world market. The textile sector was unable to develop export markets beyond Spain's remaining colonies; when these were lost in 1898, it quickly declined.

The conservative and foreign-influenced model of capitalist development which emerged from Spain's bourgeois revolution found its political expression in the Restoration monarchy, which succeeded the short-lived 1874 Republic. The new king, Alfonso XII, presided over a constitutional régime which was ostensibly modelled upon the British parliamentary system of two political parties taking turns holding office. In reality, it was a complete distortion of the British model. Under the so-called *turno pacífico*, the Conservative and Liberal parties alternated in office. The desired

---

33    The political groupings that developed in the second part of the nineteenth century were as follows. First, the Conservative Party, which represented agrarian and financial interests and was favourable to foreign capital, especially French; the interests it represented covered landowning, railways, banking and speculation. Secondly, the Progressive Party, or Liberal Party, as it became known, represented commercial interests; it was linked to English capital and committed to the doctrine of free trade. Finally, the Democratic Party (founded in 1849) and the Republican movement had a social base among the urban petty-bourgeoisie. It sought modernising reforms such as political democracy, a republic, federalism and agrarian reform.

government was ensured by agreement between the two main parties, both of which recognised the Crown as arbiter and the king's right to dissolve parliament irrespective of the distribution of seats. In order to guarantee the success of these electoral agreements, it was often necessary for the party whose turn it was to negotiate with local political power-brokers, the *caciques*.[34] The advent of universal male suffrage in 1890 meant that new, more representative political parties began to contest elections. The old parties' response was to resort even more to their traditional methods of electoral fraud, corruption and intimidation.

The loss of Spain's remaining American colonies and the Philippines in the war with the United States in 1898 marked the beginning of a crisis of the Restoration state which would ultimately prove terminal. The external context of this crisis was the intense rivalry between the major industrial powers that characterised the age of 'high' imperialism through to the First World War. Domestic factors included the growth of a concentrated industrial proletariat increasingly organised by trade unions and political movements of the Left, the resurgence of regionalist demands in Cataluña and the Basque Country, and a growing conviction among sections of the bourgeoisie that the constitutional monarchy posed an obstacle to further economic development.

Indicative of Spain's continuing crisis was the violent urban popular protest sparked off by the mobilisation of Catalan reservists to fight a new colonial war in Morocco in late July 1909. 'Tragic Week', as it became known, saw popular protest met with state repression in Barcelona, a pattern that would be repeated over the next three decades. Spain's neutrality during the First World War boosted both industry and agriculture; in 1917 the industrial bourgeoisie and workers' organisations collaborated for the first time in an attempt to transform Spain's failing Restoration political system. The resulting general strike and efforts to establish a parliamentary assembly in Barcelona were suppressed, but the following six years witnessed more strikes and violent confrontations between the workers' movement and the authorities, especially in the south and in Barcelona. The Catalan industrial bourgeoisie also politically attacked the ruling agrarian and financial oligarchy under the guise of Catalan nationalism. This ongoing

---

34   The word *cacique* derives from the Indian name given to the chiefs through whom the Spanish colonial system in the New World had partly been administered. In rural Spain, *caciquismo* referred to the practice of employing local political bosses to ensure the 'correct' result in elections. These local despots were often landowners who employed a combination of threats, bribery and intimidation to deliver the desired result, often with the connivance of the local police (Cattell 1955, p. 215, note 2). Gabriel Jackson remarks that importing a colonial apparatus into domestic social life indicates the political psychology of the ruling classes. Having lost their colonial empire in the nineteenth century, they had a tendency to treat the peasantry and rural proletariat in the same way they had the American Indians (Jackson 1976, p. 27).

political crisis was sustained and further aggravated by a post-war economic depression, unemployment and military setbacks in Morocco. In response to this instability the Restoration régime found its only response in the old formula of a military *pronunciamiento.*

General Primo de Rivera came to power in 1923 with the support not only of the hegemonic fractions of the bourgeoisie, the king, the army and the Church, but also with the approval of Catalan industrialists. The reason for this about-face by the modernising bourgeoisie was that it recognised both the short-term benefits and its own structural weakness. In the first place, the Restoration Liberal administration sought to lower the high tariff barriers which since the 1890s had offered protection to the high-cost agrarian producers of central Spain and the developing industries of the periphery. Second, and perhaps more importantly, was the looming threat of an organised and militant working class whose numbers had grown as industry expanded and which had already indicated its revolutionary inclinations in the years between 1917 and 1923. Faced with such an uncertain political and economic climate, an authoritarian regime that professed sympathy for Catalan business interests proved irresistibly attractive.

The historical debate regarding the character of the Primo dictatorship need not detain us, other than to note that the disagreement hinges more upon whether it presided over significant economic modernisation than whether or not it can be labelled 'fascist'.[35] The onset of the world depression from 1929 sealed the fate not merely of a dictatorship that had become increasingly unpopular but also of the Restoration monarchy. Primo resigned in January 1930 and was replaced by the short-lived *dictablanda* ('soft dictatorship') of General Dámaso Berenguer. During 1930, the Republican movement began to win broad popular support and the monarchy became increasingly

---

35    Shlomo Ben-Ami has argued that Primo's régime was the forerunner of Franco's. He stresses the ideology of economic nationalism, as opposed to economic liberalism, that characterised both dictatorships. Primo's government was decidedly interventionist, giving public projects to Spanish rather than foreign companies. It offered state subsidies and favoured monopolies, even setting up a national oil-purchasing company, CAMPSA, in 1927. The state promoted tourism and public works (roads, railways and irrigation), raised tariffs to the highest in Europe and tried to boost exports. It also gained the cooperation of the Socialist Union (UGT) over industrial arbitration (Ben-Ami 1983). Jordi Nadal and Josep Fontana, on the other hand, do not equate Primo with fascism at all. They argue that Primo's economic policies were a failure despite the relatively favourable economic conditions of the mid-1920s. The result was public debt and a fall in the value of the peseta. Rather than fascist, the dictatorship was traditionalist, conservative and paternalistic. It represented 'debased capitalism, on the defensive' (Fontana and Nadal 1976, pp. 473–9). For a discussion of the Spanish economy under Primo, see Harrison 1985, Chapter Three.

unpopular among its traditional supporters. A tide of Republican sentiment swept Republican candidates to victory in the major cities during the municipal elections of April 1931; the king, now without the support of the army, was advised to abandon his throne and leave the country.

### The Workers' Movement

By 1931, the Spanish labour movement could already boast a long history of participation in economic and political struggles. Although the activities of its organisations only involved large numbers of workers after 1914, the roots of its dominant forces, reformist socialism and anarcho-syndicalism, can be traced back to the beginnings of Spain's industrial development in the middle of the nineteenth century. Its history sets the Spanish Left apart from its Russian counterpart and is important in understanding the immense problems facing the communist movement. The events of the Republican period, from 1931 to 1939, cannot be fully comprehended without an appreciation of the origins and development of Spain's unique labour movement.

The origins of Spanish workers' self-organisation can be traced to the Barcelona textile industry in the 1840s, as wage labour became predominant. At this time, the industrial workforce was very small, confined to certain regions of Spain and rarely concentrated in large factories. Yet, as Marx noted, the textile workers of Barcelona played a significant part in the revolution of 1854 to 1856. Industrial workers initially organised into workers' associations whose political orientation was usually reformist. Their demands seldom exceeded those of universal suffrage, moderate labour reforms, and the freedom to organise. In the absence of a political movement of their own, they tended to support the petty-bourgeois Republicans. This tendency persisted well after the emergence of the Socialist Party in 1879. It was to be 30 years before the socialist Partido Socialista Obrero Español (PSOE) would begin to make serious headway and another 20 before it participated in government. Only from the 1980s, after a hundred years of existence, could the PSOE be said to have achieved lasting political success. The failure of one of Europe's oldest socialist parties is often attributed to the strength of anarchism, the uneven and backward development of industry or circumstantial factors. More recently, historians have begun to question the internal contradictions of Spanish socialism, many of which stem from its weak theoretical grasp of Marxism and fundamental misunderstanding of Spanish society.[36]

The origins of the PSOE lie in the struggle within the First International between Marx and Bakunin. During the 1870s, the International's Spanish section (Federación Regional Española) had become dominated by Bakuninists. But a small group of

---

36    See Heywood 1990. Heywood refers to the socialism of the PSOE as 'decaffeinated Marxism'.

pro-Marx members in Madrid formed a rival federation with the help of Paul Lafargue, Marx's son-in-law. This became the PSOE. Despite its avowed Marxism, the party's early programmes actually owed more to the ideas of Bakunin and Proudhon. As it became better established, the tendency concentrated more on problems of organisation than on political and economic theory. Indeed the PSOE's version of Marxism was second-hand, coming to Spain through personal contacts with the French socialist Jules Guesde.[37] Consequently, it rested upon a highly deterministic and reductionist version of Marxism that bore little relation to Marx's actual ideas. The party also suffered from being based in Madrid, where there was little industry and thus few industrial workers. This meant that in the formative years of the Spanish labour movement the PSOE could not offer any serious compettyion to the anarchists in Spain's major industrial region, Cataluña.

The Spanish section of the First International was organised after Giuseppe Fanelli's influential visit to Madrid and Barcelona in 1868. The fact that Fanelli represented Bakunin's Alliance of Social Democracy meant that the movement was from the outset prejudiced against the alleged authoritarianism of Marx and Engels. As Engels wrote in 1872, after the split in the International:

> In Spain the International has been founded as a pure nexus of the secret society of Bakunin, the Alliance, to which it may serve as a kind of recruiting camp and at the same time a lever allowing it to lead the whole proletarian movement.[38]

Yet the remarkable success of anarchist ideas in Spain cannot simply be explained in organisational terms. Its success among southern rural proletarians and poor peasants has long been explained in terms of an organic appeal. Anarchism, it has been argued, was the form of politics most suited to the temperament and experience of Spanish labour. The academic Américo Castro, who served as the Second Republic's ambassador to Berlin, noted:

> Fascism and communism, socialism and the constitutional régime were all injected into Spanish society as a consequence of impulses coming from outside; anarchism, on the contrary, was the emanation and expression of the structure, of the functioning reality of the social life of Spanish people.[39]

Hence anti-statism, apoliticism and direct action are often seen as the natural expressions of Spain's mainly rural labouring population. The various rural revolts and land

---

37    Guesde's ideas owed much to the influences of Lassalle, Malthus and Ricardo.
38    Quoted in Iglesias 1977, p. 49.
39    Quoted in Iglesias 1977, p. 48.

occupations of the nineteenth century, which were fuelled by disentailment, rural unemployment and starvation wages, are referenced. These tended to be localised outbursts that were harshly suppressed by governments. One of the focuses of rural popular revolt was the hated Guardia Civil, a paramilitary police force established in 1844 precisely in order to crush such uprisings.

It has to be said that the argument that anarchist ideas enjoyed organic currency among impoverished rural proletarians and peasants does not explain why anarchism also took root among industrial workers in Cataluña. Nor does it hold true for the entire rural workforce, since the Socialist Party later gained support among the same groups in Andalucía and Extremadura. Part of an explanation for the early strength of anarchism may well lie in the Socialists' slowness of to organise in rural areas and in Cataluña, compared with the anarchists' willingness and ability to do just that. The Socialist trade union, the UGT (Unión General de Trabajadores) exemplifies the slowness of this development. Founded by Pablo Iglesias in 1888 with 3,355 members, by 1899 the UGT had only increased its strength to 15,264.[40] One might compare this with the Agrarian Federations, which had some fifty thousand affiliates in 1882, thirty thousand of whom were in Andalucía.[41] But the problems faced by organised labour were also caused by the highly uneven nature of the country's development.

As a consequence of its marginalisation, the PSOE concluded an agreement with the Republicans which had as its aim the replacement of the constitutional monarchy with a liberal republic. This effectively converted the Socialists into a national party and drew in the intellectuals who were to help to shape its particular brand of reformist socialism. As Paul Heywood has noted, Spanish socialism adopted a humanist and moralistic stance not dissimilar to that of the British Fabians. 'Evolution' and 'gradualism' became its watchwords; it is possible to detect the influence of Karl Kraus as well as that of Second International Marxists such as Kautsky.[42] This period also confirmed in the minds of PSOE intellectuals the belief that, however inevitable the victory of socialism might be, Spain had first to witness its bourgeois revolution. They considered it their moral duty to assist in bringing this about.

One result of the agreement with the Republicans was the election of the Socialist leader Pablo Iglesias to the Cortes in 1910. This raised the profile of the party to a national level for the first time. The membership of the UGT increased by leaps and bounds, rising from 40,000 in 1910 to 119,114 in 1914.[43] This no doubt reflected both the expansion of industry and an increase in political awareness. But, in 1914, the industrial proletariat still comprised less than 20 per cent of the working population. What would alter this,

---

40   According to the table reproduced in Shubert 1990, p. 131.

41   These figures are from Brenan 1943, p. 155 and p. 159.

42   Heywood 1990, pp. 21–4.

43   Shubert 1990, p. 131.

providing both the UGT and the newly founded Confederación Nacional del Trabajo (CNT) with a base for mass industrial unionism, was the First World War. As a neutral country, Spain was able to supply both sides in the conflict and its economy enjoyed an export-led boom that had deep structural effects. The rapidly rising demand for industrial goods served to deepen the contradictions between modernising and conservative forces. The very forces that would overthrow the Restoration monarchy in 1931 gained a great deal of ground in this period.

With the increase in industrial activity, the urban working class grew in size, especially in the north of Spain. The upturn also boosted the profits of the industrial and financial bourgeoisie. In the Basque Country, these profits were ploughed back into industrial diversification and modernisation, but, in Cataluña, the new wealth was often squandered on high living. Exports of foodstuffs also increased, yet returns from these were seldom reinvested in modern technology. The *latifundios* of the south remained as inefficient and backward as ever, yet, along with the financial bourgeoisie, they still constituted the dominant force in the power bloc. But the industrial bourgeoisie's impatience was growing along with its economic power. Many northern industrialists now came to see regionalist movements like the Lliga Regionalista Catalana (Regionalist League), which became the party of the Catalan bourgeoisie, as a means of achieving political and economic modernisation. An attempt by the Madrid government to tax war profits merely served to confirm such anti-centralist views.

During the summer of 1917, the anarcho-syndicalist CNT participated in a purportedly revolutionary strike. This anti-government rebellion was to be staged by a supposed alliance of three highly diverse groups: army officers, Catalan business interests and the workers' movement. It appeared that their wholly separate grievances had come together at the same moment. The UGT, wildly misjudging the motives of the officers and industrialists and failing to coordinate with any other political action, called a general strike in August 1917 with the intention of creating the conditions for a 'bourgeois-democratic revolution'. The strike was a complete fiasco, collapsing within a week in most of Spain, although miners in Asturias and Vizcaya held out longer. Contrary to expectations, the workers' movement received no support from other quarters. The Lliga Regionalista quickly distanced itself from the workers' movement and the military obeyed the orders of Eduardo Dato's government to crush the strike.[44]

Although the 1917 strike was a failure, the actions of both the Socialists and anarchosyndicalists were to be rewarded with increased support. The wartime economic boom brought with it very steep increases in food prices; this led almost inevitably to serious labour unrest. Strikes became more widespread, culminating in a three-year period of social conflict from 1919 to 1921 known as the *trienio bolchevique*. The 1918 elections gained the Socialists six deputies in the Cortes, a success that served to confirm their

44    Arranz, Cabrera and del Rey 2000, p. 198.

commitment to parliamentary socialism in spite of the savage government repression their members had suffered. For its part, the CNT gained considerable support, rising from 11,000 affiliates in 1911 to 114,000 by 1918 and 745,000 in 1919.[45] During the *trienio bolchevique* the anarcho-syndicalists were able to extend their influence among the poor peasantry and rural proletariat through the Agrarian Federation. The UGT was also beginning to gain support among agricultural workers and by 1920 had attracted some 61,000 to its ranks.

A major turning point in the already turbulent industrial relations of Cataluña was the 44-day general strike in February 1919 launched by the CNT against the Anglo-Canadian hydroelectric company La Canadiense, which was trying to reduce wages. The strike spread to other sectors, including textile workers and print workers, and paralysed transport; it is estimated that 70 per cent of all factories in the industrial region of Barcelona closed. Rural disturbances broke out in Andalucía as well as bread riots in Madrid. The UGT appeared likely to join the strike, which threatened to escalate the situation. Faced with a national crisis at a moment when the shock waves of the Bolshevik Revolution were still reverberating across Europe, employers and government had little choice but to reach a settlement with the unions.[46] However, the ensuing repression by the state and the employers led to a deep split in the anarcho-syndicalist movement between moderates who favoured syndicalist tactics and the more anarchist-minded, who turned to terrorism. The period between 1919 and 1923 witnessed a virtual civil war in Barcelona between anarchists and the employers' hired assassins. This period ended the CNT's brief phase as a mass organised labour movement and signalled a turn to insurrectionary tactics.

The repression of 1917 and the example of the Russian Revolution also inspired a revolutionary current within the PSOE. This intensified during the violent social conflicts of the following years, especially in Barcelona. PSOE militants in Asturias and the Basque Country became increasingly radicalised, criticising their leadership's insistence on the bourgeois-democratic stage and dismissal of the Bolsheviks as 'adventurists'. The party's left wing also pointed to the failure of the 1917 strike and the desertion of the very bourgeois elements it was intended to bring to power. However, PSOE-UGT leaders such as Largo Caballero showed no interest in revising their orthodox Marxism to take account of events either in Russia or in their own country. The December 1919 PSOE congress expressed sympathy with the Bolshevik Revolution, yet refrained from immediately affiliating with the Third International. A 1921 report-back by the PSOE's delegates to Moscow, Fernando de los Ríos and Daniel Arguiano, finally enabled the leadership's view to prevail. The PSOE now chose to adhere to the 'Reconstructionist' International led by the Austrian Social-Democratic Party, which stood aloof from

---

45    Shubert 1990, p. 131.
46    Meaker 1975, pp. 158–61.

both the Second and Third Internationals.[47] This decision led the PSOE's youth movement to break away and form a Communist Party.

The PSOE leaders' victory on this issue provoked a second, more damaging split. This time the party lost a number of older and experienced members, who promptly founded another Communist Party. Moscow soon directed this party to merge with the one set up in April 1920 to form the Partido Comunista de España (PCE). However, there was barely time for the fledgling party to find its feet before the political restrictions of the Primo dictatorship greatly reduced workers' organisations' freedom to operate.

Under Primo, the CNT was outlawed, but the PSOE-UGT collaborated with the régime in order to preserve its monopoly position as the legal representative of labour. The party lost a significant number of members in the early 1920s, which increased its desire to recuperate and consolidate by taking advantage of the suppression of the CNT. Largo Caballero became a state councillor and worked to push labour reforms through. But as the dictatorship began to show signs of weakening, the Socialists sought an alliance with various Republican groups. It is noteworthy that, during the years of dictatorship, the UGT steadily increased its strength, so that membership stood at 277,000 by 1930.[48] Thus, by the time Primo fell, the Socialists had established themselves as key players in a future Republican government.

The CNT, by contrast, was forced underground and suffered a decline in membership during the Primo years. This period was also one of bitter conflict within the CNT itself. Its moderate elements sought joint action with the UGT. The assassination of their leader, Salvador Seguí, dashed the CNT's hopes of breaking with the utopian anarchism which had always presented an obstacle to effective action. In July 1927, the Federación Anarquista Ibérica (FAI) was established by the 'pure' anarchist elements in the CNT. With its belief in libertarian communism and putschist tactics, the FAI drove out many syndicalist elements and, most would agree, became the dominant force in the CNT.[49]

The newly founded Communist Party was unable to gain a sufficiently high profile within the workers' movement for the Primo régime to consider it a serious threat. Its membership was about five hundred in 1923; its influence was restricted to Cataluña

---

47     Established in February 1921, the International Working Union of Socialist Parties (IWUSP) was also referred to as the 'Vienna International' and the 'Two-and-a-Half International'.

48     Shubert 1990, p. 131.

49     Juan Gómez Casas dissents from this view. He argues that the FAI was only one of three factions in the CNT and never possessed enough membership to exercise control (Gómez Casas 1986, pp. 132–134). However, the FAI was able to gain major influence in Barcelona, the key locus of power for the CNT. Moreover, the FAI represented a militant anarchism that had always been part of Spanish anarcho-syndicalism. The FAI's appeal within the CNT stemmed from a fear that the CNT's ideals were being diluted by reformist elements or, worse still, that it was open to Communist infiltration. See Fraser 1981, p. 548, note 1.

and the mining areas of the Basque Country. As was the case with many other national Communist Parties, the PCE was under Comintern control from the outset. Direction from Moscow effectively ruled out any constructive discussion of strategy and tactics and ultimately drove out the handful of talented and perceptive intellectuals who had been among its founding members.

If Stalin and Trotsky's power struggle in the USSR had a belated effect on the Spanish party, the adoption of the ultra-left 'social-fascist' line by the Sixth Congress of the Comintern in 1928 had an immediate impact. Joaquín Maurín, a member of the party's regional organisation, the Federación Comunista Catalano-Balear (FCCB), argued that the Comintern's slogan of 'democratic dictatorship of the workers and peasants' merely proposed to replace Primo with another dictatorship. For the PCE to support this policy would be, he maintained, 'political suicide'.[50] It ignored what was evident to Maurín, namely that Spain was on the verge of a democratic revolution that could only be carried through by the working class at the head of an alliance of oppressed classes. Maurín also felt that the struggle against Primo had to be conducted alongside a struggle for regional autonomy, since this was a key issue in Cataluña, the Basque Country and, to a lesser extent, Galicia. The FCCB's alternative slogan called for a 'democratic federal republic'.

Not surprisingly, the pro-Moscow faction denounced this as 'rightist'. At the Paris congress of the exiled PCE in August 1929, the FCCB delegates (Maurín and Pere Bonet) were excluded, along with their political theses, on the bizarre grounds that their residence in France made them members of the French, not the Spanish, Communist Party. This was part of a manoeuvre by Moscow to suppress internal opposition to the newly chosen leadership of Bullejos, Adame and Trilla. After the Paris affair, dissidents who belonged to the FCCB began to look for allies beyond the official Communist movement. This was the state of play within the Spanish Communist movement when Nin returned to Barcelona in September 1930. But, if Maurín and his co-thinkers rejected the imposition of general political directives that seemed to take no account of Spanish conditions, they certainly did not wish to break with the PCE or foster a split in the Comintern at a time when the forces of the Right were gaining the upper hand in Europe. For its part, the PCE leadership still considered the FCCB to be a section of the party because it needed the forces the FCCB commanded in Cataluña. From this brief outline, we can see that the state of Spain's Communist movement in 1930 was one of numerical weakness, little real political influence and internal division.[51]

---

50    Maurín 1932, *El Bloque Obrero y Campesino*, Barcelona, quoted in Alba and Schwartz 1988, p. 15.

51    Much of this outline of the internal conflicts in the Spanish Communist Party draws upon the following works: Bonamusa 1977; Alba 1974; Alba 1975; Alba and Schwartz 1988; and Pagès 1978a.

## The Second Republic

The provisional government that was established in April 1931 as king Alfonso was making his way into exile was an uneasy alliance of petty-bourgeois Republicans, Socialists, Catalan nationalists and some traditionalist politicians who had 'converted' to Republicanism at the eleventh hour. To many of its members, certainly to those from the PSOE, the task of the Socialist and left-Republican coalition government that received a popular mandate in the June elections was to carry through the long-awaited 'bourgeois revolution'.

Over the following two years, this government introduced a series of social and economic reforms which, while addressing all of the 'democratic' issues to a greater or lesser extent, tended to be partial and inadequate. The most significant measure, the Agrarian Law, was designed to create a class of small proprietors with an economic stake in the Republic. In practice, this reform merely alarmed the large landowners while failing to satisfy the poor peasants' and rural workers' hunger for land. The left-Republican government was simply unable or unprepared to allocate the financial resources necessary to carry through the radical land redistribution laid down by the law.[52]

Passing the regional autonomy statute for Cataluña is often considered to be the first Republican government's principal achievement. It re-established a Catalan regional government, the Generalitat, with powers over local administration, health, poor relief and civil law. Defence, foreign affairs and border control, however, remained in the hands of the Madrid government, so this reform did not meet the criteria of the statute for which the Catalan people voted in the 1932 plebiscite. The statute was therefore much less successful than is often claimed. On the one hand, it failed to fully satisfy the Catalans' regionalist aspirations; on the other, it provided another focus for the anti-Republican Right, which could portray it as the beginning of the break-up of the Spanish nation. It also gave a boost to Basque claims for regional autonomy, which the government at this time had no intention of dealing with in a similar fashion.

Perhaps the least urgent of reforms, that of the influence of the Catholic Church, was carried through with the greatest vigour. It was pursued almost without heed to the enormous propaganda opportunity it afforded the Right. Separating church and state, attacking the Church's traditional control of education, placing limits on Church property and business activities, legalising divorce and elevating civil marriage were all grist for the mill of those who claimed the Republic was 'alien' to the Spanish people. The Right could easily portray the May 1931 outbreaks of church- and convent-burning as manifestations of 'Republican anarchy'. Later on, the radical Right gained considerable propaganda benefit by depicting both physical and political attacks on the Church as evidence that the Republic represented 'anti-Spain' forces.

---

52    For a classic study of the Republic's agrarian reform, see Malefakis 1970.

Other reforms, such as an attempt to reduce the size of the officer corps, met with little success. Nor were there any accompanying reforms to the composition and structure of the existing state apparatus. By attempting to use the machinery of the old régime for their own purposes, the Republican reformists left untouched the very instruments of their own future destruction. The unsuccessful *pronunciamiento* of General José Sanjurjo in August 1932 ought to have served as a reminder that the officer corps still fervently believed in its sacred right to intervene in politics. The irony of the situation lay in the fact that this self-proclaimed 'workers' republic' used the Guardia Civil, police and army to suppress worker and peasant unrest.

The failure of the *bienio reformador*, as the two-year period of left-Republican government from 1931 to 1933 is known, probably had as much to do with the enormity of the task facing the Republicans and Socialists as it did with conjunctural factors such as the economic depression or the undoubted mistakes of the politicians. As Ronald Fraser has remarked:

> In essence, the Republic's task was to reform the socio-economic structures of the Spanish state with the dual but complementary objectives of 'modernizing' capitalism while preventing proletarian revolution (or nationalist secession). This entailed finding new forms of legitimizing the capitalist system which – thanks to the reforms involved – would serve to incorporate the proletariat (and the nationalist petty bourgeoisie) into the new political system.[53]

If these could be said to constitute the outstanding 'democratic tasks' of Spain's bourgeois revolution, then the Socialists ought to have been aware that the bourgeoisie itself was not going to support them. For not only did the agrarian bourgeoisie – those landowners whom the PSOE wrongly considered feudal – feel threatened by the agrarian reforms, but the financial and industrial bourgeoisie and sections of the petty-bourgeoisie also rejected them. In other words, if there were to be a bourgeois-democratic revolution, it would have to be carried out against the very class that bore its name.

The government had also made itself unpopular through its failure to tackle unemployment and its overreaction to anarchist risings, especially the one in Casas Viejas that led to a massacre by the Guardia de Asaltos. New elections in November 1933 returned a right-wing coalition which would govern until the end of 1935.[54] This government enjoyed the parliamentary support of the Confederación Española de

---

53    Fraser 1981, pp. 41–2.
54    The Socialist and left-Republican vote was further reduced by the CNT electoral boycott and the fall in agricultural prices that hit small producers hard. But the main reasons for the Right's success were the electoral bloc it was able to forge and the breakdown of the Left electoral bloc. Despite winning fewer votes than the PSOE and left-Republican parties put together, the Right won twice as many seats.

Derechas Autónomas (Spanish Confederation of the Autonomous Right, CEDA), which formed the largest single grouping in the Cortes. The CEDA, a broad alliance stretching from monarchists to Christian democrats, was led by José María Gil Robles, widely considered a fascist.[55] For the time being, however, the CEDA remained outside of the government.

The following two years of right-wing government, known to partisans of the Left and Centre as the *bienio negro*, were characterised by a sustained attack upon the modest reforms enacted under the previous government. The Agrarian Law was ignored, those responsible for the Sanjurjo coup were released and the Jesuits were soon teaching again. Erosions of workers' rights and the licence given to employers to reduce wages and to landlords to raise rents and evict tenants inevitably provoked violent civil conflict. The UGT, especially its agricultural workers' branch, moved sharply leftward, as did a large section of the PSOE.

On the extreme Right, the admirers of Hitler and Mussolini started to arm and organise themselves. José Antonio Primo de Rivera, the son of the former dictator, was the parliamentary representative of Spain's fascist movement, the Falange Española. Spanish fascism possessed all the trappings of its Italian and German mentors: military-style rallies, uniforms, street-fighting, extreme nationalism and quasi-revolutionary rhetoric. However, it derived much of its support from the middle classes; José Antonio himself came from the old ruling élite. Catholicism was also an important element in its ideology. Its financial backing came from large landowners and business interests; it also had a measure of support within the officer corps.

The unbearable tensions caused by the increasing polarisation between Left and Right came to a head in October 1934. The inclusion of three CEDA deputies in the cabinet provoked the UGT into calling a general strike, which soon collapsed in Madrid after the UGT and CNT failed to cooperate. In Barcelona, an autonomous Catalan state was proclaimed, but once again the CNT stood aloof and the alliance of workers and petty-bourgeois political elements was crushed. In Asturias, however, the militant miners headed a broad workers' alliance that held out against the army for two weeks. Fears that the new government was a precursor to a fascist régime had led to the creation of a genuine united front. Unlike in other parts of Spain, the Asturian Workers' Alliance (Alianza Obrera) enjoyed the cooperation of the PSOE, UGT, CNT and PCE as well as the dissident communists. They set up revolutionary committees to direct resistance to the government forces. But the failures of strikes in other areas and the superiority of the opposing military force (commanded by Generals Goded and Franco) ensured defeat.

---

55    Gil Robles was certainly an admirer of Dolfuss's corporate state in Austria. He nevertheless vacillated between legalist and conspiratorial methods of destroying the Second Republic. In July 1936, he gave financial support to the military rising.

The severity of the subsequent repression gained the workers' movement a great deal of popular sympathy. It also accelerated the radicalisation of key elements in the PSOE and UGT toward a revolutionary position. The next actions of the Alejandro Lerroux government were also provocative: Gil Robles was appointed Minister of War and General Franco was made Chief of Staff. Lerroux also initiated negotiations with Germany over arms purchases. The government appeared to intend to prepare Spain's army to crush any possible resurgence of revolutionary activity. To many, particularly radicalised Socialist youth, it seemed that only a full-blown proletarian revolution could now prevent fascism from taking over.

The Alianza Obrera spread nationally during 1934 and 1935, but despite its promising beginnings failed to develop into a united front organisation. The CNT could not be persuaded to join; the PSOE sought to utilise it as a means of dominating the labour movement. During this period, moderates in the Socialist Party and among the left Republicans sought to rebuild the original Republican coalition. Fears of another electoral victory for the Right and the influence of the Comintern's newly adopted tactic of the 'Popular Front' also won over many left Socialists. The broad appeal of this strategy finally overcame Largo Caballero's professed objections to yet another alliance with the left Republicans.

The electoral pact that brought the new left-Republican government into office after the February 1936 elections had a far broader base than its 1931 forebear. In addition to the left Republicans and PSOE, the so-called Popular Front pact had been signed by the Juventudes Socialistas (Socialist Youth), PCE, Partido Obrero de Unificación Marxista (Workers' Party of Marxist Unification, POUM) and Partido Sindicalista. All agreed upon certain measures a new government should implement forthwith: the restoration of civil and political liberties; amnesty for those imprisoned and sacked for their part in the October 1934 uprising; continuation of the reforms begun during the *bienio reformador*. Unsurprisingly, the CNT refused to participate as an organisation, although its sympathisers voted *en masse* for Front candidates, thereby ensuring victory.[56]

The initial popularity of the Popular Front and its perceived radicalism certainly raised workers' and peasants' expectations to a far higher level than had been the case during the *bienio reformador*. This reflected the far greater polarisation and instability of the international and domestic political climate of 1936 compared with the early days of the Second Republic. After its electoral defeat in February, the Right lost patience with legalistic solutions, as the growth of fascist and monarchist movements committed to the violent overthrow of the Republic shows. Even those political representatives of the big bourgeoisie who had formerly accepted the Republic now looked toward authoritarian methods to further their political aims.

---

56    The debates around the Spanish Popular Front are discussed in Chapter Six.

On the Left, however, the unity the Popular Front agreement achieved proved to be a fleeting illusion. Many of the pact's signatories rapidly distanced themselves from the new government and, resuming his revolutionary posture, Largo Caballero refused to participate. For its part, the still-numerically-small PCE dutifully followed the resolution passed at the Comintern's Seventh Congress and implemented the new general line by supporting what it believed was an anti-fascist Popular Front. According to the Comintern, this Front would both provide a bulwark against fascism *and* complete the bourgeois stage of the revolution. But in stating that this was 'the particular form in which the Spanish revolution was unfolding at that stage',[57] the Communists again showed themselves to be completely incapable of grasping the dynamics of the revolutionary process they were witnessing.

The initial wave of popular enthusiasm that followed the elections soon dissipated as the promised reforms failed to live up to expectations. In the following months, the workers' organisations became increasingly radicalised. The number of strikes mushroomed: by June, there were up to 20 a day. Strikers now made revolutionary demands for bread, land, work, to smash fascist organisations and to overthrow capitalism. Although such slogans were hardly new, the occupations of large estates in the south and the level of political violence convinced many that the country was entering a revolutionary crisis.

### The Civil War

On 17 July 1936, a group of generals, headed by Sanjurjo, Goded, Mola, Fanjul and Franco, began a military rising against the Second Republic that would initiate a civil war. The officer corps had the support of key figures associated with the old régime, such as Catholic traditionalists, monarchists, bankers, industrialists, large landowners and fascist groups. They were also to enjoy military support from Italy and Germany. By the end of July, the Nationalists occupied roughly one-third of the country. Hastily organised and often spontaneous resistance by workers' organisations and what police and paramilitary forces remained loyal to the Republic ensured that the military garrisons' revolts did not succeed in most major cities. Owing to the impotence of the Madrid government, the workers' militias were forced to arm themselves and assume control of local defence, administration and the economy. By the time Madrid had caught up with the situation, it found that its authority had been usurped by the various local Anti-Fascist Militia Committees.

---

57    Such was the view of Palmiro Togliatti, a leading Comintern figure and one of the key influences on the PCE, quoted in Claudín 1972, p. 7.

The Committees presided, with varying degrees of control, over what many historians consider to have been an ongoing social revolution.[58] Questions such as the Church, the army and agriculture were all being addressed in ways that went far beyond the legal limits accepted by the Republic. Many industrial enterprises either came under joint government and union control or were completely taken over by their workforces. Both Socialists and anarcho-syndicalists carried out the collectivisation of agriculture in many areas. But, however profound some of these revolutionary changes may have been, the revolution itself lacked a central organisation and did not even begin to address the problem of state power. Moreover, the early defeats inflicted upon Republican militias by the Nationalists demonstrated the need for a single military command. The central government was seen as best suited to fulfil this role. Having lost its coercive apparatus, the Republican government had to rely upon the workers' parties and unions to restore its authority. This posed the now-accurately-named Popular Front government – headed by Largo Caballero from September 1936 and including Republicans, the PSOE, the PCE and later the CNT – the task of arresting the Revolution's development and redirecting the workers' and peasants' energies toward fighting the War.

It became evident to many in the government that re-establishing the authority of the Popular Front was the price Stalin demanded for providing the Republic with much-needed military assistance. Soviet ambassador Marcel Rosenberg argued that, if Britain and France were to be persuaded to support a fellow democracy, its government could not be seen as socialist. In his famous letter to Largo Caballero, Stalin reiterated this, even though it was by then obvious that Britain and France would not intervene.[59] By this time, it was also becoming clear that Moscow expected the Revolution not merely to be halted but completely reversed.

Thus, from late 1936, the Popular Front government and the Catalan Generalitat began to neutralise and then dismantle the organs of workers' power, although Largo Caballero did attempt to institutionalise some of the revolutionary advances. The Committees were replaced by local councils which included bourgeois elements; the militias were replaced by a 'popular army'. This facilitated what could be seen as a process of counterrevolution that, by early 1937, was actively reversing the Revolution's achievements. Among the most active participants in this process were the official Communists, assisted by a handful of Soviet agents.[60]

---

58     To cite three prominent historians not noted for their left-wing sympathies but who see these events as a social revolution: Thomas 1986, p. 268 and pp. 290–312; Jackson 1976, pp. 249–56; and R. Carr 1977, Chapter Six.

59     Stalin's letter and Largo Caballero's reply are reprinted in E.H. Carr 1984, pp. 86–8.

60     This is discussed at some length in Chapter Seven.

The timely arrival of Soviet aid in October 1936 certainly prevented the fall of Madrid, and the Communist-organised International Brigades undoubtedly contributed greatly to the defence of the city. This early success gained the Soviet Union and Stalin a great deal of popularity among supporters of the Republic. Bathing in reflected glory, the PCE and its Catalan counterpart, the PSUC, were able to increase in size from between 30,000 and 40,000 members in July 1936 to some 250,000 by December.[61] The PCE's national leadership was heavily reliant upon Moscow's lead and Soviet military advice. However, there is much debate over the extent of Soviet political interference with the Republican government and even within the functioning of the PCE.[62] In terms of its political 'line', PCE propaganda portrayed Spain as a still-semi-feudal country that had yet to experience its bourgeois revolution. The Civil War was depicted solely as a struggle against fascism, certainly not a social revolution akin to the Russian Revolution. Those groups which defended revolutionary gains, such as the POUM and CNT, were denounced as agents of fascism. Thus, without abandoning the long-term aim of a socialist revolution, the official Communists were able to exploit the common-sense argument that a bourgeois democracy was infinitely preferable to a fascist dictatorship and that winning the War was separate from any question of social revolution.

From the beginning of 1937, the process of restoring the bourgeois Republic began to take on a more sinister character. During the early part of that year, there were several armed confrontations between anarcho-syndicalists and Communist-controlled forces in Cataluña. On 3 May, a PSUC-led unit took over the Barcelona Telephone Exchange, which had been held by the CNT since July. This sparked a spontaneous insurrection by CNT and POUM workers, who held out for four days against the PSUC, Esquerra, Estat Català (a Catalan pro-independence party) and the police. Although none had sought this confrontation, the POUM leaders supported their rank and file. CNT leaders, however, repeatedly called upon their militants to end the insurrection. Finally complying with this advice, the CNT workers laid down their weapons and brought to an end the armed opposition to Communist and Republican domination.

The Barcelona defeat also marked the end of the Spanish Revolution. As a consequence of the May Days, the revolutionary forces (the POUM, CNT-FAI and some left Socialists) were progressively deprived of any power they still retained. In the case of the POUM, this reached the extent of physical liquidation, most notoriously of Andreu Nin, and what has been seen as an attempt to stage a 'show trial' of its surviving leaders. Largo Caballero was forced out of office. The bourgeois Republicans and reformist Socialists took advantage of the situation to reassert their authority from key positions in the government, administration and the army. The PCE, whose only political

---

61    Graham 2002, p. 183. Some estimates put PCE membership by mid-1937 as high as one million. Broué and Témime 1970, p. 229.

62    See Chapter Seven for some discussion of this.

strategy had been to support the bourgeois Republicans and roll back the Revolution, gained nothing. No aid was forthcoming from the Western democracies, whereas Franco received a great deal of assistance from the Axis powers. It became increasingly clear, even to some Communists, that certainly Britain and perhaps France and the United States were tacitly supporting Franco. The Republican forces were finally defeated in late March 1939, ushering in 36 more years of dictatorship.

# References

## Libraries and Archives Consulted

John Rylands University Library, Manchester
Hemeroteca Municipal, Madrid
Fundación Andreu Nin, Madrid
Fundación Pablo Iglesias, Madrid

Acosta Sánchez, José 1975, *El desarrollo capitalista y la democracia en España*, Barcelona: Dirosa.

Alba, Víctor 1974, *El marxisme a Catalunya, 1919–39, Volume IV: Joaquím Maurín*, Barcelona: Pòrtic.

——— 1975, *Dos revolucionarios: Joaquín Maurín y Andrés Nin*, Madrid: Seminarios y Ediciones.

——— 1977, *La Alianza Obrera. Historia y análisis de una táctica de unidad en España*, Madrid: Ediciones Júcar.

——— (ed.) 1977, *La revolución española en la práctica: Documentos del POUM*, Madrid: Ediciones Júcar.

Alba, Víctor and Stephen Schwartz 1988, *Spanish Marxism Versus Soviet Communism: A History of the POUM*, New Brunswick and Oxford: Transaction Books.

Alexander, Robert Jackson 1999, *The Anarchists in the Spanish Civil War*, Volumes 1 and 2, London: Janus.

Anderson, Perry 1974, *Lineages of the Absolutist State*, London: New Left Books.

——— 1979, *Considerations on Western Marxism*, London: Verso.

——— 1983, 'Trotsky's Interpretation of Stalinism', *New Left Review*, I/139: 49–58.

Andrade, Juan 1971, 'Introduction', in *Los problemas de la revolución española (1931–37)*, by Andreu Nin, Paris: Ruedo Ibérico.

——— 1986, *Notas sobre la guerra civil: Actuación del POUM*, Madrid: Ediciones Libertarias.

Aracil, Rafael and M. García Bonafé (eds.) 1976, *Lecturas de historia económica de España*, Volume 1, Barcelona: Oikos-Tau.

Arranz, Luís, Cabrera, Mercedes and Fernando del Rey 2000, 'The Assault on Liberalism, 1914–1923', in *Spanish History Since 1808*, edited by José Alvarez Junco and Adrian Shubert, London: Arnold.

Balcells, Alberto (ed.) 1973, *El arraigo del anarquismo en España: Textos de 1926–32*, Barcelona: A. Redondo.

Barnes, Jack 1983, 'Their Trotsky and Ours: Communist Continuity Today', *New International*, 1: 9–89.

Beetham, David 1983, *Marxists in the Face of Fascism*, Manchester: Manchester University Press.

Beevor, Anthony 2007, *The Battle for Spain: The Spanish Civil War 1936–1939*, London: Phoenix.

Ben-Ami, Shlomo 1983, *Fascism from Above: The Dictatorship of Primo de Rivera in Spain*, Oxford: Oxford University Press.

Blackbourn, David and Geoff Eley 1984, *The Peculiarities of German History*, Oxford: Oxford University Press.

Blanco Rodríguez, Miguel 1982, 'Le livre que Trotsky n'a pas écrit sur l'Espagne', *Cahiers Léon Trotsky*, 10: 115–7.

Bolloten, Burnett 1979, *The Spanish Revolution: The Left and the Struggle for Power during the Civil War*, Chapel Hill: University of North Carolina Press.

Bonamusa, Francesc 1973, 'La segunda muerte de Joaquín Maurín', *Triunfo* 583: 18–19.

——— 1974, *El Bloc obrer i camperol: Els primers anys (1930–32)*, Barcelona: Editorial Curial.

——— 1977, *Andreu Nin y el movimiento comunista en España (1930–37)*, Barcelona: Editorial Anagrama.

Bonet, Pedro 1989 [1973], 'En la muerte de Joaquín Maurín', *La Batalla*, December, reproduced in '*Dossier' Joaquín Maurín*, Barcelona: Fundació Andreu Nin.

Borkenau, Franz 1963 [1937], *The Spanish Cockpit*, London: Pluto Press.

Brenan, Gerald 1943, *The Spanish Labyrinth*, Cambridge: Cambridge University Press.

Brossat, Alain 1974, *Aux origenes de la révolution permanente: La pensée politique du jeune Trotsky*, Paris: Maspero.

Broué, Pierre 1966, *Trotski y la guerra civil española*, Buenos Aires: Jorge Alvarez.

——— 1967, 'Trotsky et la révolution espagnole', *La Vérité*, 537: 23–31.

——— 1975, 'Introduction', in Leon Trotsky, *La Révolution Espagnole 1930–1940: Textes recueillis, présentés et annotés par Pierre Broué*, Paris: Les Éditions de Minuit.

——— 1977, *La revolución española (1931–1939)*, Barcelona: Ediciones Peninsula.

——— 1982, 'Cartes et lettres d'Andrés Nin a Trotsky', introduction, *Cahiers Léon Trotsky*, 10: 35–45.

——— 1983, 'Quand Carrillo était gauchiste… les Jeunesses Socialistes d'Espagne (1934–35)', *Cahiers Léon Trotsky*, 16: 17–53.

——— 1988, *Trotsky*, Paris: Fayard.

Broué, Pierre and Emile Témime 1970, *The Revolution and Civil War in Spain*, London: Faber and Faber.

Carr, Edward Hallett 1982, *The Twilight of the Comintern, 1930–35*, London: Macmillan.

——— 1984, *The Comintern and the Spanish Civil War*, London: Macmillan.

Carr, Raymond 1977, *The Civil War in Spain 1936–1939*, London: Weidenfeld and Nicolson.

Carr, William 1972, *Arms, Autarky and Aggression: A Case Study in German Foreign Policy, 1933–39*, London: Edward Arnold.

Casanova, Julián 2002, 'Barcelona, May, 1937', *International Journal of Iberian Studies*, 20, 2: 155–8.

——— 2010, *The Spanish Republic and Civil War*, Cambridge: Cambridge University Press.

Cattell, David T. 1955, *Communism and the Spanish Civil War*, Berkeley: University of California Press.

Claudín, Fernando 1972, 'Spain – The Untimely Revolution', *New Left Review*, I/74:. 3–32.

Clavero, Bartolomé 1976 [1974], 'Mayorazgo: Propiedad feudal en Castilla 1369–1836', in *Lecturas en la historia económica de España*, Volume 1, edited by Rafael Aracil and M. García Bonafé, Barcelona: Oikos ediciones.

Company, Enric 1992, 'In Memoriam: Andreu Nin (1892–1937)', *El País*, 6 November.

Comunismo 1978, *Revista Comunismo (1931–34): La herencia teórica del marxismo español*, Barcelona: Editorial Fontamara.

Conquest, Robert 2008, *The Great Terror: A Reassessment* (revised edition), London: Pimlico.

Cotterill, David (ed.) 1994, *The Serge-Trotsky Papers*, London: Pluto Press.

Cusick, Lois 1979, *The Anarchist Millennium: Memories of the Spanish Revolution 1936–37*, unpublished manuscript.

Day, Richard B. and Daniel Gaido (eds.) 2009, *Witnesses to Permanent Revolution: The Documentary Record*, Leiden: Brill.

Deutscher, Isaac 1954, *The Prophet Armed: Trotsky 1879–1921*, Oxford: Oxford University Press.

——— 1959, *The Prophet Unarmed: Trotsky 1921–1929*, Oxford: Oxford University Press.

——— 1963, *The Prophet Outcast: Trotsky 1929–1940*, Oxford: Oxford University Press.

——— 1966, *Stalin*, Harmondsworth: Penguin.

——— 1984, *Marxism, Wars and Revolutions*, London: Verso.

Dukes, Paul 1979, *October and the World*, London: Macmillan.

Durgan, Andrew 1989, 'Dissident Communism in Catalonia, 1930–36', doctoral dissertation, University of London.

——— 1991. 'Spanish Trotskyists and the Foundation of the POUM' in 'The Spanish Civil War. The View from the Left', *Revolutionary History*, 4, 1 and 2: 11–53.

——— 1996, *BOC 1930–1936: El Bloque Obrero y Campesino*, Barcelona: Laertes SA de Ediciones.

——— 2004, 'International Volunteers in the POUM Militias', Madrid: Edición Digital Fundación Andreu Nin.

——— 2007, *The Spanish Civil War*, London: Macmillan.

Ealham, Chris 2005, 'The Myth of the Maddened Crowds: Class, Culture and Space in the Revolutionary Urbanist Project in Barcelona, 1936–1937', in *The Splintering of Spain: Cultural History and the Spanish Civil War 1936–1939*, edited by Chris Ealham and Michael Richards, Cambridge: Cambridge University Press.

———— 2010, *Anarchism and the City: Revolution and Counter-Revolution in Barcelona, 1898–1937*, Oakland: AK Press.

Elliot, J.H. 1963, *Imperial Spain 1469–1716*, Harmondsworth: Penguin.

Elorza, Antonio 1987, 'La estrategia del POUM en la guerra civil', in Institució Valenciana D'estudios i Investigació, *La II República: una esperanza frustrada*, Valencia: Ediciones Alfonso el Magnànium.

Esenwein, George and Adrian Shubert 1995, *Spain at War: The Spanish Civil War in Context, 1931–1939*, Harlow: Longman.

Ensner, Clara and Pavel Thalmann 1983 [1977], *Pour La Liberté*, Paris: Spartacus.

Etchebehere, Mika 1976, *Ma guerre d'Espagne à moi*, Paris: Denoël.

Evans, Les 1973, 'Introduction', in Leon Trotsky, *The Spanish Revolution (1931–39)*, New York: Pathfinder Press.

Evans, Richard 1985, 'The Myth of Germany's Missing Revolution', *New Left Review*, I/149: 67–94.

Falkus, M.E. 1972, *The Industrialization of Russia, 1700–1914*, London: Macmillan.

Fatherree, Ben H. 1978, 'Trotskyism in Spain, 1931–37', doctoral dissertation, Mississippi State University, Starkville, MS.

Fitzgerald, C.P. 1977, *Mao Tse-tung and China*, Harmondsworth: Penguin.

Fontana, Josep and Jordi Nadal 1976, 'Spain 1914–1970', in *The Fontana Economic History of Europe*, Volume 6, Part 2, edited by Carlo M. Cipolla, Glasgow: Fontana/Collins.

Frank, Pierre 1979, *The Fourth International: The Long March of the Trotskyists*, London: Ink Links.

Fraser, Ronald 1981, *Blood of Spain: The Experience of Civil War 1936–39*, Harmondsworth: Penguin.

Fundació Andreu Nin 1988, *El proceso de 1938 contra el POUM: Barcelona no fue Moscú*, Barcelona: Fundació Andreu Nin.

————1989a, *'Dossier' Joaquín Maurín*, Barcelona: Fundació Andreu Nin.

———— 1989b, *Acotaciones para la historia del POUM*, Barcelona: Fundació Andreu Nin.

———— n.d., 'Mesa redonda' (typescript of a round-table discussion on Trotsky and Spain between Javier Maestro, Juan Pablo Fusi, Wilebaldo Solano and Pierre Broué), Madrid: Fundación Andreu Nin, available at <http://www.fundanin.org/nin7.htm>.

García Sanz, Angel and Ramón Garrabou (eds.) 1985a, *Historia agraria de la España contemporánea*, Volume 1, Barcelona: Editorial Crítica.

———— (eds.) 1985b, *Historia agraria de la España contemporánea*, Volume 2, Barcelona: Editorial Crítica.

Geary, Dick 1987, *Karl Kautsky*, Manchester: Manchester University Press.

Genovès, María Dolors and Llibert Ferri 1992, 'Operació Nikolai', Televisó de Catalunya.

Geras, Norman 1986, *The Literature of Revolution*, London: Verso.

Gerschenkron, Alexander 1964, 'The Early Phases of Industrialization in Russia and their Relationship to the Historical Study of Economics of Growth', in *The Economic Take-off into Sustained Growth*, edited by W.W. Rostow, London: Macmillan.

Getty, John Arch and Roberta Thompson Manning (eds.) 1993, *Stalinist Terror: New Perspectives*, Cambridge: Cambridge University Press.

Giner, Salvador 1973, *Continuity and Change: The Social Stratification of Spain*, Reading: University of Reading Graduate School of Contemporary European Studies, Occasional Papers No. 1.

Giner, Salvador and E. Sevilla 1977, 'The *Latifundio* as a Local Mode of Class Domination: The Spanish Case', *Iberian Studies*, VI, 2: 47–58.

Gómez Casas, Juan 1986, *Anarchist Organization: The History of the FAI*, Montreal: Black Rose.

Gorkín, Julián 1973, *El proceso de Moscú en Barcelona: El sacrificio de Andrés Nin*, Barcelona: Aymá.

Graham, Helen 1986, 'The Road to a Popular Front', *History Today*, 36, 7: 19–23.

———— 2002, *The Spanish Republic at War*, Cambridge: Cambridge University Press.

———— 2004, 'Spain Betrayed? The New Historical McCarthyism', *Science and Society*, 68: 364–369.

———— 2005, *The Spanish Civil War: A Very Short Introduction*, Oxford: Oxford University Press.

Graham, Helen and Paul Preston 1987, *The Popular Fronts in Europe*, London: Macmillan.

Granell, Eugenio F. 1937, *El ejército y la revolución*, Barcelona: Editorial Marxista.

Hallas, Duncan 1979, *Trotsky's Marxism*, London: Bookmarks.

Hansen, Joseph 1975, 'Introduction', in Leon Trotsky, *My Life: An Attempt at an Autobiography*, Harmondsworth: Penguin.

Harrison, Joseph 1985, *The Spanish Economy in the Twentieth Century*, Kent: Croom Helm.

Hassel, Keith 1988, 'Trotsky and the POUM', *Revolutionary History*, 1, 2: 18–19.

Heywood, Paul 1990, *Marxism and the Failure of Organized Socialism in Spain, 1879–1936*, Cambridge: Cambridge University Press.

Hilton, Rodney 1984, 'Feudalism in Europe: Problems for Historical Materialists', *New Left Review*, I/147: 84–93.

Howe, Irving 1978, *Trotsky*, Glasgow: Fontana.

Ibárruri, Dolores et al. 1960, *Historia del Partido Comunista de España*, Paris: Ediciones Sociales.

Iglesias, Ignacio 1974a, 'Joaquín Maurín, guía excepcional', *España Libre*, New York, January–February.

———— (as Andrés Suárez) 1974b, *El proceso contra el POUM: Un episodio de la revolución española*, Paris: Ruedo Ibérico.

———— 1976, *Trotski y la revolución española*, Madrid: Zero.

———— 1977, *León Trotski y España 1930–39*, Madrid: Júcar.

Jackson, Gabriel 1976, *La república española y la guerra civil, 1931–1939*, Barcelona: Orbis.

Juliá, Santos 1979, *Los orígenes del Frente Popular en España (1934–36)*, Madrid: Siglo XXI de España.

———— 1989, 'The Origins and Nature of the Spanish Popular Front', in *The French and Spanish Popular Fronts: Comparative Perspectives*, edited by Martin S. Alexander and Helen Graham, Cambridge: Cambridge University Press.

Kahan, A. 1967, 'Government Policies and the Industrialization of Russia', *Journal of Economic History*, 27: 460–77.

Kemp, Tom 1969, *Industrialization in Nineteenth-Century Europe*, London: Longman.

Kitchen, Martin 1976, *Fascism*, London: Macmillan.

Kowalsky, Daniel 2001, *Stalin and the Spanish Civil War*, New York: Columbia University Press.

Krassó, Nicolas 1967, 'Trotsky's Marxism', *New Left Review*, I/44: 64–86.

———— 1968, 'Reply to Ernest Mandel', *New Left Review*, I/48: 90–103.

Landau, Katia 1988, 'Stalinism in Spain', *Revolutionary History*, 1, 2: 40–55.

Lenin, Vladimir Ilyich 1964, *Collected Works*, Volume 24, London: Lawrence and Wishart.

———— 1970, *Two Tactics of Social Democracy in the Democratic Revolution*, Peking: Foreign Language Press.

———— 1980, *Lenin's Unfinished Fight*, New York: Pathfinder Press.

Leval, Gaston 1975, *Collectives in the Spanish Revolution*, London: Freedom Press.

Lipietz, Alan 1982, 'Marx or Rostow?', *New Left Review*, I/132: 48–58.

Low, Mary and Juan Breá 1979 [1937], *Red Spanish Notebook. The First Six Months of the Revolution and the Civil War*, San Francisco: City Lights.

Löwy, Michael 1981, *The Politics of Uneven and Combined Development*, London: Verso.

Maestro, Javier 1978, 'Los orígenes del movimiento trotskista en España', *El viejo topo*, 27: 34–37.

Malefakis, Edward E. 1970, *Agrarian Reform and Peasant Revolution in Spain*, New Haven, CT: Yale University Press.

Mandel, Ernest 1968, 'Trotsky's Marxism – An Anti-Critique', *New Left Review*, I/47: 32–51.

———— 1971, 'Introduction', in Leon Trotsky, *The Struggle Against Fascism in Germany*, New York: Pathfinder Press.

———— 1978b, *The Second Slump*, London: New Left Books.

———— 1979a, *Trotsky: A Study in the Dynamic of His Thought*, London: New Left Books.

———— 1979b, *Revolutionary Marxism Today*, London: New Left Books.

———— 1986, 'In Defence of the Fourth International – Against the Split of the Australian Socialist Workers Party', *International Viewpoint*, 93, 24 (special supplement): 7–10.

———— 1989, *Beyond Perestroika: The Future of Gorbachev's USSR*, London: Verso.

———— 1995, *Trotsky as Alternative*, London: Verso.

Márquez, Reviriego, 1975, 'España 1916: Trotsky, turista sin libertad y viajero excepcional', *Tiempo de historia*, 1: 116–20.

Marx, Karl 1843 [2000], 'On the Jewish Question', in Karl Marx, *Selected Writings*, [Second Edition], edited by David McLellan, Oxford: Oxford University Press.

———— 1844 [1967], 'The Holy Family', in *Writings of the Young Marx on Philosophy and Society*, translated and edited by Lloyd D. Easton and Kurt H. Guddat, Indianapolis: Doubleday.

———— 1973a, *The Revolutions of 1848*, Harmondsworth: Penguin/New Left Review.

———— 1973b, *Surveys from Exile*, Harmondsworth: Penguin/New Left Review.

Marx, Karl and Friedrich Engels, 1975, *Revolution in Spain*, Westport: Greenwood Press.

Maurín, Joaquín 1932, *El Bloque Obrero y Campesino*, Barcelona.

———— 1966 [1935]. *Revolución y contrarrevolución en España*, Paris: Ruedo ibérico.

———— 1977a [1930], *Los hombres de la dictadura*, Barcelona: Editorial Anagrama.

———— 1977b [1931], *La revolución española. De la monarquía absoluta a la revolución socialista*, Barcelona: Editorial Anagrama.

Meaker, Gerald H. 1975, *The Revolutionary Left in Spain, 1914–23*, Stanford: Stanford University Press.

McLellan, David (ed.) 1977, *Karl Marx: Selected Writings*, Oxford: Oxford University Press.

Mills, C. Wright 1963, *The Marxists*, Harmondsworth: Penguin.

Milward, Alan and S.B. Saul 1977, *The Development of the Economies of Continental Europe, 1850–1914*, London: Allen and Unwin.

Monreal, Antoni 1984, *El pensamiento político de Joaquín Maurín*, Barcelona: Península.

Mooers, Colin 1991, *The Making of Bourgeois Europe*, London: Verso.

Moore, Barrington Jr. 1966, *Social Origins of Dictatorship and Democracy*, Harmondsworth: Penguin.

Moradiellos, Enrique 1999, 'The Allies and the Spanish Civil War', in Sebastian Balfour and Paul Preston (eds.), *Spain and the Great Powers in the Twentieth Century*, London: Routledge.

Munis, Grandizo 1977 [1948], *Jalones de derrota, promesa de la victoria*, Bilbao: Zero.

Nadal, Jordi 1972, 'The Failure of the Industrial Revolution in Spain 1830–1914', in *The Fontana Economic History of Europe*, Volume 4, Part 2, edited by Carlo M. Cipolla, London: Fontana.

Nin, Andrés 1923, *The Struggle of the Trade Unions Against Fascism*, Chicago: Trade Union Educational League.

———— 1971, *Los problemas de la revolución española (1931–37)*, Paris: Ruedo ibérico.

———— 1977a [1930], *Las dictaduras de nuestro tiempo*, Barcelona: Editorial Fontamara.

———— 1977b, *Los movimientos de emancipación nacional*, Barcelona: Editorial Fontamara.

———— 1978a, *Por la unificación marxista*, Madrid: Castellote Editor.

———— 1978b, *La revolución española*, Barcelona: Editorial Fontamara.

———— 1982a, Letters in Pierre Broué, 'Cartes et lettres d'Andrés Nin a Trotsky', *Cahiers Léon Trotsky*, 10: 35–45.

———— 1982b, letters to Maurín 1928–30, in Pelai Pagès, 'Correspondència Nin-Maurín', *L'Avenc*, (Barcelona) May–June and July–August, pp. 24–35.

———— 1987 [1932], *Los soviets*, Madrid: Editorial Revolución.

Nin, Andrés and Joaquín Maurín 1977 [1935], *¿Qué es y qué quiere el POUM?*, in Alba (ed.) 1977.

North, David 2010, *In Defense of Leon Trotsky*, Michigan: Mehring Books.

Novack, George 1972, *Understanding History: Marxist Essays*, New York: Pathfinder Press.

Nueva Era 1976, *La Nueva Era: Antología de una revista revolucionaria, 1930–36*, Madrid: Ediciones Júcar.

Orozco, Miguel 1977, 'Introduction', in Leon Trotsky, *Obras 2: España 1930–36*, Madrid: Akal Editor.

Orwell, George 1979 [1938], *Homage to Catalonia*, Harmondsworth: Penguin.

Pagès, Pelai 1975, *Andreu Nin: Su evolución política (1911–37)*, Bilbao: Editorial Zero.

———— 1977a, *El movimiento trotskista en España 1930–35*, Barcelona: Ediciones Peninsula.

———— 1977b, 'Introduction', in Andreu Nin, *Las dictaduras de nuestro tiempo*, Barcelona: Editorial Fontamara.

———— 1977c, 'Introduction', in Andreu Nin, *Los movimientos de emancipación nacional*, Barcelona: Editorial Fontamara.

———— 1978a, *Historia de Partido Comunista de España*, Barcelona: Ediciones Rincón.

———— 1982a, 'Andreu Nin al Moscou de Stalin: Correspondència Nin-Maurín', *L'Avenc* (Barcelona), May–June, 24–35.

———— 1982b, 'L'obsessió de Nin: Marxar de Rússia: Correspondència Nin-Maurín', *L'Avenc* (Barcelona) July–August, 30–9.

———— 1988, 'Assassinat d'Andreu Nin', *El Temps*, 236: 42–4.

———— 2007, '"Estalinistas y alborotadores": La campaña contra el POUM', *Viento Sur*, 93: 51–6.

———— 2010, 'El asesinato de Andreu Nin, más datos para la polémica', *Ebre 38, Revista internacional sobre la guerra civil*, 4: 57–76.

———— 2011, *Andreu Nin: Una vida al servicio de la clase obrera*, Barcelona: Laertes S.A. de Ediciones.

Pagès, Pelai and Xavier Virós 1971, 'El POUM ante la revolución española' (unpublished), Barcelona.

Pastor, Manuel 1975, *Los orígenes del fascismo en España*, Madrid: Tucar.

———— 1978, 'Notas para una interpretación de la dictadura primoriverrista', *Revista de estudios políticos*, 6: 137–43.

Patenaude, Bertrand M. 2009, *Stalin's Nemesis: The Exile and Murder of Leon Trotsky*, London: Faber and Faber.

———— 2011, 'Book Review', *American Historical Review*, 116, 3: 900–2.

Payne, Stanley 1970, *The Spanish Revolution*, London: Weidenfeld and Nicolson.

———— 1999, *Fascism in Spain 1923–1977*, Madison: University of Wisconsin Press.

———— 2004, *The Spanish Civil War, the Soviet Union, and Communism*, New Haven: Yale University Press.

———— 2005, 'Prologue', in José María Zavala, *En busca de Andreu Nin: Vida y muerte de un mito silenciado de la Guerra Civil*, Barcelona: Edición DeBOLS!LLO.

Peirats, José 1990, *Anarchists in the Spanish Revolution*, London: Freedom Press.

Plekhanov, Georgi 1969, *Fundamental Problems of Marxism*, London: Lawrence and Wishart.

Portela, Luis 1973, 'La única muerte de Joaquín Maurín', *Triunfo*, December: 13–15.

Portuondo, E. 1981, *La Segunda República: Reforma, fascismo y revolución*, Madrid: Ediciones Revolución.

Preston, Paul 1981, 'Spain', in *Fascism in Europe*, edited by S.J. Woolf, London: Methuen.

———— 1983, *The Coming of the Spanish Civil War*, Cambridge: Cambridge University Press.

———— 1986, 'The Struggle Against Fascism in Spain: *Leviatán* and the Contradictions of the Socialist Left 1934–36', in *Spain in Conflict 1931–39: Democracy and its Enemies*, edited by Martin Blinkhorn, London: Sage.

———— 1987, 'The Creation of the Popular Front in Spain', in *The Popular Fronts in Europe*, edited by Helen Graham and Paul Preston, London: Macmillan.

———— 1999, *¡Comrades! Portraits from the Spanish Civil War*, London: Harper-Collins.

———— 2006, *The Spanish Civil War: Reaction, Revolution and Revenge*, London: Harper Perennial.

———— 2012, *The Spanish Holocaust: Inquisition and Extermination in Twentieth-Century Spain*, London: HarperCollins.

Radosh, Ronald, Mary R. Habeck. and Grigory Sevostianov (eds.) 2001, *Spain Betrayed: The Soviet Union in the Spanish Civil War*, New Haven and London: Yale University Press.

Reed, Dale and Michael Jakobson 1987, 'Trotsky Papers at the Hoover Institution: One Chapter in an Archival Mystery Story', *American Historical Review*, 92, 2: 363–75.

Rees, Tim 1998, 'The Highpoint of Comintern Influence? The Communist Party and the Civil War in Spain', in *International Communism and the Communist International, 1919–43*, edited by Tim Rees and Andrew Thorpe, Manchester: Manchester University Press.

Rees, Tim and Thorpe, Andrew (eds.) 1998, *International Communism and the Communist International, 1919–43*, Manchester: Manchester University Press.

Revol, René 1979, 'Procès de Moscou en Espagne', *Cahiers Léon Trotsky*, 3: 121–32.

Richards, Vernon 1972, *Lessons of the Spanish Revolution (1936–1939)*, London: Freedom Press.

Rimlinger, G.V. 1960, 'Autocracy and the Factory Order in Early Russian Industrialization', *Journal of Economic History*, xx: 67–92.

Rovida, Giorgio 1980, 'La rivoluzione spagnola e gli insegnamenti del 1917 russo', *Il ponte*, 36 2: 1355–401.

Schwartz, Stephen 2010, 'Reading the Runes. New Perspectives on the Spanish Civil War', in *Arena Two: Anarchists in Fiction*, edited by Stuart Christie, Oakland: PM Press.

Schwartz, Stephen, George Esenwein, and Irving Louis Horowitz 1989, 'Communications', *Labor History*, 30, 1: 153–7.

Schlögel, Karl 2012, *Moscow 1937*, Cambridge: Polity Press.

Segal, Ronald 1983, *The Tragedy of Leon Trotsky*, Harmondsworth: Penguin.

Seidman, Michael 1991, *Workers Against Work: Labor in Paris and Barcelona during the Popular Fronts,* Berkeley: University of California Press.

——— 2002, *Republic of Egos: A Social History of the Spanish Civil War*, Madison: University of Wisconsin Press.

Service, Robert 2009, *Trotsky*, London: Macmillan.

Shub, David 1966, *Lenin*, Harmondsworth: Penguin.

Shubert, Adrian 1987, *The Road to Revolution in Spain: The Coal Miners of Asturias*, Champaign: University of Illinois Press.

——— 1990, *A Social History of Modern Spain*, London: Unwin Hyman.

Smith, Steve A. 2002, *The Russian Revolution: A Very Short Introduction*, Oxford: Oxford University Press.

Snow, Edgar 1968, *Red Star over China* (revised edition), New York: Grove Press.

Solano, Wilebaldo 2008, 'La larga marcha por la verdad sobre Andreu Nin', *Nodo 50 Contrainformación en la Red*, 7 July 2008, available at <http://info.nodo50.org>

Swain, Geoffrey 2006, *Trotsky: Profiles in Power*, Harlow: Pearson.

Takahashi, Kohachiro 1978, 'A Contribution to the Discussion', in *The Transition from Feudalism to Capitalism*, edited by Rodney Hilton, London: Verso.

Thatcher, Ian D. 2003, *Trotsky*, London: Routledge.

Thomas, Hugh 1986 [1965], *The Spanish Civil War*, Harmondsworth: Penguin.

Thornberry, Robert S. 1978, 'A Spanish Civil War Polemic: Trotsky versus Malraux', *Twentieth Century Literature*, 24: 324–33.

——— 1982, 'Trotsky', in *Historical Dictionary of the Spanish Civil War*, edited by James W. Cortada, Westport: Greenwood Press.

Tosstorff, Reiner 2009, *El POUM en la revolució espanyola*, Barcelona: Editorial Base.

Trotsky, Leon 1958 [1935], *Diary in Exile*, Cambridge, MA: Harvard University Press.

———— 1929 [1969], *The Permanent Revolution* and *Results and Prospects*, New York: Pathfinder Press.

———— 1970a, *Leon Trotsky on the Paris Commune*, New York: Pathfinder Press.

———— 1970b, *The Third International After Lenin*, New York: Pathfinder Press.

———— 1970c, 'Luxemburg and the Fourth International', in Rosa Luxemburg, *Rosa Luxemburg Speaks*, New York: Pathfinder Press.

———— 1970d, *Stalin: An Appraisal of the Man and his Influence*, New York: Stein and Day.

———— 1970–9 [1929–40], *Writings of Leon Trotsky*, Volumes 1–12, New York: Pathfinder Press.

———— 1971, *The Struggle Against Fascism in Germany*, New York: Pathfinder Press.

———— 1972a, *The Revolution Betrayed*, New York: Pathfinder Press.

———— 1972b, *Writings of Leon Trotsky (1937–1938)*, New York: Pathfinder Press.

———— 1973a, *The Spanish Revolution (1931–1939)*, New York: Pathfinder Press.

———— 1973b, *1905*, Harmondsworth: Penguin.

———— 1973c, *Writings of Leon Trotsky (1930–31)*, New York: Pathfinder Press.

———— 1973d, *In Defence of Marxism*, New York: Pathfinder Press.

———— 1975a [1929], *León Trotski en España* [*Mis peripecias en España*], Madrid: Akal Editor.

———— 1975b, *My Life: An Attempt at an Autobiography*, Harmondsworth: Penguin.

———— 1976, *Writings of Leon Trotsky 1934–1935*, New York: Pathfinder Press.

———— 1977, *Obras II: España 1930–36*, Madrid: Akal Editor.

———— 1978, *Writings of Leon Trotsky 1936–1937*, New York: Pathfinder Press.

———— 1979a, *Leon Trotsky on France*, New York: Pathfinder Press.

———— 1979b [1929–33], *Supplement to Writings of Leon Trotsky 1929–40*, Volume 1, New York: Pathfinder Press.

———— 1979c [1934–40], *Supplement to Writings of Leon Trotsky 1929–40*, Volume 2, New York: Pathfinder Press.

———— 1980a, *The Death Agony of Capitalism and the Tasks of the Fourth International*, London: New Park.

———— 1980b, *The History of the Russian Revolution*, New York: Pathfinder Press.

———— 2009, *The Hidden Dynamics of Chinese Revolution. Writings and Speeches of Leon Trotsky on China (1925–1940)*, Delhi: Aakar.

Tuñón de Lara, Manuel 1977, *Estudios de historia contemporánea*, Barcelona: Nova Terra.

Ucelay-Da Cal, Enric 2005, 'Catalan Populism in the Spanish Civil War', in *The Splintering of Spain: Cultural History and the Spanish Civil War 1936–1939*, edited by Chris Ealham and Michael Richards, Cambridge: Cambridge University Press.

Velarde Fuentes, Juan 1968, 'Una nota acerca de Trotsky y sus ideas sobre la realidad económica y social de España', *Revista de trabajo*, 4–8: 31–8.

Vilar, Pierre 1977, *Spain: A Brief History*, Oxford: Pergamon Press.

Von Laue, T.H. 1961, 'Russian Peasants in the Factory 1892–1904', *Journal of Economic History*, 21: 61–80.

Warren, Bill 1980, *Imperialism: Pioneer of Capitalism*, London: Verso.

Zavala, José María 2005, *En busca de Andreu Nin: Vida y muerte de un mito silenciado de la Guerra Civil*, Barcelona: Edición DeBOLS!LLO.

Zeman, Z.A.B. and W.B. Scharlau 1965, *The Merchant of Revolution: The Life of Alexander Israel Helphand (Parvus)*, Oxford: Oxford University Press.

# Index